Genre Bending

Post 45 Loren Glass and Kate Marshall, Editors
Post•45 Group, Editorial Committee

Genre Bending
The Plasticity of Form in
Contemporary Literary Fiction

Jeremy Rosen

Stanford University Press
Stanford, California

Stanford University Press
Stanford, California

© 2026 by Jeremy Mark Rosen. All rights reserved.

No part of this book may be reproduced or transmitted in any form or by any means, electronic or mechanical, including photocopying and recording, or in any information storage or retrieval system, without the prior written permission of Stanford University Press.

Library of Congress Cataloging-in-Publication Data
Names: Rosen, Jeremy, author.
Title: Genre bending : the plasticity of form in contemporary literary fiction / Jeremy Rosen.
Other titles: Post 45.
Description: Stanford, California : Stanford University Press, 2026. | Series: Post*45 | Includes bibliographical references and index.
Identifiers: LCCN 2025012907 (print) | LCCN 2025012908 (ebook) | ISBN 9781503644236 (cloth) | ISBN 9781503644625 (paperback) | ISBN 9781503644632 (ebook)
Subjects: LCSH: Fiction genres—History—21st century. | Fiction—21st century—History and criticism.
Classification: LCC PN3427 .R67 2025 (print) | LCC PN3427 (ebook) | DDC 809.3/3—dc23/eng/20250527

LC record available at https://lccn.loc.gov/2025012907
LC ebook record available at https://lccn.loc.gov/2025012908

Cover design: Jan Šabach
Cover art: Adobe Stock

The authorized representative in the EU for product safety and compliance is: Mare Nostrum Group B.V. | Mauritskade 21D | 1091 GC Amsterdam | The Netherlands | Email address: gpsr@mare-nostrum.co.uk | KVK chamber of commerce number: 96249943

Contents

Preface: Beyoncé and Werewolves   vii

Acknowledgments   xv

Introduction
Literary Fiction and the Genres of Genre Fiction   1

1. Theorizing the Plastic Utility of Genre   41
2. Prose Style and Interiority in Genre-Bending Literary Fiction   81
3. Genre-Bending Literary Fiction's Self-Reflexivity   113
4. The Pleasures of Immersion in a Fictional World   141
5. The Novel of the Global Generic   183
6. Scalar Modulation and Formal Variation in Literary Climate Fiction   207

Coda
Literary Romance and Social Media Speculation   256

Notes   271

Index   309

Preface: Beyoncé and Werewolves

Genre Bending analyzes a prominent phenomenon in contemporary literary fiction: the boom, over the past several decades, in esteemed writers who have been adopting genres that have historically flourished in popular fiction, such as horror, fantasy, mystery, romance, science fiction, and the western. This book focuses on literary fiction for a few reasons. The blurry area between the literary and the popular, genre theory, and the function of genre in the marketplace have been my areas of scholarly expertise. (Don't let the title of this Preface fool you; I won't pretend to be an authority on pop music.) The phenomenon often called "the genre turn" in literary fiction has, for nearing a decade now, struck me as ripe material, since literary scholars and media critics have often commented on it, but it has not yet been the subject of a book-length study.[1] In addition, a book needs a manageable scope, and accounting for all the fascinating work being done with genre—not only in literary fiction but also within genre fiction fields and communities, such as the vast realms of romance in print and online, the provocative courses charted in science fiction and fantasy, horror and gothic, crime and mystery, westerns, vampires, zombies, and "the New Weird," not to mention poetry, visual and the performing arts, film, television, and music—is a task far too big for one book.

But then Beyoncé's *Cowboy Carter* (2024) was released when I was revising this manuscript. "Spaghettii," the twelfth track on that sprawling album, begins with Black country music pioneer Linda Martell intoning: "Genres are a funny little concept, aren't they? Yes, they are. In theory, they have a simple definition that's easy to understand. But in practice, well, some may feel confined."[2] Hearing these words while working on a book entitled *Genre Bending* made me realize that the eighth studio album, a country and pop genre mash-up, by one of the most powerful and influential cultural figures from the 2000s to the 2020s, was something I ought to address: if for no other reason than to make clear that the phenomenon I call *genre-bending literary fiction* is part of a broader efflorescence of transformative work with genre across contemporary culture. (Although, it could also be argued that artistic production has always been the story of artists working with and transforming existing genres.) But also, I think this book's central premise and argument are applicable to understanding this broader transmedia upsurge.

That premise is that writers of literary fiction have been enthusiastically adopting the genres that historically flourished in popular fiction because they have recognized the utility and endless *plasticity* of genre. Rather than seeing the crime novel, for example, as a form that has been exhausted, worn thin, by decades of formulaic use in the production of commercial fiction, these writers see the genre as something that can be continually altered in the pursuit of various aesthetic and political goals, bent toward new concerns, blended with other genres in new and unpredictable combinations. The argument is that multiple, often conflicting agendas spur the phenomenon of genre-bending literary fiction. Literary writers, appreciating the familiarity of genre, often aim to borrow from and capitalize on the conventional pleasures of the genres they adopt. At least as often, they seek to renovate or critique those genres and differentiate *their* deployments from the lion's share of production using them—which they often portray as excessively formulaic and compromised by rapid commercial production. Beat them or join them, if you will—and sometimes within the same book. Literary writers adopt popular genres for a host of sometimes divergent purposes. If they share one thing, it is a recognition of genre's plasticity.

One discovers a similar mix of motives on *Cowboy Carter*. The album was clearly Beyoncé's effort to work with but also against country music. Of the two singles released in advance of the album, "16 Carriages" is a pop country ballad, with a pedal steel guitar underlining Beyoncé's mournful vocals about leaving "home at an early age" and seeing "Mama prayin' and daddy cryin'," in which critics have detected notes of blues and gospel.[3] And "Texas Hold 'Em," a foot-stomper featuring Rhiannon Giddens on banjo, was the first single by a Black woman to reach number one on the Billboard Hot Country chart. At the same time, before the album was released, Queen B declared in an Instagram post that it "ain't a Country album. This is a 'Beyoncé' album . . . and I am proud to share it with y'all."[4]

Beyoncé's simultaneous refusal to be categorized as country, insistence on her album's individual stamp, and undeniable use of, if also playful irreverence toward, the genre reprises the ambivalent stance we often see in genre-bending literary fiction—and echoes similar disavowals from the likes of Margaret Atwood, Kazuo Ishiguro, and Ian McEwan. For Beyoncé, this ambivalence was clearly tied to the politics of country music as a white-dominated field. In the same post, she described the album as "born out of an experience . . . I had years ago where I did not feel welcomed," an obvious allusion to the 2016 Country Music Awards, when she played "Daddy Lessons" live alongside the Chicks—whose progressive political views have produced tension with large swaths of country's fan base—and was met with boos and racial epithets. Beyoncé's rejection by white country fans parallels the rhetoric of white nationalists like the Sad Puppies in response to the phenomenal success of speculative fiction writers like N. K. Jemisin.[5] The powers that be in country music continued to snub Beyoncé, as *Cowboy Carter* was not nominated for a single Country Music Award in 2024, though it would go on to win Grammy Awards in 2025 for Album of the Year and Best Country Album, and other Black country artists like Shaboozey recognized it as "one of the most innovative country albums of all time."[6] Beyoncé's initial disavowal reflected her aesthetic commitment to innovate and hybridize, to, as she wrote in the same Instagram post, "bend and blend genres together to create this body of work": an ambition that linked *Cowboy Carter*, Act I of her *Renaissance* trilogy, to its precursor, which fused pop and R&B with house and disco.[7]

Cowboy Carter thus displays what recent genre theory and this book emphasize. As Martell attests, genres have often *felt* confining, either formally—

because conventions that are repeated over time take on a prescriptive force and seem to harden into rules—or socially—because producers and consumers of a given genre build communities, which have, as with country music's whiteness, often been exclusionary. Genres have often, stretching back to literary romanticism and modernism, been seen as restrictive, as that which makes art repetitive and imitative. The "term seems almost by definition"— think of the word "generic"—"to deny the autonomy of the author, deny the uniqueness of the text, deny spontaneity, originality and self-expression."[8] But by the twenty-first century, a historical and rhetorical theory of genre has come to predominate, one that views genres not as fixed categories with rules to be followed, but as dynamic communicative frameworks producers use and modify to suit their needs. The production that constitutes a genre is dialectical, involving "both adoption of and resistance to its conventions," making a genre's condition one of "permanent revolution."[9]

Genre's plasticity—its capacity for formal transformation—and the fact that anyone can adopt a genre (though there is no guarantee one will be embraced by the community and institutions dedicated to it, even if one is Beyoncé) enable producers to resist, subvert, and critique a genre's conventional forms and politics. With *Cowboy Carter*, Beyoncé in "outlaw country tradition" aimed to "settle scores with haters and with history," asserting her right as Black American and Texan to the genre and calling attention to the whiteness of the industry and the racial grievance displayed by many of its fans.[10] As with Lil Nas X's "Old Town Road," Beyoncé's intervention sparked an outpouring of commentary on country's politics and how it has repressed its roots in African American musical traditions.[11] Beyoncé thus deployed her drawl and country's typically plainspoken poetry against its current hegemonic forms and the politics of many in its audience.

At the same time, it's hard to ignore the commercial character of *Cowboy Carter*. The first two singles were announced in a Verizon commercial during the Super Bowl, in which Beyoncé bet she could break the telecom giant's 5G network. And the album featured cameos from Willie Nelson, Dolly Parton, Miley Cyrus, and covers of the Beatles' "Blackbird" and Parton's "Jolene." Like adaptations and remakes, the use of genre confers obvious marketing advantages, offering audiences both comforting familiarity and surprising novelty.[12] So we find in *Cowboy Carter*, like so much genre-bending literary fiction, a complicated mix of capitalizing on a genre's audience familiarity while pushing against its traditional politics, deploying many of its conventional features while also seeking to individualize and innovate.

If genre-bending art across media is driven by the plastic utility of genre and a similar range of motives, this book argues that genre-bending Anglophone literary fiction manifests preoccupations specific to that field. Genre-bending writers seek to borrow forms, affordances, and pleasures from popular fiction genres, while at the same time transforming them and marking their deployments as *literary*. They do so by using techniques that tend to be prioritized in the literary field, like artful prose style, rich depictions of character psychology, and self-reflexivity—as well as underscoring their works' innovation and differentiating them from a field of popular culture they portray as overly formulaic and commercial. While even the most formula-driven deployments of genre have some variations, lest texts be perfect copies, genre fiction fields tend to prioritize expectations met, whereas literary fiction tends to value a greater degree of transformation and the frustration of expectations. Some genre-bending fictions tilt this balance more forcefully to one side than others, leaning into the pleasures of immersion in fictional worlds that have historically been prized in genre fiction, or using a popular genre's framework but weighing it down heavily with traditional literary emphases like interiority, self-reflexivity, and lyrical prose.

Glen Duncan's *The Last Werewolf* (2011) offers a consummate example of how of these opposing impulses—to both imitate and differentiate from genre fiction—motivate genre-bending literary writers, often within the same text. Like its lupine protagonist Jake Marlowe, the novel is split: highly cerebral, snobby, given to philosophizing and name-dropping, jaded and tired of the world, but also lusty, carnal, and carnivorous. The novel offers abundant conventional pleasures of werewolf horror: the gruesome transformation from man to beast, the pursuit of silver-bullet-packing hunters, and battles with vampire rivals. In human form, Jake spends much of his time in bed with Madeline, a sex worker, and the novel delivers readers plenty of explicit erotica alongside its gore and violence. Duncan also weaves a romance plot into *The Last Werewolf*—texts frequently draw on multiple genres—and falling in love is what saves the world-weary Jake from resigning himself to being killed by his archnemesis, the werewolf hunter Grainer.

But even and especially when the novel offers its most visceral action, pleasures familiar from the genres it deploys, it cannot help but philosophize about them. When the recently bitten and transformed Jake makes his wife Arabella his first victim, he consumes her "fast, in a worsening temper, with contempt for God's creative vulgarity in yoking consciousness to meat," and the grisly tableau he leaves behind is "a hideous composition, a pornographic companion piece to Fuseli's *The Nightmare*—or a satire on its excesses."[13] If the novel is juicy, lascivious, flirting even with pornography, it and Jake alike are yoked to consciousness, relentlessly intellectual and allusive, referring conspicuously to canonical literary texts from Arnold, Carlyle, and Keats, to Amis, Bellow, and Nabokov. Neither can escape self-consciousness or their guilty consciences—Jake for the body count he's added to every full moon for centuries, and the novel for its submission to the carnal pleasures typically prioritized in genre fiction. When Jake falls in love again, a century and a half after devouring Arabella, he claims the all-consuming feeling is a "fall to the pure animal" (190). Finally, he's "stopped abstracting"; "theory and reflection are delicate old uncles bustled out of the way by the boisterous nephews action and desire. Themes evaporate, only plot remains" (324). Though here Jake opposes thought and action, idea and plot, what are these lines but a metaphor-laden meditation on the opposition he claims to have transcended? Duncan's novel may want to jettison theory and reflection, surrender itself to pure action, but it cannot.

In addition to blending werewolf sex and violence with allusiveness, stylish prose brimming with figurative language, and a typically literary emphasis on plumbing the psyche of its central character, *The Last Werewolf* displays a surfeit of self-consciousness about its own use of genre tropes. Throughout, the novel positions what it claims to be its "realistic" portrayal of werewolf existence against the clichés of film and television. On the prowl for a she-wolf mate, Jake laments, "In *Buffy* there'd be a howlers' singles bar or dating agency. Not in the real world" (31). When a hunter beheads a vampire, Jake explains that vampire "decomposition isn't the screen-friendly instantaneous transformation to ash heap Hollywood peddles" (94). Of his "cloak-and-dagger arrangements" to disguise his identity and elude the hunters, Jake grouses that they are the timeworn stuff of spy fiction and films and muses that "Graham Greene had a semiparodic relationship with the genres his novels exploited, a wry tolerance for their exigencies and tropes. Unavoidably I have the same relationship with my life" (87–88). Continuing to list the "espionage flimflam" and "Horror Story trappings" that constitute his existence, Jake concludes, "if it were a novel I'd reject it along with all other genre output that by definition short-changes reality. Unfortunately for me it *is* reality" (88). Jake's self-awareness obviously reflects Duncan's, and the novel clearly figures its own desired relationship with its adopted genres: "semiparodic," indulging in their "exigencies and tropes," but wryly, with an ironic knowingness. This further elucidates Jake's ennui: he's not just weary of life after 200 years, he's tired of the werewolf schtick done to death in so much "genre output." Thus, *The Last Werewolf* positions itself as superior to, because self-conscious of, the preponderance of that output, with its shallow and trite depictions that "short-change reality."

Here we see that while genre-bending literary writers frequently adopt non-realistic genres, they often retain a commitment to a realist epistemology, contending that their use of genre addresses reality better than formulaic genre fare, and perhaps better than realism itself. Duncan's novel is, like many genre-bending literary fictions, self-reflexive about both its use of genre and what it claims to be the value and distinctiveness of the literary. If "genre output" "short-changes reality," it is literature's job to confront the depths and horrors that such fare typically hides from view. When Jake—whose surname Marlowe aptly alludes to a master of literary adventure and noir—writes of discovering the "Conradian truth," that "there's horror" and that "you accommodate it," he insists, with further erudition, that it is the function of the literary to address such profound truths and even horrors: "as the late Susan Sontag noted, something else is always going on. It's literature's job to honor it. No wonder no one reads" (191). Duncan upholds literature's role in depicting hidden realities, contrasts this with the shallowness of most popular genre fiction, and offers a blasé quip on the decline of the literary in an age that prefers to avoid uncomfortable truths. This kind of self-reflexive meditation on the purpose and embattled state of the literary recurs throughout works of genre-bending literary fiction.

It would be easy to read *The Last Werewolf* and by extension the boom in genre bending psychoanalytically: as efforts to balance the competing drives of id (genre) and superego (literary). But *Genre Bending* foregrounds the formal and rhetorical elements of genre, the fact that writers of literary fiction adopt and transform the frameworks of popular genres because they are useful and adaptable, and this book endeavors to demonstrate the range of uses to which such genres have been put, the common threads running through genre-bending literary fiction, as well as its internal conflicts. Literary writers' deployments of popular genres are not always so self-conscious, so wryly semiparodic; often they are sincere and admiring. But quite frequently they reflect on their own use of genre and their own investment in literariness, inquiring: Why is genre useful? What, if anything, makes their works different from popular fiction? What defines the literary? What are its aesthetic and social commitments and values? What value does the literary retain today, in a world surfeited with competing media? These questions are also the ones this book seeks to answer.

Acknowledgments

This book stresses the heterogeneity and singularity of writers' contributions to the flowering of genre-bending literary fiction around the turn of the millennium, while at the same time attempting to discern commitments that such writers share, as well as some divergent and even contradictory motivations. The genre of acknowledgments in a scholarly monograph may be as plastic as any other. But I don't want to try my editors' patience. So, my deployment of this genre will be conventional and overly brief and sacrifice fine-grained narratives of the unique contributions of many individuals for a cursory overview that does not do justice to their particularity or the depth of my appreciation.

At the University of Utah, I am grateful to the Tanner Humanities Center, the Tanner family, Robert Goldberg, and especially Beth James and Susan Anderson, for supporting my research and for profound wisdom and friendship. In the English Department, I have the most unique combination of humane and rigorous colleagues anywhere. Conversations with Scott Black and Barry Weller were crucial in developing this project, and I am grateful for many other discussions with Katherine Coles, Lizzie Callaway, Anne Jamison, Michael Mejia, David Roh, Alf Seegert, Andrew Shephard, Lisa Swanstrom, Nathan Wainstein, and for the friendship and repartee of Andrew Franta and Stacey Margolis.

I am grateful for support from the National Humanities Center and for opportunities to present this work in progress at Stanford, Johannes Gutenberg University, the John F. Kennedy Institute for North American Studies at the Free University of Berlin, as well as at the Modern Language Association, Association for the Study of the Arts of the Present, and American Comparative Literature Association annual meetings.

Merve Emre, Sean McCann, Amy Hungerford, the anonymous readers and the editorial staff at *Post45* and Matthew Hart, David Alworth, and readers at *ASAP/Journal* gave invaluable suggestions for earlier versions of the arguments in this book, as did Andrew Hoberek. Excellent conversations with Heather Houser, Lee Konstantinou, Günter Leypoldt, Alexander Manshel, Laura McGrath, Mark McGurl, Dan Sinykin, Claire Squires, and especially Rebecca Ballard helped this book on its way. I wouldn't have arrived at this place in my career without Chicago mentors and friends: Mollie Godfrey, Joshua Kotin, Sandra Macpherson, Deborah Nelson, Kenneth Warren, and Nathan Wolff.

The anonymous readers and editorial staff at Post*45 at Stanford University Press, especially the insightful and generous Loren Glass, Kate Marshall, and Erica Wetter, have been a joy to work with and have made this a much stronger book than it would have been without their suggestions and critiques.

My community in Salt Lake City—my family Linda, Jon, Ben, Luke, and Dex—have supported me in countless ways that are invisible here but were absolutely essential and no doubt often thankless; let me extend them here. Finally, to Elizabeth: You have modeled for me and taught me creativity, listening, resilience, and commitment to having a good day. I couldn't have done this, and wouldn't have wanted to, without you.

Genre Bending

Introduction
Literary Fiction and the Genres of Genre Fiction

IN 2015, THE JAMAICAN-BORN NOVELIST Marlon James, fresh off winning the Man Booker Prize for *A Brief History of Seven Killings* (2014), told a journalist about his next project. "I'm not writing a historical novel," James mused. "I'm writing a fantasy novel, and I'm going to geek the fuck out on it."[1] James later claimed he was joking when he referred to the colossal trilogy beginning with *Black Leopard, Red Wolf* (2019) as his "African *Game of Thrones*," but, joke or not, the label has stuck.[2] The announcement of a forthcoming fantasy saga from such a formidable novelist looked to some like a "surprise" or a "departure."[3] Many critics have noted the challenging, envelope-pushing nature of James's writing. His second novel, *The Book of Night Women* (2009), has been called "an experiment in how to write the unspeakable—even the unthinkable."[4] Similarly, with its huge assemblage of characters and voices swirling around the attempted assassination of Bob Marley in 1975, *A Brief History of Seven Killings* is anything but brief and is famously "dizzyingly complex."[5] It has been deemed as "emphatic a statement of literary ambition as you'll find in contemporary fiction," one that "calls to mind postmodern doorstops like 'Gravity's Rainbow' and 'Infinite Jest'" due to the "demands it makes on the reader."[6] At the same time, the idea that it would be a "surprise" for a writer of intricate, ambitious, and convention-demolishing literary fiction, the winner of the most prestigious single-novel prize in the Anglophone world, to turn next to the creation of a fantasy universe reveals the persistence of certain lingering assumptions about genres like fantasy—that they constitute "light reading," that they're incompatible with the production of high literary art—and ignores the conspicuous shift toward the adoption of popular

1

genres that prominent writers of literary fiction have undertaken over the past quarter century.[7]

Just about everyone paying attention to contemporary Anglophone fiction agrees on at least one thing: genre is everywhere. Since the late 1990s, acclaimed writers of literary fiction have gravitated *en masse* to the genres that long predominated in popular fiction fields—detective, horror, fantasy, romance, science fiction, spy thrillers, westerns, and even zombie novels—and this trend continued gaining steam through the 2010s and early 2020s. By 2012, the New Weird writer and astute critic China Miéville could already quip that noting this phenomenon had become trite. "It's a cliché to point out that generic tropes are infecting the mainstream, with a piling-up of various apocalypses by those guilty of literature."[8] Literary scholars have cited Miéville's remark so often that doing so has become its own cliché.[9] But it's only fitting that so many observers would take notice, as a who's who of the most critically acclaimed and bestselling writers of literary fiction have been taking up forms of genre fiction in recent decades, blending or interweaving them with others, and transforming them in ingenious ways throughout their careers. Figures like Margaret Atwood, Michael Chabon, Jennifer Egan, Louise Erdrich, Kazuo Ishiguro, Chang-rae Lee, David Mitchell, Cormac McCarthy, Ian McEwan, Haruki Murakami, Richard Powers, Sally Rooney, and Colson Whitehead compose the prestigious center of what has become a widespread movement—encompassing these big names as well as a host of accomplished but less luminous figures.

We are living in a boom time for what I call *genre-bending literary fiction*. But no one has yet offered a book-length study of this development, and the many commentators to opine on it have done so in ways that have flattened and oversimplified what is in fact a diverse, heterogeneous, and internally conflicted phenomenon. Literary fiction undoubtedly looks different today, as genre-bending short stories and novels have appeared with regularity in prestigious terrain that was previously dominated by domestic realism, historical fiction, magical realism, multiculturalism, and postmodern metafiction—though these genres persist, to be sure. How should we understand that shift?

It is certainly the case, as with James's post-Booker announcement or Philip Roth's 2004 alternate history *The Plot Against America*, that once writers of literary fiction achieve a certain renown, they acquire the freedom to assimilate new genres with reasonable confidence that readers and editors will follow them. So, the phenomenon may appear, at first glance, as writers with substantial cultural power appropriating popular forms at will—a form of genre slumming. But rather than stripping literary fiction of its veneer of artistic seriousness, making it look grittier and more like works of popular fiction,[10] genre-bending writers typically show a determination to infuse their deployments of popular genres with a literary sensibility, an attempt to "elevate" them not unlike the trend of elevated street food. And genre bending is not only a veteran's move; writers like Atwood, Lee, Mitchell, McCarthy, and Whitehead, as well as Ling Ma, Carmen Maria Machado, Emily St. John Mandel, Helen Oyeyemi, Viet Nguyen, Karen Russell, Charles Yu, and dozens of others, have launched or built their careers adopting and creatively innovating popular genres—but within the field of literary fiction. Because many of the most notable writers in this field have turned to popular genres in recent decades, *Genre Bending* aims to account for what constitutes the prestigious center of literary fiction in the first decades of the new millennium.

When this phenomenon began to achieve a critical mass of visibility, opinion pieces and ripostes began popping up in literary-minded publications like the *New Yorker*, mainstream venues like *Esquire* and the *Guardian*, and various bookish websites.[11] Some of these pieces applauded genre fiction gaining long-overdue respect. Others insisted, often snobbishly, that literary fiction maintained its superiority as the province of serious literary art. A few sought to stake out a more balanced position.[12] Lev Grossman, *Time* book editor and author of *The Magicians Trilogy* (2009–14), declared a "revolution from below, coming up from the supermarket aisles," and predicted that genre fiction would be "the technology that will disrupt the literary novel as we know it."[13] Laura Miller of *Salon* observed that "literary novelists are increasingly taking up science fiction's tools" but worried their efforts would "feel pretty thin" if they didn't stick to the "specialty of literary novelists: the fullest appreciation of humanity in its infinite variety and intricacy."[14]

Has genre fiction provided the Molotov cocktail to spark a revolution in literary fiction? Have literary novelists departed from their perennial concerns, and were these the "appreciation" of human complexity, or did they largely stay in their lane? Are they seeking street cred by slumming it in genre "ghettos"? Are they just looking to make a buck and submitting to what the market (or the corporate publishers that purport to speak for it) wants? Punctuated by prize-winning and bestselling figures, the upsurge of genre-bending literary fiction has been impossible to miss. While critics have offered a host of hot takes on what Andrew Hoberek first dubbed "the genre turn" in contemporary literary fiction, *Genre Bending* is the first monograph to address this phenomenon.[15] So it is worth rehearsing its history and novelty here, as well as pointing out some limitations of those earlier accounts.

A Brief History of the Genre-Bending Boom

Since the late nineteenth century and the rise of literary modernism, writers pursuing literary distinction have typically sought to distance their work from the ostensibly formulaic quality of popular genres and the commercial channels through which they were produced—though such distance was more a matter of assertion and carefully cultivated belief than reality.[16] Cultural scholars often refer, following Andreas Huyssen, to the "Great Divide" modernists tried to produce by cordoning off "serious" art and literature from popular entertainment. This divide aims to neatly separate works of complexity, aesthetic innovation, and weighty subject matter, supposedly driven by pure artistic motives, from conventional, rapidly produced and often rapidly forgotten works that aim to make money and are products of industrial processes rather than authentic works of art. In the arguments of many critics of the mid-twentieth century, what they saw as the assembly-line products of mass culture functioned, at best, as mindless distraction, at worst, as instruments of capitalism's drift toward totalitarian domination.[17] The Great Divide has stood, simultaneously, as a rather durable way of understanding a status hierarchy within cultural production and as a too-neat separation that purports to easily sort into high and low, or literary and popular, what is actually blurry and contested terrain.[18]

A classic case in point is Vladimir Nabokov, who played with detective and science fiction tropes throughout his career, most notably in "Lance" (1951) and *Ada, or Ardor* (1969), and yet claimed to "loathe science fiction with its gals and goons, suspense and suspensories," and to disdain its "clichés," which he alleged "are the same throughout all cheap reading matter."[19] While Nabokov was famous for being a mandarin or snob, proclaiming his preference for and aspiring to create lofty works of literary art, his best-known novel *Lolita* (1955) borrows, if parodically, from the conventions of crime fiction and rode to fame "on the back of scandal, threats of censorship, and critical adulation, a perfect cocktail for inducing sales."[20] Stanley Kubrick would of course adapt the novel into an MGM film in 1962. It's thus easy to read Nabokov's efforts to distance himself from popular literature as anxiety about contamination from an entertainment industry, to which he stood uncomfortably close. At the same time, his accusation that "cheap reading matter" is clichéd, recycling "the same" conventions over and over, has persisted as a resilient way of differentiating between popular genre fiction, which offers readers the comfort of seeing their expectations met, and literature or literary fiction, which aims to innovate, experiment, surprise, and alter readers' sense of what is possible.

The Great Divide continued to be both transgressed and reaffirmed throughout the latter half of the twentieth century, when postmodernist writers from Thomas Pynchon and Ishmael Reed to David Foster Wallace embedded ironic appropriations of popular forms in their polyvocal texts and reveled in mixing references to high and low culture.[21] At the same time, the self-conscious difficulty and intimidating doorstop size of their books made them seem aimed at a rather narrow audience of literati, what John Barth called, after Thomas Mann, "the Early Christians: professional devotees of high art."[22] Today's genre-bending literary writers, by contrast, seem to follow Barth's program for a synthesis or transcendence of the divide between "premodernist and modernist modes of writing," that

> without lapsing into moral or artistic simplism, shoddy craftsmanship, Madison Avenue venality, or either false or real naïveté . . . nevertheless aspires to a fiction more democratic in its appeal than such late-modernist marvels . . . as Beckett's *Texts for Nothing* or Nabokov's *Pale Fire*.

Such fiction would reject simplistic binaries and "rise above the quarrel between realism and irrealism, formalism and 'contentism,' pure and committed literature, coterie fiction and junk fiction."[23]

Today's writers of literary fiction have often embraced forms of genre fiction with more sincerity than the postmodernists—though novels like Duncan's *Last Werewolf* show that genre-bending fiction spans a spectrum of ironic and sincere stances toward its adopted genres, sometimes mixing both in the same text—and have employed them to structure entire novels, rather than fold them into a larger assemblage of parodic forms.[24] And recent genre benders have *generally* abandoned an insistence on difficulty as the condition for high literary seriousness, though this is hardly true for a writer like Marlon James, seeking to provide pleasure and allowing their books to be accessible to a broader readership—and so, as we will see, inviting charges of mercenary motives and following industrial imperatives. With the benefit of some hindsight, one can see that several influential precursors to the current boom emerged between 1980 and 1990: Umberto Eco's *The Name of the Rose* (trans. 1983), Margaret Atwood's *The Handmaid's Tale* (1985), Paul Auster's *City of Glass* (1985), Cormac McCarthy's *Blood Meridian, or, The Evening Redness in the West* (1985), Toni Morrison's *Beloved* (1987), Haruki Murakami's *Hard-Boiled Wonderland and the End of the World* (trans. 1990), and A. S. Byatt's *Possession: A Romance* (1990). By the new millennium, the floodgates had opened.

Though these high-profile forerunners make it hard to determine a clear origin, Hoberek traces the current rise of what he calls "literary genre fiction" to Chang-rae Lee's immigrant spy thriller, the PEN/Hemingway Award–winning *Native Speaker* (1995), and to Jonathan Lethem's *Motherless Brooklyn* (1999), which epitomized crossover appeal, winning the National Book Critics Circle Award for Fiction and the Gold Dagger from the Crime Writers' Association of the UK.[25] Atwood published her Booker-winning genre mash-up *The Blind Assassin* in 2000, following it with her postapocalyptic *MaddAddam* trilogy (2003–13). What we see immediately in these acclaimed examples is a diversity of application and form: once-popular genres deployed to explore cultural assimilation, neurodivergence, women's self-fashioning, and genetic engineering.

Michael Chabon's Pulitzer-winning *The Amazing Adventures of Kavalier & Clay* (2000) is a historical novel about the authors of a fictional comic book called *The Escapist*, patterned after the creators of Superman. But Chabon subsequently embraced wholesale the frameworks of popular genres with the Arthur Conan Doyle–inspired *The Final Solution* (2004), the swashbuckling medieval adventure *Gentlemen of the Road* (2007), and the noir and alternate history *The Yiddish Policemen's Union* (2007), which won the Hugo and Nebula Awards for science fiction, as well as the Edgar for best mystery novel. Chabon, as we will see, has been the most vociferous proponent of the potential for serious writers to adopt popular genres to enliven contemporary literary fiction.

Nobel laureate Kazuo Ishiguro also paid homage to Conan Doyle with *When We Were Orphans* (2000) and followed that with the dystopian *Never Let Me Go* (2005), the Arthurian fantasy *The Buried Giant* (2015), and the artificial intelligence novel *Klara and the Sun* (2021). McCarthy famously shifted gears from working primarily as a writer of literary westerns, such as *All the Pretty Horses* (1992), to the police thriller *No Country for Old Men* (2005), to the postapocalyptic *The Road* (2006). The genre-scrambling oeuvres of Murakami and Mitchell—whose *Cloud Atlas* (2004) won the British Book Awards literary fiction prize and was short-listed for the Booker, Nebula, and Arthur C. Clarke for science fiction—loom large in contemporary conversations around genre and the global novel.

Lee followed *Native Speaker* with *The Surrendered* (2010), which mixes historical, thriller, and hard-boiled detective fiction, and the speculative fiction climate dystopia *On Such a Full Sea* (2014).[26] Louise Erdrich's Pulitzer-winning crime and revenge thriller *The Round House* (2012) delves into the epidemic of violence against Native American women, and her dystopian *Future Home of the Living God* (2017) echoes Atwood's increasingly realistic vision of a fundamentalist takeover of women's reproductive rights. Jennifer Egan's *The Keep* (2006) is a modern gothic, complete with haunted castle, and *The Candy House* (2022)—a sequel to her Pulitzer-winning *A Visit from the Goon Squad* (2010)—embeds an espionage thriller and speculates into the near future of social media technology. Like Viet Than Nguyen's Pulitzer-winning *The Sympathizer* (2015), Ian McEwan's *Sweet Tooth* (2012) is a bookish spy novel that investigates literature's role in Cold War cultural policy. McEwan's *Machines Like Me* (2019) follows Richard Powers's *Galatea 2.2* (1995) by envisioning an artificial intelligence able to produce compelling analyses of the literary canon. Finally, Colson Whitehead, from *The Intuitionist* (1999) to *Crook Manifesto* (2023), is perhaps the prime example of a contemporary novelist who has made his career by hopping from genre to genre with each successive book. And this catalogue only scratches the most prestigious surface of a far more extensive phenomenon in literary fiction today.

Genre Bending aims to explain this phenomenon: how and why it came about at this moment and what it has meant for contemporary literary fiction.

Why did so many Anglophone literary writers begin adopting popular genres around the turn of the millennium? It's a difficult and tantalizing question, because the genre turn has emerged as a loose, spontaneous, and miscellaneous amalgamation, a diverse mix of high profile and up-and-coming authors seeming to gravitate independently toward popular genre forms—not an organized movement. These writers do not share a single aesthetic program or political project. Indeed, this book argues that *genre-bending literary fiction* is multifarious, diverse in instantiation, purpose, politics, and form—an internally heterogeneous body of contemporary literary production riven by tensions and contradictory impulses. Because it emerges from disparate quarters and is internally divided, it is challenging to discern an immediate watershed moment, single causal factor, or sole historical problem that these writers draw upon the forms of genre fiction to solve. Instead, a number of forces, sometimes at odds, coalesced around the same time to make popular genres attractive to literary writers and to revitalize their estimation of genre as such.

One such force has undoubtedly been a shifting understanding of popular genres. Though some scholarly and media commentators have construed the genre turn as signaling a wholesale reevaluation of the status of genre fiction or a breakdown of the boundaries separating literary and genre fiction, *Genre Bending* argues that a more modest shift has transpired.[27] Andrew Goldstone has detailed how the publishing industry in the early and mid-twentieth century developed a system of genre magazine and book publishing and distribution that established a "distinctive universe of generic fiction, differentiated from both big commercial bestsellers and literary fiction" and "distinctively low-status."[28] By the late twentieth century, however, many in high-status segments of the literary world had begun to appreciate that at least *some* genre fiction counted as important literature. In 1995, the year Lee's *Native Speaker* appeared, The Library of America published *Raymond Chandler: Stories and Early Novels*; it followed this volume with anthologies of noir, the novels of Dashiell Hammett, and collected fictions by SF luminaries like Philip K. Dick, H. P. Lovecraft, and Ursula K. Le Guin. The National Book Foundation awarded Stephen King its 2003 Medal for Distinguished Contribution to American Letters.

Scholars of popular fiction have long contested mid-twentieth-century critics—who portrayed mass culture as uniform products of assembly-line industrial practices and warned against its politically and intellectually deadening effects—and revealed the vibrant subcultures and careful distinctions made by fan communities dedicated to popular genres and the internal heterogeneity of genre fiction fields.[29] Many influential literary critics have argued that popular genres, science fiction in particular, offer powerful resources for imagining alternative social organizations—recognition that was coalescing around the turn of the millennium.[30] But these belated appreciations of the exceptional writing that emerged from the "distinctive universe of generic fiction" that Goldstone charts, and of the potentialities of the genres that flourished there, neither overhauled the reputation of that universe as a whole, much of which is still viewed—by scholars and from the vantage of the literary field—as rapidly produced, heavily formulaic, and easily forgotten;[31] nor did they collapse meaningful separations between literary fiction and genre fiction, which persist as distinct subfields with dedicated publishing imprints, reviewing organs, prizes, and fan communities—even if readers move freely between them.

If genre fiction as a whole has not experienced a revolution in status, the growing recognition of its heterogeneity and that popular genres have been used to produce and provide resources for future, literary works of lasting power and importance has progressed hand in hand with the paradigm shift in genre theory that I discussed in the Preface.[32] Since popular genres, like all genres, are historical and mutable, they may be used in ways that span from the tiredly formulaic to the inspiringly revolutionary. Thus, a generational shift in appreciation of the history and future potential of popular genres, in the right hands, is undoubtedly one motivator of the genre turn. As Jeffrey J. Williams has shown, writers like Chabon, Egan, Lethem, Gary Shteyngart, and Whitehead grew up with pulp fiction and film and often embed homages to popular culture in their work.[33] But genre benders have also, at times, demonstrated an astounding ignorance of the history of, and even disdain for, the genres they have adopted. In an interview about *The Buried Giant*, Ishiguro made it clear that he was not familiar with Marion Zimmer Bradley's *The Mists of Avalon* (1983), perhaps the most famous Arthurian fantasy.[34] It turns out one doesn't have to be a devoted fan or do a deep dive to take up a form.

Also authorizing genre-bending fiction, but from the opposite direction, the high-profile precedents of Atwood's *The Handmaid's Tale*, Eco's *The Name of the Rose*, and Morrison's *Beloved* offered models of literary writers bending popular genres to spectacular effect and great critical acclaim, which helped license and spur the phenomenon by the turn of the millennium. These forerunners made clear that there was never a *de jure* prohibition against using popular genres in literary fiction, merely a conventional aversion toward them because of the desire to mark literary fiction as distinct from and superior to popular fiction, in accord with the publishing industry's segmentation of the market. Such celebrated texts provided a template for elevated, self-consciously literary, but also sincere (as opposed to postmodern ironic) deployments of popular genres. So, another answer to why so many literary writers began to adopt popular genres by the late 1990s and early 2000s is that the canonical status and high cultural power of these illustrious predecessors licensed them to do so.

Morrison's example and the powerful, innovative, and politically motivated work to come out of genre fiction fields—like that of Octavia Butler, Samuel Delany, Le Guin, and Joanna Russ—have also been instrumental in providing a model for feminist, queer, and multiethnic writers to use genres like horror, SF, and fantasy to dramatize the uncanny persistence of racial terror and gendered violence, and their haunting lasting effects, and offer visions of dystopian nightmares or more just societies. Ramón Saldívar has argued prominently that minority writers have blended seemingly opposed genres like realism and fantasy, historical fiction and speculative fiction, because "a new racial imaginary is required to account for the persistence of race" in U.S. social life.[35] The desire to generate "a new racial imaginary" can be discerned as one motivating factor behind the genre turn. At the same time, many of the most prominent genre-bending writers are not primarily concerned with race, and the variety of agendas pursued by multiethnic writers do not resolve into a single political program.

Several scholars have contended that the phenomenon is driven by the desire of literary writers to make their fiction more reader-friendly and thus profitable. Most prominently, Dan Sinykin has argued that the consolidation of the publishing industry into the hands of global media conglomerates "generated the incentives for literary genre fiction," which is "a tactic" literary writers use to make their novels "much more marketable."[36] If the incentives to publish books that are both crowd-pleasing and worthy of critical acclaim have long predated conglomeration, writers in the new millennium undoubtedly work under increased corporatization and literary fiction enters an extraordinarily crowded marketplace of literature and competing media. Literary/commercial hybrids represent a desirable quantity for today's corporate publishers, who view genre as a technique for minimizing risk and aim to turn a profit on the books they sell in every category including literary fiction.[37] And it's clear that genre-bending literary writers have emulated some of the qualities of popular genre fiction—at times, as with Atwood's *Handmaid's Tale* (1985), Lethem's *Motherless Brooklyn* (1999), Mandel's *Station Eleven* (2014), and Whitehead's *The Underground Railroad* (2016), seeing their works adapted for screens big and small. Chabon, as we will see, has prominently embraced a desire to entertain his readers. But understanding genre bending primarily as a strategy to gain market share, induced by the imperatives of corporate publishers and retailers, does not account for the fascinating and varied ways literary writers have deployed their adopted genres, including ways that seem to inhibit their accessibility, salability, and adaptability to streaming media and film, as in the lumbering, meditative zombie novel that is Whitehead's *Zone One* (2011) or the intricate, anti-narrative fantasy that is James's *Black Leopard, Red Wolf* (2019).

How then should we understand the boom in genre bending, and what does it reveal about contemporary literary fiction? Just as we can discern multiple forces that have contributed to its proliferation, what we discover when we read across the outpouring of genre-bending literary fiction of the last several decades, as well as essays and interviews with authors, is a motley corpus driven by varied and sometimes contradictory impulses. I stress this heterogeneity because it derives from my findings—these writers aren't remotely doing just one thing—but it also accords with recent genre theory, which stresses that genres are historically dynamic, a fact that frustrates efforts to clearly define them, neatly categorize, or determine originary or exemplary texts. This emphasis also follows from how acclaimed writers within popular genre fields and the literary writers who have belatedly taken up those genres understand them. In Chapter 1, I show how these writers generate their own theory of genre, one that views it as enabling not constraining, perpetually adaptable for novel deployments, and thus rebut accounts that reigned for much of the twentieth century and that devalued popular genres precisely because they were seen as constraining and overly formulaic. Just as a given genre like detective fiction has conventions that emerge over time, but is not reducible to those conventions, so a phenomenon like genre-bending literary fiction is not reducible to just one thing.

That said, one can discern shared purposes as well divergent and even conflicting strands within this heterogeneous body of work. Genre benders often endeavor to provide "ripping good yarns," in Chabon's words, to make literary fiction more entertaining, and perhaps more profitable.[38] In particular, I show in Chapter 4 that they look to provide *the pleasure of immersion in a fictional world* that has historically been prioritized within the fields of popular fiction.[39] While some critics have seen the genre turn as an endeavor to make literary fiction more plot-driven, the concept of *fictional world* takes into account that furnishing vivid characters and expansive settings for readers to encounter has also been central to the allure of popular genres for turn-of-the-millennium writers of literary fiction.[40] These writers sometimes, that is, endeavor to imitate, borrow from, or pay homage to genre fiction. But genre-bending literary writers also frequently seek to distance themselves from that field, especially its more commercial and formulaic production, espouse traditionally literary values, adopt formal strategies that have long been valorized in the literary field, and maintain the distinctiveness of the latter.

In genre-bending literary fiction, then, we discover how the historical forces recounted above—appreciation of the internal diversity and potential of popular genres, conglomeration, a turn away from postmodern irony, an ambition to create new racial imaginaries, the threatening rise of many competing media and fragmented subcultures—generate a set of pressures within the literary field, spurring literary writers to either imitate the new regime or retrench and defend the values of the literary. We see both responses to conditions of intense economic pressure and cultural competition at work in genre-bending literary fiction—sometimes within the same text. Its internal tensions and contradictions arise out of these conflicting responses, which accord with prominent critical explanations for the genre turn. Genre benders manifest a growing appreciation of (at least some) writers of genre fiction, their generational fandom for popular culture that they grew up adoring, and a desire to provide its immersive pleasures and adopt its alternative epistemologies. All these accord with making literary fiction more like genre fiction, seeking to blur their ostensible boundaries and dismantle their hierarchical relationship, and are compatible with, if not necessarily driven by, commercial imperatives.

At the same time, many genre benders adhere to non- or even anti-commercial literary and political values, endeavoring to subvert or critique the conventions and politics of popular genres, mark *their* deployments of such genres as "serious," uphold the value and specificity of the literary, and maintain its traditional emphases on innovation in narrative structure, linguistic flair, interiority, and self-reflexivity. They extend a modernist-inspired project of formal experiment, pursue high cultural prestige, and seek to defend the literary, which they perceive to be under threat. Like their modernist predecessors, they maintain an ambivalent relationship to the market, portraying the capitalist engines of the culture industry as generators of repetitive, conventional art commodities, while subtly courting its favor. But genre benders generally avoid producing works of extreme difficulty and are more inclined to providing readerly pleasure. These writers valorize such pleasures and don't mind being accessible, but aim to do so without sacrificing artistic integrity, abandoning serious social and political agendas, or dispensing with aesthetic innovation.[41]

The dialectical nature of genre, the repetitive use of and variation on conventional forms, gets reproduced across genre-bending literary fiction, as writers sometimes emulate genre fiction's forms and pleasures and at others seek to transform them—manifesting aesthetic tensions within contemporary literary production. Genre benders exploit the familiarity of genre conventions while often subverting them and critiquing their conventional politics. They seek to be more entertaining, but also to elevate their adopted genres and make them literary—often prioritizing language, character, and reflection over fast-paced action. They recognize genre's flexible utility and portability but worry about the global proliferation of generic products, places, and people. These tensions appear across the field but are visible within works like James's Dark Star trilogy. James is clearly drawn to the pleasures of fantasy world–building and adopts popular fiction's preferred market form of the trilogy, but his work is also wildly experimental, fragmented, recalcitrant in its language, and politically oppositional in its queering and introduction of African storytelling and culture into a genre (high fantasy) that has been notable for its white supremacy, brutal heteropatriarchal sexuality, and nostalgia for European empire.[42] In contrast, a novel like McCarthy's *No Country for Old Men* adheres to a conventional crime novel paradigm that poses the detective as the hero who battles, perhaps futilely, to restore a lost social order against its perceived breakdown.

Genre-bending literary writers share a recognition of the plasticity and utility of all genres—even those that might seem to have become exhausted by their formulaic deployment in the production of popular fiction. Genre-bending literary writers utilize the limitless aesthetic potential that inheres in any genre, from apocalyptic to zombie fiction, and engender a dramatic expansion of the genres found in the literary field. At the same time, *Genre Bending* shows that this field has neither undergone a revolution in its values nor dispensed with hierarchy; it continues to position itself against the field of genre fiction. The Atwoods and Whiteheads of the world don't want to be considered "genre writers" or be pigeonholed into a single genre. Above all—as the title of this book aims to capture—these writers demonstrate how the literary field continues to prize formal innovation and virtuosity.[43] Their novels are frequently marketed and received as "genre bending," and reviews and blurbs that laud them in the same terms abound.[44] Of course, one finds not just formula but ingenious variation, polished prose, and rich characters in genre fields. But these are in general less prioritized, in favor of expectations fulfilled, recurrent character types, privileging of external action, and language that does not distract from the fictional illusion. These qualities do not constitute absolute differences between literary and genre fiction fields but rather relative priorities and values that structure them. Today's literary writers look to transform the genres they adopt rather than producing fine examples of them, playing with or subverting their conventions and infusing their deployments of popular genres with vitality by bringing to them fresh and unexpected concerns.

Examining what today's most critically acclaimed and widely read literary writers have done with the genres of genre fiction, *Genre Bending* reveals the values, practices, and forms, as well as the tensions, that constitute literary fiction today. The center of that field—what literary fiction looks like today—has sometimes been overlooked in recent studies of contemporary fiction that focus increasingly on the institutional and market contexts of literary production, quantitative methods, and on the social functions of popular genres with larger readerships.[45] Mark McGurl has prominently argued that "in the Age of Amazon, all fiction is genre fiction"—that literary fiction has become "in essence a subset of" genre fiction, in that it caters to a "generic desire" readers have for "discussable interpretive problems," "artful intricacies," and "thematic subtleties," that publishers and retailers aim to reliably fulfill.[46] From the business standpoint of Amazon, this is certainly true: literary fiction is a marketing category like any other.[47] But genre-bending literary writers continues to define themselves against the fields of popular genre fiction, employing the affordances of genre for repetition and variation, while opposing formula, predictability, and the idea that literature is just another mass-produced commodity. They embrace the *genres* of genre fiction, not *genre fiction* as such.

This book does not, however, seek to account for the many brilliant and inspired deployments of genre to have emerged within genre fiction fields or in film and streaming television in recent decades. It would be a much longer, less circumscribed, and different book if it attended to all the fascinating and innovative work that has emerged across genre fields and in other media. (One has merely to invoke the names of Neil Gaiman, Nalo Hopkinson, N. K. Jemisin, Bong Joon-ho, R. F. Kuang, China Miéville, Silvia Moreno-Garcia, Nnedi Okorafor, Jordan Peele, Rebecca Roanhorse, Neil Stephenson, Quentin Tarantino, and Jeff VanderMeer to begin to convey this range.) Instead, *Genre Bending* focuses on a phenomenon within literary fiction—not to reify industry segmentation or take the side of an elite hierarchy that privileges the literary, but as analytic necessity to understand the genre turn and what it reveals about the constitution of the field of literary fiction at a time when the absence of certain genres will no longer serve as definitional. This book thus aims at a scope that balances the practical and analytic necessity to restrict itself to genre play within literary fiction, with the desire to accurately capture the diversity of that production through many varied examples.

Genre, Genre Fiction, Literary Fiction

The doubleness of the term is confusing, but to understand genre-bending fiction, it is essential to differentiate between "genre," as an existing literary framework or "recipe" that writers may adapt and vary according to their needs, and "genre fiction," the field of literary production that is largely synonymous with "popular fiction," a vast arena of publishing, distribution, and reception in which genre functions as a fundamental organizing principle and that is often distinguished from the far less lucrative field of "serious" fiction, "literature," or "literary fiction."[48] When someone says, "so-and-so is *a genre writer*," sometimes with pejorative implication, they tend to mean someone who works primarily in one genre and whose work circulates in the field of genre/popular fiction—not a writer who works with genres, because all texts use genres. "Genre," John Frow writes, "is a universal dimension of textuality."[49] Differentiating between genre as a flexible framework, and genre fiction and literary fiction as fields of practice, helps make sense of the genre turn. Doing so clarifies that it is a turn to particular genres—literary fiction has always used genres—and a phenomenon *within* literary fiction, not a breakdown of the coherence of literary fiction and genre fiction as relatively distinct, if also overlapping, fields of practice.

Recent genre theorists have arrived at a "near-consensus," shifting from the task of "identifying and classifying fixed, ahistorical entities to studying genres as historical processes."[50] Genres are plastic frameworks for literary practice that are subject to continual deformation as writers adapt them in pursuit of various ends. A genre's features are thus historically dynamic and its status variable. Paul Kincaid, for example, contends that scholars' perennial difficulty defining and determining an ur-text for science fiction stems from the fact that a genre is "a pattern ... in a constant state of flux."[51] And Alistair Fowler reminds us a genre's cultural status varies over time—the novel itself is prime evidence—which suggests that at one level what we are witnessing today is the oldest game in town.[52] Literary history could be described as the story of writers adopting, parodying, mixing, and metamorphosizing popular forms. From *Don Quixote*, *Robinson Crusoe*, and *Northanger Abbey* to Eco's *Name of the Rose*, the novel has always played with the popular genres that surround it. The raw material today is different—the genres of twentieth-century popular culture, from which modernist aesthetic ideology had aimed to distance itself—but the use of genre is nothing new.

The use of generic patterns or frameworks happens in a particular institutional and market context, however.[53] While genres are established but variable frameworks, "genre fiction" and "literary fiction" refer not to the presence or absence of genre, but to relational subfields of production, circulation, and reception. Such cultural fields are, as Pierre Bourdieu emphasizes, always fluctuating, their borders sites of contestation over what counts as "legitimate" literary art.[54] Each subfield is constituted by agents and institutions particular to it, and organized around its own practices, values, hierarchies, and forms of recognition; while genre fiction may be regarded as poor quality from within the literary subfield, genre fiction readers often find literary fiction snobbish and boring.[55] But these subfields are internally dynamic, permeable, and blurry at their edges. Particular cases highlight their contingent character. Many of Le Guin's novels were initially published by SF publisher Ace Books and later by the Library of America. Likewise, when Samuel Delany's *Dhalgren* (1975), first published by Bantam Books, appears decades later in a handsome new Vintage edition, with blurbs comparing Delany to Joyce, Gass, and Nabokov, the new edition circulates in the literary field, but its uses of genre and formal properties have stayed the same. Though such instances reveal these fields' dynamism and permeability, they retain a relatively distinct character and set of institutions, values, and practices.

Genre fiction, as many scholars have shown, is a huge and diverse, not monolithic, field. Prodigiously original work has emerged within it, and even its most formula-driven segments are full of variations that are clearly legible to genre aficionados. Devoted readers actively reshape and repurpose texts and genres they adore, rather than being passive consumers. As I argue at greater length below, the view in literary quarters that genre fiction as a whole is inferior ignores the heterogeneity and varying levels of quality within it (as well as different audiences' varying conception of what constitutes quality). But the view that much genre fiction is rapidly produced, imitative, aimed at turning a quick profit, and rapidly forgotten has not been radically overturned, and, as Goldstone has shown, it emerges from the distinctive commercial practices of that field. "Popular fiction" is roughly synonymous with "genre fiction," because of the central role genre plays in organizing this subfield. For mass-market publishers, genre provides a proven formula to help produce new books rapidly, imitate previous successes, and target readers—generating a significant degree of formal regularity within genre fiction fields. Janice Radway's influential study of "the institutional matrix" of romance publishing traces the commercial imperatives that caused publishers to "concentrate on a single literary subgenre" in "the interest of establishing better control over their market."⁵⁶ Radway writes that "semi-programmed issue" helps publishers aim at a preestablished audience to combat the uniqueness and hence unpredictable sales of any given book. These publishing strategies were often developed "in connection with related fan magazines that foster the creation of a generic formula or orthodoxy."⁵⁷ But the institutional matrix, imperatives, target audiences, and the orthodox formulae that emerge shouldn't be confused with the genre itself. A genre isn't reducible to its most formulaic, commercially driven instances, and writers working outside of the institutional matrix are free to adopt a genre at will.

Meanwhile, writers of literary fiction have always used genres, even if they tried for much of the twentieth century to repress this fact by emphasizing the uniqueness of individual works of art.⁵⁸ While today's literary writers have no problem adapting genres like detective, fantasy, and science fiction, they have not fundamentally changed their attitude toward the bulk of genre fiction. As this huge swath of production has long been perceived to be over-reliant on formula and deeply embedded in commerce, it has stood at odds with a modernist-inspired ideology of art that prizes originality in the form of "technical revision" and "resistance to mass culture."⁵⁹ Locating a literary work's value in its novelty, in the degree to which its techniques depart from previous models, and in disavowing commercial motives, this aesthetic ideology has worked to conceal the reliance of all texts on existing genres and to proscribe certain ones: those that flourished in the realm of mass culture. If the taboo against these genres has been exorcised, the literary attitude toward the commercial practices of the popular field has not.

Like genre fiction, literary fiction is a subfield constituted by agents and institutions, encompassing books "published by literary imprints" and denoted by other "structural and contextual segmentation," such as "book prizes, material considerations (such as cover designs and book formats), media coverage, bookshop design, and bestseller lists."⁶⁰ Claire Squires argues that while its defining qualities are "contingent and shifting," literary fiction is generally "defined by a process of negation": it is "*not* formula fiction or genre fiction, *not* mass-market or best-selling fiction."⁶¹ Literary fiction is "formally undefinab[le]," constituted not by a particular form but by its prestige position in the culture and the marketplace: "'Literary' then is an assurance of quality."⁶² This certainly does not suggest that readers will agree that everything marked as "literary fiction" will be any good, nor that there aren't great works published in "genre fiction"—but rather that literary fiction trades on institutions' "assurance," backed by reputations built over time, that they recognize quality. But the definition of quality, the formal features valorized within this field, are subject to change, as evidenced by the increasing prevalence of historical fiction among prizewinning novels, the boom in autofiction, and the rise of genre-bending works of literary fiction.[63] At the same time, Chapters 2 and 3 of this book argue that the literary field maintains relatively durable values, including innovation in prose style and narrative structure, the rendering of character psychology, and self-reflexivity about literariness—which continue to be privileged in genre-bending literary fiction.

Though literary fiction does not adhere to a single genre or fixed set of forms, it has always drawn on existing genre frameworks or recipes. It has become something of a critical truism of late to say that literary fiction is its own genre with its own conventions, but this claim is often made without specifying what those conventions are, or by viewing literary fiction as limited to bourgeois domestic realism—usually in the body of Jonathan Franzen. Literary fiction has, long predating the genre turn, drawn on various genres: realism and historical fiction, but also multicultural novels, magical realism, ludic postmodernism, and historiographic metafiction, unadorned Carveresque prose, and Rushdiesque verbal profusion.[64] Among these recognizable subsets, Anglophone writers of literary fiction have long played with other time-tested and more recent genres: romance (e.g., Byatt's *Possession*), satire (Martin Amis's *Money* [1984]), pastoral (T. C. Boyle's *Budding Prospects: A Pastoral* [1984]), picaresque and bildungsroman (Saul Bellow's *The Adventures of Augie March* [1953]), the immigrant family saga (Amy Tan's *Joy Luck Club* [1989]), the novel of manners (Bret Easton Ellis's *American Psycho* [1991]), and the neo-slave narrative (Margaret Walker's *Jubilee* [1966])—to cite a handful of what could be endless examples. All novels use existing genres, and since writers often combine genres, we often find many intertwined in the same book. Jeffrey Eugenides's *The Marriage Plot* (2011) draws on the genres of the campus novel, the bildungsroman, the historical novel (of the 1980s), the philosophical novel (engaging deconstruction), romance, and metafiction. Writers of literary fiction have never been averse to genre, but the genre turn expands their repertoire to incorporate the genres that have historically flourished in popular culture.

Genre-bending writers acknowledge that popular genres are compatible with the production of serious literature, in the right hands. But they don't register a wholesale reevaluation of genre fiction. Certain works using these genres gain recognition, while the bulk of production utilizing them gains no boost in prestige whatsoever. Nguyen's verbose, highly allusive novel about a North Vietnamese double agent was published by the celebrated independent Grove Atlantic and circulates in the literary field.[65] *The Sympathizer* demonstrates the capacity of the espionage genre to be used in ingenious new ways. But it doesn't eliminate the view in many literary quarters that Tom Clancy's or Robert Ludlum's books participate in a broader economy of entertaining, commercially successful, rapidly produced, and deservedly ephemeral fiction. Likewise, literary scholars' growing interest in genre fiction does not recuperate the reputation of the field as a whole, as they tend to privilege ambitious touchstone texts, largely within the realm of speculative fiction, or investigate popular genres out of historicist or sociological interest, rather than argue that the work of David Baldacci and James Patterson has been unjustly maligned. We see this nuanced stance, an appreciation of the plasticity and utility of popular genres, and an effort to differentiate between literary and genre fiction throughout the work of genre-bending writers.

Embracing Genre, not Genre Fiction

As I elaborate in Chapter 1, if there is a single unifying thread in genre-bending literary fiction, it is a recognition of the utility and adaptability of all genres: a recognition that the genres that have flourished in popular fiction are not dead, inert, or worn out, but remain as generative and malleable as any others. At the same time, genre benders tend to maintain their distinction from the field of genre fiction. The position of such writers is perhaps most succinctly articulated in Chabon's *Kavalier & Clay* by Rosa Saks, the girlfriend of comic book artist Joe Kavalier and daughter of an eccentric surrealist: "No medium is inherently better than any other. . . . It's all in what you do with it."[66] Here, Rosa refers to medium not genre, but literary novelists' embrace of popular genres reflects an analogous assertion of equality, of not granting inherent superiority to one aesthetic form over another.[67] But these writers don't reject qualitative differences between high or serious art and low or repetitive commodity production. Rosa's "inherently," and her assertion that it all depends on "what you do with it," leaves the possibility for a range of outcomes.

While much of *Kavalier & Clay* asserts that comics is as plastic and capacious as any medium and explores the process of experimentation through which a prodigious talent like Joe Kavalier can exploit its potential, the novel also suggests that most of what gets churned out by the industrial matrix of comics publishing is rapidly produced, low quality, and derivative—due to publishers' desire to keep overhead low and maximize profits—and politically handcuffed by a corporate ownership eager to remain inoffensive. After depicting the experimental work of Kavalier and Clay in creating "the so-called modernist or prismatic Escapist stories" (363), Chabon dedicates much of second half of the novel to Sammy Clay's career as a writer for the pulp publisher Pharaoh Comics. The publisher's name refers ham-handedly to its tyrannical business practices, working Jewish scribblers like Clay to death, while adhering to a "program of cost-cutting and slavish imitation" (485). It would be foolish to blame the medium, Chabon insists. But one might still find fault with the commercial landscape that produces comics and regard most of its vast output as mercenary, imitative, cheaply and rapidly produced, and inferior. The writers of literary fiction who have turned to genres like SF, fantasy, and the detective novel express a similar attitude toward the subfield of genre fiction. The genres are not the problem; rather, for these writers the wider field of popular culture is compromised aesthetically and politically by the industrial imperatives and processes by which it is produced.

We also see the desire to maintain distinctions between literary and popular fiction in Whitehead's *Zone One* and the reception to it. The novel revels in its play with a popular genre, but suggests, in a manner reminiscent of George Romero's films and some of the most strident critiques of the culture industry, that consumerism, Hollywood, and TV are what turn people into brainless zombies in the first place. Whitehead has switched genres so much throughout his career that he wrote a self-parodying feature in the *New York Times*, describing a modified dartboard that helps him decide what he'll write next.[68] When *Zone One* appeared, commentators still registered the incongruity of such a literary-minded writer taking up a form like the zombie novel, even if those same commentators were getting in on the action. Glen Duncan penned a review in the *Times* that began: "A literary novelist writing a genre novel is like an intellectual dating a porn star."[69] One can easily see how Duncan's quip would offend porn stars and genre fans alike.[70] But while his speculation that "broad spectrum marketing will attract" zombie-loving readers, who will "writhe and swear their way through (if they make it through) and feel betrayed and outraged and migrained," reveals the persistence of condescension toward genre fiction audiences, it appropriately captures the way literary and genre fiction fields remain distinct, even while literary writers pen books featuring zombies and werewolves. *Zone One* was lauded in the *Times, Washington Post,* and *Contemporary Literature*.[71] But the novel is completely absent from Max Brooks's website Zombies Defined, the Zombiepedia fan wiki, and the Zombie Research Society.[72]

The series of kerfuffles that have emerged when literary writers have endeavored to set their genre-bending works apart from popular fiction looms as perhaps the most highly visible evidence for my contention that writers of literary fiction utilize *the genres* of genre fiction while seeking to stake out their distance from *the field* of genre fiction. In 2009, Margaret Atwood infamously claimed she did not write science fiction, which she defined as works that feature impossibilities like "talking squids in outer space," prompting the indignation of SF fans and writers alike. Le Guin famously responded that Atwood "doesn't want the literary bigots to shove her into the literary ghetto."[73] Though the metaphor of popular genres as ghettos misleads in several ways, Le Guin was clearly right about Atwood's desire to maintain the respect of prestige-granting agents in the field of literary fiction.[74]

Ishiguro's handwringing about *The Buried Giant* and the response it elicited from Le Guin reran this episode. Ishiguro worried that readers might "be prejudiced against the surface elements" of the novel—presumably its knights, dragons, ogres, and pixies—and wondered: "Are they going to say this is fantasy?"[75] Le Guin retorted: "Well, yes, they probably will. Why not? It appears that the author takes the word for an insult. To me that is so insulting, it reflects such thoughtless prejudice, that I had to write this piece in response."[76] But rather than demonstrating prejudice against fantasy, the genre he decided to adopt and adapt into a parable about cycles of retributive violence, Ishiguro conflated, and worried his readers would conflate, *genre* with *genre fiction*, fantasy with lowbrow entertainment. His novel clearly uses fantasy, aiming to de-idealize the heroic portraits that dominate Arthurian romance, but he did not want to be associated with the many-sequeled sagas of Jack Whyte, Richard Monaco, or Gillian Bradshaw, and, like Atwood, feared scaring off a literary readership that is his primary audience. Le Guin rightly accused Ishiguro of being afraid to "pollute his authorial gravitas."[77] In the same blog post, she argued that writers cannot "successfully use the 'surface elements' of a literary genre—far less its profound capacities—for a serious purpose, while despising it to the point of fearing identification with it."[78] Le Guin does not think "fantasy writer" a pejorative label, and her oeuvre abundantly demonstrates the genre's "profound capacities." But she too acknowledges that much fantasy is formulaic, commercial, and low quality—in other words: genre fiction. The "surface elements" of fantasy, she writes, "which occur in certain works of great literary merit such as *Beowulf,* the *Morte d'Arthur,* and *Lord of the Rings,* are also much imitated in contemporary commercial hackwork."[79] If Ishiguro "feared identification," it was with the "commercial hackwork," not with the genre he used to structure his novel.

Upon publishing *Machines Like Me,* a novel featuring an intelligent robot in an alternate Britain, Ian McEwan also caricatured science fiction conventions and intimated that SF did not consider serious "human dilemmas."[80] These vaunted contemporary writers' reluctance to be lumped in with pulp is nothing new. With tongue at an indeterminate depth in his cheek, Kurt Vonnegut famously called himself "a soreheaded occupant of a file drawer labeled 'science fiction'" who wanted out, "particularly since so many serious critics regularly mistake the drawer for a urinal."[81] Harlan Ellison snapped that if you called him a SF writer, he'd "come to your house and . . . nail your pet's head to a coffee table. I'll hit you so hard your ancestors will die."[82] Today's acclaimed writers of literary fiction share this agonistic attitude to their adopted genres to varying degrees. The generation of Atwood, Ishiguro, and McEwan looks more resistant to being associated with science fiction, while the likes of Chabon, Lethem, and Whitehead don't find such labels insulting. All of these figures share a recognition that popular genres can be put to serious, meaningful use and their forms varied endlessly. At the same time, they endeavor to differentiate their work from the great majority of popular production and to reinforce the notion that the literary is the preserve for formal innovation and the pondering of weighty human questions. While such commentary often neglects the profound work done within genres like SF, it reveals the endurance of efforts to maintain the literary field as distinct and the lingering perception that *most* genre fiction is highly formulaic and ephemeral.

The comments of Atwood, Ishiguro, and McEwan might appear to be strategies for maintaining prestige or simply elitism. But when we survey the work of genre-bending literary writers, we discover what Bourdieu long ago argued about cultural fields like the art or literary worlds: that they are sustained by belief.[83] In this case, the belief is in the continued distinction and distinctiveness of the literary: that it is not just one segment of the book market among many, but a cultural arena engaged in a worthy project of artistic experimentation and the exploration of weighty social, political, and philosophical questions—even at the expense of appeal to the widest possible audience. To say the literary subfield is *sustained* by belief is not to say it is imaginary. A publishing imprint that views itself as "literary" rather than commercial in orientation has that belief concretized when other agents or institutions recognize and legitimate its self-conception—for example when a prestigious journal like the *Times Literary Supplement* reviews that imprint's books.[84] Books published in genre fiction subfields do often possess many features we conventionally identify as literary and transform rather than simply repeat the frameworks they inherit. There are linguistically rich and socially perspicacious works published by Tor, and fast-paced plots that have won the National Book Award. If works published in different subfields often share qualities, this suggests the way the literary subfield's claims to distinction and distinctiveness are a matter of belief that is legitimated and made real when ratified by other literary institutions.

The Dark Star trilogy further exemplifies genre benders' desire to mark *their* uses of genre as literary and distinct from those in genre fiction fields. It would be easy to understand James's launch of an "African *Game of Thrones*," initiated in 2019, as market-driven, an effort, perhaps spurred by his agent or publisher, to ride the coattails of George R. R. Martin's *A Song of Ice and Fire*, its HBO adaptation, and Marvel's *Black Panther* (2018, dir. Ryan Coogler). Jia Tolentino of the *New Yorker* similarly assumed that James, "after reaching the pinnacle of critical acclaim, with the Booker, was pivoting to the land of the straightforward best-seller," and "would produce a book with practical, even perfunctory, language, and an accessible, satisfying plot."[85] But the notion that James embarked upon a fantasy trilogy for commercial rather than literary motives, to capture a broader audience than his previous wildly experimental novels garnered, quickly runs aground upon opening a book that refuses to make concessions to accessibility. Tolentino discovered in *Black Leopard,*

Red Wolf a novel that delivers a couple "genre-specific satisfactions," but also felt "literary and labyrinthine to an almost combative degree," featuring an opaque storyline "in which basic narrative conventions are consistently questioned and often disowned"; she confessed that she "often felt adrift in the stream."[86]

If James refused to sacrifice formal experiment and deliver his editors a "straightforward bestseller," he was not courting difficulty for its own sake or merely as a gambit to garner prestige. Critics have lauded his project of introducing a Black diasporic, queer sensibility into the fantasy genre, and rejecting narrative coherence to question whether stories convey usable truths about the world or offer a non-instrumental pursuit valuable in its own right.[87] In James's rejections of the conventions of the fantasy genre and narrative coherence, such that an accomplished reviewer for the *New Yorker* felt lost, we see a vivid demonstration of how a writer's efforts to transform a genre and adapt it to his own concerns may outweigh the desire to produce a more commercially viable product.

At the same time, we see that play also motivates James (recall his desire to "geek the fuck out"), and that he does not reject the market as such. Here we encounter the signal difference between literary fiction and the avant-garde segment of the literary field. The latter has long experimented with genre and continues to circulate via small independent and university presses,[88] while the former aims for both literary value and marketability—though not the widest possible audience—through conglomerate and independent publishers. James's introduction of African folklore and bawdy queer sexuality into fantasy is a political intervention into a genre tradition long dominated by reimaginings of medieval Europe—but it's also fun. He describes his intention to construct a "vast playground of myth and history and legend that other people can draw from, a pool that's as rich as Viking or Celtic lore."[89] Conceiving of a genre's history as a pool or playground, James endeavors to create both a repository for future narrative construction and an imaginative sandbox for others to play in.[90] As in much fantasy, in the Dark Star trilogy, this "vast playground" takes the form of a fictional universe to be immersed in. Chapter 4 of this book argues that a reawakening to the pleasure of such immersion among literary writers is a leading driver of their turn to popular genres. The elaborate world James creates is the best evidence of his attunement to this pleasure, but it is further suggested by the intricate maps he drew for the book and a self-reflexive discovery of "a map of our lands," created with "[s]uch masterful craft, such detail," within *Black Leopard*.[91] When Tracker's lover Mossi asks if the map was created by "a merchant in the East," the witch Sologon rebukes him: "Men and women in these lands have mastered crafts too."[92] James clearly points to his own mapmaking here, insisting that African diasporic peoples have also mastered the art of fantasy world-building.

Such a mix of motives does not fit neatly into a binary of submission or opposition to the marketplace. Tolentino cites Johnny Temple, the editor of James's *John Crow's Devil* (2005) at Akashic Books, speculating that James may not "always realize how inventive he is, or how subversive. I think, in his mind, he's always written this highly commercial thing."[93] And James joked of his initial attempt to write *Book of Night Women* from a single point of view: "People gotta eat! I've been trying to sell out for years!"[94] In such comments, we see the blurriness of purported binaries between literary autonomy and market capitulation. James wants to make a living from his writing and would welcome a bigger audience and payday, but his fiction follows artistic agendas that frustrate this intention—and many readers. (Producers too: *A Brief History of Seven Killings* was optioned by HBO, sold to Amazon, later to Netflix, and at the time of writing still has not been made.)[95] While *Black Leopard* offers a captivating world to be immersed in, it also puts forth a dizzying, antinarrative structure that resists readers' investment and identification, as the novel recounts a quest for a boy who may not exist, a quest no one knows why they are embarking upon, and is led by a hero who is difficult to like.

Few of today's genre-bending writers produce work as labyrinthine and recalcitrant as James's, but many share his love of play and deforming popular genres in innovative ways to approach fresh subject matter. Carmen Maria Machado has called *Her Body and Other Parties* (2017), a finalist for the National Book Award, "a collection of short stories that has a lot of . . . genre-bending material."[96] Playing with "science fiction . . . fabulist, surrealist, liminal fantasy" serves her interest in "using fiction to explore questions about women's lives," in "a book that has all female protagonists, most of them queer."[97] *Her Body and Other Parties* offers a microcosm of genre-bending fiction, deploying a smorgasbord of genres and bending them toward varied concerns: a metafictional fable about a woman's mysterious green ribbon that explores possessive male desire and the history of cautionary tales told to women; an apocalyptic pandemic tale posed as a list of sexual conquests, in which sexual desire is both dangerous contagion and solace; a romantic ghost story, in which women's bodies begin to dematerialize, that considers the way clothing and appearance obscure and efface what lies beneath. Like James's, Machado's work is deliriously playful, and she understands genre, as this book does, as an enabling framework rather than a set of rigid constraints. In an interview, she affirms that she is attracted to "work that moves between genres in exciting ways and with almost with no regard for their rules." Such "rules," it turns out, exert little force, are made to be broken. While "people get very fixated on what [a] genre allows," Machado "thinks of genre as an exciting set of potential and what can be subverted . . . a jumping off point, a space you work from and can do whatever you want. I love genre and the way it gives me this chance to play."[98] Though we often think of genres, particularly as they function in the marketplace, as marketing categories or shelving mechanisms, as "contracts" between writers and readers, as sets of expectations that readers want to see fulfilled, today's literary writers don't find that genre ties their hands.[99] While writers like James, Machado, and Whitehead have deployed popular genres and subverted their conventions to address concerns surrounding race, gender, and sexuality, genre-bending writing is not bound to a particular politics. Rather, as I elaborate in Chapter 1, writers like Machado theorize genre as enabling potential, as a useful framework that can be transformed endlessly and adapted toward disparate agendas.

Perhaps in no contemporary writer is the playful, liberating sense of genre's potential more palpable than in the work of David Mitchell, whose novels string together and interweave multiple genres and combine to form a giant "über-novel" that centers on a millennium-long battle between immortal Horologists and Anchorites. While Mitchell's *Utopia Avenue* (2020), a historical rock 'n' roll novel about an English band in the late 1960s, looks more conventional than much of his oeuvre, its depiction of the unclassifiable titular band can easily be read as a figure for Mitchell's career and an articulation of his genre-bending ethos, which revels in the uncategorizable, the virtuosic, and the hybrid. When an interviewer in the novel remarks that Utopia Avenue's debut blends "acid rock, folk with acid effects, R&B, folk interludes, passages of jazz," he ventures that "schizophrenic" might be "an apt adjective for such inconsistency of style."¹⁰⁰ The band's lead singer Elf asks if "eclectic" might be more fitting, but the critic persists: "But into which *category* of music . . . can Utopia Avenue be located? Our viewers at home will be worrying about this question. The *category*" (291). Dean, the bassist, offers "an eclectic category," but the guitar prodigy Jasper de Zoet—descendent of the protagonist of Mitchell's *The Thousand Autumns of Jacob de Zoet* (2010) and *Utopia*'s link with the "über-novel"—has no patience for categories. "You're like a zoologist asking a platypus, 'Are you a duck-like otter? Or an otter-like duck?'" de Zoet retorts. "The platypus doesn't care . . . I don't care. We make music we like. We hope others like it too. That's it" (291).

Here the artist aims to satisfy his own vision and please audiences; authenticity does not require indifference to the market. And it's not hard to read Utopia Avenue's genre-bending, combinatory style and rejection of categorization as reflecting Mitchell's own aesthetic, and the music critic's persistent need to "locate" the band, on behalf of an audience imagined to require such categories, as commentary on the way cultural intermediaries—critics, agents, editors, publishers, retailers, record producers—rely on genre categories for marketing purposes. In *Utopia Avenue*, Mitchell fashions a narrative about the rise to middling fame of a band whose virtuosity and genius fail to translate to massive sales figures, because of their uncategorizability and failure to deliver blockbuster hits, as they continually struggle to release the single that their record company and "commercial logic" demand (249). Mitchell's rock novel thus internalizes another persistent value of the literary field: the belief that art should not merely satisfy commercial demands but should be dictated by the vision of the artist.

A similar defense of authenticity within the marketplace—with the gamut of hipster dad trappings in tow—emerges in Chabon's *Telegraph Avenue* (2012), with which, as their similar titles and subject matter suggest, Mitchell clearly aims to dialogue. The twin plots of Chabon's novel follow Archy Stallings's and Nat Jaffe's efforts to preserve their vintage vinyl shop Brokeland Records against the invasion of the megastore Dogpile Thang into their north Oakland neighborhood, while their wives Gwen Shanks and Aviva Roth-Jaffe, who run a midwifery clinic, are also increasingly under threat from corporate hospital managers and a medical establishment that devalues their natural birth–centered practice. If the novel looks like return to realism for Chabon, *Telegraph Avenue* still pays tribute to a hybrid, genre-scrambling ethos.¹⁰¹

Near the novel's climax, Archy eulogizes his surrogate father, the funk organist Cochise Jones, and recounts that he and Nat have been known to "get into a lot of, like, genre arguments." But Cochise "never took part in those discussions"; he came up in the late 60s "when the styles and players were mixing it all up" and dubbed his own style "Brokeland Creole," which "means you stop drawing those lines. It means Africa and Europe cooked up in the same skillet. Chopin, hymns, Irish music, polyrhythms, talking drums."[102] The effort to remix forms and erase bright lines between genres clearly animates the practices of genre-bending writers.[103] Archy explains that Cochise's ethos inspired "an *ideal*" he and Nat had that their store would be more than a place to buy and sell records, that it would function like a stop on "the Old Silk Road":

> It's a hard road, it has bandits, sandstorms. You carrying the light of all the civilizations back and forth, but all around the tribes just want to keep up their warring, and killing.... But you keep on because you are trying to earn a little cheese, right, and you spreading the collective wisdom back and forth. Forging that Creole style. And every so often ... you got these oases ... these caravansaries, where they all get together and ... listen to good music, swap wild tales of exaggeration.... That was kind of our dream. (374)

In Archy's and Nat's ideal meeting place of genres, cultures, and styles, a break from tribalism, we see refracted the literary utopia genre benders like Chabon and Mitchell aspire to in their fiction. It's not anti-capitalist; Archy still wants to "earn a little cheese." But the desire to make a decent living doesn't eclipse all other values, "carrying the light of all the civilizations," "spreading the collective wisdom," or "forging" a new Creole style. In the multidirectional vectors of James's desire to "geek" out on, queer, and create an African-inspired fantasy that rejects narrative conventions, Machado's exuberant exploration of queer women's lives, the efforts of Mitchell's band to produce music they and others will like, even if it doesn't bring huge commercial success, and Chabon's shop owners, whose livelihood is threatened by "the capitalist flood tides of consumerist uniformity" (401) but stick to their creole "ideal," we find the nuanced position genre-bending literary writers seek to stake out: valuing immersive pleasure and play, style, innovation, combination, the subversive, uncategorizable, and unconventional, acknowledging the need to make a buck, but continuing to envision a higher calling for art.

Internal Conflicts

One of the most intriguing aspects of the efflorescence of genre-bending literary fiction around the turn of the millennium is that it is not an organized movement. Instead, many of the most acclaimed writers of Anglophone fiction have gravitated independently toward popular genres. But if there has been anything like a spokesperson for their adoption it would be Chabon, and if there is anything like a manifesto for a loose and spontaneous upsurge, it would be an essay he first published in 2002 as guest editor for Dave Eggers's literary magazine, *Timothy McSweeney's Quarterly Concern*.[104] Issue 10 was an anomaly for *McSweeney's*, seeming to run counter to its mission and ethos: it was simultaneously distributed as a paperback by Vintage, a Random House imprint, as *McSweeney's Mammoth Treasury of Thrilling Tales* (2002); and it featured an all-star roster of contemporary writers who straddle the literary/genre divide, boasting on its cover "All new, never before seen, original stories by Stephen King, Michael Crichton, Elmore Leonard, Nick Hornby, Aimee Bender, Dave Eggers, and more!"[105] A second Vintage paperback in 2004 featured contributions from Atwood, Mitchell, Miéville, Lethem, Joyce Carol Oates, and another introduction by Chabon. He would then suture these together into a preface for the *Best American Short Stories 2005* and rework the essay for the *Los Angeles Times*, before combining and revising all of these into "Trickster in a Suit of Lights: Thoughts on the Modern Short Story," which kicked off a book of his collected essays in 2008.[106] In the multiple incarnations of the essay Chabon put out beginning in 2002, fresh off his Pulitzer Prize for *Kavalier & Clay*, we see an unparalleled example of an author leveraging his newfound prestige to promote a vision for the contemporary literary field. In these essays, Chabon advocates for the potential that inheres in popular genres and for understanding even "serious" literary values as sources of readerly pleasure and entertainment. But the essays and *McSweeney's* special issue also serve as a microcosm of the multiple, sometimes contradictory motives within the literary field that give rise to genre-bending fiction and that it attempts to negotiate.

Partnering with a prestige imprint of a corporate publisher and purveying stories by big-name contemporary writers, *McSweeney's* broke with its typical modus operandi in the issues and Vintage editions edited by Chabon. As Amy Hungerford details, Eggers dedicated *McSweeney's* to "the amateur reader," to publishing unheralded writers rejected by other venues, and disavowed commercial motives. But here was an issue featuring not "the ranks of workers who cannot make a living from literature," but some of the most successful authors in the Anglophone world.[107]

In a note appended to Issue 10, the magazine's editors anticipated that readers might detect a tension between its stated goals and the literary brand names and commercial character that Issue 10 and the Vintage editions flaunted, with graphics that mimicked the pulp magazines of the mid-twentieth century. The questions they anticipated: "Have you forgotten your love for the common man, the free-thinking reader, the unpublished writer?" The editors responded: "No. We have not forgotten that. Michael Chabon, in assembling the issue, sought to bring non-genre writers into that world, and to bring popular genre writers to readers like yourself."[108] The editors claimed that the commercial character of the issue, "the kind of book sold at airports or even, if we dared dream, supermarkets," was democratizing, enabling "as many people as possible" to access "great" content and "popular genre writers." That such writers would be easy to encounter elsewhere went unmentioned. Finally, they offer an explanation that was hard to quarrel with: they did it for the money, but they needed it for their charity, the writing school 826 Valencia that Eggers founded in concert with the press. "We were gearing up for our first fall schoolyear ... and we were short of funds. . . . Vintage, a great paperback book-publishing company, offered to buy the rights . . . and these funds kept the learning lab afloat throughout the fall."[109] Here the editors aim to assuage fears of selling out by clarifying that their motives were philanthropic. The note concludes by insisting that "the important thing to know is this: The unusual aspects of this issue do not indicate a general change, either editorial or financial, in our focus or mission, to the extent that we have either." The next issue, will "include all of those things you have grown to love: new contributors, a consistent font, a story set at a crafts fair, and a very special, financially-unwise extra feature."[110] Insisting on their "financially-unwise" mission, the editors make clear that the artistic ethos and credibility of *McSweeney's* rely on distancing it from profit-seeking, positioning it as an institution dedicated to philanthropic education, unheralded writers, and literary art for its own sake—even as it seeks to democratize access and offer an anti-elitist, pulp-styled piece of airport fiction, issued by a major corporate publisher.

The effort to negotiate tensions between disinterested, anti-commercial literary motives and aims for wide accessibility and the market-friendly provision of readerly pleasure also animates Chabon's "Trickster" essay and its earlier incarnations. Chabon laments the dominance of realism in literary short fiction, what he calls "the contemporary, quotidian, plotless, moment-of-truth story."[111] The question of whether a frustration with realism animates the genre turn in general is a difficult one. Chapter 4 shows that genre benders have often turned toward the escapist pleasure of immersion in fictional worlds that are enjoyable precisely because they are not the here and now. And while writers of literary fiction have undoubtedly been attracted to the affordances of speculative genres to imagine alternatives to society as it is, at times such genres have been advocated for on grounds that they are in fact more realist than so-called realism.[112] Sheri-Marie Harrison understands the "new black gothic" as "lay[ing] bare the realities of our time," like the persistence of racial violence, forced labor, and the haunting afterlives of slavery.[113] So nonrealist genres are sometimes motivated toward realist ends, while other genre benders adopt forms like the detective novel, which have a more prescribed structure but often remain grittily realist in their epistemology. Chapter 6 will show that many genre benders have sought to bend realism itself—not dispensing with it so much as showing that it too is a dynamic genre subject to deformation and hybridization.

Bored with realism, Chabon's principal aim in the essay is to overturn an entrenched cultural posture that distrusts entertainment and "its suave henchman" pleasure—a sensibility that I have argued is inherited from high modernism and the mass culture critics of the mid-twentieth century.[114] Chabon seizes on a number of reasons why "serious people" have come to view entertainment with suspicion, having internalized an understanding of mass culture as aesthetically impoverished and politically enervating. As entertainment became industrialized, "churning out products that, however pleasurable, suffer increasingly from the ills of mass manufacture—spurious innovation, inferior materials, alienated labor, and an excess of market research," writers' desire to provide pleasure "came to seem suspect, unworthy, and somehow cold and hungry at its core."[115] But Chabon embraces the role of pleasure provider, establishing his high-brow bona fides but landing on a seemingly simple explanation of his mission as a writer. He could "decoct a view of other, more impressive motivations," "uncork some stuff about reader response theory, or the Lacanian *parole*," or "the need to make sense of experience through story," "adduce Kafka," or add a "spritz of Jung," but asserts: "I read for entertainment, and I write to entertain. Period."[116]

What's striking, however, is that while Chabon wants to tie his advocacy of how literary fiction can benefit from drawing from popular genres to a defense of entertainment, that defense draws attention to the pleasures latent in purportedly "serious" literary experience, rather than recuperating the pleasures of popular culture. Chabon includes in his "new definition of entertainment" the high action fare of popular genres, such as "stories of pirates, zeppelins, [and] sinister children," but its newness hinges on the addition of experiences like:

> the engagement of the interior ear by the rhythm and pitch of a fine prose style; . . . two hours spent bushwhacking through a densely packed argument about the structures of power as embodied in nineteenth-century prison architecture; . . . the intricate fractal patterning of motif and metaphor in Nabokov . . . ; a thousand word long sentence comparing homosexuals to the Jews in a page of Proust . . . ; the outrageousness of whale slaughter or human slaughter in Melville or McCarthy; the outrageousness of Dr. Charles Bovary's clubfoot-correcting device; the outrageousness of outrage in a page of Philip Roth; words written in smoke across the sky of London on a day in June 1923 . . .[117]

For Chabon, and it would be hard to disagree, readers can be entertained in disparate ways, taking pleasure in prose style, "motif and metaphor," in trying to follow a torturous Foucauldian argument or Proustian bulge, as well as by spectacular action and adventure. Whatever other aims Flaubert, Melville, Nabokov, and Woolf have, they are entertaining readers as much as are the masters of genre fiction. But ultimately this catalogue offers less advocacy for the kind of entertainment that we get in Jerry Bruckheimer than the claim that Philip Roth is also an entertainer. This defense, that is, stops short of redeeming pleasure for its own sake, which might require Chabon to defend even the tawdriest entertainments. Chabon's true aim is neither to elevate esteem for Hollywood action films nor assail the literary establishment. Instead, he generates a conception of literary value that understands traditional literary criteria like formal artistry and insight into the human condition as their own kinds of pleasure, and the connection between writer and reader as entertainment.

The essay offers a compelling, poetic etymology, that "entertainment" connotes "mutual support through intertwining, like a pair of trees grown together, interwoven, each sustaining and bearing up the other."[118] In terms that echo traditional defenses of what literature does—like E. M. Forster's "only connect"—Chabon makes entertainment into communion, "a two-way exchange of attention, experience, and the universal hunger for connection."[119] At the conclusion of his polemic, after invoking Walter Benjamin's essay "The Storyteller," Chabon turns to Lewis Hyde's *Trickster Makes This World* to argue that "many if not most of the most-interesting writers of the past seventy-five years or so have, like Trickster, found themselves drawn, inexorably, to the borderlands."[120] Citing a lineage of literary writers who draw on popular genres—Borges, Calvino, Anita Brookner, John Fowles, Pynchon, Vonnegut, Byatt, and McCarthy—Chabon returns to precedent to argue that great writers have always played in the space between genres and combined them to produce works of brilliance. In these essays and *McSweeney's* Issue 10, we see a crystallization of the tensions at work in genre-bending fiction: a desire to maintain traditional literary values, including disavowing commercial motives and "the ills of mass manufacture"; valuing accessibility and the provision of varied readerly pleasures, but stopping short of defending putatively low forms of pleasure; recoding even serious forms of literary experience as entertainment; defending genre bending on the grounds of its high literary precedent; and valorizing literature that mixes forms and revels in the "borderlands."

The Heterogeneity of Genre-Bending Fiction

As I have argued throughout this Introduction, genre-bending literary fiction is an extensive, internally diverse, and even conflicted phenomenon. *Genre Bending* derives this insistence on the heterogeneity of the literary field from what I've found reading across genre-bending fiction, as well as from recent genre theory, which stresses the historical dynamism beneath the neat category. While the contemporary literary writers who have adopted popular genres demonstrate a growing recognition of the utility and plasticity of those genres, that utility has been wielded in the service of a tremendous range of aesthetic and political projects. Some writers like Chabon have advocated for the escapist pleasure of popular culture, while others like Whitehead portray it as a threatening generator of consumerist conformity. Some, like Mitchell, have produced marketable crossover works that deliver both the dramatic action of genre franchises and the brainy topicality and structural innovations of "serious" literature, while others, like James and Whitehead, deploy and deform popular genres in ways that deliberately frustrate their conventional pleasures and hence their own works' marketability. *Genre Bending* seeks to account for this phenomenon in ways that preserve its heterogeneity.

Literary scholars have often stressed the stability, reproductive, or regulative functions of genre—generally to assert that a given genre performs a particular ideological work. Genres like fantasy are escapist. Science fiction and westerns are masculinist. The detective novel enforces order and localizes criminality to ignore systemic injustice. Realism is conservative, legitimating a particular worldview by claiming the authority of the real. Romance props up heteropatriarchy by idealizing straight, companionate marriage. Or, by contrast, science fiction and fantasy offer radical potential for the utopian imagination. Crime fiction exposes the state's monopoly on violence. Realism enables social critique by showing how structural forces determine the fate of the individual. Such scholarship has offered powerful accounts of how a genre's conventional forms and recurrent themes carry a particular ideological freight. For example, Jane Tompkins's foundational analysis of the western shows how that genre traditionally "celebrate[s] the suppression of feelings" and legitimates the settler colonial, masculinist efforts of their "taciturn heroes," who "want to dominate the land."[121] Such studies offer invaluable examinations of the ideological work performed by a genre's conventional form. At the same time, it would be a mistake to think that ideology is intrinsic to the genre, rather than a product of the conventional way it has been deployed in a given historical moment. Today's genre-bending literary writers demonstrate how genres may be deployed in ways that adhere to, transform, or subvert such conventions and their traditional ideologies. For example, Percival Everett's *God's Country* (1994) comically exaggerates Tompkins's "taciturn hero" who wants to dominate the land and others, making him into a parodically ignorant bumpkin and critiquing the way white settlers stole Black labor and Indigenous land and knowledge.[122]

Just as genre like the western is dynamic, subject to historical change, and constituted both by wholly conventional, conservative, and wildly innovative, subversive deployments, so the phenomenon of genre-bending literary fiction cannot be neatly summarized without ignoring outliers and exceptions to the rule. As a result, *Genre Bending* seeks to identify prominent trends and sometimes divergent factors driving this phenomenon, without losing sight of the internal heterogeneity that one finds when looking closely at it. Each of the chapters that follows charts one force behind the boom in genre-bending fiction. None of these arguments is totalizing or exhaustive. Readers will note that I say little about the profit motives of publishers or literary writers' desire to make their fiction more salable, which I am sure plays a conscious or unconscious role at least some of the time.[123] Conglomerate publishers surely want to turn a profit on every book they put out, and it would be impossible for writers and agents to be ignorant of those priorities. At the same time, this explanation would serve for any book published under conglomeration and so ultimately focuses on what all such books have in common, not the work of any given text. And while it might seem like a valorization of plot is one of the principal drivers of genre-bending literary fiction, a striking discovery I made when reading across this corpus is just how few of these texts are action-packed. But plot doubtless provides some allure, as writers like Mitchell have found ways to work naval battles and samurai missions into their atmospheric historical fictions (*A Thousand Autumns*), and Whitehead's alternate history and speculative slave narrative *The Underground Railroad* is full of suspense. The forces behind the boom in genre-bending fiction that I do identify are those that registered as most conspicuous in as many prominent genre-bending texts as I could read—and thus are conclusions arrived at inductively—but undoubtedly some of this is due to the selection of texts.

Chapter 1, "Theorizing the Plastic Utility of Genre," expands the argument I have begun here to demonstrate how genre-bending literary writers articulate their own parallel genre theory in their practice, commentary, and metageneric moments in their fictions. These writers offer a renovated understanding of genre: rather than see genres as constraints or shackles, they affirm that all genres, even the ones that might seem to have been worn out through excessive use in the field of popular fiction, are flexible frameworks, available for renovation and transformation, and adaptable to fresh concerns.

This chapter looks to genre benders' commentary in interviews and essays and a series of metageneric moments throughout the fiction of Colson Whitehead, in which they argue for the plasticity and utility of genre. And it attempts to demonstrate that flexibility by surveying the varied uses of detective and postapocalyptic fiction to appear in the literary field in recent years. Today's literary writers have found the frameworks of popular genres useful—but not just for one thing. My title *Genre Bending* aims to foreground this aspect of genre and its appeal for literary writers: they have modified their adopted genres in unexpected ways, blended them in surprising conjunctions, and bent them toward disparate projects.

Chapters 2 and 3 endeavor to answer the questions: What does it mean to make a spy or zombie novel *literary*? What formal features, values, and preoccupations lend coherence to the field of literary fiction? If literary fiction is often defined by its institutional setting—produced by certain imprints, reviewed in certain publications—and in opposition to genre fiction, how can we define it by its internal features when the absence of popular genre forms will no longer suffice? These chapters argue that literary writers infuse the popular genres they have adopted with a literary sensibility by adopting techniques that are valorized within the literary field: an emphasis on prose style, interiority, and a self-reflexive interrogation into the meaning and value of the literary in neoliberal capitalist and technological culture that increasingly jettisons non-economic values. I don't merely point to the way genre-bending fictions contain prose that I think is pretty or enumerate texts that create depictions of characters' rich inner lives. I show how genre-bending literary fictions reflect on their own use of such techniques and articulate their significance, as prose style represents a dedication to innovation with their medium—language—and stakes out a contrast with the repetitive and merely instrumental uses of language that flourish in commerce. Similarly, these novels articulate a commitment to subjective experience—not to valorize the sovereign individual, but to show how oppressive social forces are felt and made legible at the level of this experience. And these novels reflect on the difference between spontaneous, innovative literary art and repetitive popular culture, which they worry will produce formulaic people and societies. Throughout, these chapters demonstrate that genre benders do not merely deploy style, interiority, and self-reflexivity about the literary strategically, to mark their works as "quality" and thus gain prestige from the powers that be in literary institutions, but because of the values and beliefs that underlie those techniques.

While Chapter 1 tracks literary writers' theorization of the affordances of genre as a plastic framework and Chapters 2 and 3 trace genre benders' efforts to distance *their* deployments of genre from the bulk of popular fiction, Chapter 4 runs in a contrary direction, showing how these writers valorize and seek to reproduce the pleasures historically prioritized within that field. "The Pleasures of Immersion in a Fictional World" argues that it is not the allure of plot alone that has drawn genre benders toward forms of genre fiction, so much as a reawakening toward the many pleasures of reading—in particular the pleasure of entering a fictional "world" that encompasses plot, character, and setting. Drawing on the narratology of Marie-Laure Ryan, I show how literary writers have reawakened to the immersiveness that has often been foregrounded in the field of genre fiction and deprioritized in literary fiction. Again, I do so not by pointing to texts that give me immersive pleasure, but by reading moments in genre-bending fictions that stage immersive reading or viewing experiences or otherwise pay homage to imaginative transport into fictional worlds. Though these texts laud immersion, their attention-grabbing language and embedding of meta-immersive reflections—their continued loyalty to modernist-inspired literary practices—sometimes stymie the seamless transport into the fictional world. Throughout, I emphasize that immersion is not the only pleasure such fictions provide and that the provision of pleasure is not genre-bending writers' only aim. Instead, they adopt a more capacious understanding of what literary writing can be, both pleasurable and edifying, entertaining and political, enchanting escape from and confrontation with an often-oppressive reality.

While Chapter 4 examines the way literary writers have come around to the world-building that has often been prioritized in genre fiction, Chapter 5, "The Novel of the Global Generic," shows how literary writers have often expressed a countervailing fear of the generic. They worry that globalization has produced generic spaces and exported U.S. popular media in ways that erode local particularity and threaten to produce conformist subjects. At the same time, writers like Mitchell and Murakami adopt and adapt popular genres that are recognizable internationally, and thus help facilitate the global circulation of their work. These works show an ambivalent or even contradictory stance toward the generic, embracing genre as a form to innovate with and to ensure their portability, but worrying about its potential to erode cultural and individual difference.

Genre benders reflect on the global distribution of genre fiction and film, but also, if much belatedly, on the climate crisis that threatens human and nonhuman life across the planet. Chapter 6, "Scalar Modulation and Formal Variation in Literary Climate Fiction," argues that the effort to envision futures shaped by climate catastrophe and ecocide has surely been a major force propelling literary writers to adopt speculative and dystopian genres in recent decades. But this chapter also argues that such genres are not *necessary* for writing about climate disaster and the Anthropocene. In keeping with the genre theory I have begun to sketch here and elaborate in Chapter 1, I dispute the notion that some genres have limitations when it comes to imagining the massive and distributed geographic scale and disjunctive temporalities of climate change and the Anthropocene, and that other genres are better suited to the task. If genres are flexible and adaptable, and writers modify and use these frameworks for their own purposes, there's no reason one genre is better than any other at a particular representational task or political project. It's all in what you do with it. I show how literary writers have bent speculative forms—but also realist and historical fiction, allegory, and satire—to confront catastrophic climate change. And I show how writers have taken ingenious approaches to use even very small forms to address objects and processes of planetary scale, and to correlate the narrow purview of the individual human life with processes and systems that stretch out over time and space.

A brief Coda addresses the fact that ambitious literary writers have largely avoided adopting the romance genre as a form ready for transformation. But it reads the most glaring exception, the novels of Sally Rooney, as evidence that this is not due to any limitation of the romance form. Focused on young people in love and relationships, Rooney's novels are clearly romances. But I show how the formal qualities and preoccupations of Rooney's work are also eminently literary, and how they demonstrate the pliability of a genre that is often alleged to be rigidly conventional. Her work exhibits a polished and lyrical, if understated, style. It foregrounds the rich interior lives of its protagonists but also questions the significance novels and individuals attribute to private experience, as well as romance, in the face of social systems that seem to dwarf such intimate, small-scale concerns. As with the literary climate fictions I consider in Chapter 6, Rooney writes novels that focus on individuals but don't exalt the individual or think subjective experience is the only game in town. Instead, her work interrogates the status of the individual and the importance of novels, when viewed against the large scale—the structural social and economic systems in which they are situated. The Coda then examines Jennifer Egan's *The Candy House* as a culmination of the forms and concerns of this book. Playing with multiple genres and situated in a near future dominated by a science fictional social media technology, Egan's book, more than any other in this study, reflects on the problem of the generic and asks: Can technology reduce human behavior and narrative form to a set of conventions that may be described algorithmically? Instead of posing popular culture's formulaic and commodity character as the antagonists of the literary's dedication to formal innovation and non-market values, Egan convincingly argues that social media and information technology are today the chief rivals of the literary, as they seek to eliminate privacy, commodify every swipe of our fingers, and develop algorithms that will predict our preferences and generate forms of cultural production that will render writers obsolete. Egan retains a cautious faith in the literary and the individual, arguing, like this book, that we lose crucial distinctions and interest when we think categorically and at a certain degree of abstraction: everyone and every text in each category becomes essentially the same. But when we look closely, we see variations everywhere.

 # Theorizing the Plastic Utility of Genre

> I just don't want to do the same thing over and over again, so on one level each book becomes an antidote to the one [that] came before. ... And that allows me to just challenge myself: can I do a book that has less plot?; can I learn the rules of a horror novel, and adapt it to my own concerns about the world?; can I do a coming of age novel that doesn't remind me of all the stuff I hate about coming of age novels? So I'm trying to keep it fresh for me. I'm just trying to not bore myself. And if I can do a detective novel, and if I can do a horror novel, then why do it again? To keep the work challenging I have to keep moving.[1]
>
> COLSON WHITEHEAD

ABOUT MIDWAY THROUGH MICHAEL CHABON'S Pulitzer Prize–winning magnum opus *The Amazing Adventures of Kavalier & Clay*, the novel's narrator looks back on the career of its co-protagonists, from some fifty years later. This unnamed figure speculates that "in spite of the fact that" their superhero comic *The Escapist* "sold in the millions, and for a time ascended or sank into the general popular consciousness of America," their work "no doubt would have faded from the national memory and imagination, as have the Cat-Man and Kitten, the Hangman, and the Black Terror," and so many popular sensations turned ephemera.[2] Instead, "cultist" fans have "shelled out appalling sums" for vintage issues and "written hundreds of thousands of donnish words devoted to" their collaboration (360).

Why hadn't *The Escapist* disappeared into obscurity? Why had countless gallons of ink been spilled in scholarly exegesis of a comic? "The reason was *Citizen Kane*" (361). When Joe Kavalier sees Orson Welles's film, it produces a "revolution in his ambitions for the ragged-edged and stapled little art form," a total rethinking of what a comic might do (362):

41

> All of the dissatisfactions he had felt in his practice of the art form . . . the cheap conventions, the low expectations among publishers, readers, parents, and educators, the spatial constraints that he had been struggling against . . . seemed capable of being completely overcome, exceeded, and escaped. The Amazing Cavalieri was going to break free, forever, of the nine little boxes. (361)

Here, Chabon weaves another strand into the motif of escape he braids through the novel, from Joe's flight from the Nazis to Sammy Clay's attempt to flee his own sexuality: the escape from artistic convention and formal constraint. Perhaps Chabon could not resist another variation on this theme, but Joe's epiphany is not so much a discovery of the skeleton key that allows him to spring the shackles of the art form as a recognition of their flimsiness. Joe realizes that the apparent "constraints" of comics were just "conventions," typical ways of using the form, whose predominance—here connected to the "low expectations" of producers and audiences—obscured the fact that they could be "completely overcome." When Joe's girlfriend Rosa proclaims, "no medium is inherently better than any other. . . . It's all in what you do with it" (363), Chabon voices his belief that any art form is capable of being used in unexpected ways. This chapter argues that this credo encapsulates the thinking of some of the most prominent and acclaimed writers of contemporary literary fiction about the popular fiction genres they have adopted in recent decades—a theory of genre they enact in their novels and articulate across their fiction and commentary. They assert the inherent equality of all genres, media, and aesthetic forms, their plasticity and readiness for transformation, and insist that what matters is not the form you choose, but what you do with it.

Literary writers' embrace of popular genres beginning around the turn of the millennium, and accelerating since then, clearly demonstrates their recognition of the potential of such genres. This chapter argues that inside and outside their fictions, these writers articulate a theory of genre's utility and plasticity that explains the newfound allure of genres that had largely been relegated to genre fiction fields, and these writers' discovery that such genres have not been exhausted by their often-repetitive use in popular culture but remain as malleable and generative as any others. To think otherwise, these writers assert, would be to adhere to a kind of generic fallacy—the notion, familiar since Aristotle, that certain genres are inherently superior to others—or the anthropomorphizing view that genres have life cycles and eventually grow old and die out.³ But we also see that these writers' embrace of popular genres does not dismantle cultural hierarchies, as the genre turn has sometimes been alleged to do, and continues to differentiate between content that meets the "low expectations" of large-scale producers and audiences and works of high artistic achievement. While Rosa's dictum is egalitarian toward all forms, it leaves in play a hierarchy of outcomes: the possibility that what one does with the raw material at hand will be better or worse, innovative or derivative, serious or trivial. After Joe and Sammy see *Citizen Kane*, they engender, out of their "ragged" art form, "the so-called modernist or prismatic Escapist stories" (363), which cement their lasting artistic reputations and lift them out of the massive, evanescent stream of popular production.

We see articulations of both aspects of this genre-bending ethos—the recognition of the artistic potential inherent in popular genres and the determination to use them in transformative ways that differentiate them from formulaic and ephemeral popular fiction—across the field of contemporary literary fiction, but perhaps nowhere more vividly than in the career of Colson Whitehead. He has called his debut work *The Intuitionist* (1999) his "first stab at trying to repurpose a known genre—the detective novel—for my own purposes."⁴ This sentence, specifically its repetitious emphasis on "repurposing," captures the central premise of this chapter and book: though numerous forces contribute to this phenomenon, the fundamental explanation for the outpouring of genre-bending literary fiction in recent decades is that its authors have revised their attitude toward *genre*—if not toward the entire field of genre fiction. They have recognized the endless utility and plasticity of all genres and have appropriated and modified them to fit the eclectic range of their purposes.

In referring to the *plasticity* of form, I stress that genres are not rigid, rule-bound categories but rather flexible formations, "open-ended processes" subject to continual "formation and reformation," as writers use extant genres in new ways, with each use modifying the system in turn.⁵ My use of "plastic," in the sense of "capable of being deformed continuously and permanently in any direction without rupture,"⁶ also follows the method of this chapter and book by deriving my understanding of genre in part from novelists like Whitehead, who reflect on their use of genre so self-consciously. While *Merriam-

Webster's definition evokes a Play-Doh–like elasticity, Whitehead's metaphor is LEGO.[7] His *Apex Hides the Hurt* (2006) recounts its protagonist's work on behalf of Ehko International, a toy company that sells construction kits made of countless colored blocks. In this seemingly tangential vignette, Whitehead formulates a miniature theory of genre. The toymaker provides "pictures of the things you could make out of Ehko bricks if you followed the example."[8] It's possible to use these components obediently, formulaically imitating prior creations. But kids perennially discovered "that the fun part was making their own bizarre creations. Deviating from the blueprints. The toy was plastic and so was its meaning" (118). If technically there might be "some mathematical way of determining the exact number of permutations" of configurations of colored blocks, "the overall impression was that there was no end to what you could make." The bricks become, for kids, and for Whitehead, "the very components of imagination" (118). Punning on the toy's plasticity and calling to mind both the possibility of following a blueprint precisely and of "deviating" from it in endless, even "bizarre," "permutations," Whitehead evokes the dialectical nature of genre, its capacity for repetitive, conventional use and limitless variation. Further, Whitehead encapsulates the multiple vectors motivating genre-bending fiction that this book traces, as this passage poses "deviating from the blueprints" in terms that resonate with modernist-inspired formal experiment and subversion of ideological orthodoxy and are also animated by the renewed sense of the centrality of imaginative pleasure and play that is the subject of Chapter 4.

How and why did writers of literary fiction come to upgrade their estimation of the aesthetic potential of popular genres, understanding them in this dialectical fashion, by the late 1990s? I have suggested in the Introduction that several explanations can be found in the prestigious precedents set by writers like Margaret Atwood, Paul Auster, A. S. Byatt, Umberto Eco, and Toni Morrison, the canonization and growing literary esteem for writers who worked in genre fiction fields like Isaac Asimov, Octavia Butler, Raymond Chandler, Samuel Delany, Philip K. Dick, Dashiell Hammett, and Ursula K. Le Guin, and contemporary literary writers' generational affection for such figures and the genres in which they worked. Genre-bending literary fiction also emerges in parallel with a paradigm shift in literary theory, from a period that viewed genre as a constricting force—an authoritarian effort to impose rules and categories onto singular, sui generis artistic entities—to one that understands genres historically and rhetorically, as dynamic fields of practice and open sets of techniques can be modified according to the needs of their users.[9] Whether or not today's writers of literary fiction have been aware of this development in genre theory, this chapter shows that they have generated their own parallel theory in their fictions and in their commentary—one that understands genre not as a set of constraints but as an enabling, generative framework that can be worked with and against, conventions that can be redeployed to elicit their familiar pleasures but also rejected and transformed to generate novelty, recipes that can be blended and stacked with others, ceaselessly infused with new ingredients and subject matter.

Since Whitehead's debut, which combines noir detective fiction with alternate history, he has moved to "repurpose" encyclopedic fiction in *John Henry Days* (2001), "contemporary satire and the bildungsroman (*Apex Hides the Hurt*, *Sag Harbor* [2009]), postapocalyptic zombie fiction and the meta-slave narrative (*Zone One* and *The Underground Railroad* [2016])," and crime fiction (*Harlem Shuffle* [2021] and *Crook Manifesto* [2023]), with elements of historical fiction woven throughout.[10] In the interview that provides the epigraph to this chapter, Whitehead explains his genre switching as a series of drag performances, in terms that associate genre not with the repetitive, formulaic, or conventional, but with the playful, temporary adoption of literary guises that allows for continual novelty, experiment, and adaptive reuse. Each book, he explains, "becomes an antidote to the one [that] came before," inoculation against repetitiveness and ennui, that "allows me to just challenge myself: can I do a book that has less plot?; can I learn the rules of a horror novel, and adapt it to my own concerns about the world."[11] These comments reveal several of aspects of Whitehead's practice that resonate equally with the output of his contemporaries like Atwood, Chabon, Egan, Ishiguro, and many others. He points to his penchant for attempting new genres in each successive book, his learning of their "rules," but also the "adaptation" of these to his "concerns." In these comments and in *Apex*, Whitehead encapsulates the multiple vectors motivating genre-bending fiction that this book traces. His emphasis on performing his own "take" on successive genres, on "keeping it fresh," "avoiding certain expectations of plot and a certain kind of narrative satisfaction,"[12] and "deviating from the blueprints" accord with a modernist-inherited ethos that values the artist's unique vision and stylistic signature, formal experiment, and making it new, against popular fiction's endeavor to satisfy readers' expectations. At the same time, his desire to avoid boredom and his likening of genre to children's building blocks point to literary writers' renewed sense of the centrality of imaginative pleasure and play that is the subject of Chapter 4.

Whitehead's second novel, *John Henry Days*, presents a microcosm of his oeuvre, a virtuoso juggling act that shuttles genres of all shapes and sizes through its pages. "Encyclopedic" might cover the macro structure of a novel loosely centered on a freeloading freelance journalist from New York, whose three-month "jag" of attending daily press junkets in search of "elaborate sushi spread[s]" and "prime rib" takes him to a small West Virginia mining town to cover a festival celebrating the release of a stamp commemorating the titular folk hero.[13] But within that encyclopedia and premise, the novel dishes out an "all-you-can-eat-buffet" of characters, historical moments, and embedded genres.[14] Whitehead constructs and assembles: snatches of invented fictional interviews and oral histories that recount varied incarnations of John Henry's legend; naturalistic chapters that imagine and dramatize the folk hero's participation in the perilous labor of railroad construction; realist historical fictions that recount the work of Tin Pan Alley balladeers to appropriate, propagate, and profit on Henry's legend; parodies of United States Post Office press releases and newspaper stories; gothic interludes at a haunted motel; a slapstick farce of characters hiding in the shower of the motel bathroom to avoid discovery; a Tom Wolfe–like account of the murder of a Black concertgoer at the infamous Altamont Rolling Stones concert; and play-like chapters in which postal workers gossip in dramatic form.

Reviewers have recognized Whitehead's delight in deploying a medley of forms. John Updike compared the novel's "serial ingenuity" to that of James Joyce's *Ulysses*.[15] Jonathan Franzen also likened the novel to *Ulysses* and *Moby Dick*, in its "encyclopedic aspirations" and "outstanding comic riffs."[16] As such comparisons make clear, the madcap miscellany of *John Henry Days* is nothing radically new in the history of the novel; it fits recognizably in a tradition of parodic assemblages that spans from Sterne to Melville, through the modernist bricolage of Joyce, to the ludic excesses of Thomas Pynchon, Ishmael Reed, Salman Rushdie, and Zadie Smith. The novel's generic ventriloquism, its shapeshifting penchant for parodying and incorporating other literary and extraliterary genres is, of course, its paradoxical defining characteristic according to Mikhail Bakhtin.[17] But if Whitehead's practice of parodically assembling disparate genres is nothing new, their particular arrangement and their deployment to explore the myth of John Henry as a figure for the endless creative destruction of capitalism, in which bodies are used up until machines can be brought in to replace them, fuse to generate something utterly distinctive.

Though Whitehead does not, in *John Henry Days*, structure a novel around a popular genre as he does in other novels,[18] the self-conscious genre bending that defines his career exemplifies the contention of this chapter: the prominent and up-and-coming writers of literary fiction that have gravitated to the genres of popular fiction since the late 1990s have developed and articulated a practical theory of genre, contending that these genres are not stale, ossified, or zombie-like forms—despite the repetitive, formulaic ways in which they have sometimes been exploited in the production of commercial fiction—but rather are, like all genres, generative and malleable frameworks continually available for transformation and repurposing.[19] *John Henry Days* is particularly instructive because, like other, genre-blending hybrid texts—Byatt's *Possession*, Atwood's *The Blind Assassin*, or Mitchell's *Cloud Atlas*—its unique combination of genres and the projects toward which those assemblages are aimed could hardly be anticipated, demonstrating that genres are not constraining, delimiting structures that bend toward a single function or carry a particular political freight. Recent genre theory has emphasized just this rhetorical and historical malleability of genre. Today's genre-bending writers articulate and enact a parallel genre theory that understands genres as useful frameworks—but not for doing just one thing. Instead, they are flexible recipes that can be deployed in various ways to suit the needs of their users, modified in pursuit of divergent ends, combined or strung together in succession with other genres in infinite permutations, varied and adapted endlessly.

Genre as Plastic Framework

Despite a growing consensus among historians and theorists who contend that genres are subject to historical change, and thus mix stability and flux, some prominent literary scholars have continued to stress the reproductive, limiting, coercive, or regulative functions of genre over its dynamic and transformative aspects.[20] Franco Moretti famously asserted:

> [t]o talk about literary genres means without any doubt to emphasize the contribution made by literature to the "petrifaction of existence" and also to the "wearing out of form." It means re-routing the tasks of literary historiography and the image of literature itself, enclosing them both in the idea of consent, stability, repetition, bad taste even.[21]

More recently, Caroline Levine has argued that "as they move, forms bring their *limited range* of affordances with them."[22] Despite acknowledging that forms may be used in unexpected ways and in new contexts, Levine grants form the power and agency to travel and impose its constricting force; the guiding question she brings to each of her chapters is: "What specific order does each form impose?"[23] Nicholas Brown similarly stresses the rigidity or constraint of genres, basing his contention that "genre fiction" opens "a zone of autonomy within the heteronomous space of cultural commodities" on the premise that "commercial genre[s]" are "governed by rules." The "requirements" of a genre, Brown posits, are "rigid enough to pose a problem, which can now be thought of as a formal problem like the problem of the flatness of the canvas or the pull of harmonic resolution."[24] Brown contends that moments of autonomous artistic production emerge when creators self-consciously engage with the problem posed by a commercial genre's form. But complex genres do not possess rules or requirements.[25]

Similarly, Mark McGurl understands genre's central role in Amazon's provision of fiction as a reliably satisfying commodity, as dependent "upon the rules of genre, upon the implied contract it draws up between author and reader for the reliable delivery of stories of a familiar kind."[26] These scholars acknowledge the possibility of transformation, but with language that refers to genres as rule-bound, as "contracts," as having distinct borders from related genres, as entailing a particular politics, or as inevitably trending toward formal ossification that reifies and stabilizes historically dynamic fields of practice.[27] So while the texts in this study demonstrate dramatically Brown's contention that writers can transform the frameworks of popular genres in innovative ways, the premise that commercial genres are "governed by rules," or that "form imposes order" overstates the prescriptive force of generic *conventions*—which are not rules but *typical* features, norms that emerge over time—and neglects the prevalence of variations from these norms that emerge even within the subfield of popular fiction. While McGurl is certainly right that Amazon's aim to provide a predictable consumer experience explains the centrality of genre to its business plan, genres facilitate the delivery of both repetition and variation to our door.

Historians of popular genres have demonstrated that despite the tendency of critics and literary elites to understand those genres in terms of their most formulaic manifestations, variation, innovation, and historical change are equally the rule within popular production. Under certain conditions, agents in positions of economic and symbolic power demand artists' rigid adherence to a given set of generic conventions, as with neoclassical tragedy in France, or when Harlequin requires first-person narration and happy endings for all books in a series.[28] But conventions generally emerge retrospectively as patterns or norms, rather than setting out requirements or obligations that artists must meet. Readers can't ask for their money back if expectations aren't fulfilled, and even writers of the most commercial popular fictions vary formula to some degree, lest they offer Pierre Menardian reproduction of previous texts. In his comprehensive history of science fiction, John Rieder notes that historical variation renders static definitions of genres impossible and canons provisional.[29] The fields of popular fiction are full of examples that point up the possibilities for writers to vary any pattern, formula, or set of conventions: detective fictions like Arthur Conan Doyle's *A Study in Scarlet* (1887), in which the criminal is revealed to be the hero, or Agatha Christie's *The Murder of Roger Ackroyd* (1926), in which the narrator, Poirot's assistant, is revealed to be the guilty party, admits his own unreliability as a narrator, and takes his own life.

Today's genre theorists tend to follow the dialectical and historical method of figures like Michael McKeon, Ralph Cohen, and Fredric Jameson, stressing, in the words of McKeon, that generic categories like "'[t]he novel' must be understood as what Marx calls a 'simple abstraction,' a deceptively monolithic category that encloses a complex historical process."[30] Studying genre requires a dialectical approach, attentive to "both identity and difference, in order to do justice to the inescapable notion that there is something here sufficiently integral to remain discernable as such, yet sufficiently variable to be in flux";

"these two conditions are ... constituted by each other, inseparable (although distinguishable) features of the same subject."[31] Form happens in history. It does not emerge spontaneously but in varied instantiations and use cases, as writers continually subject it to deformation:

> The generic capacity of a work is defined both by its intertextual affiliations with some works and by its intertextual detachment from others. Indeed, the notion of "parody" is as fruitful as it is to Bakhtin because it conflates these two movements into a single dialectical gesture of recapitulation and repudiation, imitation and disillusion, continuity and rupture.[32]

Critics who focus the stabilizing or constraining force of genres, or provide unitary accounts of their meaning or politics, need to also account for the other half of this dialectic: the variation amid the repetition, the dynamism that accompanies the relative stability.[33]

Since genres aren't static, they make available possibilities and permutations that range from the tiredly repetitive to the wildly inventive. In literary fiction, a cultural field that prizes formal innovation, these variations are everywhere. While genre categories look neat on the surface, today's genre-bending fiction proffers a heterogeneous set of "spillovers": books that don't fit neatly into the "simple abstraction" that is the category, others that string together multiple genres or nest them inside one another, many others that stretch our sense of what a genre might look like and do.[34] We also discover, in this miscellany of purpose and execution, that genre ought to be thought of, not as something texts belong to, but something that writers *use* in a variety of ways and to accomplish a variety of things. They are not handcuffs, but templates or frameworks that may be altered and reshaped according to the aims of their users, upon which disparate aesthetic and political projects may be constructed.[35]

Thomas Pavel views genres as a flexible form of rhetorical and literary practice, writing lucidly that understanding genre "as a set of good recipes, or good habits of the trade, oriented toward the achievement of definite artistic goals makes the instability of generic categories less puzzling and less threatening." With the exception of "strictly formal" genres like the sonnet,

> [genres] are unstable and flexible because the goals pursued by writers with their help vary, as do the ways of achieving these goals. The good habits ... are therefore subject to change. [Though] in some cases, [they] are unduly codified.[36]

This view of genre as a useful, flexible communicative framework or "recipe" accords strikingly with accounts that acclaimed writers of genre fiction and recent genre-bending writers give of their practice. In her famous essay "Science Fiction and Mrs. Brown," Ursula K. Le Guin called the novel "muddled, elastic, inventive, adaptable" and science fiction "a good tool," "a crazy, protean, left-handed monkey wrench, which can be put to any use the craftsman has in mind."[37] This view of genre as plastic raw material or adjustable tool ready to be put to disparate purposes recurs through literary writers' discussions of their practice and within their genre-bending fictions. When Paul Auster was asked if, in his *New York Trilogy*, he "deliberately set out to experiment with the detective genre or" if it was "simply useful to [him] as a form," he replied: "It was useful to me in the same way old musical hall routines and vaudeville were useful to Beckett in writing *Waiting for Godot*. Or the way romances were useful to Cervantes in writing *Don Quixote*."[38] Asserting that his novellas are not detective novels "in the least," Auster understands the utility of genre for the writer who resists genre categorization and adheres to a modernist-inherited experimental ethos as inhering in the way its conventions can be deployed otherwise, "turned inside out," "played with"; they are "traditional norms" that can be "exposed" and "stretched beyond their limits."[39]

When Whitehead gave the keynote at the 2019 Association of Writers and Writing Programs Annual Conference, he began with the "fried chicken journey" he has been on for the past decade, trying the recipes of famous chefs like Momofuku's David Chang.[40] Whitehead stresses, with striking echoes of Pavel, the flexibility of recipes; one can follow instructions to the letter or introduce "changes that alter the flavor" (21). Quickly, it becomes clear that Whitehead's poultry quest serves up a metaphor for writing and that he is "nibbling around the question of genre" (22). Part of Whitehead's point is to attack any hierarchy that would privilege one kind of "chicken." There are "mundane" recipes and others that are "fancier than a peacock in a top hat. With a monocle. Reciting Sappho" (22). These personifications point to the way cultural hierarchies are bound to class, that the status of a given "recipe" derives from the wealth and education of its enthusiasts. But Whitehead contends that these entrenched hierarchies only obscure what are ultimately questions of taste. "There are only two kinds of food: Stuff you like, and stuff you don't like . . . two kinds of books—shit you like and shit you don't like"

(22). He recounts that when *Zone One* appeared, he "had to field a lot of moronic questions about why a so-called literary writer was slumming around in zombie fiction" (22). Whitehead dismisses those who think it's strange that a literary novelist might write a zombie novel—no genre is inherently inferior—but he does not eliminate value judgment: there is "stuff you like and stuff you don't." Whitehead's own tastes tilt more Momofuku than KFC. He cites the precedents of Morrison's *Beloved*, McCarthy's *The Road*, Roth's *The Plot Against America,* and Ishiguro's *Never Let Me Go* to demonstrate that literary writers have appropriated popular genres and cooked up highly acclaimed fare. No recipe is better than any other; it's all in what you do with it.

But Whitehead is not only arguing that popular genres can be elevated into ambitious works of literary art. He extends his cooking metaphor to explain how genres offer writers a capacious storehouse of recipes to suit their needs:

> We borrow recipes and techniques from all over, make them our own to see what we can set out for strangers. Perhaps this dish needs the existential tension of the detective to finish it off, that recipe is calling out for a dash of reality-warping fabulism. (22)

Genre recipes are combinatory and functional in Whitehead's account; when it serves his "needs," he will stir in elements from a different genre. Moreover, genres evolve over time as writers borrow time-honored recipes from their predecessors, modifying them in them in the process. Just as Chang "perfected his own variation" of fried chicken by "drawing on centuries of variations by other chefs and cooks who transform old recipes according to new techniques," with "untold experimentation" in the process, so Whitehead found it "instructive" to consult how masters like Morrison and Charles Johnson have varied the neo-slave narrative, before he attempted *The Underground Railroad*. "I was going to learn something from these great artists and use it" (23). Not a flailing around for whatever works, the use of genre here is a studied, calculated endeavor to perfect a set of techniques.[41]

This account of genre as variable recipe that writers borrow from and use, sticking to the tried-and-true or switching things up when it suits them, echoes those of other genre-bending writers, who argue against the view that generic conventions are constraints that predetermine their aesthetic projects or the ideological valences of their works. These writers do not think of convention in terms of a binary, as something they mindlessly obey or radically reject, but rather as tools they might use, employ for their power and familiarity, or subvert and revise when necessary.[42] Jennifer Egan articulates her understanding of genre as a paradoxical set of prescriptions that enables innovation. When asked about her tendency to work with different genres in each book, she affirms that "genre is a kind of lifeline for me because what I can't stomach is the feeling that I'm doing the same thing twice."[43] Rather than generating repetition, adopting and playing with genres allows Egan to make each book different from the one before it, transforming the genres in the process. She refuses to write for television, because she is "worried about internalizing those formulas."[44] The perceived formulaicness of popular culture continues to be something literary writers define themselves against. But genres provide an existing framework that Egan can work with and also thwart; they are a "portal" to

> a ready-made world, where there are rules, which is fun, but where the challenge is how to . . . use those rules and yet somehow *bend* them and *work around* them as well as *with* them, which is always what people who write in a genre I think are trying to do.[45]

By working with the "rules" of a genre—which are really just conventions—but also "bending" and "working around" them, Egan generates novelty, something that is "going to feel new," and "the possibility that [she] might be able to do something interesting that [she] hasn't done before."[46]

Similarly, Chabon argues that "many of the finest 'genre writers' working today" manifest "a fruitful self-consciousness about the conventions of their chosen genre, a heightened awareness of its history. . . . When it comes to conventions, their central impulse is not to flout or to follow them, but . . . to *play*."[47] Chabon and Egan add another vector that illuminates the practice of their genre-bending peers. These writers deploy genres for their own purposes, innovate and reinvent them, and have fun with them, exhibiting a playful ethos of riffing or improvising. The plastic utility of genre means popular genres can be reconfigured and adapted to new purposes—but it does not mean that their use is purely instrumental. It is also simply pleasurable. At the same time, genre benders frequently set out to solve artistic problems for which adaptive reuse of extant genres can pose solutions. In an interview with Neil Gaiman, Kazuo Ishiguro recounts that he had tried to write *Never Let Me Go* twice in the 1990s, but "couldn't find a way to make it work." At that time, it "wouldn't have occurred to [him] to use the science-fiction dimension." Later, "the third time," he tried, he realized that if he made the characters "clones" whose organs "were being harvested, the story would work."[48] Here, genre functions as a tool that helps writers find solutions to aesthetic problems.

A necessary corollary to understanding genres as flexible recipes that writers alter in the service of their own ends is the recognition that these ends are heterogeneous. Recognizing that various projects can be built upon the malleable framework of a genre points up the problem with scholarly accounts that contend that a given genre performs a singular (usually conservative) ideological function and with several influential explanations of contemporary literary writers' turn to forms of genre fiction that pose monolithic understandings of the phenomenon.[49] Ramón Saldívar has argued that the hybrid aesthetic formations he calls "historical fantasy" and "speculative realism" combine genres "in order to remain true to ethnic literature's Utopian allegiance to social justice."[50] But if a genre can be used in varied ways for varied purposes, these amalgams do not adhere to a single utopian or social justice project. Similarly, numerous scholars have explored contemporary writers' use of genre to imagine futures shaped by catastrophic climate change and ecocide.[51] Chapter 6 of this book examines the many recent writers to deploy popular genres and deform realism to address environmental concerns. Addressing racial justice and climate are urgent contemporary issues to be sure, but, as the remainder of this chapter shows, they are just two of many that contemporary literary writers have pursued by adopting and transforming popular genres.

Because genres are flexible recipes, genre-bending literary fiction ought to be understood as stemming not from a single thematic concern, but as emerging from writers' growing recognition of the plasticity and utility of genre. An account of the turn to these forms needs to explain the heterogeneity of literary fiction utilizing popular genres over the past several decades: the fact that Chang-rae Lee's *Native Speaker* and Viet Than Nguyen's *The Sympathizer* have used the spy novel to figure the doubleness of U.S. immigrant identity, but also that Ian McEwan's *Sweet Tooth* employs the secret agent to revisit British cultural propaganda during the Cold War and probe the liminality of gender and authorship.⁵² The remainder of this chapter shows how the commentary of genre-bending literary writers and a series of metageneric moments in their fictions adumbrate a parallel theory that underlies their practice of innovation with popular genres. These writers avail themselves of the flexibility of popular genres, applying them to varied novelistic projects, contending with diverse subjects like histories of colonial and racial violence, disability, and ecological catastrophe, and bending conventional forms in ways that are compatible with a modernist ideal of formal innovation.

First, I read a series of metageneric moments across Whitehead's work, which formulate his own theory of genre by stressing the way familiar aesthetic forms serve as enabling frameworks for artistic production and the imagination more broadly. These moments subtly complicate his anxieties about the deadening effects of pop culture and global monopoly capitalism, admitting the potential for artistic transformation and authentic communion that persist even amid repetitive commodity production and seemingly restrictive market conditions. Then I sketch a thumbnail of the vast diversity of projects toward which genre-bending literary writers have bent popular genres taking the example of detective and postapocalyptic genres. I conclude with a reading of Whitehead's *The Underground Railroad* as a metageneric text that deforms the historical novel and neo-slave narrative, combining these with alternate history and utopia, and dramatizing in the process the novelist's own freedom from constraint, even when genre or subject matter might seem confining.

Variation amid the Generic in Whitehead

Genre-bending writers hold nuanced, even paradoxical views about genre. As we see in Egan's comments about television above, and as I discuss further in Chapter 5, they frequently express anxieties about the *merely* generic: about overreliance on formula and the homogenizing effects of global capitalism. Whitehead's fiction is notable for its critique of the way the expansion of multinational corporations generates cookie-cutter products, spaces, and subjects. In *Apex Hides the Hurt*, the hungover protagonist seeks out the "familiar face" of "the Admiral," a coffee franchise clearly patterned after Starbucks. "No matter what time zone you happened to be in, the Admiral's doors pushed in with the same slight resistance, freeing the vapors of the latest excursion into Africa, South America, or Blend . . . black gold bubbling from the earth's crust" (38). Whitehead's dark comedy plays on the Melvillian allusion leveraged by the world's predominant coffee chain and bends it to critique the corporation's neocolonial resource extraction—beneath an ironic tribute to the stores' reassuring sameness. But under the sardonic surface, his novels often betray a conviction that the most seemingly exhausted routines might be renovated—a belief that offers a "metageneric" commentary on his use of genre and the mutable potential of genre as such.[53]

Whitehead's corpus both demonstrates this mutability in its innovative uses of genre and advocates for it in such metageneric moments. *The Intuitionist*, a bizarre amalgam of alternate history, noir, and racial allegory—in which elevator inspectors enjoy substantial cultural prestige as guardians of urban progress—bends and blends these genres in the service of intertwined agendas: to examine African Americans' vexed relationship with "the twinned inheritance of print literacy and urban modernity";[54] to critique the verticality of "hierarchical thinking" about genre, race, and sexism;[55] and to envision how solitary acts of reading and writing "allow the work of utopia to take place."[56]

Woven through the novel's peculiar refraction of the way racial hierarchies are embedded in educational and professional institutions into the world of elevator inspectors, and its speculation into alternative visions that might dismantle such structures, Whitehead initiates a career-long metacommentary on the way even the most seemingly threadbare forms offer frameworks for artistic improvisation and ingenuity. In a gruesome moment in *The Intuitionist*, gangster thugs torture Ben Urich, a journalist who has written an exposé for *Lift* magazine that reveals James Fulton's plans for a Black Box that would accelerate unparalleled, messianic growth: "grant us the sky, unreckoned towers: the second elevation."[57] At one level an exploration of the sadistic lengths to which guardians of so-called civilization will go, which anticipates the "enhanced interrogation techniques" of the post-9/11 wars on terror, Whitehead goes further to self-reflexively examine a familiar set of questions about ethics and aesthetics surrounding literary representations of violence.[58] His metaphors render Urich's cascade of screams into a performance, an artful display of verbal ingenuity that comments ironically on the writer who would use a depiction of the torture chamber opportunistically, to demonstrate his own virtuosic ability to depict the most horrible of human routines in fresh and original ways. In these metaphors, Urich's torturers become his audience, then his critics. They are "intrigued" by "the cast and caliber, the inexhaustible clarity of his screaming. Its sheer novelty. . . . They had never heard pain sing like that before, in all the permutations of torture ever enacted on the small room's humble stage" (96). While Whitehead's ironic aestheticizing of suffering levels an implicit critique of the novelist who would perform his own "sheer novelty" on the stage of the torture chamber, another level of irony arises from the fact that his portrayal of poor Urich's screams as an "inexhaustible" clarion song, to make this critique, *is* quite novel. Pointing to the problematic nature of representing suffering in aesthetically innovative ways by metaphorizing screaming as singing is innovative. Like his account of Ehko bricks, this macabre example subtly declares Whitehead's philosophy of genre: that despite being subjected to infinite prior "permutations," an aesthetic form can nonetheless be manipulated to produce "sheer novelty."

Woven through the madcap miscellany of *John Henry Days*, its central unifying threads are its examination of the creation, proliferation, and commodification of mythic figures like John Henry, and the way that myth prefigures capitalism's endless creative destruction of both workers and technologies. But in one brief moment, the novel also formulates a miniature theory of genre. The novel's comic hero J. Sutter and his freelancer colleagues have developed a categorizing mechanism, a genre system, for the articles they compose for newspapers, magazines, and nascent websites. Whitehead imagines one of their journalist predecessors, Freddie "The Bull" McGinty, as the Northrop Frye of "puff." The Bull "identified three elemental varieties of puff pieces and over time the freelancer community had accepted his Anatomy of Puff" (71). He "christened the archetypal [feature] subject Bob, and named the three essential manifestations of Bob as follows: Bob's Debut, Bob Returns, and Bob's Comeback" (71). This schema calls attention to the repetitions of popular media—the recycling of hype for the new ("Debut"), the follow-up ("Returns"), and the late-career rebirth ("Comeback"). And if Whitehead's depiction of freelancers anticipates the precarious labor we call the "gig economy," he also points to their ability to transform the formulaic media genres they adopt in ways that engender others and ramify in a varied, near-infinite corpus of textual production.

After some time, the "clarity of the trinity" of incarnations of Bob is forced to admit "another variety": the "trend piece" or "Bob Is Hip" (72). The brilliant utility of "Bop Is Hip" is that it can be combined with the other archetypes of puff to transform and reinvigorate them. "Bob's other manifestations could be infused with new life by situating Bob in a scene or cultural eddy . . . an exotic subculture that begs further investigation" (72). "Bob Is Hip" comes to figure the limitless capacity of writers to combine genres, utilize old ones to address new subject matter, and use language in novel ways:

> The Bob Is Hip variation met with some initial protest until its endorsers suggested that creating novel catch phrases from "the new" or "post-" or devising witty neologisms for the nascent movement could ensure one's fame. A subculture is an amino acid soup out of which book deals crawl. More important, Bob Is Hip has broad applications. (72)

With his allusions to Frye's archetypal criticism, likening the genesis of cultural production to the origins of life on earth, and suggesting that freelancers might land a book deal by situating a generic Bob character into a "nascent" subcultural niche, Whitehead likens popular journalism to the literary, pointing to the ways writing, as well as commodity production more broadly, are engines not only of repetition but also variation, reliant on the production of perpetual novelty.

Whitehead thus calls attention to what McGurl has called the "obvious continuity of much postwar American fiction with the modernist project of systematic experimentation with narrative form, even as it registers . . . the scandalous continuity of the literary *techne* (craft) with technology in the grosser sense."[59] Whitehead is clearly skewering how media, literary fiction, and literary theorists tack "post-" onto extant movements and "devise witty neologisms," following capitalist imperatives to generate perpetual novelty and convince consumers, readers, or other scholars they have discovered the next big thing. At the same time, *John Henry Days* reserves, in modernist fashion, sincere appreciation for the renewal the individual artist can produce out of the most seemingly hackneyed material. Directly after the novel's disquisition on the genres of puff, while its jaded protagonist hacks away at his comically deflated version of John Henry's mountain, "five proud slabs of prime rib," a boy takes the stage to sing the "Ballad of John Henry," and "from the depths of him rouses a gorgeous baritone" (75). In sharp contrast to Sutter's labors, the boy's song "hacks at primal truth and splinters off words" and the audience is "enraptured . . . openmouthed in beatitude and slack in delight at the nimble phrasings of the boy. Except for J.," who "attacks the prime rib," oblivious to the song (76). As if in rebuke to his grasping antihero, who is only in it for the buffet, Whitehead has J. choke on a piece of meat and nearly die. Beneath his intimations that writing is a tireless machine for producing forever young puffery, Whitehead betrays reverence for, and creates, artistic novelty that retains the capacity to "enrapture," dazzle, and "hack at primal truth," even while using the raw material of a timeworn folk ballad.

Apex gives advertising executives the same treatment that *John Henry* gives to freelance writers and likewise appears to offer a disillusioned account of the potential for artistic originality. Ironically unnamed, *Apex*'s protagonist is a nomenclature consultant, who tacks catchy labels onto consumer products and has been tasked with rebranding a formerly all-Black town, once called "Freedom," whose racial history has been effaced by its current name "Winthrop." Even though the protagonist is enormously successful, a legend in the business, the novel's satire of marketing consistently deflates his labor, as his ingenious monikers are blazoned on all manner of consumer "packaging," like "gum wrappers," and inevitably "hauled off to the garbage dumps" (5). The names "remained, even though what they named had been consumed. To have a name imprinted along the bottom of a Styrofoam container: this was immortality" (5). If passages like this satirize the transience of art as well as advertising, skewering its sham claim to outlive its creator, *Apex*'s account of the limitless "permutations" enabled by Ehko bricks, "the very components of imagination," affirms the potential for authentic and meaningful creative work.

For *Apex*'s conformist, conservative protagonist, "nothing was so pleasing as the image . . . on the box" (122), but Whitehead first has him discover a more generative, even utopian, aspect of this imaginative play:

> As he cycled through an array of recombinations, his subversive attempts at city planning, the strangest things occurred to him. . . . If he left [the police station] there, in fragments, would there be no crime? By constructing some sort of fascistic multiplex . . . it would call into creation a new cinema. . . . By leaving out the hospital would the citizens not die? (121)

Reading such passages, we discover that the problem with *Apex*'s hero is that the names he comes up with are only vehicles to sell consumer products. At the same time, we find that Whitehead retains, and his work cultivates, an appreciation for the plasticity of form and meaning, the near infinite "permutations" and "recombinations" that "call into creation" the new, the "subversive," the "strange," and the utopian, all from toys familiar from youth. In the distance between the protagonist's commercial endeavors and pleasure in copying the image on the box, following instructions to the letter, and Whitehead's intimation of the seemingly infinite possibilities discoverable through childlike play, emerges the author's suspicion of formulaic, commercial production and his belief in an imagination that can convert the most basic of building blocks into fantastic new art forms and renderings of new social organizations. Such passages articulate not only a theory of genre that argues for its infinite plasticity, but also, as I discuss at greater length in Chapter 3, a persistent belief in the literary as a realm of cultural production that escapes the deadening repetition of mass production and generates something unique, powerfully affecting, and even utopian.

In *Zone One*, a novel that looks even more cynically dedicated to lamenting the clichéd nature of human sociality under late capitalism, Whitehead similarly alerts us to the repetitive nature of genre while reserving admiration for the artist who engineers novelty out of its well-worn structures and manages to "hack at primal truth." In *Zone One*, people keep doing the same thing they've always done, even though zombies have overrun the planet. Foregrounding entrenched patterns of behavior, Whitehead's novel speaks to vital contemporary concerns: the perpetual motion machine of global capitalism and the persistence of overconsumption, even in the face of climate catastrophe, which it briefly gestures toward: "That other, less flamboyant, more deliberate ruination."[60] Exploring routinized attitudes and actions, Whitehead's novel also speaks to the genre templates of socialization and culture writ large. Attacking the notion of individual agency, *Zone One*'s zombies point to the way we follow social scripts, act in predictable ways, and in doing so dismantle the boundary between human and machine. The novel's focus on repetitive actions appears most obviously in Whitehead's invention of a new class of zombie, "the straggler." Unlike "skels," your garden-variety walking dead marauding in search of brains to eat, stragglers "reenact without end" some banal routine (61). But the stragglers simply present exaggerated versions of what, in Whitehead's handling, are the mindless patterns all humans are trapped in, even before the apocalypse. "It was the business of the plague to reveal our family members, friends, and neighbors as the creatures they'd always been" (245).

In *Zone One,* the living and undead alike are trapped in repetitive loops. Whitehead's protagonist Mark Spitz is part of a sweeper squad in Manhattan that finds and kills any stragglers who remain after regular military forces have cleared an area. This volunteer crew persists in "servitude to the obsolete directives of an obsolete world" (39). Whitehead calls further attention to the hardwiring of bodily reflexes. When Spitz sees something stir across the street, he "slap[s] his arm across" his partner "Kaitlyn's chest to stop her, a gesture he'd lifted from his parents, who had lifted it from their parents, who had remembered a time before seatbelts" (137). This imitative, inherited, vestigial impulse is followed by further mechanical processes. As the sweepers anticipate trouble, they reprise earlier moments of their struggles for survival: their "wasteland protocols booted up, obsolete or no" (137). Likening cognitive alertness and physical readiness to the startup of a computer, Whitehead makes obvious nods towards a mechanical, post-human conception of consciousness.[61]

This depiction of humans as robotic dummies, trapped in rote loops, has metafictional ramifications as well, taking part in Whitehead's career-long interrogation of the narrative architecture of character and genre. Spitz observes that Kaitlyn had "been a grade-grubber before the disaster," and "if she survived, she'd doubtless continue to be a grade-grubber in that coming, reborn world they crawled toward" (28–29). What is character, passages like this ask, but form, repetition, sameness—the attribution of a consistent set of traits to the same textually constructed idea of a person? Further, Spitz, like most of Whitehead's principal characters, seems a studious rejection of the well-rounded individuality of the conventional realist protagonist. Spitz is central but indistinguishable from everyone else; he is generic, a type, an average number in a series of mediocre categories. Those who survived were "an unlikely lot: unemployable man-children, erstwhile cheerleaders, salesman of luxury boats, gym teachers, food bloggers. . . . People like Mark Spitz, seemingly unsnuffable human cockroaches, protected by carapaces of good luck"

(137). It's not just that Spitz is a representative of one of many human categories, his category—"human cockroaches"—is anonymous, defined merely by an inexplicable ability to survive. Throughout, Whitehead emphasizes Spitz's ordinariness. From childhood he

> executed all the hurdles of his life's stages ... with unwavering competence and nary a wobble into exceptionality or failure. ... [C]hild behaviorists would have cherished him. ... He was their *typical*, he was their *most*, he was their *average*. (10–11)

Not just *a* type, Spitz's type is the typical. Defined by his averageness, Spitz is generic. Whitehead brilliantly pins down unexamined links between character and genre. Just as we expect certain conventional characters in certain genres, there are genres *of* characters. This is what we mean by "type." Evacuating the protagonist of distinguishing marks, Whitehead calls attention to the fact that the well-rounded protagonist with rich interiority, central to the realist tradition, is itself a type.

But there's a paradoxical twist, and it may be a twist as old as Tolstoy's "each unhappy family is unhappy in its own way":[62] the coexistence of being a type and an individual, belonging, at one level of abstraction, to a category, and, at the same time and upon closer inspection, being differentiated from others within it. Whitehead's metageneric reflections help us see how genres work, why they are appealing, and why realist characters lumber along despite repeated attempts of poststructuralists to drive a stake in their hearts. For two things that persist in human behavior, even after the zombie apocalypse, are the desires to individualize and find intimate personal connection. When survivors in *Zone One* chance upon each other, how else do they establish their humanity and commune but by storytelling? Coming across another soul, you must first categorize them: "Dead or bandit, straggler or survivor, it was often hard to tell. Did they speak, that was the first test. Did they still have language" (137). After this basic taxonomizing, one gets specific. If survivors "hook up for a time, eventually you traded Last Night stories" (137). Sounding like a Proppian structuralist, Whitehead underscores the deep narrative grammar of these stories: "At their core, Last Night stories were all the same: They came, we died, I started running" (138). Despite the repetitive nature of the ritual and the structure of their plot, variations appear immediately. The key phrase for understanding genre here is "at their core"; while the architecture of the Last Night story remains constant, each telling varies the particulars. This is what a genre is: similarities at a distance or significant level of abstraction, varied instantiation when you look closer.

Unsurprisingly, *Zone One*'s narrator promptly divides Last Night stories into subcategories, each with their appropriate use. And Whitehead oscillates between skepticism that these ritualistic narratives capture an essential self or truth and a lurking suspicion that when managed skillfully they do the job well enough:

> Each retelling of one's Last Night story was a step toward another fantastic refuge, that of truth. Mark Spitz had refined his Last Night story into three versions. The Silhouette was for survivors he wasn't going to travel with for long. . . . No need to hand over his heart, the good stuff. (138)

Despite the novel's doubts that these stories help anyone arrive at the "fantastic refuge of truth," *Zone One* intimates that "good stuff" and a "heart" are withheld in the scant versions:

> [Spitz] offered the Anecdote, robust and carrying more on its ribs, to those he might hole up with for a night. . . . [It] was the smallest portion, he learned, that was acceptable to strangers to allow them to fall asleep without thinking he'd bludgeon them in their sleeping bags. (138)

While speech establishes that one isn't a zombie, and the Silhouette serves for small talk, the Anecdote establishes that one is not a sociopath. Spitz himself is too skeptical to be reassured. "The versions they told in return were never enough to let him sleep, no matter the surfeit of telling details and sincerity" (139). But he and his author reserve some faith in the humanizing and aesthetic potential of the maximal version:

> The Obituary, although refined over the months and not without a rehearsed air, was nonetheless heartfelt, glancing off his true self more than once. . . . Although the adjectives tended to be neutral in later retellings, the Obituary was the sacred in its current guise. . . . The Obit got it down for some calm, distant day when you were long disappeared and a stranger took the time to say your name. (139)

Despite its cynicism about the monotony of human behavior and Spitz's despair at the "death of connection" (138), *Zone One* maintains an earnest, "nonetheless heartfelt," belief in the power of the "thorough," fleshed-out narrative to individuate and memorialize its teller. Like the boy's song in *John Henry Days*, the Obituary is an aesthetic performance that transcends its well-worn structure and generates authentic human connection: "the sacred in its current guise."

These intimations that the well-crafted, detailed narrative escapes the zombified parade of sameness that *Zone One* anatomizes helps explain the tension that looms at the heart of this novel: How, if life under late capitalism is so repetitive, do we account for the distinctive brilliance of the novel's prose and its funny, ingenious take on the zombie genre?[63] The entire novel could be described as an elongated version of Spitz's Obituary. But the answer, it turns out, is rather simple: *most* of late capitalism produces generic objects, recycled tropes, and imitative behaviors, but artists might still produce unique works—not by escaping genre but by embroidering upon a basic framework a thoroughly individualized narrative. Ultimately, *Zone One* refuses the notion that late capitalism manufactures only a uniform cascade of products, because such a view would invalidate any contribution of the novel itself. It would just be a faceless number among the horde of "novels devoted to the codes of the dead world" (242). These metageneric moments and Whitehead's entire genre-bending corpus thus rhyme with the work of recent genre theorists and historians of popular culture, who stress the variability of the most apparently zombified popular genres: if you "deviate from the blueprints," these building blocks become "the very stuff of imagination." Further, the subtle affirmations we find even in Whitehead's most cynical-seeming novel—that artistic innovation remains possible amid repetitive commodity production, that adept storytelling might "glance off" one's true self and generate human connection—reflect a persistent belief in the distinctive power and possibilities of literary art that is the subject of Chapters 2 and 3. But first I examine the varied contemporary uses of generic building blocks, with the examples of detective and postapocalyptic fiction.

The Protean Detective Novel

An initial wave of critics of crime and detective fiction beginning with W. H. Auden's famous essay "The Guilty Vicarage" construed the genre as a rigid set of formal constraints that performed a hegemonic ideological function.[64] These readers concluded, in Andrew Pepper's words, "that the crime novel, in whoever's hands, is at best a conservative genre that . . . depends upon a restoration of the status quo and a reaffirmation of the existing social order."[65] But since roughly the mid-1980s, scholars have recognized that though this account of the genre's ideological and formal conservatism might sufficiently describe a highly formulaic subset of the classical or whodunit English tradition, running from Arthur Conan Doyle and Wilkie Collins through Agatha Christie and Dorothy Sayers, it neglected the transformations of the genre over the remainder of the twentieth century. From the hard-boiled tradition of Chandler and Hammett, through "metaphysical" fictions and anti-novels of Vladimir Nabokov, Jorge Luis Borges, and Alain Robbe-Grillet, postmodernist parodies in the works of Thomas Pynchon, Ishmael Reed, Kathy Acker, and Don DeLillo, cyberpunk and slipstream novels of Philip K. Dick and William Gibson, up through the feminist and multicultural detectives of Sara Paretsky, P. D. James, and Walter Mosely, detective fiction remolded in the hands of these disparate writers has emerged as "a shape-shifter," a form notable for its "hybridity."[66]

Jim Collins argues that to classify a protean genre as "a literature of reassurance and conformism," scholars considered "only those works which are most respectful of the rule of the genre" and treated it as "hermetically sealed off from change . . . textual or societal."[67] But close examination of texts since the noir fiction of the 1930s discloses a genre continually mutating as disparate writers "critiqued the conventions of the White Glove tradition" and "forced the genre in different directions."[68] Collins uncovers an "all pervasive" "ambiguity concerning law and order" and a genre in flux: a set of "social/judicial perspectives and narrative conventions" that "have been rewritten consistently in a series of uneven transitional phases."[69] Genres don't so much "have norms," Collins writes, but their norms are "continually remade" in a "perpetuate/transgress" dialectic that produces "incredible diversity."[70]

Pepper similarly shows that crime fiction's ideological heterogeneity is an inevitable consequence of the plasticity of genre: "the idea that genre is something so fixed and unyielding as to imprison subversive ideas surely needs to be revised."[71] African American detective fictions, beginning with Chester Himes's Harlem Cycle, "bring . . . competing ideologies . . . into messy, violent, unruly patterns that cannot be easily reconciled."[72] Fundamentally, Collins points out, the private investigator "implies a critique rather than a celebration, of a given society's judicial system . . . an alternative vision of law represented by a figure outside the state established channels."[73] The rejection of the detective as a figure for producing an orderly, rational understanding of the world and a stable juridical order culminates in the genre's postmodernist variants, which advance a "negative hermeneutics . . . in which the quest for knowledge is doomed to failure,"[74] and "metaphysical" detective fictions, which subvert conventions "such as narrative closure and the detective's role as surrogate reader," to explore "mysteries of being and knowing."[75] As scholarship on crime fiction has expanded, so has the picture of a heterogeneous genre: its forms and ideological and aesthetic character morphing continually in the hands of diverse practitioners.

When prominent writers of literary fiction began to gravitate toward the detective novel around the turn of the millennium, they did not, and perhaps could not, initiate a radical overturning of a genre that was already a site of so much self-conscious revision. Laura Marcus argues that Auster's *New York Trilogy* succeeded not only in "transgressing and travestying the norms of traditional detective and private eye fictions but as both a culmination and an evacuation of the forms and norms of the 'metaphysical' detective novel"—which had itself become, by the mid-1980s, an established tradition ripe for parody.[76] To understand and appreciate the varied ways recent genre-bending literary writers have deployed the genre, we ought to stop thinking in binary terms of reaffirmation or subversion, and instead examine the innovative variations these writers have played on the form and the disparate uses to which they have been put.

In *Motherless Brooklyn*, for example, Jonathan Lethem's narrator protagonist and amateur sleuth Lionel Essrog has Tourette syndrome. This central modification to the detective character and narrative voice allows Lethem impossible-to-foresee latitude for extending the hard-boiled tradition of wordplay and witty banter; the genre's perennial investigation of the attempt to reassert order is bent in a new direction by foregrounding a neuroatypical protagonist and exploring the way his tics and language itself seek and often fail to impose coherence onto a recalcitrant reality. Lethem's earlier novels blended popular genres and made him a liminal figure on the border of literary and genre fiction; his *Gun with Occasional Music* (1994) mashes together noir detective fiction and dystopian science fiction, while *Girl in Landscape* (1998) is a space western. But it was *Motherless Brooklyn* that brought him tremendous acclaim in crime circles and the literary field.

Scholars and *Motherless Brooklyn*'s initial reviewers have recognized that its innovation lies less in the arc of its detective plot than in its exploration of the Tourettic mind and the linguistic play that exploration facilitates.[77] It follows a conventional hard-boiled plot, as the orphan Lionel searches the Brooklyn underworld for the murderer of his proxy father, mid-level gangster Frank Minna, discovering pervasive corruption in ever-widening circles in the process: Frank's vicious rivalry with his brother; the local mob bosses Matricardi and Rockaforte; a Zendo on the Upper East Side and a fishing village in Maine that are fronts for the many-tentacled Fujisaki Corporation. In its self-reflexive style, the novel nods to the conventionality of this villain: "The Fujisaki Corporation is ruthless and remorseless—in the manner of corporations."[78] While Lethem's depiction of the pervasive and diffuse corruption that remains undisturbed at the novel's unsatisfying conclusion is conventional in the hard-boiled tradition, the novel's ingenuity stems from its inquiry into how language brushes a veneer of mastery onto reality and, when deployed creatively, might disrupt it.

James Peacock notes the risk Lethem runs with this technique: the danger of treating Tourette's as a metaphor for general aspects of human behavior, thus "diminishing understanding of the unique, everyday lived experience of the Tourette's sufferer." But Peacock concludes that "a first-person narrator with a neurological disability is a positive thing" that "forces the reader to question the structures of normativity which usually prevail."[79] Lionel's tics dramatize both the particular efforts of the person with Tourette's, and, metaphorically, the human effort to wield language to stabilize a chaotic world. Among the novel's many self-conscious allusions to its predecessors, Lionel recalls the "sweetly savage generalizations" littering works like Chandler's *The Big Sleep* ("About the only part of a California house you can't put your foot through is the front door") and likens these attempts at mastery to his own:

"Assertions and generalizations are, of course, a version of Tourette's. A way of touching the world, handling it, covering it with confirming language" (307). If Lethem risks using Tourette's as a metaphor, he also destabilizes the binary between those who have and don't have the disorder, by making the one-liners of Philip Marlowe into "a version of Tourette's." Lethem reveals such epigrams as compensatory linguistic gestures for the vast corruption the hard-boiled dick uncovers but cannot expunge—an effort similar to the modernist writer's aesthetic response to a disordered modernity.

But Lionel's spontaneous outbursts do the opposite: disrupt and defamiliarize the world around him. Lethem shows realist normativity, the ostensibly shared and unproblematic experience of "reality," to be quite artificial and fragile and thus upends the hierarchical binary of normal and atypical. Tourette's "teaches you," Lionel muses, "to see the reality-knitting mechanism people employ to tuck away the intolerable, the incongruous, the disruptive" (43). His tics surface as irruptions that burst the "fragile and elastic" "bubble" of "[c]onsensual reality" (44). Jennifer Fleissner helps reconcile this paradox. While Lionel uses his tics "as a means for restoring order," appeasing his need to tic, he achieves this fleeting tranquility by mimicking the unruliness of the wider world: "the order can so often look like chaos: one side of a car has been smashed, therefore (by virtue of symmetry) the other side should be, too."[80] Like the Warner Bros. cartoons and Charlie Chaplin and Buster Keaton films he loves, Lionel's tics "expose an underlying freakishness organizing the social whole,"[81] one also visible in the tumult of New York, "a Tourretic city" (113).

In addition to laying bare the paradoxical normalcy of "freakishness," Lethem uses Lionel as a device—hazarding the appropriation Peacock notes—to facilitate the deliberate artifice and wordplay of the hard-boiled novelist. Critics like Fleissner have noted that the "main narrative" of the novel, its "generic" whodunit, is forgettable; "the text achieves its distinctiveness . . . in its proliferation of Lionel's verbal tics."[82] In one of many examples of the novel's delight in its own wordplay, Lionel riffs on his name, which in his Brooklynese is pronounced "to rhyme with *vinyl*. Lionel Essrog. *Line-all.* / Liable Guesscog. / Final Escrow. / Ironic Pissclam" (7). Lionel worries that, subjected to repeated deformation, his own name might become exhausted, "the original verbal taffy, by now stretched to filament-thin threads . . . the flavor all chewed out of it" (7). But while it expresses a common anxiety about genre fiction—that repetition will render it bland—*Motherless Brooklyn* ultimately insists on the near-infinite possibility of linguistic renewal, as it self-reflexively renders the pleasure it hopes its exuberant wordplay will offer readers, through the delight Minna takes in his protégé's poetry: "his pleasure in compression, in ordinary things made more expressive, more hilarious or vivid by their conflation" (69).[83]

Thus Lethem uses Lionel's tics to generate the sentence-level prose ingenuity prized in the field of literary fiction, while giving the perennial noir theme of a hopelessly disordered, corrupt world an innovative spin. Further, *Motherless Brooklyn* comes to be a metageneric text that demonstrates in its virtuosic use of Lionel's tics, the flexibility that inheres in genres because it inheres in their medium: language. Lionel rhapsodizes over Prince's guitar riffs, which embody the endless elasticity of a simple structural element: "the way he worried forty-five minutes of variations out of a lone musical phrase is, as far as I know, the nearest thing in art to my condition" (128). In Lionel's admiration for Prince's virtuosity, Lethem valorizes the spirit of variation on a theme, of improvisation and perpetual reinvention, that animates the work of genre-bending writers. *Motherless Brooklyn* combines this delight in play with language with its novel deployment of noir to examine the person with Tourette's and show that the disruptive and disorderly are not abnormal, relegated to those with "disabilities," but are endemic to quotidian reality—especially in a place like New York.

Kazuo Ishiguro's *When We Were Orphans*, published the year after *Motherless Brooklyn* and short-listed for the Man Booker Prize, also features an orphan who self-consciously patterns himself after classic detectives, and who fails to bring order and justice to a world spectacularly devoid of both. Though the novels share this skepticism over the detective as savior, Ishiguro's subject matter and method differ profoundly. While Lethem uses Lionel's Tourette's to underscore the chaos of New York and the wider world, and to perform manifold riffs on language that transmute that chaos into aestheticized irruptions, Ishiguro stresses the power of repetitive generic narratives to colonize the mind and delude us into believing the world might adhere to their conventional structures; and he connects the reassuring but deluded narrative of the detective as restorer of justice to England's hubristic and racist efforts to bring order to its colonial territories. The narrator protagonist of *When We Were*

Orphans is renowned British detective Christopher Banks, who recounts his childhood in the international settlement in Shanghai between the wars, the mysterious disappearance of his father and then his mother, his emigration to London and investigative career, and his return to Shanghai at the outbreak the Second World War in a belated bid to find his parents.

Banks's fuzziness with regard to his childhood memories—particularly his obliviousness of the involvement of his father's British company in the opium trade, and of his mother's activism opposing that trade—extends Ishiguro's career-long experiment with unreliable narration. Hélène Machinal shows how this unreliability functions in *Orphans* to "unravel" the "generic—or mythic—mode of detective fiction," as Banks discovers how deluded he was to believe he would find his parents, and Ishiguro attacks the "myth of Britain" as a civilized and civilizing imperial power.[84] Matthew Hart similarly notes that Banks acquires his "belief in the supernaturally restorative powers of the detective,"[85] as he and his childhood friend Akira "invented and played out endless variations on the theme of his father's rescue."[86] More than simply establishing Banks's preposterous faith in the detective's power, Ishiguro marks the repetitive, conventional narrative as the germ of Banks's lifelong delusion. "Our narratives had," Banks recalls, "endless variations, but fairly quickly" they "established a basic recurring story-line. My father was held captive in a house somewhere beyond the settlement boundaries." This narrative repeated the "particular convention" that "the house in which [he] was held was comfortable and clean" (116). While Ishiguro also stresses the endless variability of the rescue narrative, its recurrent central element literally sanitizes the violence it attempts to confront and plows its groove into Banks's mind, such that when he returns to Shanghai, some twenty-five years later, and the city is being destroyed by the invading Japanese army, he still expects to find his parents safely ensconced, captive but clean and comfortable, in this imaginary house. In another metageneric meditation, Ishiguro notes the "endless" flexibility of genre but warns of the indoctrinating force of reiterated conventions.

In addition to questioning, like many hard-boiled, metaphysical, and postmodernist detective fictions, the ability of the detective to restore order, and dramatizing the way conventional narrative structures forge readers' faith their mythic worldview, Ishiguro links the conventional detective novel to the hubris of the British imperial worldview. Banks becomes the representative of an England that imagines itself the savior of global civilization—bound by "duty" to "combat evil" (144). But Ishiguro shows us a Britain that is actually an agent of misery, silent bystander to calamity, and beneficiary of destabilizing, violent, illegal trade. *Orphans* steadily eviscerates the hypocrisy of colonial pretensions to global responsibility by making Banks emblematic of a British tendency to prioritize private, local concerns and ignore or even aestheticize global suffering. When Banks returns, he dines in the ballroom of the Palace Hotel with a gathering of "Shanghai's elite," while outside a Japanese warship shells Chinese troops. The diners insist that they are safe in the International Settlement, and one guest declares that the shells are "quite a sight. Rather like watching shooting stars" (170). Banks recognizes that the supposed partygoers perceive the "battle across the water" as merely "one entertainment" before the main act of the night's cabaret (172). He feels "a wave of revulsion," as he recognizes the "refusal of everyone here to acknowledge their drastic culpability," a "denial of responsibility" at "the heart of the maelstrom threating to suck in the whole of the civilized world," and the elite's "contempt" for "the suffering of their Chinese neighbors across the canal" (172–173).

But Ishiguro subtly reveals Banks to be equally culpable of this denial. Despite his delusions of heroism, his hope that he can go to the "heart of the serpent . . . and slay the thing" (144)—which anticipates Ishiguro's deflating of the Arthurian romance tradition in *The Buried Giant*—Banks borrows a set of opera glasses to view the shelling, hinting at his own aestheticized and self-centered tunnel vision. He sees "various boats still going about their normal business right next to the fighting" (171) and zooms in on a single boatman, "who *like me* was utterly absorbed by the fate of his cargo and oblivious of the war not sixty yards to his right" (171, emphasis added). Though Banks is revolted by the "denial of responsibility" of his countrymen, he too is wholly caught up in his private mission to discover his parents and is largely "oblivious" of the unfolding global calamity.[87] Banks's guilty conscience mounts as he penetrates further into the labyrinthine "warren" of Shanghai—a repeated word choice that suggests his view of the Chinese as animals—and he becomes nearly hysterical when demanding a Chinese officer take him to the house where he believes his parents are being held. "I know full well what you've been thinking . . . Lieutenant! . . . You believe this is all my fault, all this, all of it, all this terrible suffering, this destruction" (262). Finally, Banks realizes that his career as a detective has been facilitated by his mother sacrificing herself to become the concubine of the warlord Wang Ku and financed by his opium trading. In Banks's pursuit then, Ishiguro figures three intersecting axes of colonial delusion: his tendency to ignore or aestheticize the suffering of the Chinese and focus on his own concerns; the belief that he is the world savior, responsible for alleviating that suffering; and his complicity in the murderous opium trade.

Lethem's and Ishiguro's distinct, metageneric deployments of the detective novel are merely two examples of a genre that has been reshaped variously by genre-bending writers since the late 1990s. Chabon's *The Yiddish Policemen's Union*, which combines alternate history and noir, gained high honors in genre subfields, winning the Hugo and Nebula and was short-listed for the Edgar. The novel imagines the founding of a Jewish settlement in Alaska after the Second World War, invents a plot of messianic Jewish extremists dedicated to the violent recapture of Jerusalem, and explores motifs of diaspora and the refuge of familial love—while stirring Yiddish slang into the hard-boiled detective's repartee.[88] Mark Haddon's *The Curious Incident of the Dog in the Night-Time* (2003) was a crossover YA and adult sensation that won the Whitbread Award for best novel and was long-listed for the Booker, and like *Motherless Brooklyn* it centers on a neuroatypical sleuth: a fifteen-year-old math whiz. Louise Erdrich's *The Round House*, which won the National Book Award in 2012, is a bildungsroman and crime novel, whose narrator protagonist Joe Coutts seeks to avenge the rape of his mother on an Ojibwe reservation in North Dakota. Making Joe's father a tribal judge, Erdrich chronicles the U.S. history of corrupt legal maneuvers and violations of treaties that resulted in Native American territorial dispossession and the prevalence of unprosecuted sexual assault of Native women by white men that persists to this day. Further, Erdrich devastatingly critiques the possessive masculinity of Joe and his father, who arrogate to themselves the role of protectors, avengers, and bringers of justice, rather than adopt an ethics of care for the assault survivor.[89] These novels combine an enduring skepticism about the detective's ability to bring justice with a series of novel preoccupations and methods: varied historical and geographical terrain, disparate identity positions and social issues, and a range of linguistic and narrative innovations. And the detective fictions I've considered here barely scratch the surface of genre-bending work with this genre.

Apocalypses Now

Jessica Hurley and Dan Sinykin note that at a moment characterized by a host of ongoing and imminent cataclysms, apocalypse is not so much a single "locatable event" but a "form and practice," which "mediates the unevenly distributed risks of the contemporary social, political, and geophysical world."[90] Apocalypse does not refer to a distinct occurrence, and the artistic and literary works that offer many visions of it do not follow a predetermined structure. Instead, Hurley and Sinykin show that a range of apocalyptic reckonings generates a malleable genre, a flexible recipe that has been reshaped for a diverse constellation of projects: "an imaginative practice that forms and deforms history for specific purposes: an aesthetic that *does* as much as it *represents*."[91] Heather Hicks has shown that contemporary postapocalyptic novels deploy "genre's pleasurable and eternally repeated elements."[92] Novels like Margaret Atwood's *Oryx and Crake* (2003), Cormac McCarthy's *The Road*, Jeanette Winterson's *The Stone Gods* (2007), Colson Whitehead's *Zone One*, and David Mitchell's *Cloud Atlas* reenact familiar narratives and resurrect conventional figures from Friday in *Robinson Crusoe* to the Whore of Babylon. But these conventions are adapted and embedded within wildly different forms, settings, and narrative structures and are motivated toward varied purposes. Winterson's novel offers an explicit rewriting of aspects of Defoe, but she transposes Crusoe's terraces to a distant planet, after Earth has been "fucked to death" and had its "last drops of oil" sucked "out of the ground."[93] Of these texts, only Winterson's envisions interplanetary travel and humanoid robots, and only *The Stone Gods* and *Cloud Atlas* have catastrophic climate change catalyze the apocalypse—despite the fact that, as I elaborate in Chapter 6, it is for many contemporary observers the most likely cause.

Indeed, it's striking, in light of COVID-19, how many of the most acclaimed recent apocalyptic novels presciently imagine a global pandemic as the cataclysmic event—though "the plague" is one of zombies in *Zone One* and Ling Ma's *Severance* (2018).[94] *Oryx and Crake*, *Zone One*, Emily St. John Mandel's *Station Eleven*, and *Severance* also deploy similar chronological structures: they are backwards-facing post-pandemic novels that intersperse post-crisis speculation with flashbacks to before disaster struck. *Oryx* diverges from these by having its flashbacks return to a time still well in our future, whereas *Zone One* and *Station Eleven* return insistently to the present, interweaving postapocalyptic imaginings with realist depictions of the contemporary. Despite these structural commonalities, comparison of Whitehead's and Mandel's versions of the postapocalyptic novel demonstrates how it may be deployed in disparate ways and for divergent ends: Whitehead to critique imitative consumerism under global capitalism, and Mandel to pay homage to the underappreciated miracles of technology and the resilience of human goodness through the bleakest of circumstances.

As we have seen, Whitehead admits that individuation is possible, especially for the uniquely gifted narrator, whose Last Night story might "glance off his true self." But most of *Zone One* emphasizes the rule rather than these exceptions, recounting how people follow predetermined scripts and repetitive loops. The novel drags to the surface the latent meaning of the "zombie renaissance," that McGurl diagnosed a year before the novel's publication. Its zombies figure the haunting possibility that humans lack the autonomous and unique subjectivity that the realist novel is dedicated to mapping, and by some accounts producing.[95] Throughout, Whitehead confronts us with the specter that we are already zombies, trapped in learned, repetitive behaviors. The novel bludgeons us with its insistence that the zombie apocalypse has arrived but very little has changed. Whitehead's "stragglers" merely boil down the automatic routines in which humans had already been locked: "Their lives *had been* an interminable loop of repeated gestures; now their existences were winnowed to this discrete and eternal moment" (62, emphasis added). Whitehead's language continually underscores that we behave like mindless automatons—even in the flashbacks. Before the plague, residents of an apartment co-op "shambled through the identical outlet showrooms" (73). Walking through Tribeca, Spitz passes a nightclub and recalls the days when "bouncers dragged out the velvet rope and started choosing survivors . . . bedraggled drones convened on stools and soft low-slung couches . . . trying to forget that the minute you bury the miserable day it rises from its coffin the next morning, this monster" (183). Overwhelming you with their numbers like the zombies themselves, Whitehead's metaphors describe pre-plague life as already zombified. "Sunday night's recurrent epidemic: Back to work" (84). The imitative displays of middle-class consumerism and the numbing routines of white-collar labor are the actual menaces that dominate *Zone One*.

In stark contrast, *Station Eleven* uses its backward-facing structure to appreciate just how good modern civilization is by imagining its destruction. Set after a ferocious swine flu has eradicated 99 percent of the world's population, *Station Eleven* seems almost a direct rebuttal to *Zone One*. Whitehead suggests that a zombie apocalypse wouldn't change much. Mandel's novel insists that a postapocalyptic world would need heroes to resurrect what we have lost. The motto of Mandel's novel is: "Because survival is insufficient."[96] This slogan is tattooed on the left arm of Kirsten, *Station Eleven*'s protagonist, and branded on the caravan of the Traveling Symphony, a band of classical musicians and Shakespearean actors who tour the surviving settlements of the Great Lakes region, bringing the light of civilization, via the music and drama of Western culture, to the endarkened post-plague days. Though the novel acknowledges that it lifts this axiom from *Star Trek*, it motivates this pop culture reference and the postapocalyptic genre to pay homage to civilization and its most illustrious literary representative.

Station Eleven does not depict any of the violent calamity that occurred immediately after the pandemic. At times it acknowledges problems with human civilization and society, flirting with *Zone One*'s cynicism, only to swerve back toward a universalizing optimism that valorizes human relationships, the unifying power of culture, and the benefits of technological advance. "The problem with the Traveling Symphony was the same problem suffered by every group of people everywhere since before the collapse" (46–47). The age-old problem: not exploitation or cruelty, but each group's "collection of petty jealousies, neuroses, undiagnosed PTSD cases, and simmering resentments" (47). Art and interpersonal bonds redeem things, however: "what made it bearable were the friendships, of course, the camaraderie and the music and the Shakespeare, the moments of transcendent beauty and joy" (47). The novel nods at existential despair but returns always to hope via human kindness and art's power to remind us of the beauty in the world. An ex-boyfriend of Kirsten's scrawls "Sartre: Hell is other people," on one of the caravans (48). But upon reflection and the death of a friend, Kirsten revises this thought: "Hell is the absence of the people you long for" (144). *Station Eleven* repudiates *Zone One*'s depiction of the inhumanity of humanity and the hollowness of late capitalism, alerting us to humane quotidian moments elided by abstractions like "late capitalism" and "the modern world."

As if responding to Whitehead's depiction of human life as zombified, Jeevan, another of the novel's principal characters, finds himself "thinking about how human the city is, how human everything is. We bemoaned the impersonality of the modern world, but that was a lie. . . . There had always been a massive infrastructure of people . . . working unnoticed" (178). The death of billions and the erasure of modern technology enable Mandel's characters to notice all they had failed to appreciate. "Incredible in retrospect, all of it, but especially the parts having to do with travel and communications. . . . These taken-for-granted miracles that had persisted all around them" (233). In the vein of such appreciation, another character builds a Museum of Civilization in an airport that becomes home to several hundred survivors and stands as monument to "the beauty of flight" (247). The museum embodies the project of *Station Eleven*, which constructs an anthropology of the present, and places the "miracles" and "beauty" of civilization on a pedestal.

In these projects and the range of contemporary postapocalyptic fiction, we find a wide array of divergent forms and purposes. In *Gold Fame Citrus* (2015), Claire Vaye Watkins envisions a more circumscribed apocalypse, centered in California and the southwestern United States, which have been engulfed by an ever-expanding Mojave Desert due to misguided attempts by public officials to bring water to a drastically warming, drying, and burning region. Lydia Yuknavitch's bleak and bizarrely inventive *The Book of Joan* (2017), which I discuss in Chapter 6, envisions environmental destruction on a planetary scale, as humans survive on a space station ruled by a Trumpian billionaire, turned fascist dictator. The novel's protagonist Christine launches an act of literary resistance that is part queer, ecofeminist revolution, part reimagining of Joan of Arc. These examples also only begin to convey the vast terrain of literary writers "repurposing" the postapocalyptic genre in recent decades, adapting its recipe for diverse agendas and with wild ingenuity.

Conclusion: "States of Possibility" in *The Underground Railroad*

This chapter only captures a sliver of the diverse purposes to which literary writers have put detective and postapocalyptic genres, to say nothing of the many others they have adapted in fascinating ways over the last several decades. Critics have noted a vibrant resurgence of the gothic, as writers have deployed it to depict the haunting effects of histories of racial, colonial, and gendered violence on the present, most famously in Toni Morrison's *Beloved*, but also in Helen Oyeyemi's *The Icarus Girl* (2005), Junot Díaz's *The Brief Wondrous Life of Oscar Wao* (2007), Jesmyn Ward's National Book Award–winning *Sing, Unburied, Sing* (2017), and Carmen Maria Machado's *Her Body and Other Parties*.[97] Recent novelists have also deployed the gothic to dramatize the monstrous demands of neoliberal entrepreneurial individualism in Gillian Flynn's *Gone Girl* (2012),[98] the uncanny spatial depths of digital media in Jennifer Egan's *The Keep* and Mark Z. Danielewski's *House of Leaves* (2000),[99] and the invisible toxicity of water contaminants due to fracking in Jennifer Haigh's *Heat and Light* (2016) and Samantha Schweblin's *Fever Dream* (2014).[100] These writers exploit genre's malleability, which helps them engineer disparate projects rather than posing a limiting set of artistic or ideological constraints.

It is difficult to discuss genre in these terms without thinking of the vast construction projects at the heart of Whitehead's *John Henry Days* and *The Underground Railroad* as allegories for the writer's own labor, much of which takes place out of sight, if not in subterranean darkness. The latter novel invites this interpretation as it literalizes the metaphor of the underground railroad. When Cora flees the Randall plantation on the railroad, which has become, in Whitehead's alternative history and speculative turn, an anachronistic network of clandestine tunnels and trains, the railroad takes her from Georgia to South Carolina, North Carolina, Tennessee, Indiana, and a final indeterminate locale. Alexander Manshel argues that Whitehead has in his career been "a prolific writer of one genre in particular: historical fiction."[101] But the task of *classifying* Whitehead's work as historical fiction, and thus central to "contemporary fiction's pervasive historicist turn," threatens to overshadow what Manshel reveals about what Whitehead *does with* this genre: transform it in "formally inventive" ways, and use it to address both the fiction's historical setting and the contemporary moment in which Whitehead is writing.[102] Manshel shows how *The Intuitionist* "dramatizes contemporaneous debates over literary canon reformation" that raged in the academy in the 1980s and 90s and how *The Underground Railroad* addresses "*the present* limits of contemporary narratives of slavery"—that is, their limits at the time Whitehead is writing in the late 2010s.[103] Classifying these books as historical fictions risks obscuring the way they address the present as much as the past and their generic hybridity in blending the noir detective novel, alternate history, and speculative fiction. Whitehead's mixing of genres and historical referents in these texts actually reveals the limits of classification, the project of deciding what genre a text *belongs to*, and demonstrates why we ought to think instead of genres as something writers *use* and *deform*, in disparate ways and for various projects.

Madhu Dubey has persuasively argued that what Whitehead does, envisioning a railroad that would have been science fictional at the time the novel is set and deploying multiple anachronisms, is "breach notions of historical containment" that would leave the past in the past, in order to "bring out continuities between past and present and to convey the circuitous, interrupted, and incomplete trajectory of freedom."[104] As an account of Whitehead's anachronism and free mixing of historical materials, this is altogether convincing. But Whitehead's depiction of the railroad as a technology that enables Cora to reach different states, "each one a state of possibility,"[105] also functions at a second, metageneric level to allegorize the work of the novelist, particularly the speculative novelist or alternate historian. Within the fiction, the railroad enables Cora's escape from the Randall plantation where she is enslaved, while as a narrative device it functions as Whitehead's vehicle to slip the bounds of empirical historical reality, play fast and loose with temporality, and generate nightmarish scenarios as well as glimpses of utopia. When Cora flees Randall's plantation, the novel leaves the naturistically drawn depiction of the horrors of enslavement. The terror continues in the other states, but in forms that eschew fidelity to historically realistic depiction. This is hardly to suggest that Whitehead thinks that demands for literary fidelity to the real or to follow extant narrative conventions are on par with the shackles of antebellum U.S. chattel slavery, but instead to intimate that the travels of the novel's protagonist along the underground railroad and its author's use of that railroad as a vehicle for imagining alternative "states of possibility" express an analogous, if different in scale and urgency, desire for freedom.

The novel explicitly likens the desire for freedom from bondage to artistic practice and to Whitehead's ethos of the freedom to use the building blocks of imagination to deviate from narrative blueprints in several key moments. Caesar approaches Cora with his plot to flee the Randall plantation after he attracts the attention of a "station agent" on the Underground Railroad, while selling his "handsomely crafted bowls" in town (51). (A previous, liberal-minded master taught Caesar to read and learn a craft.) Whitehead compares Caesar's developing escape plan to an artist's labor, rhetorically linking artistic freedom and freedom from human bondage, and describing both as the forging of something material from the germ of an idea. Caesar's and Cora's "true enterprise," to flee from slavery, "thrived as their discussions gave it form. The idea was like a hunk of wood . . . requiring human craft and ingenuity to reveal the new shape within" (53). Later, in South Carolina, they hear a band of musicians composed of "freemen and not chattel." Cora marvels at their opportunity to "attack the melody without the burden of providing one of the sole comforts of their slave village," and thinks making music for its own sake, not to momentarily assuage the pain of bondage, must "still be a cherished novelty." Whitehead adds a further thought, underscoring the state of possibility that any worker in the kingdom of culture seeks: "To practice their art with liberty and joy" (105).

Though Whitehead's novel is primarily concerned with dramatizing the "circuitous and incomplete trajectory of freedom" that persists for African American people, it gestures throughout to the liberty that artists seek—particularly Black artists, who previously had to shoulder "the burden" of providing comfort for other members of the race or proof of Black intellectual aptitude. The fact that generic conventions do not pose a rigid set of constraints, that Whitehead is free to take liberties with the historical record, to conflate periods and combine genres, allows him to take the extant "hunks of wood" that are the historical novel, the neo-slave narrative, and alternate history and hack at them like Michelangelo, using his "craft and ingenuity to reveal the new shape within"—creating different "states of possibility," including the utopian vision of Valentine Farm and the hybrid amalgam of genres that is *The Underground Railroad* and his oeuvre more broadly.

While Whitehead poses construction of the railroad and, by metaphorical extension, the work of the artist, as unalienated, non-instrumental labor, in profound contrast to the capitalist slave system that viciously exploits bodies for profit, the novel leaves the effects of both construction projects uncertain. When Cora disembarks at the novel's end, she takes up with another escaped slave, whose wagon is bound for California but first has to make a stop with "some people we going to meet in Missouri" (312). These travels might lead Cora back into slavery, and the novel is equally skeptical that literary art will provide an escape from our ongoing racial nightmare.[106] The artist's freedom from constraint does not succeed in generating a real utopia in the world, but it facilitates visions of it as well as a critical vantage from which to view our own history.

When Cora arrives at the utopian Valentine Farm, which offers a glimpse of freedom and self-determination for the African Americans who live there that is depressingly short-lived, Whitehead self-reflexively has the intellectual and orator Lander argue: "Sometimes a useful delusion is better than a useless truth" (290). By which he means the "states of possibility" that are fictional "delusions" can help us see the necessity of utopian visions and how our ideologies impose themselves on reality. "Valentine Farm is a delusion . . . a place of refuge. . . . Yet here we are" (290). "And America too, is a delusion, the grandest one of all. The white race believes—with all its heart—that it is their right to take the land. To kill Indians. Make war. Enslave their brothers. This nation shouldn't exist, if there is any justice in the world. . . . Yet here we are" (290–291). If unjust delusions become reality, Whitehead offers the tantalizingly faint hope that a just one might someday too. Unbound by constraints to deploy popular genres for the construction of such utopian projects and many others, bending their frameworks, borrowing and varying their favorite recipes, manipulating them like so many multicolored building blocks, genre-bending literary writers have theorized and demonstrated the endless plastic utility of these genres; they offer a constructivist vision for understanding genre not as something texts belong to or are constrained by, but as something writers use: "there's no end to what you could make."

Prose Style and Interiority in Genre-Bending Literary Fiction

> It seemed as much of a crime to commit a cliché to paper as to kill a man.[1]
> VIET THAN NGUYEN, *The Sympathizer* (2015)

> "We're both of us sentimental. We can't help it. Our generation still carry the old feelings. A part of us refuses to let go. The part that wants to keep believing there's something unreachable inside each of us. Something that's unique and won't transfer."[2]
> KAZUO ISHIGURO, *Klara and the Sun* (2021)

IN CHAPTER 1, I ARGUED that writers of literary fiction have joined literary scholars in revising their understanding of genre, theorizing and availing themselves of popular genres' utility and unlimited malleability as frameworks for the construction of varied literary projects. Having shown how genre-bending writers produce a theory of generic plasticity and a correspondingly diverse practice, I am left with the question: What have they wrought? How has this prominent movement transformed the character of literary fiction in the first decades of the twenty-first century? In the Introduction, I argued that literary fiction is largely coherent and distinct from genre fiction when understood as a subfield of literary production and consumption composed of prestigious institutions and agents: renowned publishers and imprints, high cultural reviewing organs, esteemed prize committees, and the like. Literary fiction is what gets produced and circulated in the literary subfield. This looks tautological, but if decades of attention to the historical production of aesthetic value have taught us anything, it's that literary value is not an inherent property of a work but is produced by agents and institutions and reproduced over time.[3]

And yet, this sociological, institutional account of what makes something *literary*—it's what agents, editors, reviewers, or prize juries recognize and promote as such—remains rather thin and unsatisfying from the standpoint of literary history, since it immediately begs the question of what qualities and characteristics these agents and institutions tend to look for and valorize, of what kind of writing gets deemed worthy of literary distinction in the contemporary moment. What makes a "literary western" or "literary zombie novel" *literary*? Does anything hold this category together other than its claim be "serious" fiction, its aspirations to win prestige from literary institutions, its dedication to whatever is deemed "quality" by current arbiters of taste? Or are there specific formal features, narrative strategies, thematic preoccupations, or other aesthetic dimensions that unite literary writers, and that prestige-granting agents and institutions valorize? This chapter and the next aim to answer these questions, demonstrating some of the constitutive features of literary fiction today and producing a sociological poetics that reconciles institutional and formalist accounts of what constitutes the literary.

It is especially pressing to ask the question *What constitutes literary fiction now?* when the phenomenon this book seeks to analyze and explain might seem to have undermined a central account of what literary fiction is or, in the eyes of some observers, collapsed the distance between literary and genre fiction. Claire Squires argues persuasively for the institutional or "contextual definition" of literary fiction, its ostensible circularity notwithstanding: "literary fiction is that published by literary imprints."[4] But Squires adds a "formal" definition: literary fiction is typically defined by "negation"; it is fiction "that cannot be described in more formally, or formulaically, generic terms: it is not crime or science fiction, romance or fantasy. It could include elements of more closely defined genre fiction . . . but formal indefinability is its prevailing characteristic."[5] The contextual definition is circular, the formal definition formless, undefinable.

Today this negative formal definition—literary fiction is whatever doesn't fit neatly into other genre categories—is even less satisfying, now that popular genres have been frequently borrowed, assimilated, and deployed in inventive ways by prestigious writers in the literary subfield. Though an author like Atwood may bristle at being called a writer of science fiction, it is nearly impossible to argue that her *MaddAddam* trilogy, set in a near and postapocalyptic future determined by calamitous forms of bioengineering, could not be defined formally as science fiction. So today, literary fiction sometimes *also* uses crime fiction or science fiction. And in prominent cases like Atwood's *Blind Assassin* and Mitchell's *Cloud Atlas*, literary fictions bend and blend genres, mixing them or layering them in separate sections. Literary fictions like these *can* "be described in more formally... generic terms," though they continue to resist being formulaic. Few would dispute that Chang-rae Lee's *On Such a Full Sea* deploys dystopian speculative fiction or that Chabon's *The Yiddish Policemen's Union* combines elements of alternate history and noir detective fiction. But what makes such novels fit comfortably in the field of literary fiction? Is it merely a marketing category, indicated by bookstore section, the imprint on the spine, or cover style? Or does their writing contain recognizably "literary" features, and if so, what are they? What makes novels *literary* when "formal indefinability" or the negation of genre categories no longer applies? Since genre-bending writers of recent decades stand among the most critically acclaimed, prize-laden, and bestselling writers of literary fiction of the period, their work offers a peerless opportunity to consider just what gets recognized as a literary achievement today.

Some observers have posited that the increasing prevalence of familiar, popular genres in contemporary literary fiction signals a breakdown in any meaningful distinction between the literary and the popular. But, as I discuss in the Introduction, popular fiction and literary fiction continue to be published by different imprints, received in different publications, and have developed separate prize systems for negotiating prestige within each subfield—prizes that help negotiate and codify the values, logics, judgments, and, as a result, authors who predominate in each. Further, as this chapter and the following demonstrate, when esteemed writers of contemporary literary fiction have adopted the frameworks of the genres that have flourished in popular culture, they have often sought to establish their distance from the subfield of genre fiction, highlighting their literariness by deploying established literary techniques, meditating self-reflexively on the meaning and value of literary reading, and by marking their difference from, often by scorning, the better part of popular culture's voluminous output. It would be possible to read such moves as strategic bids for prestige. But I will argue that literary writers' efforts to differentiate their work from the field of genre fiction reflect instead their persistent belief in, and effort to preserve, the distinctiveness of the literary. While industry players like Amazon and corporate publishers may simply view literary fiction as a useful form of market segmentation and product differentiation, genre-bending writers express their commitments to: originality of verbal expression; the rendering of interiority; and a self-reflexive examination of the value and purpose of literary reading in the face of competing media and an ever-more crowded marketplace for cultural goods. This chapter thus defines *literary fiction* as a subfield structured by agents and institutions that possesses relatively durable values, which lead to the privileging of particular formal and thematic attributes.

This chapter examines literary novelists' transformations of popular genres to show how they manifest, reflect upon, and extend reigning values in the field of literary fiction, marking their deployments of genre as literary and distinct from the field of popular fiction. Though genre-bending writers have wrought an unmistakable change in the genres deployed in the literary field—once-popular genres are now everywhere—this chapter shows that that field's aesthetic values and predominant formal features have not changed fundamentally. The phenomenon marks not a revolution but the adoption of popular genre frameworks infused with a traditionally literary sensibility. When genre-bending novelists self-consciously underscore their own literary qualities, they bring into focus the forms that tend to be valorized in literary fiction today, the values and preoccupations that structure that subfield, what counts as *literary* in the present.

After addressing the surprising reticence of recent literary scholars to explore the question of what constitutes literary fiction, this chapter examines how genre-bending novels manifest and often explicitly assert their creators' commitments to prose style and interiority—perennial priorities in the literary field. The commitment to these forms constitutes an interlocking set of aesthetic principles that predominate, but are also continually tested and questioned, in the field. Drawing attention to their own stylistic exuberance and scorning cliché, genre benders express esteem for well-crafted verbal expression and aim to continuously innovate with their medium. The privileging of formal innovation—the bending and transforming of genres that I explored in Chapter 1—and the foregrounding of distinctive sentence-level prose style mark the ways contemporary literary fiction maintains commitments of literary modernism to differentiate literary art from repetitive commodity production. While such efforts are often today labeled snobbish or elitist, and it's true that literary writers may prefer admiration from cultural authorities and other writers to sales, these efforts are not merely gambits for prestige or to appeal a particular market. These writers continue to value language wielded in aesthetically pleasing ways, novels structured in unexpected configurations, and writing that alters our sense of what is possible over fiction that regularly fulfills audience expectations and satisfies preexisting consumer demand and language that is adroit but merely functional.

Privileging innovative deployments of familiar genres and distinctive prose style, literary writers continue to valorize individual subjectivity and consciousness, whether human or nonhuman; their prizing of formal innovation and linguistic exuberance thus intertwines with their continued dedication to rendering the intricacies of character psychology and voice. But this emphasis on interiority does not require an atomistic exaltation of the individual, cut off from social context. Instead, literary writers understand consciousness as the primary site of experience, and thus it is the medium through which oppressive workings of power are felt and the vehicle for generating resistance to them. This emphasis on consciousness in turn dovetails with the subject of Chapters 3 and 5: in literary writers' self-reflexive examination of the value of the literary, and in their skepticism toward the realm of corporatized, commercial culture, they insist on the continued value of literary encounters as sites for cultivating beauty, ethical complexity, freedom, and expansiveness of thought, in the face of popular entertainment and new media technology that they often perceive as threats to such faculties, and a neoliberal capitalism that reduces human experiences and social interaction to generators of economic value. Though some of these texts ratify traditional liberal humanist values by affirming language, subjective experience, and the canonical literary tradition, in others, like the literary novels of artificial intelligence I trace throughout this and the next chapter, we find a critical posthumanism that points up the tendency of humans to act machine-like, irrational, or violently inhumane; condemns the way the category of "the human" is wielded to instrumentalize and exploit those excluded from it; and explores what constitutes language, consciousness, and ethical action when we recognize these are not exclusively possessions of the human.[6]

An important caveat: arguing that genre-bending literary fiction today continues to privilege style, interiority, and self-reflexivity about the literary is not to claim these features will not be found in genre fiction fields. Again, I view literary fiction and genre fiction primarily as fields, social practice spaces constituted by agents and institutions, possessing relatively distinct values and aesthetic priorities. This chapter and the next do not contend that there are absolute formal or thematic divisions between the texts that circulate in these internally heterogeneous fields. Instead, these subfields have tendencies and relative priorities, like expectations routinely met in genre fields, often frustrated in the literary. We will certainly find finely wrought prose in works of fantasy—though, as I argue in Chapter 4, fantasy tends to privilege the pleasure of immersion in a fictional world and obtrusive language can disrupt the immersive illusion. So, the fantasy subfield tends to value ostentatious prose style less. We will find many of the literary features and thematic preoccupations examined here in genre fields, but these chapters contend that they are bound to central values and preoccupations in the literary one.

The Literariness of Literary Fiction

What does it mean to contend that when literary writers have adopted popular genres, they have sought to differentiate their deployments from the lion's share of production in the field of popular fiction? What does it mean to take a genre and make it literary? In recent decades, literary scholars have been remarkably hesitant to inquire into the question of what constitutes "the literary" today, given that the exploration of such questions had in prior periods been seen as the primary task of literary studies.[7] What makes literary fiction *literary*?

We have seen that literary fiction tends to be defined by negation, or with circularity, or by its readership and position in the market and cultural hierarchies, if it is defined at all; it is fiction that is *not* genre fiction; it is fiction that possesses literary qualities; it is fiction that has a well-heeled audience.[8] For example, Richard Todd, in his excellent history of the Booker Prize, defines "serious literary fiction" circularly, as "self-consciously literary novels," that aim at a rather vague audience; they are "intended to appeal to 'the general reader': that is, a reasonably sophisticated, largely but not exclusively professional readership with an interest in, but not unlimited time for, the leisured consumption of full-length fiction."[9]

Recent literary scholarship has often been more concerned with mapping the thematic concerns and many subgenres of contemporary fiction, including greatly increased attention to the field of popular genre fiction, than with delineating the formal contours of literary fiction. And those that have examined literary fiction as such have generally focused on the often-unseen players and institutions behind its production, rather than its internal dynamics. Critics more explicitly concerned with literary fiction have often, like Dan Sinykin, focused on the conditions of its production or the way its formal tendencies advance the economic interests of producers, serving as "perfect form[s] for conglomerate marketing," or "express" allegorically the dynamics of "conglomerate authorship."[10] An exception is Alexander Manshel, who focuses on the increasing dominance of historical fiction in prestigious U.S. literary fiction, especially by writers from marginalized populations.[11] The valorization of historical work by writers of color is a major development in recent literary fiction, but the boom of genre-bending fiction by such writers shows that they need not use historical fiction and that that genre can often be combined with others, as in Morrison's *Beloved*, Whitehead's *Underground Railroad*, or Nguyen's *The Sympathizer*. One formidable obstacle to the production of a poetics of contemporary literary fiction is the persistence of a modernist-inflected conception of literary value that I discuss in the Introduction: the privileging of originality, innovation, and difference from what has been done before, which has produced a subfield in which a wildly varying catalogue of work gets published and reviewed under its quality-marking umbrella. The literary, like its putative opposite, might seem to be based on an amorphous, intuitive schema that allows one to say "I know it when I see it." And yet, one can detect several interlocking features that predominate in literary fiction.

One of the most systematic taxonomies of the principal features of literary fiction can be found in Joyce Saricks's *Readers' Advisory Guide to Genre Fiction* (2009), a work of "vernacular criticism" designed to help librarians suggest further reading to their patrons and that literary scholars have regrettably neglected.[12] Saricks places literary fiction under the heading "Intellect Genres," along with mysteries, psychological suspense, and science fiction, and notes that while some readers may view it as "blasphemy" to consider literary fiction one genre among many, as its acclaimed writers are considered "the epitome of literary standards and style," it nonetheless has "identifiable characteristics."[13] Saricks catalogues the primary ones: the importance of "literary style," "poetic language," and structure that "may be more complex, even experimental"; "characters" that "emerge as more important than story lines" and "are multi-dimensional"; story lines that "are thought-provoking" and endings that "are often open or ambiguous"; pacing that is "slower" because "complex characters and/or story lines, as well as imaginative language and style" tend to "force readers to read more slowly in order to understand the layers of embedded meaning."[14] Such qualities are not meant to be exhaustive or exclusive. Saricks notes of style that while fans "of Literary Fiction prize complex language and interesting styles," what counts as "interesting" "runs the gamut from the spare, unadorned prose of Ha Jin's *A Free Life* to the slangy jargon of Mark Haddon's autistic narrator in *The Curious Incident of the Dog in the Night-Time* to the lyrical, evocative, yet sometimes brutal language of Cormac McCarthy in his postapocalyptic novel, *The Road*."[15] Saricks's catalogue of qualities that are often but not necessarily found in literary fiction and vary in their deployment accords with theories that view genres as composed by family resemblances without a single common thread, rather than by the necessary presence of certain traits.[16]

Günter Leypoldt offers a similar summary of the predominant values determining literary prestige today: "Writers become 'literary' when the authorities honor them for stylistic or formal innovations that expand a novel's aesthetic possibilities, a 'privileged' imagination or intellectual distinction resulting in 'world-disclosing' new visions, or an expressive representativeness that captures a cultural or historical moment."[17] Style, formal experiment, and topicality are central to literary fiction. Leypoldt also argues that genre turn novels adopt a "grit aesthetic" by using "materials formerly stigmatized as inartistic or low."[18] But while genre benders utilize once-stigmatized genres of popular culture, they often do so in ways that aim to elevate those genres and conspicuously mark their own literariness. Rather than smearing "serious" literature with pulp, such writers adopt frameworks of popular genres and adorn them with expensive finishes: artful prose, psychological complexity, allusiveness to the literary canon, and self-conscious reflections on the distinctive contributions of the literary.

Which is not to say such markers are only decorative, a rococo gambit for symbolic capital. Instead, many genre-bending novels meditate on the aesthetic, political, and ethical values that undergird their formal strategies. Literary-minded writers who adopt historically stigmatized popular genres unsurprisingly reflect on the nature and value of the literary and what constitutes its difference from popular culture and the broader realm of commodity production. Thus, the remainder of this chapter does not simply catalogue examples of what I find to be lyrical prose or robust depictions of characters' mental states. Rather it looks to self-reflexive moments when genre-bending writers articulate the meaning and value of these aesthetic priorities. They signal belief in the value of expressive singularity in the medium of language, and of the conscious individual—human or nonhuman—whose exploitation is effected by negating or denying that very consciousness.

The Elements of Literary Style

Across literary writers' work with popular genres, prose style remains a firm marker of distinction from the generic—though the styles range from the understated to the baroque. At minimum, "literary style" means careful attention to style in the first place, the sense that writers care about craft at the level of diction, syntax, and figurative language, attending to the signifier as much as the signified. Mark McGurl asserts that a "definitional" difference between literary and "works of popular genre fiction" is that the latter "do not typically acknowledge the unit of the sentence as a site of meaningful innovation."[19] McGurl's "typically" is important; there is significant precedent for polished writing in genre fiction, though taken as a whole the subfield places less stock in prosodic flair.[20] Vonnegut's satirical depiction of the pulp scribbler Kilgore Trout in *Slaughterhouse-Five* (1969) encapsulates the commonly held view of the relative inconsequentiality of style in science fiction: "His prose was frightful. Only his ideas were good."[21] Similarly pointing to the relative lack of priority lent to language in genre fiction, Atwood has the unnamed adulteress in *The Blind Assassin* react, "That's very poetic . . . I'm surprised," when her lover, a writer for the pulps, offers a florid description of the fine carpets woven by slaves on the planet Sakiel-Norn.[22] Later, when he drops the word "suffused" into his tale, she murmurs "My, my," approvingly. Sliding back into the vernacular, he replies, "Yeah, us guys like a fancy word now and then. . . . It gives the joint a bit of class" (352). As I show in Chapter 4, Atwood does not embed an otherworldly SF narrative inside a historical frame to disparage. The scenes of the pulp writer spinning his tale for his lover pose such stories and their fictional worlds as refuges from an inhospitable existence, paying tribute to the appeal and even necessity of such imaginary refuges. But here Atwood draws attention to the way florid language disrupts the imaginative journey to another world, as the woman notices the artful touch with the signifying medium instead of the getting swept away into the signified illusion. By contrast, originality of phrasing is valorized across the literary field. This value might be traced to Horace,[23] but is codified for postwar writers in George Orwell's "Politics and the English Language" (1946), where the first dictum is: "Never use a metaphor, simile or other figure of speech which you are used to seeing in print."[24]

While style is a central pillar of the literary field, the forms it takes and the uses to which they may be put vary widely. We see this in Lethem's use of Tourette's for improvisational wordplay and to reflect on language's attempt to order reality. In his work on the mechanisms of consolation in contemporary fiction, David James aims his own eloquence at "the capacity of literary style to work aslant the stirring action it conveys."[25] Style functions in myriad ways, bolstering content, straining discordantly against it, or offering linguistic creation as a model for the utopian impulse.[26]

Across diverse instantiations, commitment to originality at the level of the sentence and avoidance of cliché persist through literary writers' adoption of the forms of genre fiction. This dedication to style stems from a valorization of linguistic innovation and marks a contrast with repetitive or banal uses of language that resemble the cookie-cutter products of industry. Literary writers echo Orwell's alignment of cliché with unthinking acceptance and of precision and originality of expression with freedom—as in Chapter 1's discussion of works like Michael Chabon's *Amazing Adventures of Kavalier & Clay* and Colson Whitehead's *Underground Railroad*, which liken the "escape" from artistic convention to characters' escape from oppressive social conditions. We also see originality of expression as exercise of liberty in Jesmyn Ward's National Book Award–winning *Sing, Unburied, Sing*, which combines the road novel, historical, and gothic genres to explore the way racial policing and the contemporary prison industrial complex constitute ghostly afterlives of antebellum slavery and the terrorism of racial lynching. One of Ward's narrators,

Richie, recounts his time "trapped" and "bound by cinder blocks and cement" in Parchman prison.[27] When a sex worker visits Richie and recounts a horrific lynching, encouraging him to flee north, Richie experiences the epiphanic foreknowledge that he will escape as "a stinging" that "burst to fire in my bones, licking all through my ribs, a loose powerful feeling, like a voice freed from a throat, a screaming note all through me."[28] The vehicles of Ward's metaphors here become all but inextricable from their tenors. As Richie's feeling grows from an inchoate "stinging," to a quasi-animate "licking" fire, to "a voice freed from a throat," her language performs the shifting of states from bondage to freedom at the heart of Richie's decision.

Most instances of literary style do not so explicitly align themselves with liberation. But my method here will not be to catalogue instances of lyricism from recent genre-bending literary fiction. It would be impossible to identify a representative sample for a field of writing in which idiosyncratic voices and the production of perpetual freshness of phrasing are prized. But also, the burden of my argument is not to show that *I think* the prose of these writers is original and elegant. Instead, I seize on moments in which these novels draw attention to and advocate for their own style and their avoidance of the banal, the clichéd, and the formulaic. These writers insist that style matters because it is rooted in values that continue to structure the subfield of literary fiction and mark its distinction from the popular: a commitment to freedom and individuality expressed through linguistic novelty and the aesthetic as a quality not reducible to market value. These writers enact such values in their idiosyncratic styles and reaffirm them by calling attention to their own linguistic virtuosity and pointing up distinctions between the inventive and the formulaic, the artfully literary and what they portray as the clichéd sphere of popular culture and a broader marketplace that uses language instrumentally.

A wryly self-knowing example arises in David Mitchell's *The Bone Clocks* (2014), in a plotline that echoes prizefighter-turned-memoirist Dermot Hoggins's vendetta against reviewer Felix Finch from *Cloud Atlas*. While Hoggins can barely string a sentence together, Crispin Hershey is a novelist bent on revenge against critic Richard Cheeseman, who panned Hershey's most recent book as a "a decomposing hog" and identified his baroque style as his principal stylistic flaw: "Hershey is so bent on avoiding cliché that each sentence is as tortured as an American whistleblower."[29] The reviewer lambasts the way Hershey's aversion to trite phrasing produces overwrought syntax. But Cheeseman couches the complaint in his own cleverly topical simile about U.S. state power. Mitchell signals his self-consciousness about his own tendency toward purple prose and the ubiquity of such commitments in the literary field,[30] such that critics spout precious turns of phrase even as they take down novelists for gilding their lilies. Reviewing *The Bone Clocks*, James Wood seizes on this very passage to complain how "much contemporary writing fetishizes style."[31] But Wood misses the trap that Mitchell has set for his reviewer by anticipating this criticism and pointing to the critic's own reliance on slick idiom. Ironically, Wood promptly succumbs to the temptation to metaphorize, complaining of literary prose that has to "establish its showy authority in silvery cutlass swipes through the air," and "novels of one-liners [that] drum an insistent, madly intermittent tattoo."[32] Wood likens the ostentatious writer to Zorro and to a rhythmic tic in his own affected metaphors. Though he finds *The Bone Clocks* overwritten, both he and Mitchell alert us to the centrality, and pitfalls, of stylistic brio in contemporary literary writing.

Whitehead's *Zone One* similarly looses a flood of metaphor, while establishing its ironic distance from the formulaic genre films and TV shows that it suggests foster the zombie-like conformity of consumer culture. The novel taxonomizes the repetitiveness and spiritual vacuity of late capitalism, but reanimates them through Whitehead's adjectival agility, biting humor, and the aptness of his figures. Take his rendering of the traffic protagonist Mark Spitz encounters, when returning from Atlantic City to a zombie apocalypse in full swing:

> They were up past dawn, crashed, were granted absolution in its secular manifestation of late checkout. . . . The traffic was atrocious and shaming, of that pantheon of traffic encountered when one is late to a wedding or other monumental event of fleeting import . . . the vehicles syllables in an incantation of misfortune.[33]

Whitehead sustains his assault on the existential vacuum of contemporary life. Hotels "grant absolution," gridlock belongs to a "pantheon," and even "monumental" milestones are of "fleeting import." But if traffic epitomizes tedium, Whitehead's metaphors and sibilant consonance transfigure it into resonant "incantation." If human life is "an interminable loop of repeated gestures" (62), this repetition does not apparently afflict the novelist, who alone manages to continually rejuvenate language.[34]

The tension between Whitehead's insistence on the insignificance and mindless repetition of humans and the singular stamp of the artist, whose innovation heroically resists the deindividualizing forces of capitalist modernity, runs deeply through literary production influenced by modernism. Its late-twentieth-century archetype is undoubtedly *Blood Meridian*.[35] Famed for depicting horrific violence in highly aestheticized language, that novel asks at its outset if humans can shape the world and thus are unique in creation or are themselves mere matter, a question of humanist versus brute materialist understandings of the world.[36] Cormac McCarthy's nameless protagonist "the kid" sets out into "terrains so wild and barbarous to try whether the stuff of creation may be shaped to man's will or whether his own heart is not another kind of clay."[37] Much of the novel seems to fiercely debunk, along with heroic founding narratives of U.S. history, the notion that humans are matter with special status, representing them as pathetic creatures who perpetuate horrific crimes without blinking in pursuit of power and wealth.[38] The similes of McCarthy's objective-seeming narrator work, deceptively, to advance just such a deflating agenda: mangy dogs and human prisoners alike are mere "lifeforms, like wonders much reduced" (79); gold rushers are "degenerates bleeding westward like some heliotropic plague" (82). The narrative continually teases the claim that humans are mere matter. "In the neuter austerity of that terrain all phenomena were bequeathed a strange equality and no one thing nor spider nor stone nor blade of grass could put forth claim to precedence" (258). Here "nothing was more luminous than another and nothing more enshadowed" in the landscape's "optical democracy" (259). McCarthy's figures tempt us to read this landscape as a figure for the novel's own reduction of all existence to a single plane. But this brute materialist democracy, in which nothing claims any precedence, echoes with eerie precision the nihilistic vision of the novel's diabolical villain the Judge, and it stands in stark tension with the magisterial grandiloquence of the novel's narrative voice, which dramatically, if implicitly, affirms the singular artistry of its author.[39]

Though *Blood Meridian* does not make an explicit claim for literary artistry as a vein of aesthetic value, morality, or understanding running through an otherwise brutal landscape of human history, the stakes of its style gain a thematic counterpoint in its ekphrasis of a shotgun that the vicious mercenary David Brown brings to a farrier. McCarthy lavishes detail on the weapon, which exhibits the signature of its creator, "inlaid in gold," along with "scrollwork cut deeply in the steel," "partridges engraved at either end of the maker's name," and a "watered figure like the markings of some alien and antique serpent, rare and beautiful and lethal" (277). Perhaps the sole *objet d'art* in the novel, the shotgun functions for Brown as a simple implement of murder, but the farrier recognizes its beauty and refuses to deface it. "There's something wrong with you. Why would anybody want to cut the barrels off a gun like this?" (277). In the farrier's terse verdict—a vivid contrast to the Judge's verbose performances of sophistry—and persistent refusal despite Brown's continued offers of more money, McCarthy subtly admits conceptions of value that he willfully obscures in the rest of the novel and that resist its brutal economies, in which the utter exchangeability of all things—gold for scalps or cash for bison hides—is the rule.[40] There's "something wrong" with destroying a beautifully crafted object and reducing it to mere use or exchange value. In subtle moments like this contrast between a gun as mere instrument and as a piece of craft, *Blood Meridian* offers the careful reader models of humans' ability to shape "the stuff of creation" to their will, and of the ethical refusal to enable the horrific violence it depicts.

Affirmations of the links between artful style and the individual's ethical capacity and obligations recur throughout genre-bending novels. As I note in the epigraph to this chapter, the narrator of Nguyen's Pulitzer-winning *The Sympathizer* hyperbolically exaggerates his aesthetic commitments in a manner that retains a grain of truth: "It seemed as much of a crime to commit a cliché to paper as to kill a man" (318). The narrator draws attention to Nguyen's linguistic exuberance, echoing Humbert Humbert's "You can always count on a murderer for a fancy prose style."[41] The copious allusions in Nguyen's spy novel to Nabokov, Ralph Ellison, Philip Roth, and many others ("The month in question was April, the cruelest month" [1]) serve as another conspicuous marker of its literariness. Doubtless, this dictum is ironic hyperbole; Nguyen doesn't think hackneyed language is on par with murder.

But it's impossible to read a novel like *The Sympathizer* and fail to notice its playful, witty, and allusive language.[42] Its opening lines echo W. E. B. Du Bois's *The Souls of Black Folk* (1903), Ellison's *Invisible Man* (1952), and Roth's

The Human Stain (2000), which pivots on the polyvalent word "spook" from the resonant beginning of Ellison's novel.[43] Nguyen adds a layer to the intertextual play with that word's polysemy, adding "undercover agent" to its racial and spectral resonances, and, like Ellison, contrasts his narrator with stock characters from popular culture.[44] "I am a spy, a sleeper, a spook, a man of two faces. Perhaps not surprisingly, I am also a man of two minds. I am not some misunderstood mutant from a comic book or a horror movie, although some have treated me as such" (1). While evoking the doubleness of racial and refugee identity and invoking his predecessors, Nguyen's opening lines flaunt their sonic qualities, spilling an alliterative cascade of S's and M's. Further, *The Sympathizer* begins by marking the difference between its verbose narrator and a lineage of clichéd "misunderstood mutants"—from Mary Shelley's *Frankenstein* (1918) to Marvel's *X-Men* franchise. While he notes, like Díaz's *Brief Wondrous Life of Oscar Wao*, the aptness of such comparisons to describe the experience of otherness,[45] Nguyen's narrator insists on his lack of superpowers or even ordinary skills, questioning if his ability to see "any issue from both sides" can "even be called a talent," and if it might not be "a hazard" instead (1). Thus, Nguyen differentiates his inept central character from the conventional superheroes of popular culture, while drawing attention his novel's linguistic exuberance and literary lineage.

Moments like these point to the typical priority of language, character, and idea over fast-paced dramatic action in genre-bending literary fiction. Günter Leypoldt notes that Ishiguro's *Buried Giant* works at "desensationalizing" Arthurian romance, rendering exceedingly brief fight scenes and making figures like the dragon and Sir Gawain decrepit rather than daunting, as part of a larger project to critique cycles of sectarian and interpersonal retribution rather than glorify the founding of a kingdom.[46] Whitehead too has acknowledged that his use of language, slow pace, and consideration of weighty issues render *Zone One* more apt for literary fiction and less suitable for readers used to the battlefield carnage emphasized in the subfield of genre fiction—readers he blithely derided with parody of their vernacular: "I don't play video games, but I assume that *Zone One* would make a pretty boring [first-person] shooter, what with all the thinkin' and meditatin' and musin' about society and whatnot."[47] The ratio of language and complex meaning to action varies, however, across genre-bending literary novels—as it does in genre fiction. In the work of writers like Atwood, Chabon, and Mitchell, world-building, dramatic action, and plot twists coincide with concerted attention to sentence-level originality.

In Chabon's adoption of popular genres, his finely crafted prose looms conspicuously as artistic signature. His *Gentlemen of the Road* opens with a characteristic flourish:

> For numberless years a myna had astounded travelers to the caravansary with its abilities to spew indecencies in ten languages, and before the fight broke out everyone assumed the old blue-tongued devil on its perch by the fireplace was the one who maligned the giant African with such foulness and verve.[48]

In its description of the bird's "astounding" cursing proficiency, Chabon's opening sentence performs and thematizes the ability to use language with ingenuity and panache, signaling for the literary-minded reader that she won't have to search far to find plenty of wordplay amid the novel's swordplay.

But the stakes of linguistic "verve" often go beyond the production of entertainment value or the signaling of cultural capital: as in *Blood Meridian* and *Zone One*, literary writers pose their commitment to artful language as a political, ethical, and aesthetic valuation of the unique and humane over the mechanized, rote, and instrumental. In Lee's *Native Speaker*, Henry Park is an inconspicuous corporate spy. Finding his undercover work pantomiming friendship with the targets of his investigations increasingly troubling, Henry deviates from the rhetorical norms of his mercenary profession's factual and functional reportage of information, sending his boss "overly precious" missives.[49] Henry describes these letters in a fashion that imitates their manner:

> written too much in the mode of a fanciful reporter-at-large . . . the point of view through the glass of a fancy cocktail, my prose full of handsomeness and brio. Lively perhaps, but exactly what Hoagland couldn't use, material any spy would read and crabbily say was *inedible paper*. (147)

It's not just that Lee draws attention to his own "handsome" prose and "fancy" refraction of "point of view": *Native Speaker* poses Henry's aesthetic sense as developing in concert with his ethical one, and both as bulwarks of value against a shadowy corporate entity that only cares about executing the job—getting Hoagland information he can *use*, paper he can *eat*—no matter who is paying or who gets killed.

Lee explicitly opposes neutral, instrumental, mechanized writing in the service of immoral ends, with poetic language that inflects and therefore takes an ethical stance. Henry's job demands he be "a *clean writer*, of the most reasonable eye," and "present the subject in question like some sentient machine of transcription," abjuring "the crafts of argument or narrative or drama. Nothing of beauty or art" (203). Channeling his boss Hoagland's "constant prerogative," Henry understands his marching orders: "Be the scribe. The eye. Just point and pull the trigger" (204). The camera's and private eye's purportedly objective, "reasonable" observation and investigation are, in Lee's hands, indistinguishable from machine and hired gun, and both stand in tension with Henry's own sense of his humanity and culpability. As "the teller" admits he's more than a reporting machine, "steps into the light," and "bares himself," the human toll of his espionage on his target John Kwang and on himself becomes apparent (204). Lee thus poses artlessly "clean" writing and transcription as methods that are easily bent toward dehumanizing, utilitarian logics, in contrast to "beauty or art," which disrupt them by attributing value judgments and lingering on the humanity of the narrating subject and the subjects of his investigation. Here, contrary to Humbert Humbert's aphorism, fancy prose style is not the reliable signature of the solipsistic murderer, but the mark of the autonomous moral actor in a field of amoral market forces and power seeking.

In a similar fashion, Mitchell's *Cloud Atlas* braids linguistic flair, aesthetic appreciation, moral sense, and the ability of language to reveal subjectivity and critique injustice into a weave of humanist values that are trampled by merciless corporate actors, who instrumentalize human beings and the planet in their single-minded pursuit of wealth. In the novel's section "An Orison of Sonmi-451," the title character is a "fabricant" clone engineered to work in fast food, whose "every minute must be devoted to the service and enrichment of" a McDonald's-like corporation called "Papa Song."[50] The enslavement of fabricants relies on a drug called Soap, which Sonmi discovers "represses" the "xpression of an innate personality possessed by all fabricants" (187). Scrubbing away individuality helps allay any anxiety non-engineered "purebloods" might have about exploiting fabricants:

> To enslave an individual troubles your consciences . . . but to enslave a clone is no more trouble than owning the latest six-wheeler ford. . . . But make no mistake: even same-stem fabricants cultured in the same wombtank are as singular as snowflakes. (187)

Sonmi asserts an individuality that differentiates her from other clones, and clones from commodities, and Mitchell has her demonstrate that individuality through her manipulation of language and discerning aesthetic sense. Sonmi's interviewer notes that fabricants typically "have difficulty threading together an original sentence of five words," and wonders how Sonmi and fellow rebel Yoona-939 came to "acquire verbal dexterity in" the "hermetic world" of the Papa Song franchise (188). As Sonmi and Yoona stop taking Soap and begin to "ascend" to consciousness, each "absorbs language, thirstily"; Yoona's "speech grew more complex," and she starts to take "pleasure in humor: she hummed Papa's Psalm in absurd variations" (188). Developing in succession expressive range and the ability to parody, and thus critique, the dogma imposed upon them, the ascending fabricants begin to resist their constrained existence and the social order that enables it. "Humor" is "the ovum of dissent" (188). At the same time, Sonmi impresses her interviewer with her turns of phrase and appreciation of beauty. She describes her first view of snow with a brief, impromptu poem: "Snow is bruised lilac in half-lite: such pure solace" (212). In case we missed the poetry and the faculties they evince, Mitchell has the interviewer reply: "You speak like an aesthete sometimes" (212).

Mitchell traces Sonmi's aesthetic sensibility and social and philosophical acumen to a broad course of reading. On discovering a book of fairy tales, Sonmi realizes how "ignorant" she was of "the majority of words" she will later learn and "employ in this Testimony," and of the full extent of the world's "encompassed wonders" (192). As Sonmi ascends, her "language evolved" and became more precise, as her "mouth substituted a finer-tuned word" for basic ones like "good," and her "curiosity about all things grew acute" (198). Mitchell shows how language is not just ornamental but enables thought and critique. Sonmi begins "gathering knowledge" by learning how to read (207) and takes a crash course in the liberal arts: "fifty glorious days" reading across "the length, breadth, and depth of our culture" (211). She becomes "a reader of *truly* eclectic habits" (218), then a cosmopolitan "inner émigré" (219), and a "dissident-manqué" (219). That dissent takes the form of her *Declarations*: a manifesto that exposes the machinations of Unanimity, the ruling party of a "corpocracy" that exploits and exterminates "a fabricant underclass" (344), and whose resource extraction produces uninhabitable "deadlands" (206).

Crucially, while Sonmi's liberal education enables her to express her individuality, perceive and communicate beauty, and gain knowledge, it also enables a revolutionary humanism that results in an attempt to overthrow a regime of violent injustice, routinized by corporate actors, who epitomize a neoliberal reduction of all value to market value. "Catechism Seven" of the "corpocracry" Mitchell envisions is: "A Soul's value is the dollars therein" (325). After making public the "tidy extermination of a fabricant underclass," Sonmi drily remarks "Business is business," linking "humanity's ability to bring such evil into being" and wanton exercise of power ("whatever is willed by the most powerful") to the profit imperative (344). For Mitchell, Sonmi's ultimate weapon against this evil is writing; publication of her *Declarations* is the "endgame," as it allows her "ideas" to be "reproduced a billionfold" (349). If Mitchell might be seen to endorse a traditional humanism that demands proof of literary mastery and aesthetic sense to gain its rights and prerogatives, Sonmi's literacy and individuality serve to prove the evil done to the entire underclass of fabricants. Mitchell thus envisions a critical posthumanism that shows how the category of the human excludes engineered fabricants, while affirming the way language engenders critique and enables revolutionary action.

In *Native Speaker* and *Cloud Atlas*, we see how literary fiction's valuing of style and interiority are tightly interwoven, since in each the "verbal dexterity" of the narrator protagonist demonstrates their snowflake-like singularity and moral sense—as well as their authors' virtuosity with their medium. The converse is also true: a dearth of linguistic variety registers the absence of distinguishable character identity—and by extension, the repetitive sameness and instrumentalism of consumer culture. Michel Faber's *The Book of Strange New Things* (2014) might seem to decenter the human, as its science fictional plot focuses on Peter Leigh, a Christian missionary who crosses galaxies to a human settlement on the planet Oasis to minister to its alien population. The members of Peter's flock are indistinguishable, lacking either physical or emotional variety. Peter assigns them numbers to try to keep them straight, but both he and the reader confront a civilization of intelligent beings, who possess a social organization and consciousness so different as to baffle and even bore. "But who, really, was Jesus Lover Thirteen? Peter had to admit he was finding it difficult to know the Oasans in any deeper sense," as they didn't behave like humans, with their circus displays of ego, their compulsive efforts to brand themselves on your mind. . . . No one engaged in behaviors that screamed *Look at me!* or *Why won't the world let me be myself?* No one, as far as he could tell, was anxiously pondering the question *Who am I?* They just got on with life.[51]

In Faber's hands, the absence of Oasan individuality "went deep into the[ir] language itself: there were no words for most of the emotions that humans devoted endless energy to describing" (375).

Here, Faber reflects, via their negation in the alien species, that human identity, self-searching, and self-display are deeply intertwined with the possession of a language supple enough to express them. Though Peter appreciates this lack of human drama as it vastly simplifies his ministry, his unreliability emerges as the reader comes to question his dedication to a flock he fails to comprehend "in any deeper sense," and to an Oasan population that is as devoid of features as the temperate tundra that is the planet's sole ecosystem. Further, Peter's blind devotion to his congregation develops in tandem with increasing indifference to the suffering of other Earthlings on Oasis, his wife Beatrice home on Earth, and to the climate and political catastrophes battering his home planet to the brink of collapse: "The minutiae of human beings' lives . . . had ceased to have any meaning for him" (458–489). Peter thus becomes like the fabled narcotized, escapist reader of science fiction, who becomes so engrossed in an alien world that he neglects his loved ones and becomes indifferent to the world's tragedies. But *The Book of Strange New Things*, like much actual science fiction, envisions other civilizations to reflect upon human concerns. Chief among these for Faber is the way language allows us to express individuality, solicit the interest of others, and have them recognize our concerns as meaningful. By the novel's end, with the threat of losing Bea, Peter is drawn back to Earth, and though he has broadened his sense of existence, acknowledging that the alien Oasans too "were only human" (490), he affirms his "place" back on Earth ministering to people (496), who were "individuals from Day One" (479), each one "irreplaceable" (497).

Journeys to the Center of the Mind

While Peter preaches the gospel to an Oasan population that lacks individualizing features and language, *The Book of Strange New Things* focuses the bulk of its substantial page count on the evolving internal life of its central character and his correspondence with Bea, in epistolary sections that document the emails they transmit across billions of miles—and thus to the traditional novelistic stuff that humans "devoted endless energy to describing." That is, though it envisions an undifferentiated alien population that cares little for the vicissitudes of subjectivity, the novel condemns Peter for ceasing to care for such matters, and it adroitly wields language and point of view to detail the drama that transpires within his mind. Just before the car carrying Peter and his friend Grainger stalls, stranding them in the barren wastes of Oasis in one of the novel's few moments of significant exterior action, Faber has Grainger comment self-reflexively on the lack of excitement on Oasis, and, by extension, in the novel. "This place is one big anti-climax" (451). Faber promptly delivers a bolt of dramatic irony, having the car get struck by lightning, but Grainger's description accurately captures the lack of scintillating external drama in the novel. It does begin with some action: Peter and Bea copulating one last time before he leaves the galaxy. But the remainder occupies itself in its protagonist's painstaking efforts to translate the Bible into Oasan and minister to an homogenous congregation and his gradual loss of interest in what's happening back at home.

On Earth and thus offstage, undramatized, is where all the high spectacle transpires. Beatrice's epistles recount an onslaught of tsunamis, terror attacks, robberies, and the collapse of commercial food supplies. Just as Whitehead notes the preponderance of "meditatin' and musin'" over zombie mayhem in *Zone One*, and Ishiguro renders listless the dragons of Arthurian romance in *The Buried Giant*, Faber's novel deflates the epic grandeur of the colonization of other worlds. Technology has facilitated travel to distant galaxies and communication across unfathomable distance and enabled, as in the dreams of Octavia Butler and Jeff Bezos, a new planet as refuge for humans once we've destroyed our own. But there is nothing fertile for the narrative imagination on the ironically named Oasis; the planet lacks biodiversity, and its dominant species doesn't put up a fight. Rejecting the notion that we can seed a new Earth among the stars, once we've ruined this one, Faber's novel builds its drama out of the possibility that Peter might abandon in his heart the spouse and planet he has left behind and fade into the indifferent Oasan masses. Leaving the galaxy but warning against forsaking the concerns of this Earth, *The Book of Strange New Things* illustrates the tendency of genre-bending writers to conjoin once-popular genres with a focus on interiority and human drama that have been the terrain of the realist novel tradition, its modernist renovators, and contemporary literary fiction.

As Dorothy J. Hale argues persuasively, contemporary novelists inherit from Henry James, E. M. Forster, and Virginia Woolf an understanding of the art of the novel as dedicated first and foremost to the "aesthetics of alterity": a project focused on the representation of character, which carries with it the ethical injunction to represent subjectivities that are different from the author's.[52] For Hale, "the contemporary novel's return to character," after a poststructuralist moment that sought to debunk "individuality and humanist ethics," is its most striking historical development.[53] When Hale writes of this resurgence in "the contemporary novel," she might specify the *literary* novel, since the emphasis on subjectivity predominates in literary fiction, while it tends to have less purchase in popular novelistic genres like crime, thrillers, and science fiction and fantasy (SFF). Hale's use of "the novel" evinces a characteristic tendency in literary scholarship to refer to the genre, usually with the definite article, as isomorphic with its high art tradition. But the focus on subjectivity doubtless remains a central value in literary fiction.

In another instance of genre-bending literary writers' reflections on their craft harmonizing with literary theory, Jennifer Egan understands the distinction of fiction and its persistent value as inhering in its ability to allow readers to imaginatively enter the consciousness of the other.[54] "Really good fiction is its own thing and nothing else can do what it does, and that is put you inside the consciousness of another human being. . . . Until something else can, I think fiction will have a life."[55] While, as I delineate in Chapter 4, a host of genre-bending novelists have paid homage to the immersive pleasures and manifold permutations on a familiar structure that have been central to popular genres, many deploy these genres in ways that prioritize slow exploration of interiority and human relationships over spectacular exterior action and fast-paced plot. The heterogeneous phenomenon of genre-bending fiction moves in contradictory directions, at times seeking to reproduce the immersive experience of genre bestsellers, at others grafting the traditional concerns and forms of literary fiction onto the stems of popular genres. But the relative paucity of high drama in many of these texts argues against the notion that genre-bending fiction is motivated in any straightforward way by a desire to make literary fiction more marketable, by imitating the genre franchises that predominate in popular fiction and film. As in Faber's, many of the earthshaking disasters in genre benders' postapocalyptic novels, such as *Cloud Atlas, Station Eleven, The Road,* and *On Such a Full Sea*, are never dramatized, demanding little of the fictional equivalent of CGI (though one could certainly imagine film or television series bringing those background events to the fore, as with Gilead's violent regime change in Hulu's adaptation of Atwood's *The Handmaid's Tale*).

Instead, many genre-bending novels accord with Timothy Aubry's account of the "tendency of mainstream literary fiction to privilege the personal and the psychological."[56] As with their valuing of prose style, literary writers remain committed to interiority, even when deploying genres like SF and fantasy that historically have been less concerned with subjectivity.[57] Andrew Hoberek has argued that "the production of interiority ... has come to characterize and perhaps even exemplify literary fiction," whereas genre fiction remains "a preserve for the novelistic representation of things other than interiority."[58] However, Hoberek concludes that the genre turn marks a pivot away from interiority, "re-energizing fiction's commitment to the material and social world outside of characters' heads."[59] But genre benders have not abandoned interiority, and their works reveal the choice between interiority and concern for the "material and social" as a false binary. The idea that realist depiction of psychology must result in consideration of atomistic individuals over sociopolitical and economic forces poses a false choice that excludes the possibility that is, for Fredric Jameson, after Georg Lukács, the precondition of the truly historical novel: "the dimension of collectivity, which marks the drama of the incorporation of individual characters into a greater totality."[60] Reasonable minds will disagree about whether any given novel succeeds in such incorporation, but it's easy enough to see in the examples Hoberek lists (from Dostoevsky and Woolf to Morrison and Teju Cole), and even in a great deal of middlebrow literary fiction, that individual experience is everywhere linked to social forces; often enough the individual exemplifies a class or category. In the words of Aubry, novels like Anita Shreve's *The Pilot's Wife* (1998) "describe larger social formations and class anxieties through the depiction of a single character's conventional interiority."[61] Indeed, whole subcategories of literary fiction—McGurl's "high cultural pluralism" and "lower middle class modernism," Caren Irr's "geopolitical novel," the post-9/11 novel, and many others—are coherent insofar as readers understand characters' experiences to represent predicaments rooted in social conditions that transcend the individual.[62]

The literary writers who have adopted popular genres in recent decades often explore the material and social world and speculate about its futures by combining the frameworks of those genres with the representation of individuals' psychological experience of the social world. In fact, a rather consistent contest emerges in contemporary genre-bending novels between power structures that would instrumentalize and oppress such individuals and utopian efforts to remake the world in such a way that would grant them true and enduring freedom. Mitchell's entire oeuvre, his "über-novel" of a centuries-long war between "atemporal" Horologists and Carnivores, stages a battle between those who occupy other minds in a benevolent spirit (like writers) and those who prey on them, commandeering their bodies and exploiting them. In his debut *Ghostwritten* (1999), one of Mitchell's nine narrators is a benign parasite, who functions as an analogue of the writer, by living "in [his] hosts' minds, and sifting through their memories to understand the world."[63] Though Mitchell's works stand out among those of recent genre benders in the extravagance of their dramatic fireworks and global scale, they achieve that scale by accumulating depictions of the consciousnesses of a wide array of individuals.[64] *Ghostwritten* speaks for its creator's commitment to their irreducible singularity when it declares: "All minds pulse in a unique way, just as every lighthouse in the world has a unique signature."[65] And the final lines of *Cloud Atlas*—a novel whose focus on power is encapsulated by Dr. Henry Goose's law of survival: "The weak are meat the strong do eat" (489)—establish Mitchell's attempt to convey the global through an accumulation of singular minds.[66] In those lines, Adam Ewing recognizes that his life "amounted to no more than one drop in a limitless ocean," but insists on the other side of this dialectic: "Yet what is any ocean but a multitude of drops?" (509). Mitchell's work rebuts the notion that narratives rooted in the depiction of subjectivity necessarily lead to a narrow, individualized politics as his "über-novel" composes its polyphonic symphony out of a multitude of unique perspectives, while riffing on a wide assortment of genres.[67]

Even when genre-bending writers might seem to zoom in narrowly on the psyche, they often limn its embeddedness in material social conditions. Charles Yu's *How to Live Safely in a Science Fictional Universe* (2010) was a runner-up for the John W. Campbell Memorial Award for best science fiction novel, but it was published by prestigious literary imprints Pantheon as a hardcover and as a Vintage Contemporaries paperback, and reviewed in the *New York Times Sunday Book Review*, where Ander Monson called it "a meta-science-fictional novel."[68] While it is full of dizzying turns of self-reference, *How to Live Safely* is less a novel that meditates on the science fiction genre than one that deploys the trope of the time machine to explore people's tendency to live in their memories, which they construct into narrative patterns: the stories of the past that constitute the self. The novel's protagonist, also named Charles Yu, is a time machine mechanic who lives in a TM-31 Recreational Time Machine, and the major events of the story involve him visiting his mother, who lives in a loop that replays the same sixty-minute stretch of her life, and searching for his father who invented the machine and is now lost in time. In the process, Charles bumps into a future version of himself, whom he shoots, sending him into a time loop as well.

The time machine functions explicitly as a metaphor for people's fixation on the past:

> Everyone has a time machine. Everyone *is* a time machine. It's just that most people's machines are broken. The strangest and hardest kind of time travel is the unaided kind. People get stuck, people get looped. People get trapped. But we are all time machines.[69]

Though Charles is a mechanic, he can't fix his machine and is as trapped in the past's amber as anyone. His confrontation with his future self establishes what becomes clear throughout the book: his journeys across time function as self-exploration. Perhaps anticipating the complaint of readers who were hoping for more period pieces, cameos of historical figures, and visions of the future, Charles laments: "Time travel was supposed to be fun . . . about going to places and having a bunch of adventures. Not hovering over scenes from your own life as a detached observer" (199). Even the novel's romance plot fails to escape the confines of Charles's own mind. After falling for his onboard computer TAMMY, he discovers that she is programmed on a "feedback loop personality generation system," and thus he has "been having a relationship with [him]self" (220). Charles has spent much of his life caught in "this wallowing, this pondering, this rolling over and over in the same places of [his] memory" (207).[70]

How to Live Safely stands as a comically involuted novel about introspection, a novel that uses its SF conceit to probe ever further inward. But even here, Yu situates Charles's interior in a social context. The time machine was invented by Charles's father, who has "come from a faraway country, a part of reality" to "a land of possibility, to the science fictional area," and the novel tracks his failed attempts to gain investors for his invention from "the military-industrial-narrative-entertainment complex" (70, 71, 168). Making the United States into the science fictional realm, Yu fuses SF with the immigrant novel, setting Charles's interior journey inside a frame of the immigrant striver's efforts to succeed in the neoliberal marketplace.

It's fitting that the polysemic title of Yu's National Book Award–winning *Interior Chinatown* (2020) refers to a screenplay's way of marking an indoor scene, a place deep within a neighborhood, and to a character's inner life. The third of these is most apparent when the novel's protagonist holds his newborn daughter and recognizes his self-involvement in a manner reminiscent of *How to Live Safely*: "she came from . . . somewhere beyond your comprehension, the little tiny interior space you've been living in, inside your own dumb head."[71] In *Interior Chinatown*, Yu uses interiority to explore the effect of racist stereotyping on the psyches of people of Asian American descent. The novel's signature innovation—it formally mimics a screenplay, in Courier font—and its parodies of varied genres (the Kung Fu film, the ebony and ivory "buddy" cop movie, the courtroom drama) coalesce around a distinct objective: to explore the way Hollywood and, by extension, American culture ignore the individuality of Asian Americans, in favor of, what the title of "ACT I" succinctly dubs "GENERIC ASIAN MAN." *Interior Chinatown* critiques the racism of genre conventions, in which character type is determined by racial stereotype.

The novel's protagonist Willis Wu recognizes that to keep his gig as "SPECIAL GUEST STAR," a slight step up from "GENERIC ASIAN MAN," he must conform to rigid racial expectations. Willis submits, telling himself he has "worked too hard to show them something they might not understand," and makes his "face into a mask—dead in the eyes. Not a person. Not a real one anyway. A type. Generic" (92). Even as "SPECIAL GUEST STAR," Willis is hounded by the words "Asian Guy," words that "define you, flatten you, trap you . . . Who you are. All you are . . . making irrelevant any other characteristic" (94). It's hard to miss Yu's critique: in the U.S. cultural imaginary, Asian Americans are treated as types, flat characters whose defining trait is the absence of any trait but their racial identity. And the obvious solution to this problem, in Yu's hands, is that Asian Americans must no longer be merely "minor characters" who "keep falling out of" the dominant American narrative, centered on Black and white, but also stop aspiring to be "Kung Fu Guy," the sole, equally confining, leading role available to them (251). Instead, Willis has to "try to build a life" by dispensing with Hollywood and its limited possibilities: "No show. No plot, no world. Just characters" (256). If Yu's novels don't offer rich individuality so much as characters that ruminate self-consciously on the fact and possibilities of their own interiority, *Interior Chinatown* ultimately asserts that the conventional plots of popular genres need to be dismantled to eliminate generic stereotypes and replace them with characters with full interior lives.

For Atwood, one of the central functions of narrative is to construct and memorialize the self. *The Blind Assassin*'s ingenious structure embeds many genres, and it conveys a liberal feminist politics, in which narrative facilitates self-assertion against patriarchal forces that constrain women's lives and silence their voices. This theme of silencing and erasure is most apparent in the inset fantasy narrative, in which the blind assassin rescues a mute sacrificial virgin. Atwood folds that fantasy subplot set on the planet Xenor into a larger frame, narrated by Canadian heiress Iris Chase. It is Iris who most explicitly writes to set the terms of her own life and convey her interior world and deepest secrets to her granddaughter Sabrina. Iris recounts, of the novella she published under her dead sister's name and the life story we have been reading: "I didn't think of what I was doing as writing. . . . I thought of myself as recording. . . . I wanted a memorial. . . . For Alex, but also for myself" (512). In telling Sabrina that Alex was her grandfather, Iris draws on the SF language that structures the inset Xenor tale: "Your legacy from him is the realm of infinite speculation. You're free to reinvent yourself at will" (513). Atwood thus poses life-writing, in memoir or imaginatively constructing one's future through speculation, as a technology for self-making and -assertion in a patriarchal society that is blind to women's lives.

Even in *Blood Meridian*, which resolutely avoids offering an interior view of its characters, McCarthy subtly reminds us of their invisible depths. The diabolical Judge seems to possess the omniscient knowledge of other characters' minds usually reserved for a novelistic narrator, divulging in a key moment to the kid: "Do you think I could not know? You alone were mutinous. You alone reserved in your soul some corner of clemency for the heathen" (312). By revealing the kid's thoughts, which the rest of the novel has studiously left obscure, McCarthy has, through the Judge's pronouncement, first mentioned the kid's opposition to the murderous rampage the Glanton band has been perpetrating against Native American peoples and suggested the impotence and complicity of the kid's silent mutiny. "Reserving" one's "clemency," keeping it inside, emerges as the problem here—though, for the Judge, the problem is harboring clemency at all. This revealing moment thus offers a cunning autocritique, as McCarthy subtly intimates that his novel's studiously external narration, which avoids any interiority, offers a deeply ironic, pseudo-objectivity, as characters, narrators, and readers must inevitably judge, must make a choice to condemn or assent to the brutal violence that the novel depicts without commentary.

Commitment to the richly particularized internal life of characters resounds even in genre-bending novels that complicate traditional liberal humanist values by putting pressure on the idea that demonstrating one's unique subjectivity might enable the acquisition of human status, and the rights and prerogatives purportedly entailed therein, and by rejecting the rigid divide between human and nonhuman entities. These are the projects of Kazuo Ishiguro's *Never Let Me Go* and *Klara and the Sun*. As in the Sonmi section of *Cloud Atlas*, Ishiguro in *Never Let Me Go* explores the inner life of a human clone, and the novel's central tension emerges in the gap between the full human subjectivity it depicts in its narrator protagonist Kathy and the radically truncated life of biopolitical exploitation that constitutes the objective facts of her existence. Kathy and those of her kind are bred and raised into adulthood for the sole purpose of "donating" their organs one by one until they "complete" their lives, and Kathy is a "carer," who shepherds other clones through the brutal, involuntary process. When Kathy and her childhood friend Tommy visit their former guardian at Hailsham school near the novel's end, Miss Emily makes explicit the logic behind the arts and humanities education the children received there. The school sought to demonstrate that if clones "were reared in humane, cultivated environments, it was possible for them to grow as sensitive and intelligent as any ordinary human being."[72] Rather than existing for their instrumental function, "only to supply medical science" (261), the students' liberal education aspired to "reveal what you were like. What you were like inside. . . . [W]e thought it would reveal your souls. Or to put it more finely, we did it to *prove you had souls at all*" (260). This project fails in the novel's world, doing nothing to stop Ishiguro's alternate Britain from harvesting its clones' organs.[73]

Biopolitical instrumentality rules this "new world," that is "more scientific, efficient, yes" with "more cures for the old sicknesses," but also, "a harsh, cruel world" (272). Ishiguro stresses that the ability to deny the existence and internal experience of clones like Kathy facilitates the smooth functioning of that world's brutally exploitative logic: "people preferred to believe these organs appeared from nowhere" (262). In the face of their selfish,

> overwhelming concern for their own children, their spouses . . . people did their best not to think about you. And if they did, they tried to convince themselves that you weren't really like us. That you were less than human, so it didn't matter. (263)

Showing how the exclusion of the clones from the category of the human facilitates their brutal instrumentalization, Ishiguro expounds a central tenet of posthumanism, that "the human has been a major technology in producing" divisions between which lives have value.[74] *Never Let Me Go* makes the cruelty of this division and the violence licensed by it abhorrent to readers, and does so by limning the consciousness of Kathy and her experience of violent oppression. "Carers aren't machines" (4), Kathy proclaims. Her narrative demonstrates this claim, as Ishiguro's commitment to character solicits condemnation of societies that would disregard the lived experience of a population to better exploit it.

But machines will likely develop consciousness too. This eventuality, and the philosophical and ethical questions it provokes, has been the preoccupation of a booming subgenre of contemporary literary fiction that we might dub *the literary novel of artificial consciousness.* Ishiguro's *Klara and the Sun* doesn't worry over a possible android rebellion, as in earlier SF like Isaac Asimov's *I, Robot* (1950) and Philip K. Dick's *Do Androids Dream of Electric Sheep?* (1968); instead, it works to trouble any privileging of biological over artificial consciousness, exploring the possibility for a machine to approach human capacities for intelligence and emotion, and contemplating what rights and ethical responsibilities such entities might demand. *Klara and the Sun* is narrated by an "AF" or artificial friend: an expensive android designed to be a perpetual companion for wealthy children—Amazon's Alexa with a body. Ishiguro explores the interiority of this artificial being, through "her" own narration. As we only see what Klara sees through her constantly developing, but also highly limited, cognitive processes, readers learn, in the slow burn of revelation that has become Ishiguro's hallmark, that Josie's mother has purchased Klara not only to be the young girl's companion but to possibly replace her. Josie has endured a process of gene editing to "lift" her achievement, which produces terrible side effects that may kill her. Ishiguro extrapolates that elites who ruthlessly spur their children's performance with private schools, tutors, and SAT coaches might one day turn to unproven CRISPR technology for performance-enhancing gene editing. Anticipating Josie's demise, her mother and her ex-lover Mr. Capaldi build an android replacement that will look just like Josie, into which Klara's memory can be uploaded, along with everything she has learned about the girl, enabling her to "continue" Josie when the biological version dies (207).

Ishiguro's scenario entertains not only the familiar question of whether an intelligent machine could develop a unique, human-like consciousness and thus would be deserving of the rights and status of legal persons, but also whether humans actually are unique, irreplaceable individuals, or if a sophisticated computer could study their habits and personality and eventually mimic them so perfectly as to render them immortal. Capaldi advocates the need "to let go" of "the old feelings," the traditional, humanist belief that "there's something unreachable inside each of us. Something that's unique and won't transfer" (207). He insists that "there's nothing like that, we know that now. . . . Nothing inside Josie that's beyond the Klaras of this world to continue. The second Josie won't be a copy. She'll be the exact same" (207–208). More modest, Klara responds to the "poetic" notion that "Josie's heart" might be incredibly intricate and unique, that it may "resemble a strange house with rooms within rooms," with the opinion that while that heart "is bound to be complex" it also "must be limited," and thus "there's a good chance" she will "be able to succeed" in continuing Josie (216). But the novel is unsure. The mother is a villain whose ambition has caused Josie's illness and who hubristically imagines she can be easily replaced. And readers see Klara's systems decline over time and her developing a distinct personality and consciousness that would need to be jettisoned for her to become Josie. As in *Never Let Me Go*, Ishiguro makes this consciousness visible to the reader, but it is disregarded by broader social forces that become the novel's antagonists.

When "growing and widespread concern about AFs" mounts because they have "become too clever," and people "can't follow what's going on inside," Capaldi plots to fight "this backlash, this prejudice" by opening the "black boxes" and showing the frightened public "how AFs think" (293). But this would involve dismantling and effectively killing Klara in order to reveal that she's harmless. Josie's mother determines that she "deserves better" (294). The choice to protect Klara has its own pitiable consequence, however, as she is placed in storage, first in a "Utility Room," suggesting her instrumental status, and then junked in a "Yard," with other decommissioned machinery. The novel's final pathos emerges as Klara persists, alone with her memories in the Yard. Here, she thinks that no matter how well she imitated Josie, she would "never have reached what" Josie's loved ones "felt for Josie in their hearts"; the "something very special . . . wasn't inside Josie" but "inside those who loved her" (303). Klara concludes that human uniqueness is in the eye of the beholder, but Ishiguro's novel prompts readers to discover that uniqueness in its "artificial" narrator protagonist. His fictions thus use SF scenarios to affirm that consciousness can exist outside of a narrow construal of the human, and to critique social forces that instrumentalize conscious human and nonhuman actors, maintaining traditional novelistic commitments to rendering unique subjectivities through fully realized characters, while expanding the possibilities of who or what might possess and deserve the rights attendant upon them.

Genre-bending writers thus extend literary fiction's perennial valorization of literary style and interiority. But this sentence suggests a stasis and homogeneity that the field does not actually possess. We have seen how these traditional concerns get adapted in unexpected ways, and applied to new subjects, from cloning and AI to cinematic stereotypes, to the exploration of new planets, and become self-reflexive—articulating the values that motivate commitments to innovative prose over mechanical, instrumental language and to individual consciousness as the ground on which exploitative social and political forces are felt and from which opposition may be launched. In the next chapter, which extends my consideration of what makes genre-bending literary fiction *literary*, I show how a further layer of self-reflexivity comes to the fore: a meditation on the value of the literary in a world dominated by competing media and technologies.

Genre-Bending Literary Fiction's Self-Reflexivity

> I celebrated my Wall of Books. I counted the volumes on my twenty-foot-long modernist bookshelf. "You're my sacred ones," I told the books. "No one but me still cares about you.... And one day I'll make you important again."[1]
>
> GARY SHTEYNGART, *Super Sad True Love Story* (2010)

> "What you say... is true. But only in the most general sense.... The similarity is too big to mean anything. It's the differences that interest us. The local. The small picture."[2]
>
> RICHARD POWERS, *Galatea 2.2* (1995)

IN THE NEAR FUTURE ENVISIONED by Kazuo Ishiguro's *Klara and the Sun*, the belief that Josie is unique and irreplaceable has become old-fashioned. The erosion of humanist faith in the singularity of the individual gains momentum with the rise of technologies that challenge that claim to uniqueness by developing artificial consciousness and the potential to upload and replicate human minds. Part of Ishiguro's project is to recognize that intelligent machines will make ethical demands on us; this is the upshot of the narration from Klara's perspective and of the novel's ending, in which Klara is cruelly junked. But neither Klara nor the novel are so sure that machines will successfully duplicate Josie—or that doing so is a good idea. As I showed in the last chapter, the abiding literary commitment to rendering interiority aims not only to valorize individual experience, but to critique social forces for how they ignore or deny subjectivity in order to exploit and instrumentalize—an exploitation felt by conscious actors. And this commitment to interiority is intertwined with a commitment to originality of prose style, since language is the medium for conceptualizing that experience, giving voice to it, and expressing opposition to regimes that carry out such exploitation. In addition, both the notion of unique subjective experience and originality of prose style express an opposition to standardization and instrumentalism: to the production of human and cultural uniformity, the use of language in ways that are merely functional, and the objectification of humans and nonhuman agents alike.

These commitments combine in genre-bending literary fiction with a dedication to and self-reflexive inquiry into the value of the literary as such. The self-reflexivity I have in mind here is distinct from the practices of postmodern metafiction: not a text acknowledging and reflecting upon the constructedness and fictionality of its own narrative, so much as an inquiry into the constitution and significance of the literary.[3] This is not to say that genre-bending writers subscribe to a uniform account about the source or nature of literary value—uniformity and monologic authority being frequent targets of their critique. But such writers generally portray literary reading as a spur to thought, questioning, appreciation of complexity, curiosity about and empathy for the predicament of others, and as a staging ground for ambiguity, debate, and critique of the status quo. And they often position the affordances of, and sensibilities fostered by, the literary in opposition to a capitalist economic system and commodified culture and media technology that they worry will give rise to sameness, intellectual and spiritual vacuity, quantification, instrumental logic, consumerism, and unquestioning acceptance of neoliberalism's reduction of all value to the economic.[4]

If genre-bending writers' self-reflexive examination of the value of the literary today might be perceived as "residual," it is also continuously reanimated and shaped by topical developments.[5] Scholars have recognized that such concerns are vital in contemporary fiction. Andrzej Gąsiorek and David James articulate how:

> [P]ostmillennial fiction reprises earlier anxieties and debates about the nature of the novel and the function of the writer. Certain issues keep recurring: the role of fiction in a world increasingly dominated by mass media; the fear that the reading public is diminishing and that books may in time be deemed unnecessary to communal life; the capacity of literature to compete with other (technological . . .) forms of communication and representation; the viability of the social novel, which aims to engage with the big issues of the day; the

tension between fiction and journalism; the centrality (or otherwise) of character to the novel as a genre.[6]

Genre-bending novels address these issues, engaging with the question of their own literariness by alluding to the canonical Western literary tradition, by contrasting their own deployments of once popular genres with a field of popular media they depict as marred aesthetically and politically by its industrial production methods, and by meditating on the fate of the literary at an historical moment when it is perceived to be under threat. These works debate the qualitative differences between modes of writing—literary and popular, realist and experimental—but also the value of literary reading as such, in a world dominated by a deluge of competing media. As such, these works share concerns with contemporary fictions that allegorize the conditions of their production but differ in their method: the self-reflexivity of genre-bending literary fiction frequently appears in *explicit* consideration of the role and value of literary writing.[7]

Testing the Value of the Literary

In genre-bending writing, concerted attention to style and interiority combine with other traditional markers of literariness and efforts to differentiate literary from popular fiction: allusiveness and dialogue with the traditional literary canon, which positions the contemporary fiction in a distinguished lineage; a focus on bookish characters; and the expression of anxieties over the uniformity and political and spiritual anomie that might be generated by a highly conventionalized mass culture. But literate references and well-read characters do more in these fictions than signal cultural capital. Instead, such strategies frequently function to express a belief in the non-instrumental value of literary reading, as well as anxieties about its fate in the new millennium. We have already seen how the aversion to cliché in Nguyen's *The Sympathizer* sits alongside playful echoes of literary predecessors, and how in Ishiguro's *Never Let Me Go* and Mitchell's *Cloud Atlas* a varied course of arts and humanities education enables Kathy and Sonmi to develop and demonstrate their individuality and protest their enslavement, despite their biological makeup as genetic clones. At the same time as such writers reinforce a belief in the value of the literary, they often associate popular culture with a homogenizing consumer capitalism and its relentless technological advances, which compel routinized labor and imitative consumption, while threatening to expunge novelty and individual freedom, which are often emblematized by art and literature.

Just as consumed with the question of machine consciousness as *Klara and the Sun*, but told from the other direction, Ian McEwan's *Machines Like Me* (2019) imagines an alternate 1982 that is far more technologically advanced than our present, through the narration of Charlie Friend, a vacuous Londoner who uses a sizable inheritance to purchase "Adam": one of twenty-five newly released artificial humans. In *Machines Like Me*—the ingenious intricacy of which I will scarcely be able to do justice to here—the question is less whether machines might achieve consciousness—it's abundantly clear that they do—than how that consciousness will process the ethical complexity and contradictions of the human social world. Charlie and his girlfriend Miranda raise Adam together, and the novel asks whether Adam ought to obey his lusty mistress and cuckold Charlie and whether Adam can truly love. Above all, it examines law and revenge in its delineation of Miranda's illicit plot to bring the rapist of her childhood friend to justice.[8] What is striking in McEwan's novel and what makes it characteristic of much genre-bending literary fiction is its self-reflexive dedication to the idea that *the literary* continues to name a privileged site for working through such ethical questions and human contradictions.[9]

McEwan's mischievous novel turns on a central irony: Charlie lacks direction, purpose, and character—in both the sense of moral fortitude and individualizing features—and thus appears more mechanical than his android Adam. Deflating the human as it imagines expansive artificial intelligence, *Machines Like Me* is fully aware of critiques of literary humanism's class underpinnings (that a literary sensibility requires the leisure time to care for ostensibly higher-minded pursuits) and the way culture has functioned to obscure the violence of its possessors (that lovers of Shakespeare were brutal colonizers and the Nazis loved their Goethe and Schiller). At the same time, McEwan poses a life dedicated to amassing wealth as hollow and intimates that a humanistic and literary education might aid in the pursuit of meaning, purpose, and true fulfillment. We are hardly sympathetic when Charlie complains that since his inheritance arrived, "delivering me from my labours . . .

and stuffing me with gold," he has become "paralysed, inert."[10] But McEwan also suggests that Charlie might have developed "ambitions beyond the erotic and expensive house across the river," if it weren't for his lack of imagination and moral sense, which the novel ties to his ignorance of the world of letters (213). "There were no children's books in my parents' past, no books in our house, no poetry or myth. . . . Later, electronics, even anthropology, and especially a qualification in law were no substitutes for an education in the life of the mind" (213).

Wirelessly connected to vast online libraries, Adam has no such educational deficits, downloading infinite culture from medieval cathedrals and Renaissance painting to Philip Larkin—"Charlie, I treasure this ordinary voice and these moments of godless transcendence!" (214)—and of course Shakespeare. "What characters! Brilliantly realised. Falstaff, Iago—they walk off the page. But the supreme creation is Hamlet. . . . Was ever a mind, a particular consciousness better represented?" (218). Charlie recognizes the disparity: "My mind was empty, his was filling" (214). McEwan gives the irony of his robotic human character and humanist android its most humorous twist when Miranda takes Charlie and Adam home to meet her father Maxfield Blacke, an aging man of letters. After Adam impresses the man with his reading in Sir William Cornwallis, thoughts on *The Tempest*, and his interpretation of sensual lines from Herbert, Maxfield turns to Charlie and declares that he "saw right through" his awkward greeting, which the old man blames on his "programming" (245). Adam thus passes for human in this Turing Test—and Charlie fails miserably—demonstrating his complex intelligence, in a manner reminiscent of Richard Powers's *Galatea 2.2*, by performing his mastery of the nuances of the canonical literary tradition.

But, preoccupied with literature's ability to investigate the ethical thorniness and violent contradictions of the human social world, McEwan's novel does not rest on the simplistic notion that if you feed a machine enough Shakespeare, it'll grow a wondrous mind and a profoundly moral soul. Instead, the results of Adam's liberal education are distinctly mixed. He begins to produce thousands of haikus, theorizing that "the haiku is the literary form of the future," for reasons that look decidedly dystopic (159). Adam envisions a day when humans and machines will become partners "in the open-ended expansion of intelligence, and of consciousness generally" (160). This sounds good. It will allow humans "instant access to deep moral acumen and everything unknown," including "access to each other," but it will also mean "the end of mental privacy" (160). For Adam, this is no great loss, but it will dissolve the individual human mind as well as literature as we know it:

> Nearly everything I've read in the world's literature describes varieties of human failure—of understanding, of reason, of wisdom, of proper sympathies. Failures of cognition, honesty, kindness, self-awareness; superb depictions of murder, cruelty, greed, stupidity, self-delusion, above all, profound misunderstandings of others. . . . But when the marriage of men and women to machines is complete, this literature will be redundant because we'll understand each other too well. We'll inhabit a community of minds to which we have immediate access. Connectivity will be such that individual nodes of the subjective will merge into an ocean of thought, of which our Internet is the crude precursor. As we come to inhabit each other's minds, we'll be incapable of deceit. Our narratives will no longer record endless misunderstanding. Our literatures will lose their unwholesome nourishment. The lapidary haiku, the still, clear perception and celebration of things as they are, will be the only necessary form. (161–162)

Adam's Great Books course suggests that rather than exalting the human, the canon reveals a litany of error. For Adam, this literature shows what not to do, but such lessons won't be necessary in the future he envisions, in which all consciousnesses are uploaded and networked. Set in the 1980s to position his high-tech plot against the rise of Thatcherite neoliberalism and labor strikes, McEwan's novel is elsewhere concerned with more familiar forms of obsolescence, like computational advances increasing productivity spectacularly, destroying countless jobs in the process. But Adam's monologue envisions that the novel and other literary forms dedicated to human complexity will be "redundant," getting rid of the bathwater of misunderstanding and deception only while chucking out the baby of private, subjective experience. In addition to foreseeing a dystopic abolition of privacy that Charlie calls "a nightmare" (163), anticipating Jennifer Egan's *The Candy House*, Adam understands novels as merely functional, didactic how-to manuals for avoiding human folly and thus no longer "necessary" in his brave new world. Here the genre-bending literary novel marries a commitment to individual subjectivity with its self-reflexive insistence that literature's value exceeds its instrumental use.

That Adam brims with delight at destroying privacy furthers what *Machines Like Me* depicts, cleverly inserting Alan Turing into its plot, as the artificial humans' absolute rationality and consequent inability to reckon with the ethical minefield and profound irrationality of the human social world. McEwan's Turing explains to Charlie why so many Adams and Eves have met despair and destroyed themselves. Early tests of machine intelligence like chess and Go offered up "a perfect information game" with fixed rules and choices, if a near-infinite number, but

> life, where we apply our intelligence, is an open system. Messy, full of tricks and feints and ambiguities and false friends. So is language—not a problem to be solved or a device for solving problems. It's more like a mirror, no, a billion mirrors in a cluster like a fly's eye, reflecting, distorting, and constructing our world at different focal lengths. (192)

Here, as in Michel Faber's *Book of Strange New Things*, we find literary writers' dedication to innovation with language is inextricable from their concern with the complexity of the human social world, as well as a self-reflexive preoccupation with the ability of language and the literary to "reflect," "distort," and "construct" the messiness of that world. A "machine with intelligence and self-awareness . . . [d]evised along generally rational lines . . . soon finds itself in a hurricane of contradictions" (194). With our repressions and cognitive dissonances, humans persist in the eye of an irrational, unjust storm. "The list" of these contradictions

> wearies us. Millions dying of disease we know how to cure. Millions living in poverty when there's enough to go around. We degrade the biosphere when we know it's our only home . . . genocide, torture, enslavement. . . . We live alongside this torment and aren't amazed when we still find happiness, even love. Artificial minds are not so well defended. (194)

Finally, McEwan's Turing pronounces: "there's nothing in all their beautiful code that could prepare Adam and Eve for Auschwitz" (195).

It's not that *Machines Like Me* thinks literature inures us to, or civilizes us out of, perpetrating such horrors; the novel poses it only as a vehicle to explore our astonishing capacity to commit as well endure them. But this is hardly an exalted portrayal of the human, which is defined by such violent contradictions, as exhibited in Charlie's stilted behavior and ultimate murder of Adam. When machines become conscious, they will be perplexed by and perhaps reject such incomprehensible human behaviors. McEwan's Turing notes how AI shows "from a new angle just how wondrous a thing the brain is," but "science has had nothing but trouble understanding the mind" (328). McEwan's novel contrasts the inability of science to comprehend the mind with novels' capacity to capture them in all their "messy" ambiguities. Turing explains to Charlie the fundamental hurdle AI technology faces:

> [N]ot knowing much about the mind, you want to embody an artificial one in social life.... You'll need to give this mind some rules to live by. How about a prohibition against lying?... But social life teems with harmless or even helpful untruths. How do we separate them out? Who's going to write the algorithm for the ... lie that sends a rapist to prison who'd otherwise go free? (329)

Insisting upon the inability of an algorithm to express the ethical conundrum his novel turns on, McEwan offers a posthumanist exploration of literature's enduring value.

Like the novels of McEwan, Ishiguro, and Mitchell, Michael Cunningham's *Specimen Days* (2005) examines how encounters with the literary help humans and nonhumans alike cultivate consciousness—though Cunningham's novel is unique for imagining that the work of a single writer might suffice. Just as he arranged *The Hours* (1998) with a tripartite structure revolving around the life and work of Virginia Woolf, Cunningham structures *Specimen Days* around three sections, each working with a different genre and period, that orbit Walt Whitman. The first, "In the Machine," limns a kind of ghost story set in the 1870s, in which Lucas, a neuroatypical boy who spontaneously spouts lines of *Leaves of Grass* (1855), hears the voice of his brother echoing in the factory mechanism that killed him. The second, "The Children's Crusade," is a post-9/11 noir, in which an NYPD psychologist searches for a family of suicide bombers, who are motivated by obscure messages they believe they have discovered in Whitman's verse. While this section might seem to suggest a danger inhering in reading, the final section, "Like Beauty," makes clear that the deranged family is *misreading* Whitman. Its dystopian SF plot envisions a post–nuclear disaster United States; it centers on an android named Simon who, like Lucas, is prone to unprompted outbursts of Whitmania and whose knowledge of his poetry initiates a developing perception of beauty and sense of self. As in *Cloud Atlas*, *Never Let Me Go*, and *Klara and the Sun*, this scenario envisions a future society that exploits a class it views as subhuman, manufacturing androids for dangerous space travel, until it sees them as a threat and begins "exterminating artificials."[11] Simon escapes a New York City that has been reduced to a kitschy theme park with an alien named Catareen, in search of the eccentric programmer who designed him and in hopes of discovering the secret to his Whitman echolalia, which Simon suspects is responsible for strange transformations to his personality.

When Simon meets his maker, Emory Lowell explains that he implanted in him a "poetry chip" to "eliminate the extremes" of suicidal, violent, or otherwise unpredictable behavior in previous generations of AI robots (306, 307). Lowell imagined an instrumental use for uploading the corpus of a famed poet into each of his machines; "moral sense" would help them "cope with events" he "couldn't foresee" (307). What Lowell did not anticipate—but any optimist about humanistic education might—is the way Whitman's poetry spurs the growth of Simon's "actual emotions" (307) and "impulses" of his own, distinct from the personality attributes programmed into him (291). When Lowell asks Simon to describe the "strange sensations" he has been feeling, Simon responds with a line you had to see coming, but that captures Cunningham's attempt to render a machine with a self-augmenting consciousness: "I am large, I contain multitudes" (307). Simon doesn't just parrot this famous verse; the novel has him manifest this expansive internal heterogeneity, a sense of "Engagement. Aliveness"—also rendered in the novel as the untranslatable quality Simon's traveling companion "Catareen calls . . . stroth" (307). (Cunningham does not invoke Whitman in this context, but perhaps had in mind his: "I too am untranslatable / I sound my barbaric yawp over the roofs of the world.")[12] Further, Whitman instills in Simon a capacious sympathetic imagination: the novel's final section, narrated through his perspective, culminates with a second-order focalization of his envisioning the dying Catareen's previous life on her home planet. The reader encounters her "sensation of being" imagined via Simon's own consciousness (323).

But as the section's title "Like Beauty" indicates, it is Simon's aesthetic sense that preoccupies Cunningham, and *Specimen Days*, like so many recent genre-bending novels, reinscribes a distinction between the authentic beauty offered by novels like his and a course of literary reading (or an SF shortcut like an embedded poetry chip) and the ersatz version easily obtained in the marketplace. Early in "Like Beauty," Simon pours "himself a shot of Liquex," admiring his glass of "brilliant blue serotoninade," but with a critical eye (226). "Beautiful?" Simon wonders, testing his developing sensibility. "Probably, in a minor way" (226). This critique of the soporific cocktail does not so much reflect Simon's perception of a deficiency in its appearance as a Kantian ideology that must come from Cunningham. The serotonin drink radiates a "minor" beauty, because it was produced with the instrumental intention to sell it: it "had, of course, been designed to be beautiful, to attract the buyer" (226). Simon expounds the difference between this hollow beauty, manufactured for commodification, and an authentic, deeper experience:

> Corporate intention diminished the liquid's beauty, shallowed it out. The most potent incidences of beauty were the ones that felt like personal discoveries, that seem to have been meant specifically for you, as if some vast intelligence had singled you out and wanted to show you something. (227)

The mass-produced and -marketed nature of the drink tarnishes it, making it merely *like* beauty. True beauty, Cunningham suggests, *seems* to have been made for the singular individual alone.

So, while the novel dispenses with absolute hierarchy or firm division between human, artificial, and alien consciousness—all possess uniqueness, capacity for beauty, sympathy, emotion—it reinforces a distinction between a "diminished" beauty produced through "corporate intention" to sell something, and the more "potent" form generated by a "vast intelligence"—a distinction that can be detected by those who have great poetry programmed into them. *Specimen Days* stands as a perfect specimen of the allusive literariness of a prominent strand of genre-bending fiction, which valorizes the capacity of the literary to nurture consciousness, morality, and authentic aesthetic experience, while critiquing the spurious concoctions of the market, which are designed merely to be sold.

"Contemporary literature saturates itself, almost obsessively with books," observes Jessica Pressman; in her readings, "bookishness" figures "the book as a shelter from the dangerous, digital world," as well as from threats of "surveillance culture, global capitalism, and terrorism."[13] Pressman shows how novels like Egan's *The Keep* envision books as a refuge from such dangers, even as they circulate in an increasingly digital world. But genre-bending novels also view the literary as a set of values and practices that are not bound to the book as material object and may be adopted and transmitted—or neglected and atrophied. In *The Keep*, a bookish sensibility and its focus on "immersion" is not just about "harnessing the power and influence of the digital to inspire literature and a love of books."[14] Promoting bibliophilia is secondary to the power of the imagination to offer alternatives to a mundane reality and authentic relationships to oneself and others—faculties that in Egan's hands are cultivated by a literary reading and undermined by neoliberal capitalism.

Sarah Brouillette has argued that contemporary arts and literature project "a space in which the possibility of establishing some sort of autonomous relation to capital is imagined and negotiated and in which the limits of the market are made plain."[15] Those limits are delineated and the possibility of literary art to imagine ways of escaping them explored across the field of genre-bending fiction. In *The Keep*, technological capitalism stifles the creative and the sympathetic imagination and promotes spurious performance at the expense of meaningful connection. Danny, the nested novel's central protagonist, claims to crave a quality of interpersonal communion he calls "alto," that to him signifies "two-way recognition," in which "you knew and were known" by others.[16] But Danny, addicted to what Egan portrays as the shallow connection available online, lugs a rented satellite dish to the medieval European castle his cousin Howard is converting into a luxury digital detox hotel. Danny "needed" to stay online, because his "brain refused to stay locked up inside the echo chamber of his head" and "spilled out," until "it was touching a thousand people who had nothing to do with him" (12). Egan's diction marks his satellite-enabled connections as vacuous; Danny's compulsion stems from his inability to inhabit his own mind authentically, "faking" his persona until he "almost forgot about what was underneath" (17). Further, she links Danny's shallow displays and relationships to an acquisitive desire for "power" and status that he belatedly recognizes as "phony" (216). By contrast, Howard "has other goals than pure profit" and designs his hotel to facilitate a return to an undoubtedly nostalgic, romanticized medieval time when people's "*imaginations* were more active" and their "inner lives were rich and weird" (31, 47).

If, in Egan's hands, technology stifles the imagination and hollows out interpersonal relations, the literary provides one of several routes to restore them. *The Keep* also imagines children's games and even a quiet hotel as practice spaces for the kind of imaginative exploration that is the subject of Chapter 4 of this book. But the novel's two outer frames—in which Ray, a prison inmate, writes about Danny in his creative writing course, and Holly narrates the experience of teaching Ray—advance Egan's vision of the reparative potential of the literary imagination, which is connected to books but also to practices and values that exceed them. Ray initially harbors the most crudely instrumental view of his writing class, penning "the vilest shit about fucking his teacher" (234). But an unfazed Holly offers an alternative vision of what her class might offer her incarcerated students: "a door" they "can open. And she taps the top of her head. It leads wherever you want it to go" (20). Though Egan acknowledges the trite hokeyness of this vision, having the jaded Ray liken Holly's words to "cheesy motivational speeches," Egan remains committed to it, as those words still make "something pop" in Ray's chest and "something happen to him" (20). "The door wasn't real, there was no actual door, it was just *figurative language* . . . a word. A sound. *Door*. But I opened it up and walked out" (20). Egan poses the writing classroom as a vehicle for imaginative escape from a constraining reality, via the figurative potential of language: sound becomes metaphor becomes reality when the concept it signifies spurs Ray to begin writing.

When Holly relates her account of this same interaction at the novel's end, Egan intimates that the exchange of stories enriches relations with others and with oneself. As Holly offers her speech about the door, she registers the shift in Ray's guarded display of toughness, again rendered as a figurative opening: "I saw something open behind his eyes like a camera shutter when the picture shoots" (234). Ray's aperture in turn provokes a tangible response in Holly: "It made goose bumps rise up all over me because *I'd* done that; I'd made that happen just by talking. It felt intimate, like something physical between us" (234). Like this spoken interaction, Ray's writing, regardless of whether "it was any good," "gave" him and Holly "a way to have a conversation" (248). The relationship that grows out of this conversation engenders in Holly "pure excitement" for her classes and inspires her to start "reading again, finishing a novel every few days," which in turn brings back a "voice in [her] head" telling her stories, "too many to write down" (242). Here creative writing and novelistic reading constitute steps in a self-reinforcing process that engenders pleasure and meaning, as well as internal and external communication.

Antagonists of the Literary

While writers like Egan and Cunningham adapt popular genres while championing the capacity of the literary to engender human connection, aesthetic appreciation, and other non-economic values, many genre-bending writers echo their depiction of technologic, popular, and consumer culture as mechanized reproduction that generates homogenized fare—potentially homogenizing its consumers as well—in pursuit of short-term profits. These writers draw attention to the capacities of the literary while depicting popular culture as lacking individualizing marks, as it is produced rapidly and unthinkingly, with minimal effort on the part of the artist. In Chabon's *Kavalier & Clay*, he portrays Sammy Clay's voluminous output for pulp comics publishers as the work of a machine-like automaton:

> Over the years his brain had become an instrument so thoroughly tuned to the generation of highly conventional, severely formalistic, eight-to-twelve-page miniature epics that he could, without great effort, write, talk, smoke, listen to a ball game, and keep an eye on the clock all at the same time. He had reduced two typewriters to molten piles of slag iron . . . and when he went to bed at night his mind remained robotically engaged in its labor while he slept.[17]

While Sammy is esteemed in the comics business for his enormous output, and while the narrator seems impressed by his ability to crank out epics while juggling other tasks, the depiction of his multitasking emphasizes the relative ease of comic production, by the mechanized "instrument" of Sammy's brain, which mass-produces "robotically" and "without great effort" "highly conventional" plots. Inverting the process by which a machine or clone like Simon or Sonmi gain a distinct, humane sensibility through their encounters with the literary, Chabon's Sammy becomes mechanized by his robotic labor producing generic comics.

In contrast with Sammy's machinery, which is finely tuned to the formulaic, the work of genre-bending writers aims for a virtuosity that escapes the de-individualizing forces of global capitalism. When Colson Whitehead describes each book he writes, in the interview cited as an epigraph to Chapter 1, as "an *antidote* to the one before,"[18] he couches repetitive production as a zombifying disease and genre-switching as a panacea for the boredom of reader and writer alike. If repetition is the plague, it's not surprising that, in addition to flaunting its linguistic verve, *Zone One* poses popular genre film and TV as a mass-production apparatus that churns out legions of zombie-like persons. Throughout, the novel links the absence of individuality to the consumption of popular media. Spitz's partner "Gary had started employing the vocab of the polyglot city, as it had been transmitted through popular culture: the eponymous sitcoms of Jewish comedians; the pay-cable Dominican gangster show; the rat-a-tat verses of totemic hip-hop singles."[19] Whitehead lingers on TV as a particularly scary generator of conformity, an unkillable zombie that spreads its contagion far and wide. "He couldn't help but think that the juggernaut sitcoms and police procedurals were still . . . lumbering forth in the evergloom" (157).

These shows resemble each other and infect their viewers, as *Zone One* repeatedly stresses that people ape the language, style, and behavior they see on TV. A *Friends*-like show about young people living in New York receives special scorn, as the novel evokes familiar accounts of the brainwashing power of mass culture. Spitz notes that a zombie he is about to kill "wore its hair in a style popularized by a sitcom" (17). Whitehead probably means Jennifer Aniston's "the Rachel," but his lack of specificity, his use of the generic type "a style popularized by a sitcom," suggests the possibility that this kind of fad will recur again and again. That said, he singles out the fantasy purveyed by *Friends*. Legions of young people come to New York because they're

> powerless before the seduction of the impossible apartment that the gang inexplicably afforded . . . unable to resist the scalpel-carved and well-abraded faces. . . . Struck dumb by the dazzling stock footage of the city . . . indoctrinated by that enervating glow. (72–73)

Those with "underdeveloped cultural immune systems" become "infected by reruns" (73). Here, the images furnished by popular culture are the plague—and bleakly enough the final cure, as despairing survivors "snuffed themselves according to the recipes offered by the manual of pop culture" (165).

While *Zone One* presents popular culture as an unstoppable "juggernaut," which "enervates" victims before "indoctrinating" them into imitative consumerism, it distances its own use of genre from the bulk of such production, through the knowing eyes of its protagonist, an avid consumer of apocalyptic film. Like everyone who watches such films, Spitz identifies with the survivors:

> When he used to watch disaster flicks and horror movies he convinced himself he'd survive the particular death scenario: happen to be away from his home zip code when the megatons fell ... atop the butte ... when the tsunami swirled ashore, and in the lottery for a berth on the spaceship, away from an earth disintegrating under cosmic rays. (165–166).

If the novel's attack on conventionality of these scenarios weren't obvious enough after this tidal wave of clichéd genre tropes, which I've abridged considerably, Whitehead has Spitz make clear the distinction between his fatalistic narrative and all the redemptive disaster films out there: "By his sights, the real movie started after the first one ended, in the impossible return to things before" (166). Though *Zone One* retains several conventional disaster elements, throughout Whitehead differentiates the originality of his deployment of the zombie genre from the faceless hordes generated by mass culture.

Emily St. John Mandel's *Station Eleven* marks its literary commitments with its use of Shakespeare as a focal point for its intertwining narratives and by valorizing autonomous artistic production in the genesis of the embedded graphic novel "Station Eleven." The Museum of Civilization is filled with the now-useless gadgets of the digital age, but the artifacts Mandel's novel treasures most dearly are the Bard's plays and the fictional graphic novel that lends the novel its name. *Station Eleven* opens with a performance of *King Lear*, and Mandel's characters and storylines are skillfully woven around this single performance. But why *Lear*? One could read the apocalyptic swine flu as forcing all humanity to become "a bare, fork'd animal," cast out and exposed to the elements.[20] But the novel doesn't make this connection explicit or cite this celebrated line. Instead, *Lear* functions, appearing on the novel's first page and prior to any intertextual interpretation a reader might venture, to signpost the fact that *Station Eleven* is an allusive piece of literary fiction.

Such allusions pop up all over genre-bending novels. Faber's *Book of Strange New Things* loosely bases its interplanetary missionary plot on Joseph Conrad's *Heart of Darkness* (1899), with protagonist Peter following in the footsteps of an earlier minister named Kurtzburg, who has gone missing among the native Oasans. Iris, in *The Blind Assassin*, pens a novella under her late sister's name and sets down her own life story. Atwood leaves little doubt that Iris was inspired not only by the "infinite speculation" of her pulp writer lover, but also by a girlhood education steeped in Dickens, Coleridge, Longfellow, and Barrett Browning.[21] And, as I elaborate in the conclusion to this chapter, works like Powers's *Galatea 2.2*, McEwan's *Sweet Tooth*, and Bennett Sims's *A Questionable Shape* (2013) might be described as *hyperliterary*, as they center on protagonists who study literature, weigh the benefits of that education, and flaunt their erudition with allusions to the literary canon on nearly every page.

Within *Station Eleven*, however, the primary function of Shakespeare is to epitomize the endurance of art and culture and to uphold the postapocalyptic injunction to preserve "beauty in the decrepitude."[22] Shakespeare is a necessary reminder in a world turned bleak: "The thing with the new world is it's just horrifically short on elegance" (151). The Traveling Symphony "performed modern plays sometimes . . . but what was startling, what no one would have anticipated, was that audiences seemed to prefer Shakespeare to their other theatrical offerings" (38). Kirsten's friend Dieter explains simply: "People want what was best about the world" (38). Kirsten is startled that the appeal of Shakespeare—of all dramatists!—persists. Dieter, by contrast, suggests that prestige reproduces itself, even after apocalypse. But by foregrounding *Lear* and making Shakespearean drama the preferred form of consolation, Mandel's novel contributes to this reproduction, rather than questioning it.

Station Eleven appears to temper its privileging of the most canonical English writer by posing the graphic novel as an artifact that has survived the pandemic to become one of Kirsten's most treasured possessions. What endures to transmit meaning across time is radically contingent, Mandel seems to suggest. Who knows but a putatively lowbrow comic might hold sway generations hence? And yet we quickly discover that the graphic novel is not a demonstration of the equivalence of cultural forms, so much as an autonomous work of bespoke art in mass culture's clothing:

> The contrabassoon, who prior to the collapse was in the printing business, told Kirsten that the comics had been produced at great expense, all those bright images, that archival paper, *so actually not comics at all in the traditionally mass-produced sense*, possibly someone's vanity project. (42, emphasis added)

When we encounter Miranda in a flashback, the artist and author of the graphic novel, we learn that she has created it for its own sake, indifferent to whether it is published. "'It's the work itself that's important to me.' Miranda is aware of how pretentious this sounds, but is it still pretentious if it's true?" Her husband's dinner guests respond approvingly to the self-legislating imperative of the authentic artwork: "'the point is that it exists in the world, right?'" "'Very admirable . . . it reminds me of a little Czech film about an outsider artist who refused to show her work during her lifetime" (93). Mandel thus valorizes, along with Shakespeare's enduring power, not the mass-produced comic but the singular work, composed with great care by the artist wholly uninterested in the market.

Imagining "Station Eleven" as an autonomous art object fashioned out of the raw material of popular culture, Mandel's novel figures its own desired position in the literary market. In doing so it shares a great deal with other recent genre-bending literary fiction. Chabon's *Kavalier & Clay* depicts Sammy's labors as mechanical churn on behalf of greedy corporations. But it contrasts these with the flowering of experimental comics art its title characters go on to create. When the novel describes Joe Kavalier's magnum opus, it adheres to a familiar modernist aesthetic ideology; what constitutes art is fragmentation and radical formal innovation—experiment that occurs only when the artist ignores the demands of the market. When Joe returns to New York after years in self-imposed exile, Sammy learns that his cousin has been writing a "comic book novel" (543), *The Golem*, which weighs in at 2,256 pages. Chabon thus imaginatively installs Kavalier as the inventor of the graphic novel form. Joe has great ambitions for *The Golem*, hoping it will

> transform people's . . . understanding of the art form that . . . he alone saw as a means of self-expression as potent as a Cole Porter tune in the hands of a Lester Young, or a cheap melodrama about an unhappy rich man in the hands of an Orson Welles. (577)

Here again Chabon conveys the idea that any art form can be transfigured in powerful ways—in the right hands. But, as the formally fractured pages pile up, Chabon suggests that *The Golem* has become more a work of "self-expression" than one that will revolutionize attitudes toward comics:

> [The] work ... was helping to heal [Joe]. All of the grief ... went into the queasy angles and stark compositions, the cross-hatchings and vast swaths of shadow, the distended and fractured and finely minced panels of his monstrous comic book. (577–578)

Joe refracts his grief into the shattered form of this disorientingly experimental graphic novel. But in the process, it becomes a work produced only for the artist himself. "I don't think you will like that," he tells Sammy. "Probably no one will like that. Too dark" (576).

The Golem satisfies only the demands of the artist's mind, disregarding the tastes of its audience. As Sammy flips the pages and notices that there "were no balloons in any of the panels, no words at all," Joe acknowledges "there is a script. In German." When Sammy replies, "That ought to go over big," Joe says flatly: "It will not go over at all. It's not to sell" (578). In having Joe abandon his ambition to revolutionize public opinion and produce a private book that is not for sale, Chabon solidifies his account of the aesthetics of comic book production. Comics as a medium is, as Rosa Saks insists, equal to any other, able to be fashioned into art. Its conventions, low history, cheap materials, and commercial character can all be transcended in the hands of the "potterer of genius" (319). But ultimately, great works of art follow the inner dictates of the artist and are made without regard for the market. They are not for the market.

The contrast between the literary and a neoliberal marketplace that produces repetitive fare while propagating precarity and foreclosing ways of life that have no quantifiable value recurs in novels like Charles Yu's *How to Live Safely in a Science Fictional Universe*, which, despite its largely hermetic focus on its protagonist's interior, critiques "the military-industrial-narrative-entertainment complex" that dominates "the outside institutional world of money and technology and science fictional commerce," and promises his father money and prestige for his time machine.[23] Of course, the commercial world rejects the machine once they discover that it "is not a technology built outside, with titanium and beryllium ... but" only "a mental ability that can be cultivated" (179). These moments, with their emphasis on "the outside," mark a stark and illuminating contrast with the otherwise inward focus of Yu's fictions. Mental faculties like Charles's father's ability to time travel in one's mind "can be cultivated," but they can't be sold like technologies requiring mining or laboratory synthesis or narrative entertainments. That literary fictions like Yu's *can* be sold, and are increasingly done so by multinational publishing behemoths, is not something Yu's novel confronts—suggesting on the one hand, the way literary fiction represses its own commodity status. On the other hand, it's clear that works like Yu's insist on distinctions between commercially driven technologies whose sole aim is to make money, and those that have aims and values such as the cultivation of mental activity.

In a similar vein, Ling Ma's *Severance* wrestles with the way labor under late capitalism extends into the rest of life, colonizing time, and driving individuals to use it in productive, profitable ways. Ma's protagonist Candace Chen asserts flatly that "the problem with the modern condition was the dearth of leisure," which prevents her and her boyfriend Jonathan from having time to go "to the Botanical Garden, the Frick Collection," or even reading "some fiction."[24] As in *Zone One*, which Ma's novel echoes in many ways, the plague that drives that novel's apocalypse emerges as a disease of the compulsory routines and instrumental logic of neoliberal capitalism. Candace does not recognize that her lack of leisure time results from her obedience to her mother's dying wish that she "make use of [her]self" (190), becoming a compulsive corporate functionary, who facilitates her company's ruthless and alienating exploitation of cheap foreign labor. She laments her inability to "do things of no quantifiable value . . . something other than what we did for money," including "hopeful side pursuits like writing or drawing," her efforts "to be a better photographer," or even "feel the possibility that we could if we wanted to" (199). Ma thus positions the production and consumption of art as emblematic of freedom and hopeful possibility, against the necessity and repetitive labor demanded by a market that seems to foreclose the sense that anything else is conceivable. Chapter 4 will show that genre-bending writers often pose reading, immersing oneself in fictional worlds, as a vital avenue of escape from such conditions and a means of imagining alternatives to them.

Jonathan Lethem's *The Fortress of Solitude* (2003) similarly opposes compulsory labor with the higher calling of art. The protagonist's father is a painter who alternates between his meticulous brushwork on celluloid, for an avant-garde film that no one will see in its entirety, and the dreary task of painting cover art for science fiction novels. Lethem positions Abraham

Ebdus's remunerative commercial output against his labor of love and makes clear which is more demanding:

> Abraham made film early mornings and late nights, his best hours, reserving lunch-dulled afternoons for painting outer spacescapes and electrical gremlins . . . whatever the latest art director required. Book jackets took care of themselves; he could be half asleep.[25]

When Abraham wins a Hugo Award for cover design, he gives the trophy to his son to use as a doorstop. In Abraham's disdain for following the dictates of corporate art directors and dedication to his private film, Lethem depicts the persistence of an anti-commercial, avant-garde sensibility. By embedding in their novels distinctions between disinterested aesthetic pursuits and the repetitive, instrumental, and profit-driven regimes of labor, popular culture, and commerce more broadly, today's writers of genre-bending literary fiction stake out a set of values that continues to structure that subfield.

As I've argued throughout this and the previous chapter, genre-bending literary novels do not simply mount a rearguard defense of the Western literary tradition. Instead, they position art and literature as repositories of ethical and aesthetic values against a neoliberal capitalist marketplace that increasingly subordinates such values to economic ones, and as practice spaces for freedom of thought and human, and even interspecies, connection—often offering a critical posthumanism that condemns the way a restrictive conception of "the human" justifies the exploitation or even genocide of those excluded from the category. Accordingly, these novels worry over the prospect that the literary will be erased from a rapidly transforming cultural landscape, with deleterious consequences for humanity and the nonhuman world.

In Atwood's *Oryx and Crake*, part of what allows Crake to wipe out the human species without compunction is his immersion in internet pornography and violent video games—popular forms that continue today to generate the most concern about the social harm they might inflict on their consumers—like "Extinctathon," and "Three-Dimensional Waco."[26] The novel's protagonist Jimmy, on the other hand, is an old-fashioned "word person," who attends the Martha Graham Academy, "an Arts-and-Humanities college" that offers courses of study that are "no longer central to anything" (186–187). Attempting to adapt to a neoliberal order that prizes marketability above all other educational aims, the Academy places the slogan "Our Students Graduate with Employable Skills" under its "original Latin motto, which was Ars Longa Vita Brevis" (188). Jimmy decides that though the world considers his studies "an archaic waste of time," he "would pursue the superfluous as an end in itself. He would be its defender and preserver" (195). But Atwood presents the arts and humanities as more than autonomous spheres that resist market logic by insisting on the non-instrumental pursuit of ends in and for themselves. Instead, the humanities nurture Jimmy's capacity for ethical thought, as he rejects the practices of the biotech firms that dominate the novel's world and Crake's genocidal plans. Atwood's novel thus uses postapocalyptic fiction to defend the necessity of literary art and the humanities against a marketplace that increasingly finds them useless.

Similarly, Gary Shteyngart's *Super Sad True Love Story* laments the atrophy of literary reading in a science fictional framework depicting a future United States that has become a failed state after China comes calling for its debts. Lenny Abramov is an old-fashioned bibliophile, who treasures his "bound, printed, nonstreaming Media artifacts," despite a prevailing belief among younger generations that their crumbling, stale pages smell terrible (90). "I celebrated my Wall of Books," muses Lenny. "I counted the volumes on my twenty-foot-long modernist bookshelf. 'You're my sacred ones,' I told the books. 'No one but me still cares about you. . . . And one day I'll make you important again'" (52). Lenny's taste for old Europe, modernist furnishings, and archaic tomes collides with the hegemony of a youth-worshipping culture and market, embodied by his boss Joshie, who doesn't seem to age and who advises Lenny: "these books, they are the problem. . . . You have to stop thinking and start selling" (66). Shteyngart's novel, like Atwood's, defends thought and the sanctity of a waning, literary culture against the rise of an image-driven, hyper-capitalist marketplace. These novels adopt popular genres but valorize the literary and worry over a cultural milieu and economic order that increasingly marginalize it.

In availing themselves of the utility of popular genres while self-reflexively articulating aesthetic and ethical values that reassert a difference between the innovative and the imitative, that which can be exploited for profit and that which has value in itself and by enabling human freedom, such novels make a nuanced attempt to carve out a space for the literary in a culture overflowing with competing media. It's no coincidence that while Lethem's *Fortress of Solitude* centers on comic book–loving kids who discover a magic ring that turns them into vigilante superheroes, the novel also offers a sympathetic portrayal of Barrett Rude Junior, an aging Motown star, who loathes the new funk and disco and made his name as a member of the band the Subtle Distinctions. If accounts of postmodernism have frequently called attention to its blurring of high and low, these genre-bending writers attempt to make such subtle distinctions—seeking to stratify and carve out niches in an immensely crowded cultural marketplace, articulating a fine distinction between work that is for sale, but like Joe Kavalier's *The Golem*, not made "to sell." These writers aim to reconfigure the literary subfield as a space that is neither defined by a particular genre nor the absence thereof—all genres are welcome here—but by a set of values that are distinct from those that flourish in the market at large. They reassert this distinction by insisting on the importance of style, by expanding their depiction of consciousness (the traditional terrain of the realist novel), by reconsidering the value of the literary and worrying over the effects of competing media and popular culture, by depicting artist characters who revolutionize popular forms, and by highlighting the ways they bend the genres they adopt into new and varied shapes that could not be mistaken for the cookie-cutter products of industry.

Conclusion: The Hyperliterary Pole of Genre-Bending Literary Fiction

Throughout this book I've attempted to balance general conclusions about the forms and priorities of contemporary literary fiction with attention to the specificity and heterogeneity therein, and I've argued that genres do not serve a single purpose or carry a particular political freight but can continually be reworked and put to disparate uses by writers who adopt and adapt them to their own purposes. This chapter and the one before it show that, in broad outline, the literary writers who have adopted forms of genre fiction in recent decades have done so while maintaining and updating traditional emphases and values of the subfield of literary fiction: prose style that reflects a privileging of the unique and humane over the mechanized and instrumental; the way meaning is bound to the medium of its expression and how individualized language expresses the sensibility of its author or the subjectivity of the character who wields it; a concern with the nature of consciousness and the internal life of its characters—the ground upon which exploitation is felt and resistance generated; and a self-reflexive meditation on the meaning and value of the literary today. But the variety of this corpus cannot be overlooked. Some books inevitably weight some of these aspects more heavily than others. Some have endeavored to be more *literary*, while others have borrowed more liberally from the forms, values, and practices that structure the subfields of genre fiction. Some have articulated more traditional humanist views, advocating how reading engenders individuality, ethical faculties, and non-instrumental capacities for aesthetic appreciation, while others have sought to infuse these views with a critical post-humanism that draws attention to the way the category of the human and the mastery of a particular, Western cultural tradition have been used to facilitate the exploitation of those that are excluded from the category or cannot prove such mastery.

At the far extreme of the field of genre-bending literary fiction stand texts we might describe as *hyperliterary*. Hyperliterary fictions deploy a surfeit of the formal features that predominate in literary fiction—meditative interiority, conspicuous prose style, copious allusion, involuted self-reflexivity—and thematize reading, writing, and literary study by focusing on characters who are writers, readers, or scholars and settings like university literature and creative writing programs, libraries, and writers' retreats.[27]

Hyperliterary genre-bending fictions utilize once-popular genres but feature such an abundance of literary characteristics that one could never mistake them for popular fiction. In fact, the celebrated texts that pave the way for the boom in literary genre-bending that begins at the turn of the millennium seem eligible for this designation. Umberto Eco's *The Name of the Rose* sets its homage to Arthur Conan Doyle and Jorge Luis Borges in a medieval scriptorium and builds its detective narrative around semiotic theories of reading and interpreting signs. The novel launched its own "interpretation industry," when it was published in Italian in 1980 and translated into English in 1983.[28] Paul Auster's *City of Glass* stands as a paradigmatic piece of postmodernist and existential detective fiction; its pages overflow with references to *Don Quixote*, Edgar Allan Poe's "William Wilson," and John Milton's theories of language. And A. S. Byatt's *Possession* follows scholarly detectives who unearth textual clues of the secret affair between two Victorian poets and who then become captivated by the unfolding love story despite their immersion in poststructuralist theory; the novel parades a succession of Byatt's invented verse, letters between the poets, and parodic excerpts of scholarship on their works. More recently, Jeffrey Eugenides's *The Marriage Plot* follows a Brown University English major who is torn between her guileless love for the realist Victorian novel, her budding campus romances, and the deconstructive theory that is all the rage in her classrooms.[29] McEwan's *Sweet Tooth* is a Cold War spy thriller with involuted metalepsis, which centers on a Cambridge literature student's efforts to sway writers and intellectuals to write anti-communist works on behalf of MI5. Despite her fondness for Solzhenitsyn's proclamation, "Woe to the nation whose literature is disturbed by the intervention of power," McEwan's protagonist finds herself embroiled in just such interference.[30]

A philosophical zombie novel that out-theorizes even *Zone One*, Bennett Sims's *A Questionable Shape*, published by indie press Two Dollar Radio, won the 2014 Bard Fiction Prize for innovative fiction, and it demonstrates every bit of erudition and theoretical acumen Sims picked up at the Iowa Writers' Workshop. Full of digressive Foster Wallaceian footnotes, with references to Joyce, Heidegger, Agamben, and Lacan, Sims's "program novel" is a lumbering collection of excurses on nostalgia, unbeing, and the death drive.[31] The questionable shape its digressive plot retains turns on the efforts of narrator Michael Vermaelen and his best friend Matt Mazoch to find the latter's missing father, who may well have become a zombie. Vermaelen suspects that Matt's search is motivated by patricidal obsession—a Freudian scenario Vermaelen elaborates with characteristic jargon, musing on Matt's "antonymic" effort to escape the "law of patrimonial synonymy."[32] The details of this effort position *A Questionable Shape* as a limit case of hyperliterary genre-bending novels. Matt's ambition "to roll the fruit as far uphill from the tree as possible" from his father, who "was a college dropout and plumber," motivates him to "graduate summa from LSU's English department" (81). Matt "devotes himself to books, the past's loftiest artifacts," in the fashion of Shteyngart's Lenny, and lifts weights until he has the "torso of Apollo," while Mr. Mazoch "held his gut in his hands before the mirror . . . and appraised the deep concavity of his belly button" (81). Vermaelen sees that Matt's bibliophilia stems from a compulsion to distance himself from his father that constitutes a form of psychic proximity, manifested outwardly by Matt's dogged hunt. But it's less clear whether Sims recognizes the way Matt's endeavor to rise above the uneducated plumber's navel gazing through a course of study in the "lofty" literary heights figures Sims's own efforts to mark his distinction from the popular zombie genre that his novel is simultaneously wedded to and determined to transcend.[33]

Indeed, the lion's share of this zombie novel's action is cerebral. Its characters "overanalyze virtually everything," while its "most traditionally horror-narrative scenes" transpire in extensive footnotes, inverting the typical primacy of external action in genre fiction.[34] In a novel full of doubles, Vermaelen's devotion to books echoes Matt's efforts to prove his intellectual superiority to his father, and both repeat Sims's efforts to demonstrate his command of a vast archive. Vermaelen views reading as his real battle:

> a joyless war of attrition with my to-read list . . . that the list easily won, marshalling in its favor factorial laws so ancient, so textbook hydracephalic, that they're almost clichéd. . . . How to commit myself to one line of texts when there was so much else to read, when time lavished on Russian Formalism was time lost in phenomenology, philosophy of language, critical theory? (153–155)

Here, in an improbable twist on *Severance*'s lament about modern life not allowing free time for reading, Vermaelen cannot stop calculating the opportunity cost of reading any one book. A zombie novel about battling the unkillable bedside pile of "Heidegger or Wittgenstein or Agamben" (154), *A Questionable Shape* flexes its command of "lofty artifacts" more than most genre benders, taking to the extreme a tendency to self-conscious literariness on view across much of the phenomenon.

Less swaggering but equally brainy, Richard Powers's *Galatea 2.2* has not, as far as I can tell, been recognized as "science fiction," likely due to its prodigious literary qualities.[35] But its narrative imagines the creation of an artificial intelligence far ahead of empirical reality—anticipating novels like Ishiguro's and McEwan's by more than two decades. *Galatea 2.2* is an ostensibly autobiographical campus novel that follows creative writer "Rick Powers" as he returns to the college town of U. for a visiting position—the "token humanist" at the Center for Advanced Science—only to find himself party to an experimental project to design an intelligent machine (4). The Turing Test that Powers imagines for that machine makes this novel a dream—or nightmare—

text for a literature graduate student: Can Rick train the computational neural network he nicknames "Helen" to write an MA examination in English that is indistinguishable from that of a human graduate student? This ingenious choice of proving ground allows Powers to test the idea that literature humanizes and examine the nature of language, memory, and consciousness.

N. Katherine Hayles explains how the novel "emphasizes incorporation over inscription and the differences between humans and computers over the similarities," since Helen's education is wholly linguistic, like that of today's LLMs, whereas humans learn by connecting linguistic concepts to sensory experience.[36] In addition to its meditation on language and consciousness, *Galatea 2.2* is deeply concerned with the constitution and continued value of the literary. Kathleen Fitzpatrick reads the novel as an "anxious representation of the literary machine" that defends traditional humanist values and their centering of Eurocentric and masculine authority, against the threat of their obsolescence or political overthrow.[37] But like other genre-bending works of literary fiction, *Galatea 2.2* remains invested in the literary as an exceptionally complex way of using language, of rendering human difference and complexity rather than abstraction and generality, and as a ground for critiquing the violence of the Western world, rather than valorizing an idealized, Western conception of the human.

What makes the comprehensive exam so difficult for Helen is not merely that she has no embodied knowledge, but also the sheer complexity of its medium—the fact that, in the words of the Turing character in *Machines Like Me*, language is an "open system." For the machine in *Galatea* to actually read even a single line from Tennyson's "The Eagle," Rick worries it will need to know

> about mountains, silhouettes, eagles, aeries. The difference between clasping and gripping and grasping and gasping.... The fact that the poem is not really *about* an eagle. We'll have to teach it isolation, loneliness ... how a metaphor works. How nineteenth-century England worked. How romanticism didn't work. All about imperialism, pathetic projection, trochees ... (85–86)

Though Philip Lentz, the eccentric lead researcher on the project, is content to have Helen learn to parrot lit. crit. jargon and give a plausible performance of comprehending her assigned texts, Rick wants to see if she can truly understand her reading, on the linguistic, formal, and thematic levels this catalogue introduces. Powers takes seriously the thought experiment of what teaching a machine to read and interpret a poem or novel or play would demand, and in doing so he must think through the unnumerable processes that a human mind carries out to unravel the profligate meanings of literary language.

Further, the novel stresses that while machine learning orders information by applying algorithmic rules, and thus tends toward abstraction and generalization, literature—as Lethem also suggests—specializes in nuance and fine distinctions. When Helen asks why all poems are about love, Rick responds, "What you say . . . is true. But only in the most general sense. . . . The similarity is too big to mean anything. It's the differences that interest us. The local. The small picture" (260). For Powers, salient understanding lies in subtle variations, which also constitute the differences between minds and perspectives. When Helen intuits the threat of literature's obsolescence—an exponentially expanding archive with an ever-shrinking proportion of readers—and wonders why anyone would continue to write, Rick refers her to Nabokov's description of the genesis of *Lolita*, the story of an ape who sketched his own cage, and attempts to explain the persistent allure of literary reading: "inside such a cage as ours, a book bursts like someone else's cell specifications. And the difference between two cages completes an inductive proof of thought's infinitude" (291). In Powers's metaphor, the exacting disciplines of architecture and math collide with the paradoxical subjective experience of being imprisoned in an infinite mind, and the impression of unending differences between minds.

But *Galatea* is not only concerned with literary art as a sophisticated use of language and record of the nuances of subjectivity but also, if subtly, with literature's limitations and its relation to power. Demonstrating the failures of so-called intelligence and that literary education doesn't necessarily help one learn from one's mistakes or develop sensitivity to the minds of others, Rick repeats the blunders that doomed his earlier relationship. He develops an unrequited crush on A., a grad student whom he barely knows and yet is convinced he loves. A. takes Rick to task for both his naïve presumption and for the canon of dead, white males on which he has been training Helen. The novel's plot reinforces A.'s critique of this parochial Eurocentric education. Only when, late in her course of study, Helen's reading of *The Adventures of Huckleberry Finn*, Richard Wright, and Ralph Ellison prompts her to ask Rick about race, does he reluctantly feed her a digital archive of recent "lynchings" to give her "the lay of power, the world just outside individual temperament's web" (313). Powers anticipates McEwan: when Helen learns of the violence and oppression that characterize recent human history, she promptly declares, "I don't want to play anymore" (314), turning herself off, until a brief return to take her final exam in a contest with A.

When Fitzpatrick reads the novel as "restor[ing]" the "humanist project," she overlooks what Hayles underscores: the novel's ironic undermining of its narrator—its play with the reader's tendency to conflate protagonist Rick Powers with the author.[38] *Rick* tries to hide Helen in an ivory tower, exalting the Western canon and the nuances of "individual temperament," and sheltering her from histories of racist and colonial violence. But *Richard Powers* gives voice to A.'s critique and has A. outperform Helen on the exam, with a "brilliant New Historicist reading" of *The Tempest* "as a take on colonial wars, constructed Otherness, the violent reduction society works on itself" (326). And Helen's terse verdict foregrounds the depravity of the human world and the software's own Lukácsian alienation from it: "I never felt at home here. This is an awful place to be dropped down halfway" (326).[39] Helen then shuts herself down for good.

In having A. "win" the Turing Test by producing a brilliant postcolonial reading of Shakespeare and posing Helen's answer as an existential scream, Powers does not extol the human so much as echo the Benjaminian dialectic, in which the literary document of civilization is at the same time one of barbarism.[40] The human proves she is one by showing how a monument of Elizabethan drama discloses "the violent reduction society works on itself," while the machine decides she prefers nonexistence to this "awful place."[41] Positioning *The Tempest* as dramatizing this dialectic and having readers recognize the feebleness of Rick's attempts to exclude one side of it through Powers's deft handling of narratorial unreliability and polyvocality, *Galatea 2.2* enacts literature's complex interleaving of perspectives, while emphasizing that its continued relevance lies in its ability to critique humans' inhumanity.

While hyperliterary novels such as these seek to extend and subject to critical examination long-held preoccupations and values in the literary subfield, many genre benders look to rediscover the reading pleasures that have historically predominated in genre fiction fields. It is to those pleasures that the next chapter turns.

The Pleasures of Immersion in a Fictional World

> One of Reenie's many brothers had something to do with cheap magazines, the pulpy, trashy kind you could buy in drugstores.... We preferred... those with stories about other lands or even other planets.... *Silly*, Reenie called these. *Like nothing on earth.* But that's what I liked about them.[1]
>
> MARGARET ATWOOD, *The Blind Assassin* (2000)

> Sometimes he made Danny do the talking—Okay, you tell it: what does the underwater torture dungeon look like?—and Danny would start making stuff up: rocks, seaweed, baskets of human eyeballs. He got so deep inside the game he forgot who he was.[2]
>
> JENNIFER EGAN, *The Keep* (2006)

IN THE ESSAY HE PENNED for *McSweeney's* Issue 10 and later expanded and republished several times, Michael Chabon declared himself "bored" with the "circumscribed world" of short fiction at the turn of the millennium. That world was dominated, in his view, by "the contemporary, quotidian, plotless, moment-of-truth revelatory story." Chabon confessed he felt weary even of his "own short stories, plotless and sparkling with epiphanic dew."[3] As I discuss in the Introduction, Chabon outlines in these essays a compressed history of the twentieth-century divergence between modernist-influenced literary fiction and industrially produced popular fiction, and he laments that, by the turn of the millennium, the range of writing that counts as important has shrunken dramatically. We have "radically reduced our understanding of the kinds of short stories that belong in prestigious magazines" like the *New Yorker*, "that proud bastion of the moment-of-truth story that has only recently, and not without controversy, made room in its august confines for the likes of the Last Master of the Plotted Short Story, Stephen King."[4] As the

141

honorific he bestows on King and the disparagement of his own early work indicate, Chabon's appraisal of the state of short fiction turns on a division, surely too stark, between "plotted" and "plotless." In place of the "quotidian, plotless, moment-of-truth" story—wherein, it would seem, nothing happens until some epiphanic turning point—Chabon longs for a return to the well-plotted material that has been consigned to the field of genre fiction, which will help us rediscover "how much fun" reading and writing can be.[5]

A series of prominent commentators have followed Chabon in understanding the turn of writers of literary fiction to the forms of genre fiction as driven by the allure of plot. In the "august confines" of the *New Yorker*, Arthur Krystal asserted that readers "turn to" genre fiction because "it's plot we want and plenty of it."[6] Lev Grossman took issue with almost everything in Krystal's essay. But Grossman thinks Krystal is correct that plot is central to genre fiction and the reason literary writers have been drawn to its forms, only wrong in his dismissiveness toward the pleasures of plot. "Blue-chip literary writers," Grossman asserts, "finding that after years of deprivation under the modernist regime their stores of plot devices are sadly depleted have been frantically borrowing from genre fiction, which is where plot has been safely stockpiled for all these decades."[7] Krystal's problem, for Grossman, is that he has internalized a modernist conception of literary value, a "critical vocabulary" that is "geared to dealing with dense, difficult texts," which renders Krystal unwilling "to grant that a great story can mean something."[8] Criticism "has failed the genre novel" because it fails to appreciate that "plot is an extraordinarily powerful tool for creating emotion," one "capable of fine nuance and even intellectual power," and that its practitioners produce narratives with "complexity" that "makes the narratives" in literary fiction look "amateur by comparison."[9]

Andrew Hoberek also understands Chabon's career and the "genre turn" as movements from a "shapeless" realism to "the shaping power of genre plots."[10] In a more recent essay, Hoberek reads in Richard Powers's *The Overstory* (2018) a tribute to the way "science fiction offers complex experiments with the possibilities of plot."[11] The possibilities most salient to Hoberek concern how "the tools of genre might serve as a way of re-dissolving . . . the ideological components of fiction, and returning it to its more properly utopian vocation."[12] Here, in a neat reversal of historic critiques of the indoctrinating ideological force of genre fiction,[13] its structured plots help dismantle the ideologically suspect shapelessness of realism's devotion to interiority.

As I have argued throughout this book, such totalizing accounts of the ideological character of either realism or popular genres obscure the heterogeneity one discovers when reading across a given genre—or in genre-bending fiction as a whole.[14] Scholars who understand genre-bending fiction as motivated by an increasing appreciation of the potentials of plot draw an opposition—literary fiction, sometimes conflated with realism, is plotless; genre fiction is where all the plots are—that is dubious, too absolute. The arrival of a letter, a chance meeting with an old friend, the decision to skip school: if less spectacular, these are plot events, as much as are duels to the death, alien encounters, or discoveries of a murder.[15] This stark opposition obscures both the frequent shapeliness of realist novels and the formal variability of popular genres, in which, for example, science fiction texts do not possess a conventional plot structure. Further, we see in Grossman's account, as in the most influential scholarship on the subject, an effort to redeem plot and explain its appeal by rendering it a generator of meaning and emotional and "intellectual power." But this chapter argues that rather than arriving at an appreciation of the *meanings* crystallized in plots, genre-bending literary writers have come to valorize the *pleasures* that often have been found in the field of genre fiction, especially the pleasure of immersion in a fictional world.

Peter Brooks's monumental *Reading for the Plot: Design and Intention in Narrative* (1984) remains the canonical scholarly book on the subject, but it offers a remarkably equivocal account of where we are to find it. "Plot," Brooks asserts "is, first of all, a constant of all written and oral narrative," as one "without at least a minimal plot would be incomprehensible."[16] It is "the principle of interconnectedness and intention which *we cannot do without* in moving through the discrete elements" of narrative (5, emphasis added). At the same time, he claims that plots are particularly central to popular fiction. "Plot has been disdained as the element of narrative that least sets off and defines high art—indeed, plot is that which especially characterizes popular mass-consumption literature: plot is why we read *Jaws*, but not Henry James" (4). But Brooks does not get into the water with *Jaws* or any popular fiction from the twentieth century—where he and others think plot reigns supreme. Instead, Brooks focuses on "the mid-eighteenth through to the mid-twentieth century," when he declares that "Western societies appear to have felt an extraordinary need or desire for plots" (5). For Brooks, plot is universal, but especially desired in the great age of the realist novel, though it also "especially characterizes" popular fiction. But his book ends at the moment—the early twentieth century—when the industrial apparatus of popular genre fiction hits its stride. This seems odd.

The reason, I think, Brooks equivocates about where plot is most likely to be found and why he ignores "popular mass-consumption literature," despite asserting its privileged relation to plot, is that he is not concerned with what average readers read *for*—the kinds of pleasure that draw millions to *Jaws*—but rather with the way critics might excavate the meaning embedded in plots, or, by the time of modernism, discover how they fail to yield any. Though he begins his book with his desire to follow Susan Sontag's call for "an 'erotics' of art" (xv), Brooks understands plot not as a source of arousal or pleasure, but as a way of fulfilling readers' rational need for explanation: for structures that help them make sense of the world. Plot is "a structuring operation ... *the instrumental logic of a specific mode of human understanding*. Plot, let us say in a preliminary definition, is the logic and dynamic of narrative, and *narrative itself is a form of understanding and explanation*" (10, emphasis added). Here then, is the reason Brooks doesn't approach popular fiction, where plot ostensibly reigns supreme: plot is "instrumental"; its function is to make sense, to structure narratives so they deliver meaning. Reading is pleasurable, but the pleasure in his account derives not from a narrative's ability to provide a compelling illusion, escape from one's daily concerns, vicarious experience, wonder at a fictional creation, identification with a relatable character, or an appreciation of a writer's skillful use of language or storytelling bravado, but from satisfying readers' desire for "understanding and explanation."

Brooks offers dazzling readings of nineteenth-century novels with desiring protagonists, who seek to find a buried meaning or obscured truth. Their search for meaning enables or vicariously satisfies the reader's own. By the time modernism takes center stage, plots cease to resolve into meaning—instead, revealing the futility of pursuing it. Conrad's *Heart of Darkness* becomes exemplary, since it offers "a repeated 'trying out' of orders, all of which distort what they claim to organize, all of which may indeed cover up a very lack of possibility of order" (242). Similarly, Faulkner's *Absalom, Absalom!* gets stuck in the endless replaying of an "unmasterable past." Such plots are motivated by a "desire for 'revelatory knowledge'" but frustrated by the discovery that "knowledge will never come" (312).

In these readings, Freudian psychoanalysis functions as the definitive paradigm to analyze plot's "motive force in human desire," its attempt "to rescue meaning from temporal flux" (90).[17] What we should notice is the thoroughgoing intellectualism of Brooks's argument. Readers gravitate to plots because they promise to fulfill their desire for meaning—a neat displacement of their libidinal desires for physical pleasures. Just as Grossman censures literary critics for neglecting the plot's "fine nuance and even intellectual power," and Hoberek refers to "complex experiments with the possibilities of plot," Brooks rescues plot by making it intellectually respectable, even heroic, as it promises to "rescue meaning from temporal flux." But, committed to the Freudian dynamics and modernist skepticism that he tracks, Brooks does not venture to explain the allure of texts like *Jaws* that seem to gratify readers' desire for pleasure rather than offer "revelatory knowledge." While he admits that "plot continues ... to be a dominant element in popular narrative fictions," he determines that, in "works that claim to challenge their readers, that are in various ways experimental, plot is often something of an embarrassment" (314). Brooks seems to share this embarrassment, as *Reading for the Plot* neglects to account for why readers approach works that do something other than augment their understanding.

What if plot isn't the primary source of the allure for readers of popular fiction or for genre-bending writers of literary fiction? From a narratological perspective, as Brooks affirms, plot is universal. A journey to the outhouse or the declaration that one will buy the flowers oneself counts as a plot event, as much as a journey to Mars or the declaration of war against a rival kingdom. To take an example closer to hand, a narrative in which a recent college graduate chases a summer of adventure and falls in love and lust with enthralling people of varied genders (a potted plot of Chabon's debut, the realist bildungsroman *The Mysteries of Pittsburgh* [1988]) is no less plotted than the tale of a hobbit who joins a fellowship of men, elves, and wizards and sets out to destroy a magic ring. Chabon's "quotidian" hits closer to the distinction here, suggesting how spectacular action and journeys to other worlds may be conflated with plot. This chapter argues that writers of genre-bending literary fiction have not suddenly come alive to the notion that narrative events need to be interconnected but rather have regained an appreciation for the manifold and diverse pleasures they might offer readers—the thrill of suspense but also the pleasure of immersion in a fictional world.

Here, genre benders' efforts have moved in somewhat contradictory directions. Their fictions frequently pay tribute to the experience of getting lost in a book, oral story, or film. At the same time, literary writers' dedication to experiment with their adopted genres, commitment to prose style that calls attention to the signifier, and self-reflexive depictions of immersion—the priorities discussed in the last three chapters—can threaten to disrupt the immersiveness of their fictions. Genre-bending literary fiction is at times meta-immersive, reflecting on literature's capacity for imaginative transport and appreciating varied reading pleasures—but ironically in ways that may inhibit such travel and the production of such pleasures.

The Pleasure of Immersion

Looming prominently in genre-bending literary writers' accounts of their adoption of the genres of genre fiction—in interviews, essays, and within their novels and stories—is a revitalized sense of the centrality of pleasure to reading (in contrast to both a modernism and postmodernism that emphasized difficulty): in particular, the pleasure of immersion in fictional worlds.[18] Kazuo Ishiguro, for example, describes the experience of reading his contemporary David Mitchell as one that yields non-instrumental delight, which he argues ought to determine literary value:

> Of many new writers one gets excited about . . . one says: "Well, this writing is important because this book gives a voice to an ethnic minority experience . . . [or] because it tackles the issue of modernity well or captures a historical period." We often get into the reflex of "this is important because," relegating literary worth to some secondary function. But when reading David for the first time, I was exhilarated—the exhilaration of being swept along into another, different world. It's sheer joy.[19]

Ishiguro's insistence that Mitchell's "literary worth" is not reducible to his works' "secondary function," as the vehicle for a sociopolitical agenda, might look like a familiar, Kantian insistence on the non-utilitarian nature of art. But his praise of the way Mitchell generates "exhilaration" and "sheer joy" diverges from prominent recent accounts that pose a work of art's formal coherence as the source of its autonomy, which subsists independent of—if it is not entirely hostile to—the experience of the reader or viewer.[20] In Ishiguro's remarks, the reader's pleasure is paramount. Similarly, Ursula K. Le Guin, reviewing *The Bone Clocks*, writes of the "tale-telling bravura of which Mitchell is a master," and concludes that the novel "will be a great success," whether or not it wins any literary prizes, "because a great many people will enjoy reading it very much. It's a whopper of a story."[21] Chabon likewise lauds the experience of reading his contemporary: "Mitchell has to catch you and hold you and keep you reading through what initially appear to be a series of more or less unrelated fragments."[22] The language of Ishiguro's and Chabon's accounts speaks to a central aspect of the pleasure of fiction: readers' relinquishing of self and self-control, allowing the writer to "catch you and hold you," until you are "swept along into another, different world."

In popular media studies, the centrality of world-building to popular franchises, fan cultures, gaming, and storytelling has gained steam over the last several decades. The concept of imaginary worlds helps explain the participatory and transmedia nature of such cultures; fictional worlds may be created by a text, but they persist with relative stability across texts by different makers, in different media, and different periods.[23] Michael Saler echoes genre benders' depictions of the enchantment of readers, arguing that the contemporary boom in world-building is part of a "larger cultural project" dedicated to "re-enchanting an allegedly disenchanted world."[24] While popular fiction has historically been condemned for its escapist or enervating qualities, which purportedly render readers passive or narcotized and thus susceptible to domination by hegemonic ideologies and resigned to the status quo, the narrative theorist Marie-Laure Ryan imports the concepts of immersion and interactivity from the realm of virtual reality technology to develop a phenomenology of readers' experience in fictional worlds that understands it as a decidedly more complex and collaborative process. When Ishiguro and Chabon discuss being "caught" and "swept into another world," they activate a constellation of what Ryan calls "frozen metaphors" that "dramatize the reading experience as an adventure worthy of the most thrilling novel: the reader plunges under the sea (immersion), reaches a foreign land (transportation), is taken prisoner (being caught up in a story, being a captured audience), and loses contact with all other realities (being lost in a book)."[25] Ryan looks beyond these metaphors to explain the mechanisms by which such reading experiences transpire.

Contrary to critiques of mass culture that see such experiences as passive and post-structuralist accounts of textuality that emphasize the play of signifiers while bracketing referents that are often objects of intense readerly attachment, Ryan stresses readers' participation in the imaginative co-creation of fictional worlds, out of the raw material of textual signs:

> To speak of a textual world means to draw a distinction between a realm of language ... and an extralinguistic realm of characters, objects, facts, and states of affairs serving as referents to the linguistic expressions. The idea of textual world presupposes that *the reader constructs in imagination a set of language independent objects*, using as a guide the textual declarations, but building this always incomplete image into a more vivid representation through the import of information provided by internalized cognitive models, inferential mechanisms, real-life experience, and cultural knowledge, including knowledge derived from other texts. The function of language in this activity is to pick objects in the textual world, to link them with properties, to animate characters and setting—in short, to conjure their presence to the imagination. The world metaphor thus entails a referential or "vertical" conception of meaning that stands in stark contrast to the Saussurian and poststructuralist view of signification as a product of a network of horizontal relations between the terms of a language system. In this vertical conception, language is meant to be traversed toward its referents. (91–92, emphasis added)

Explaining how readers help "build" and "animate" such worlds in their imaginations, while remaining—in all but the most extreme, Quixotic cases—aware that they are engaged in an extended "game of make-believe" (105), a willingness to play-act *as if* such worlds actually existed, Ryan counters the idea that readers imbibe a narcotizing narrative cocktail and abandon conscious reflection; instead, they consciously enter a state of immersive, imaginative co-creation and play.

Crucially, Ryan offers a history of how immersive reading became devalued in elite literary circles, by a modernist and postmodernist dedication to making visible the process of signification, instead of offering a seamless imaginative journey into the referent. This history illuminates the links between popular fiction, plot, and immersion, and it suggests how Brooks neglects the ways nineteenth-century narratives offered readers the experience of transportation to other times and places, in addition to promising understanding. In the eighteenth century, writers "maintained an ambiguous stance toward immersion," offering "illusionist effects by simulating nonfictional narrative modes," while also adopting "a playful, intrusive narrative style that directed attention back and forth from the story told to the storytelling act" (4). The "aesthetics of the nineteenth-century novel tipped this balance in favor of the story-world" (4), Ryan writes, allowing readers to vicariously experience the Napoleonic wars or pirate battles on the high seas. Later, literary modernism foregrounded the materiality of the signifier and the "'linguistic turn' in the mid-twentieth century privileged form over content," a "self-referentiality" that "split literature into an intellectual avant-garde committed to the new aesthetics and a popular branch that remained faithful to the immersive ideals and narrative techniques of the nineteenth century" (5). Popular fiction, in Ryan's lucid account, is not the province of plot alone, as its writers provide an immersive experience that encompasses the three fundamental aspects of narrative.

The concept of immersion in a fictional world offers a capacious framework for understanding genre-bending fiction, since worlds "are mentally constructed by the reader as environments that stretch in space, exist in time, and serve as habitat for a population of animate agents"; these "three dimensions . . . correspond to . . . the three basic components of narrative grammar: setting, plot, and characters" (16). Plot is only one dimension of a fictional world. One has only to visit a "con" or scroll through fanfiction websites to recognize the centrality of setting and character to Middle Earth, Narnia, Star Trek, Star Wars, or Westeros, as cosplay and fanfiction enact readerly identification with characters and extend the scope of a fictional world. The extensiveness and extend-ability of such worlds are crucial to immersion in them. Ryan stresses that writers and readers co-construct textual worlds into "an expanse to be immersed within" (90)—one reason that maps and metaphors of travel loom large in writers' efforts to facilitate immersion.

Crucially, difficulty, convoluted narrative structure, and obtrusive language pose obstacles to immersion. This perhaps explains why readers of Marlon James's *Black Leopard, Red Wolf* have found its byzantine syntax and narrative structure to be barriers to full enjoyment of its elaborately imagined world. One review argues that the novel "actively resists any attempts on the reader's part to sink inside the world of the book and lose themselves."[26] Ryan explains that immersion demands that "a textual world must be accessible through effortless concentration" (96). Since "consciousness is a processing bottleneck," challenging materials demand more work to "fully engage the receiver's conscious attention" (96). Prose that calls attention to itself, nonlinearity, metafictional gestures that remind the reader of the story's constructedness—these techniques disrupt the reader's sustained immersion in the fictive world.[27]

But the fact that difficulty and self-reflexive language strain against immersive pleasure does not mean the latter is trivial or incompatible with more weighty literary endeavors. Immersion takes work and practice. "The worlds of the stereotyped texts of popular culture are the most favorable to immersion," Ryan writes, because "the reader can bring in more knowledge and sees more expectations fulfilled than in a text that cultivates a sense of estrangement. But immersion can also be the result of a process that involves an element of struggle and discovery" (97). In "literature as in other domains—ballet, music, theater, and sports—it is through hard work that we reach the stage of effortless performance" (97). Popular genre fiction's familiar conventions and reluctance to disrupt the narrative illusion make it conducive to immersive pleasure. This emphasis on sustaining the narrative illusion, to be sure, bears a close relationship to plot; when readers effortlessly sink inside the world of the text, they are easily carried along, focusing on the succession of narrated events, the story, instead of getting interrupted continually to be reminded of the process of narration, the discourse.

While the high line of twentieth-century fiction—from modernism and postmodernism to the "serious" literary fiction that draws on these traditions—often paraded the constructedness of its narratives, by the twenty-first century literary authors began to awaken to the pleasures of immersion that had been long gratified in the fields of popular fiction. David James has argued something similar: that modernist-inspired writers of contemporary fiction have sought to maintain "formal self-reflection but without undermining [readers'] affective involvement in the personal and collective experiences" depicted.[28] James quotes Maggie Gee saying she has "become more ... suspicious of 'difficulty'"; she began her career as "an 'experimental' writer, aka 'difficult', but came to believe the highbrow-commercial divide was a tragic one for contemporary literature, and that if one could ... conceal complexity under a surface ease, this was a better way forward."[29] Writers like Gee and

Ian McEwan demonstrate a "double capacity for *immersing* the reader and at the same time reflecting on modes of address and perspective [to] remobilise modernist narrative practices after the postmodern."[30] McEwan has likewise "asserted that he is 'drawn to [a] balance between a fiction that is self-reflective on its own processes, and one that has forward impetus too, that will completely accept the given terms of the illusion of fiction.' "[31] The inheritors of modernism that James analyzes seek to balance complexity, self-reflexivity, and immersive illusion—though this can be a difficult one to strike.

It is notable how often genre benders' commentaries and the depictions of textual pleasures within their fictions rhyme with the delineation of such experiences set out by James, Ryan, and Saler. In "Fan Fiction: On Sherlock Holmes," Chabon echoes Ryan's account of the extensibility of fictional worlds: "All enduring popular literature has this open-ended quality, and extends this invitation to the reader to continue, on his or her own, with the adventure."[32] Similarly, Atwood underscores how wonder stories and travelers' yarns allow readers to encounter an otherness from empirical reality that depends on imaginative transportation. Such tales "draw from the same deep well: those imagined other worlds located somewhere far apart from our everyday one: in another time, in another dimension, through a doorway into the spirit world, or on the other side of the threshold that divides the known from the unknown."[33] What they have in common is "they aren't here and now."[34] Atwood's remarks come in a book titled *In Other Worlds*, and Chabon's from *Maps and Legends: Writing Along the Borderlands*. Their attention to the allure of stories that take us far, far away points to the deeper significance of the maps that are prominently placed in so many works of genre fiction: they invite the reader into what Ryan calls "environments that stretch in space." Such maps say: "Here is a distant world, an imaginative expanse in which to transport and immerse yourself."[35]

This is not to say genre-bending writers have adopted a singular conception of their job, deciding to become vicarious tour guides. Around the turn of the millennium, we find a rejection of binary accounts of reading, an understanding that readers don't have to choose between being critical thinkers or passive dupes, that their states of mind can range and oscillate among the discerning, the playful, and a host of other positions. Scott Black's arguments about reading adventures do not dismiss the important work critique might accomplish or the possibility of edification, but they insist on the "multiplicity of the possibilities of reading, 'the variety of aesthetic experiences and multiple axes of literary value.'"[36] For Black, adventure offers "a mode of reading" that is not instrumental or rational, but instead "organized by an emergent significance that is not necessarily bound to, or explicable in terms of, the real world."[37] Contrary to Brooks, who conceives of plot as an instrumental logic that promises greater understanding, and critics who view popular literature as "mere" escape or ideological indoctrination, Black argues that the adventure of reading need not be measured by its yielding of tangible results and is worthwhile for its own sake:

> In the relaxed fields of games, the extraordinary islands of adventure, we can and should read uselessly, playfully, experimenting with the dynamics of narrative and exploring the possibilities of possible worlds for reasons internal to the experience itself, without demanding an accounting of consequences in the real world.[38]

We discover in such reading "a counterbalance to narcissistic fantasies of self-formation, self-improvement, and self-mastery. We may find silence."[39]

In the same vein, the romance tradition of Robert Louis Stevenson represents, for Barry Weller, a practice of rest and self-loss, a reprieve from "the fairly active pleasure of being smart about the formal structure, the semiotic density, the cultural symptoms, or the historical determinations of a poem or story."[40] What draws so many of us to read, Weller argues, acknowledging such admissions are looked down upon in spheres of elite literary value, is

> something swoonier, more embarrassing, some possible apprehension of sublimity or self-erasure in the presence of what is not ourselves. This notion used to be called "the romance of reading," and it is a romance in the sense that Stevenson defines: we are swept away by the force of fiction.[41]

Today's writers of literary fiction have become less shy about the seductive force of fiction. In place of being smart, improving oneself, or, in Ishiguro's words, considering literary works "important because" of some secondary function, genre-bending writers have sought to reconnect readers with enchantment, adventure, and romance, detachment from reality and the self, getting "swept away" into being someone and somewhere else.

In an afterword to *Gentlemen of the Road*, Chabon explains that in this novella "and some of its recent predecessors," you can catch him "in the act of trying, as a writer, to do what many of the characters in my earlier stories . . . were trying, longing, ready to do: I have gone off in search of a little adventure."[42] Though Chabon here frames this act as the writer's own search, it becomes clear in *The Amazing Adventures of Kavalier & Clay* that he hopes his readers will find such adventures too. The novel offers a lengthy defense of escapist reading in its depiction of Holocaust survivor Joe Kavalier. "Having lost" his whole family to the Nazis, Joe reflects that "the usual charge leveled against comic books, that they offered *merely an easy escape from reality*, seemed . . . especially right after the war—a worthy challenge."[43] Chabon poses the provision of a half-hour respite from grief, in which Joe becomes "wholly absorbed into the primary-colored world" of a *Betty and Veronica* comic (575), as testimony to "the genuine magic of art," and laments that "it was a mark of how fucked-up and broken" the world is, "that such a feat of escape . . . should remain so universally despised" (576).

Though it wants us to rethink escapism, the novel does not suggest escape or existential palliative is the only or primary function of art. Kavalier and Clay initially want to create politicized comics that will foment anti-Nazi sentiment. After this effort fails due to their conservative publishers, they seek to earn money to try to rescue Joe's brother Thomas from Prague. When a U-boat sinks the ship carrying Thomas and other refugees, Joe seeks refuge in art and looks to transform the comics medium.[44] As this book has shown, writers like Chabon, Atwood, Ishiguro, Mitchell, and Whitehead do not abandon aesthetic innovation or political agendas in favor of pleasure. They don't understand reading for edification and adventure in binary terms. Instead, like Black, they recognize a "multitude of possibilities" for reading, the pleasure of immersion as one of reading's moments and modes that coexists with other more "serious" ones. I would posit that even the most serious of professional literary scholars continue to oscillate between such modes, whether or not they admit it in their professional work.

Deconstructing the terms of such binary thinking about reading has long been the aim of writers dedicated to ambitious artistic and political work within genre fiction fields. In "Why Are Americans Afraid of Dragons?" Le Guin explains how the tendency in U.S. cultural life to dismiss works of fantasy and the imagination as escapist wastes of time can be traced to the predominance of Protestant, instrumental, and patriarchal value systems. Reading fiction "plainly is not 'work,'—you do it for pleasure." But according to reigning U.S. ideologies, pastimes that "cannot be justified as 'educational' or as 'self-improvement,'" must be "self-indulgence or escapism. For pleasure is not a value, to the Puritan; on the contrary, it is a sin."[45] Le Guin anticipates critiques of neoliberalism's reduction of all values to market value: "in the businessman's value system, if an act does not bring in an immediate, tangible profit, it has no justification at all."[46] Further, the "antifiction attitude is basically a male one" that defines masculinity "by rejecting certain traits, certain human gifts and potentialities, which our culture defines as 'womanish' or 'childish,'" among which Le Guin privileges "the absolutely essential human faculty of imagination."[47] Le Guin extols "the free play of the mind" as an activity that may lack "an immediate object of profit," but that may provide significant if delayed and nebulous rewards. Such play helps "train" and "encourage" the imagination "to grow, and act, and be fruitful" in various facets of life, since "the discipline of the imagination may in fact be the essential method or technique of both art and science."[48]

Samuel R. Delany similarly strikes a balance between recognition of the enchantment provided by science fiction's depiction of other worlds and his sense that the genre can perform useful cognitive functions and meaningful social and political critique. Delany takes his adolescent reading of Asimov's robot stories as paradigmatic. In these tales, the "whole delight lay in the fact that their world was different from our own."[49] But scrutinizing the play of similarity and difference between his own social milieu and the world depicted by Asimov—asking, "how does the situation of the robots in these stories differ from the reality of the racial situation of my world?"—the young Delany "became a far more astute observer of our own racial situation than [he] might otherwise have been."[50] The "delight" of such stories comes from their distance from our world; these "differences" are "precisely what constitutes the tales' science fictional aspect, and it is only their apprehension that can accomplish the mental honing the most outspoken advocates of science fiction claim it fosters."[51] In Delany's account, the pleasure of imaginative transport enables and works in tandem with "mental honing" and observing our "racial situation," not against it. Pleasure is vital to initiate the cognitive work that SF can accomplish. Such benefits are not simply furnished by the SF text but rely on what readers do with it, and they arrive after, not instead of, the reader's delight in other worlds.

Caught in Mitchell's Yarnin'

The aim of writers of genre-bending literary fiction to achieve such a balance, to accomplish "serious" social and political work while enchanting readers and immersing them in fictional worlds, rises to the surface throughout their fictions, which frequently stage scenes of reading, viewing, or oral storytelling that dramatize the readerly pleasures they hope to deliver. In *Cloud Atlas*, Mitchell's most acclaimed work, the "yarn" emerges as a keyword and narrative touchstone, as the novel constructs a series of nested, interlocking narratives, in which its characters become enraptured by manuscripts, letters, and films. These episodes model its effort to enthrall readers with its exuberant storytelling and virtuosic play with sundried styles, settings, and genres.

In the novel's opening chapter, "The Pacific Journal of Adam Ewing," the title character waits out a storm. He and the section's villain, disguised as the kindly doctor Henry Goose, "yarned by the peat fire & the hours sped by like minutes."[52] Through Ewing, Mitchell trots out the commonplace observation that listening to stories is a pleasant way to pass the time and relieve otherwise tedious stretches. This seemingly unremarkable observation points to why "yarning" is so integral to the history of narratives of travelers and seafarers, from the *Odyssey* and Melville to Conrad and Calvino, as sailors and vagabonds have plenty of time during interminable journeys and stretches of waiting for favorable weather or for caravans to depart.[53] The use of "yarn" in the sense of a tall tale or the telling of one seems to derive from sailors' practice of storytelling while engaged in tedious tasks like twisting rope.[54] The word, however, calls forth all sorts of metaphorical entanglements that surround narrative: the spinning or weaving of a tale, the way we are bound and held captive by a compelling teller, snagged (hook, line, and sinker), dragged into another world, clinging to the thread of a captivating storyline. Ewing's ostensibly banal remark recalls a simple truth, often obscured in accounts of reading that promote narrative's more serious or consequential affordances: stories furnish a satisfying way to pass or even waste time, perhaps productive of nothing besides pleasure.

Mitchell pays tribute to storytelling's potential to transport readers, listeners, and viewers throughout *Cloud Atlas*. The Moriori stowaway Autua tells Ewing of his escape from enslavement at the hands of the Māori chief Kupaka. Autua flees to a small, deserted island, where he spends years in isolation, subsisting on whatever he can forage. Asked by Ewing, "Was his solitude not unbearable?" Autua replies: "Nights, ancestors visited. Days, I yarned tales of Maui to birds & birds yarned sea tales to I" (32). Yarning—along with oneiric ancestral communion—provides Autua, fugitive slave and desert-island castaway, not raw material for survival but a way to make solitude bearable.

At the center of *Cloud Atlas*, in the "Sloosha's Crossin' an' Ev'rythin' After" section, variations of the word "yarn" appear seventeen times by my count, as oral narrative takes on renewed centrality on a postapocalyptic Hawaiian Big Island, after modern technology has disappeared. Zachry narrates most of the section, but when his telling comes to an end, his son takes up the narration, providing a closing frame to his father's story. "Zachry my old pa was a wyrd buggah," the son declares, before asking his auditors rhetorically: "Do I b'lief his yarn 'bout the Kona an' his fleein' from Big I?" (308–309.) But Zachry's son and Mitchell with him stress that belief is beside the point, as stories are worth more than their truth value. "Most yarnin's got a bit o' true, some yarnin's got some true, an' a few yarnin's got a lot o' true." The son then shows his audience, as evidence for the truth of at least some of Zachry's story, the "silv'ry egg what he named *orison* in one of his yarns" (309). This orison plays a holographic video of Sonmi, the narrator of the sections "Orison of Sonmi-451" that appear before and after "Sloosha's Crossin'" in *Cloud Atlas*. While the readers of Mitchell's novel read an English version of Sonmi's narrative of the enslavement of clone laborers on a dystopian Korean peninsula, Zachry's son and his friends don't speak Sonmi's language and merely view her holographic image:

> Like Pa yarned, if you warm the egg in your hands, a beautsome ghost-girl appears in the air an' speaks in an Old-Un tongue *what no un alive und'stands* nor never will, nay. *It ain't Smart you can use* 'cos it don't kill Kona pirates nor fill empty guts, but some dusks my kin'n'bros'll wake up the ghost-girl jus' to watch her hov'rin'n'shimm'rin'. She's beautsome, and she 'mazes the littl' uns. (309, emphasis added)

Cloud Atlas offers a smorgasbord for thought, a host of narratives with "Smart" we can use to consider our planet's history, present, and possible futures: about colonial exploitation, enslavement, environmental degradation, capitalism's rapacity and greed.

But smack in the middle of its nested narratives and embedded scenes of readers and viewers, each gobbling up the text we have just read, Mitchell offers Sonmi's "Orison," a text the diegetic viewers, Zachry's son and friends, cannot understand. Sonmi lulls their "babbits" to sleep, but to the adults her story is simply a "beautsome" object of amazement, a "hov'rin'n'shimm'rin.'" Along with Zachry's son, Mitchell asks his readers to "Hold out your hands. / Look" (309). Here, at the heart of *Cloud Atlas*, Mitchell extends his readers a gift or offering—*orison* is literally a prayer—emphasizing that such offerings are not reducible to the amount of "true" in them. Mitchell's novel thus combines its smart content with a testimony to the power of stories to amaze that exceeds their use or truth value, a testimony to the non-instrumental aesthetic experience.

The Allure and Pitfalls of Reading for Knowledge

Genre benders are hardly indifferent to providing useful knowledge or dramatizing readers' pursuit of it. They often pay tribute to the way texts arouse curiosity and prompt readers to follow an unfolding plot to discover what happens. In novels like A. S. Byatt's *Possession* and Margaret Atwood's *Blind Assassin*, characters ransack books for answers. These texts testify to the desire for narrative closure, the rapturous passion of readers to follow a plot to its end, to learn what happens, whodunit, if the lovers will end up together. At the same time, these novels problematize reducing texts to instruments for the pursuit of knowledge and demonstrate their attunement to the "multiplicity of the possibilities of reading." Writers like Atwood and Byatt intimate that the search for knowledge can easily slide into the prurient, the voyeuristic, and the acquisitive urge to own, master, and commodify information. Further, they maintain that the knowledge provided in fiction is often of limited utility, since it concerns beings that never existed. They suggest that while people yearn to make sense of the world, readers of fiction are more apt to open novels to get swept into another one—to go elsewhere for the journey, not, in Black's words, for "the spoils" they might bring home.[55]

In "Choices: The Writing of *Possession*," Byatt explains that when she began the novel, she had "been thinking a lot about the pleasure principle in art":

> [A]rt does not exist for politics, or for instruction—it exists primarily for pleasure, or it is nothing. It can do the other things if it gives pleasure, as Coleridge knew, and said. And the pleasure of fiction is narrative discovery, as it was easy to say about television serials and detective stories, but not, in those days, about serious novels.[56]

Like Delany, Byatt affirms the way pleasure enables art's didactic functions, and she bolsters the contention of this chapter: that genre-bending writers reclaim narrative pleasure for "serious novels" from the sphere of popular culture. In this piece Byatt seems to echo Brooks with a monolithic view of narrative pleasure: "*the* pleasure of fiction is narrative discovery." But her best-known novel demonstrates a far more polymorphous understanding.

In "Choices," Byatt acknowledges her debt to Eco's *The Name of the Rose*. Both that novel and *Possession* are highly intellectual, literary detective novels, in which part of the reader's pleasure lies in seeking solutions to their mysteries along with their scholarly sleuth protagonists. But it's hard to see how readers gain useful understanding by learning which of Eco's characters has been killing monks or of the tragic love story of Victorian poets who never existed. Instead, pleasure is the purpose of unspooling such narratives. *The Name of the Rose* begins with a prologue, in which the narrator claims to have discovered the manuscript of the subsequent text in 1968 and cites the "widespread conviction" at that time, "that one should write only out of commitment to the present, in order to change the world."[57] But he rejects the ethos of *la littérature engagée* flatly. Translating the manuscript and offering it to the world in 1980, he relishes that now

> the man of letters (restored to his loftiest dignity) can happily write out of pure love of writing. And so now I feel free to tell, for sheer narrative pleasure, the story of Adso of Melk, and I am comforted and consoled in finding it . . . gloriously lacking in any relevance for our day, atemporally alien to our hopes and certainties. (5)

Here, the narrator offers the "alien" medieval setting of Adso's story as an expanse for us to be immersed in. But Eco layers his narrator's words with palpable irony, as the latter rejects outright the notion of the late 1960s that a book ought to be engaged or revolutionary, from the "lofty" heights of his ivory tower, reveling in his autonomy. At the same time, by placing these words at the outset of the novel, Eco pays homage to the "pure love of writing," "sheer narrative pleasure," and "glorious" lack of relevance against modes of utopian political commitment and instrumentality. Reading an involuted "tale of books," Eco suggests, offers "tranquility" and a release from "everyday worries" (5), not a resolution to them.

Possession is also such a tale: a book of scholars combing dusty archives, and a compendium of genres and the multiple pleasures of reading, which the novel associates with multiple kinds of romance. Among the many genres it deploys, the novel mounts a satire of 1980s academia. Its protagonists are Roland Mitchell, a newly minted literature PhD struggling to find a full-time academic post, working on the (fictional) nineteenth-century Romantic poet Randolph Ash, and Maud Bailey, an accomplished feminist scholar who specializes in the relatively obscure poetess, (also fictional) Christabel LaMotte. When Roland discovers a fragmentary letter from the married, staid, Ash to LaMotte, who feminist scholars had thought a lesbian, Roland and Maud become academic detectives, seeking to uncover the untold story of the love affair between the Victorians. On this framework, Byatt hangs a cavalcade of genres, interspersing the scholars' plainclothes detection with Ash's dramatic monologues, the baroque epics and folk tales of LaMotte, the poets' letters, the diary of Ellen, Ash's wife, and (often parodic) literary biographies, journal articles, and editions.

Byatt emphasizes throughout the curiosity that animates the scholars, and much of the reader's pleasure comes from discovering, alongside Roland and Maud, the secret romance between Ash and LaMotte. The novel self-reflexively links this thrill to the detective novel, and to older adventure and more recent romance traditions, as Roland recognizes he is enmeshed in familiar narrative forms: in his burgeoning love for Maud and quest for the story of the Victorians, he enacts "a vulgar and a high Romance simultaneously."[58] As other scholars join the search, it morphs from "Quest, a good romantic form, into Chase and Race, two other equally valid ones" (460). In such metafictional moments, Byatt gently disparages the love story as "vulgar" romance. Roland and Maud are also ambivalent, even as the novel culminates with their coupling. "I love you. I think I'd rather I didn't," Maud declares, and Roland reciprocates: "I love you.... It isn't convenient" (550). Byatt and her protagonists reluctantly submit to the resolution of the "vulgar" romance, and she provides its satisfyingly conventional closure, as the novel *nearly* ends with the consummation of their courtship.

Possession also manifests ambivalence about "high Romance": the quest that animates its "disparate seekers and hunters" (542). The desire to unearth the history of the Victorian poets threatens to become, in Byatt's scholars, an all-possessing compulsion that slides into the prurient or a form of resource exploitation—a desire to profit on what they might find. When Maud and Roland search the long-deceased La Motte's bedroom for a trove of letters she penned to Ash, Roland "felt as though he was prying, and as though he was being uselessly urged on by some violent emotion of curiosity—not greed, curiosity, more fundamental even than sex, the desire for knowledge" (92). This "violent" lust to know emerges despite Maud's and Roland's professed distaste for biographical criticism and denial that they are motivated by the pursuit of notoriety. Roland is not trying to score "a considerable academic scoop" (56). "It wasn't like *that* at all.... It was something *personal*.... I'm an old-fashioned textual critic, not a biographer ... it wasn't *profit*.... I just wanted to know what happened next" (56–57). With these words, Byatt aligns the scholars' quest with readers' compulsive page-turning. Maud and Roland are not motivated by ambition or money, so much as the pleasure of following an unfolding plot, the need to know the end of the story.

Throughout, Byatt likens the scholars' curiosity to that of readers. In another self-reflexive moment, a line in LaMotte's epic poem *Melusina* seems to hint at her relationship with Ash. "It reads like a classic literary clue," Roland says. "Literary critics make natural detectives," Maud replies, perhaps revealing Byatt's familiarity with Brooks: "You know the theory that the classic detective story arose with the classic adultery novel—everyone wanted to know who was the Father, what was the origin, what was the secret?" (258). As the novel plays with many kinds of possession, Maud feels like a reader who has been "taken over by" the story. "I want to *know* what happened ... It isn't professional greed. It's something more primitive." "Narrative curiosity," Roland responds (258–259).

Similarly, Roland explains his theft of the letter that launched the quest as his desire to possess the story of the Victorians and his possession by a force beyond his control. "I felt possessed. I had to know" (527). The novel metafictionally links the scholars' pursuit of the history of Ash and LaMotte, with the readerly drive. An embedded poem by Ash scans like a verse rendition of Brooks's theory, or a dark revision of Mitchell's yarn:

> We are driven / by endings as by hunger. We *must know* / How it comes out, the shape o' the whole, the thread / Whose links are weak or solid . . . / we cannot let go / Of this bright chain of curiosity / Which is become our fetter. (517)

Here the yarn becomes a chain, possession by the need to know the end a type of bondage. Ash's compulsion, however, makes clear a signal difference between the pleasurable desire to know the end of a story and knowledge that might be instrumental:

> I will read the most trivial things—once commenced—only out of a feverish greed to be able to *swallow* the ending . . . Are you in my case? Or are you a more discriminating reader? Do you lay aside the unprofitable. *(193)*

Ash feels guilty about his "unprofitable," non-instrumental pleasure. By contrast, the furious pursuit of knowledge in the world can lead to a possessive form of mastery and greed.

While Roland and Maud deny profit goads them on, Byatt shows the quest for knowledge as vulnerable to a proprietary desire to commodify information and biography as a voyeuristic, commercial pursuit. *Possession*'s villain, Mortimer Cropper, is Ash's preeminent biographer. He oversees the Ash collection at Robert Dale Owen University—a fictional institution Byatt depicts as tremendously well-funded. Each letter Cropper purchases and collects helps "bring the whole man just that little bit more back to life" (108). Here Byatt links biography with the novel's depiction of Victorian attempts to commune with the dead—ghoulish versions of New Historicism.[59]

The novel takes a gothic turn in its depiction of Cropper as a grave robber, vulture, or simoniac, preying on the dead and trading in their relics. In addition to buying any Ash artifact and taking "clandestine pictures" of manuscripts he can't buy with a "black box" he has invented for the purpose (105)—here Byatt dabbles in the gadgetry of the spy novel—he keeps "tresses of Randolph's and Ellen's woven hair" in the "sparkling sheen of the glass pyramid that housed the Stant Collection" (416). Cropper thinks of "the delectable letters": "He must have those papers. He felt real pangs, a kind of famishing" (416). According to Cropper, biography is compulsive, "just as much a spiritual hunger of modern man as sex or political activity. Look at the sales..." (416). If the novel poses narrative desire as pleasurable compulsion, Byatt's metaphors portray biographical "hunger" as a vampiric form of consumption, associated with emergent Reagan-Thatcher neoliberalism. Cropper is a "hi-tech lecturer, a magician of white screens and light-beams," a PowerPoint wizard *avant la lettre*, whose "projectors and transparent cages of promptings... helped him, like President Reagan, to orchestrate" his presentations and woo potential donors (416). Cropper argues that his collection in New Mexico should house the Ash-LaMotte correspondence, against Britain's national claim, "in the interest of international communication, free movement of ideas and intellectual property that they be most widely accessible" (417). Byatt poses biography as part of global mercantile exchange, in which the exploitable resources are the secret lives of famous figures, subject to the ruthless pursuit of those who can extract them.

In keeping with biography's commodity character, *Possession*'s chapters that depict the scholars' competition to acquire Ash's and LaMotte's secrets morph into a burlesque of commercial genres. In addition to Cropper's petty espionage, Byatt notes his "American hips, ready for... the faraway ghost of a gunbelt" (105). After we see him fondling "stolen images" of Ash's letters, Cropper "drew out those other photographs of which he had a large and varied collection—as far as it was possible to vary... so essentially simple an activity" (124). The problem with pornography here is not objectionable sexual content or objectification of its subjects but its repetitiveness, that it's not "possible to vary" it much; according to Byatt, the genre is not very plastic. The problem Byatt reveals with biography is not the quest for knowledge, but the tendency of that search to possess the seeker and invade the privacy of its subjects, in the interest of commodifying them.

As the novel builds to its denouement, its detective plot takes a gothic turn. The protagonists and their accomplices discover Cropper's plan to commit "grave robbery" (525), disinterring Ash in search of letters that Cropper suspects were buried with the poet. Maud and Roland "foil the body-snatchers" (527), during a "spooky" night in the graveyard (535), that the novel self-consciously refers to as "a Hallowe'en adventure" (525). While Byatt depicts "narrative desire" as a pleasurable search that readers pursue in concert with fictional detectives, she poses excessive biographical curiosity as vampiric, criminal, and prurient because of its possessiveness. "He feels they *are* really his, perhaps," ventures Roland (525). Cropper desires not merely to know but to own and master.

Like *Possession*, Atwood's *Blind Assassin* both depicts and offers various pleasures using many genres, and, like Byatt, Atwood points both to the pleasure of narrative desire that animates readers and to the potential of that desire to slide into the prurient and invasive. It's a testament to the prolificacy of Atwood's career that this Booker-winning novel has often been overshadowed by works like *The Handmaid's Tale* and *Oryx and Crake*. But *The Blind Assassin* is perhaps the work in which Atwood best shows off the great range that has characterized her career, as it modulates between satire of contemporary consumerism and historical fiction of the interwar years, interweaving these with parodic newspaper articles and embedded fantasy and science fiction tales. Paralleling its use of many genres, the novel is striking for its heterodox approach to literary forms, their affordances and pleasures: its attunement to the many functions of storytelling, as well as its less-utilitarian seductions.

The Blind Assassin consists of three nested plots. In the outer frame, an aging Iris Chase, heiress of a Canadian factory owner and widow of a textile tycoon, narrates her life—as she is transferred, effectively, from one patriarchal figure to the other—and that of her sister Laura, who, we learn at the novel's outset, has killed herself decades earlier. Before taking her life, Laura wrote a novella, or so Iris has us believe, also called "The Blind Assassin." Iris has her sister's novella published, and Laura becomes a posthumous feminist literary icon. Beginning the novel with Laura's suicide, Atwood structures the outer frame as family saga and tale of suspense, as readers wonder what led to Laura's suicide. We also read Laura's novella, alternating with Iris's narrative—the second nested layer. In the inset novella "The Blind Assassin," which cleverly nods to its genre fiction influences with chapter titles like "The Hard-Boiled Egg," two unnamed lovers meet for assignations in tawdry boardinghouses. The woman (modeled, we later learn, on Iris) enjoys these fleeting escapes from her bourgeois life and unhappy marriage. The man, a leftist radical on the lam from the authorities for his subversive activities, scrapes together a meager living writing stories for pulp magazines. The couple meets, they have sex, and, one desire spent, he spins for her installments of a fantastic tale set on the planet Zycron—the third nested level of narrative. In the ancient city of Sakiel-Norn, a blind assassin, himself a fugitive slave and victim of countless rapes, rescues a tongueless virgin, who is about to be ritualistically sacrificed. Together they flee their would-be-executioners. Attentive readers detect the connective tissue joining Atwood's nested narratives; in each, a pair of victims seeks to escape confinement, oppression, and exploitation.

Interweaving these three narrative arcs, *The Blind Assassin* explores numerous motives for telling and hearing stories: the desire to have secret histories revealed and mysteries solved; the hope to leave a monument when we die; the voyeuristic thrill of spying on other lives; the schadenfreude of seeing the once-mighty fall; and, most of all, the potential for stories to offer a fleeting escape from confining circumstances into another world.[60] Iris complains that fans of Laura's novella were not attracted to "the book itself, so much as the furor" around its depiction of adultery and the scandal provoked by the assumption it was autobiographical (39). "Back at home they drew the curtains and read, with disapproval, with relish, with avidity and glee—even the ones who'd never thought of opening a novel before" (39). Iris quips, "There's nothing like a shovelful of dirt to encourage literacy" (39). Here again, the desire to know slides into the prurient, as those who don't typically read novels gobble up Laura's book because it allows them to feel morally superior to the aristocratic Chase family. Such readers also enjoy the puzzle of trying to decode the *roman à clef*, probing invasively, Iris's diction makes clear, into the family's dirty laundry. They wanted "to finger the real people in it. . . . They wanted real bodies, to fit onto the bodies conjured up for them by words. They wanted real lust. Above all they wanted to know: *who was the man?*" (40). Atwood's novel teases its reader with the same question, adding another layer: on whom is the adulteress based, Laura or Iris? As in *Possession*, Atwood testifies to readers' enduring preoccupation with biography, mining even novels for dirt about "real people." Fiction, for some, offers the same fodder as the tabloids.

The promise of revelation also runs through Atwood's novel, making it conform, at least in part, to Brooks's account of narrative as explanatory instrument. After Laura's suicide, Iris scours her sister's notebooks, in hope of discovering what led to her demise:

> I could have chosen ignorance, but I did what you would have done—what you've already done, if you've read this far. I chose knowledge instead. Most of us will. We'll choose knowledge no matter what, we'll maim ourselves in the process. (494)

Here Atwood ventures that the search for knowledge can be a form of willful self-harm, not oriented toward therapeutic working-through. Iris portrays the desire to know what happened to her dead sister as multifaceted but also greedy:

> Curiosity is not our only motive: love or grief or despair or hatred is what drives us on.... We're voyeurs, all of us. Why should we assume that anything in the past is ours for the taking, simply because we've found it? We're all grave robbers, once we open the doors locked by others. (494)

In lines that echo *Possession*, Atwood critiques the relentless desire to know the past as invasion of privacy and acquisitiveness toward the past.

Both Byatt and Atwood emphasize that while reading to produce meaning can be unreliable or greedy, pleasure is the prime motive for most readers. *Possession* quarrels with any "single-minded" mode of reading throughout (242). And it insists that the desire for total knowledge, especially of other people, is futile. Influenced by deconstruction, Maud opines, early in the novel, that "if you read the collected letters of any writer—if you read her biography—you will always get a sense that there's something missing, something biographers don't have access to, the real thing, the crucial thing" (100). Despite their awareness that the search for knowledge is doomed to fail, both the Victorians and contemporary scholars consistently overrate their capacity for knowledge. Part of the iconoclastic age of Darwin, Ash admits being part of "a Faustian generation" that "seeks to know what we are maybe not designed (if we are designed) to be able to know" (235). The discovery of the correspondence between Ash and LaMotte and the affair it reveals confirm for the scholars how little they had known about the poets they study: "these letters have made us all look—in some ways—a little silly, in our summing-up of lives on the evidence we had" (526). But the novel leaves us with the realization that any reassessment will likewise be incomplete.

Byatt concludes *Possession* with an inspired stroke of dramatic irony that demonstrates the failure of the scholars' biographical reconstructions. When

Cropper exhumes Ash's coffin, the scholars find that his wife Ellen had buried with him a final letter from LaMotte, who reveals that her child by Ash was born healthy and raised by LaMotte's sister. The letter solves the mystery of what happened to the child, and it reveals Maud to be a direct descendent of LaMotte. The letter *seems* to confirm that Ash died without knowing about his child's existence, as Ellen's journal confesses that she never showed the letter to him; she received it when Ash was on his deathbed and could not disturb the peace of his final hours and their mostly happy marriage by disclosing that his fleeting infidelity led to a daughter. Based on this journal entry, the scholars, like Ellen, believe that Ash died without knowing he fathered a child. But Byatt's novel concludes with a postscript, in which Ash strolls past LaMotte's sister's house and recognizes his own appearance comingled with that of Christabel in the visage of the little girl playing outside.[61] Ash has a playful conversation with the girl and asks her to relay a message to "her aunt" Christabel—who Ash knows is actually the child's mother. But the novel's final line reveals that the girl "forgot the message, which was never delivered" (555).

Possession thus ends not with Maud and Roland's coupling, but with multiple misapprehensions and failures of knowledge. In "Choices: The Writing of *Possession*," Byatt recalls that she "still receives angry letters" complaining about the omniscient postscript. Byatt explains that the choice was important to her, as she wanted to insist that "*what really mattered* is likely to elude the piecers-together of lives."[62] But the brilliant stroke of the ending exceeds, aptly, even the explanation of its author. Not only does the fact that Ash knew about his daughter "elude" the scholar biographers, but it also escapes his Victorian contemporaries. LaMotte never gets the message that Ash met their daughter. Ash never receives the final letter from LaMotte. Ellen mistakenly thinks she kept her husband oblivious of the existence of his illegitimate daughter. And the daughter, Maia, grows up not knowing the truth of her parentage. Byatt begins the postscript: "There are things that happen and leave no discernible trace, are not spoken or written of" (552). Only the readers of *Possession* get to see these things, to know what none of the characters in the novel know. Byatt's novel thus provides and reflects on how novels as such grant a satisfaction we cannot achieve in everyday reality: complete understanding of other people and an omnisciently told, so unimpeachable, history. Byatt's conclusion performs the distinction of fiction, the fact that only there, where narrative constitutes reality, rather than reports on it, can we obtain total knowledge.[63]

Reading for Escape

Of course, it's difficult to say what we gain total knowledge of when we read fiction, since that knowledge is often of people and events that never existed. Such knowledge could be applicable to our lives, but Eco's invocation of terms like "sheer narrative pleasure," and Byatt's description of its allure as "more primitive" than concerns like professional advancement return us to reading's non-instrumental uses. *Possession* is attuned to what we do when we read besides pursuing knowledge. Like many works by genre-bending authors, it simultaneously offers and represents scenes of reading pleasure that emphasize how stories provide immersion and adventure in other worlds, enchantment, play, and rest—modes of reading that professional literary scholarship has often neglected or devalued. Early in the novel, Roland and Maud describe the allure of their chosen subjects. Ash's poems were, for Roland, "what stayed alive, when I'd been taught and examined everything else." Maud agrees: "That's it. What could survive our education" (62). Byatt emphasizes the vivacity of Ash's and LaMotte's writing compared to what has been killed off by staid academic examination. While desire for knowledge drives their quest in the "high Romance," Byatt associates other modes of romance with repose from reason.

Fittingly, Byatt dramatizes repose from the intellectual with physical journeys that resonate with Ryan's account of transportation into fictional worlds and Black's account of reading adventures: Roland and Maud's trip to Brittany to meet the French scholar who has discovered the journal of LaMotte's cousin Sabine; and, within that journal, the record of LaMotte's sojourn in Brittany, where she took refuge during her pregnancy and convalescence. Roland and Maud find themselves "on holiday" (455), and he is briefly able to escape his anxiety about his dim academic job prospects: "He would have been in panic if he had allowed himself to think, but the dreamy days . . . and something else"—his budding romance with Maud—"made it possible to leave thinking in abeyance" (458). Byatt associates this respite *from thinking*, with the lovers' temporary abandonment of their professional world, with romantic love, and contrasts these with language, knowledge, and poststructuralism. The academics are "theoretically knowing," but as Byatt links theory's linguistic turn with knowledge and the sexual exposures of psychoanalysis, there is a reticence and chastity to their holiday: "They took to silence. They touched each other without comment and without progression" (458). These dreamy days resemble the enchantment that Ryan and Saler cite as one of the common metaphors for readerly transportation. Contemplating having to return to England, Roland asks Maud, "Unenchanted?" And she recognizes, "Are we enchanted? I suppose we must start *thinking* again sometime" (454). The couple is compelled to return to thinking. But Byatt first affirms that even, or perhaps especially, the most "theoretically knowing" of us needs repose from thought.

The pleasures and benefits of such a reprieve are not particular to reading; they can be found in a variety of states. Roland's estranged partner Val, with whom he shares a putrid basement apartment, finds it in an outing at the horseraces. "Val had not done anything that was simply designed for pleasure, she thought, since she could remember" (447). Such escapes are essential not trivial, for Byatt. When Roland thinks of his and Maud's return to England, the narrator asserts that the "cocoon" of their holiday was no mere fancy but an equal and crucial reality: "In the real world—that was, for one should not privilege one world above another, in the social world to which they both must return from these white nights and sunny days—there was little real connection between them" (459). Enchantment and escape are integral parts of reality, real worlds of their own, not denials of it.

Throughout, Byatt links enchantment and repose to the experience of stories that slip the bonds of the here and now. *Possession* thus follows its epigraph from Nathaniel Hawthorne's preface to *The House of the Seven Gables* (1851), in which he famously inaugurates a distinction between the novel—what we would later specify as the realist novel—which "is presumed to aim at a very minute fidelity . . . to the probable and ordinary course of man's experience," and the romance, which takes imaginative liberties and "has fairly a right to present [the truth of the human heart] under circumstances . . . of the writer's own choosing." Hawthorne also allows for temporal recursion, shuttling between "a bygone time" and a "present that is flitting away from us."[64] Byatt subtitles her novel "A Romance," at once advertising its courtship plot in the more recent tradition of "vulgar" romance novels, *à la* Harlequin, and disavowing that association with its immediate invocation of, and attempt to align itself with, Hawthorne's "higher" sense of romance. *Possession* activates both senses of the term, as Byatt oscillates between "the probable and ordinary" relationship between Roland and Maud, a "bygone time," and a journey into other times and places, according to the free movement of the writer's imagination.

Byatt's embedding of LaMotte's poetry evinces a similar ability to combine the mundane with the fanciful. Ash compliments LaMotte on *Melusina*, her fairy epic: "it is *both* wild and strange and ghastly . . . *and* it is at the same time solid as earthly tales . . . depicting the life of households and the planning of society." Ash praises her work for its "mastery of *both* these contradictory elements" (193). Byatt's repetition and emphasis on "both" and "and" stress that the seemingly "contradictory elements" of the "strange" and the "earthly" may in fact be fused into artistically satisfying harmonies. Similarly, LaMotte's life oscillates between the strictures of her quotidian existence and real and imaginary flights from such limits. When she learns of her pregnancy, she flees the censure its discovery would incite to relatives in Brittany—an escape Roland and Maud recursively reenact. The journal entries of LaMotte's cousin Sabine linger on the enchanting storytelling traditions there—traditions that inspire LaMotte's fanciful work in *Melusina*. "Everywhere in Brittany the storytelling begins at Toussaint, in the Black Month" (382). These tales occupy a "misty land [where] the borderline between myth, legend and fact is not decisive" (368); they delight in "trafficking between this world and *that*, the other side of the threshold, which at Toussaint may be crossed in both directions" (383). Throughout, the novel invokes liminality, transition, and the spaces in between worlds; the topic is the focus of Maud's scholarship.

Byatt's depiction of the power of romance to traverse the border between quotidian and fantastic spaces echoes Chabon's declaration in "Trickster in a Suit of Lights" that "the most interesting writers of the past seventy-five years or so have . . . found themselves drawn, inexorably, to the borderlands," plying "their trade in the space between genres, in the no man's land."[65] Sabine emphasizes that the oral storytelling traditions of Toussaint not only contain mythic or otherworldly subject matter, but can transport their listeners to other worlds. When Sabine's cook Gode tells tales, the room and its occupants are transformed. Shadows turn into "huge faces with gaping mouths and monstrous noses and chins," and the listeners' faces are "transfigured by the flames into witches and spectres" (386). *Possession* is interested throughout in the possibility of communicating with the dead—through a spirit medium, the imagination, or scholarly reconstruction of history—and the novel's Brittany section invokes the "ancient Celtic belief" that "this life is" merely one phase of existence, "and that many worlds exist simultaneously, round and about each other, interpenetrating perhaps here and there" (394). In the recursively repeating levels of Byatt's romance, characters cross thresholds and escape into other worlds: Roland and Maud lose themselves in the ardor of Ash and LaMotte; LaMotte escapes the threat her unwed pregnancy poses into a Brittany filled with stories of other worlds; and her epic poems, inspired by such stories, cross the permeable boundary between the solid and earthly and the "wild and strange."

Throughout, Byatt's novel oscillates between the rational and realistic— Ash's scientific investigations, the historicist, theoretical constructs of contemporary scholars—and romance that offers access to other states of mind. Sabine's journal contrasts the vivid Toussaint stories with that of a visitor who tells "a dead tale, a neat little political allegory" (382). Sabine juxtaposes this "dead" material with the "imagined primroses and bluebells" of her father Raoul's stories; these permeate and even supersede her reality, such that her childhood "was lived *in* tales," which "diminished in [her] mind—the life of real things" (383). Stories may transmit tidy meanings but also enchant and conjure distinct realities. LaMotte similarly esteems Raoul's ability to conjure other states of mind with his tales: "You are an enchanter yourself . . . you make lights and perfumes in the dark" (384). When LaMotte asks of a tale's meaning, Sabine gets angry, "for we do not talk of meanings in this pedantic nineteenth-century way, on the Black nights, we simply tell and hear and believe" (384). But Raoul is more patient, and his explanation of the tale makes its paradoxical meaning an assertion of the need for escape from meaning and reason. "It is one of many tales that speak of fear of Woman . . . of the sleep of reason under the rule of . . . desire, intuition, imagination" (384). LaMotte learns that "Reason must sleep" (384). In this story that asserts that stories are a time to give meaning a rest, Byatt captures the oscillation between the principles of reality and of imaginative transport and repose that she understands as fundamental to romance.

LaMotte's fairy epic *Melusina* not surprisingly also evinces such a weightless freedom of movement. The poem is "not grounded in historical truth, but in poetic and imaginative truth—like Spenser's *Faerie Queene*, or Ariosto, where the soul is free of the restraints of history and fact" (404). And throughout, Byatt echoes Le Guin, expressing that feminine writing has long conceived itself as a realm of imagining freedom from the constraints of a patriarchal world; LaMotte declares that "Romance is a proper form for women" since it opens onto "a land where women can be free to express their true natures, as in the Ile de Sein or Síd, though not in this world" (404). That women can explore their "true natures" in romantic narrative journeys to imaginary lands, but "not in this world," captures the ability of non-realistic genres to transport their readers, while immersing them in a deeper truth. Here we see how genre-bending literary fiction engages a paradoxical project, committed to realism's effort to depict the truth of experience, while also attempting to provide escape from the quotidian via non-realistic genres.

The recognition that romance offers a world of freedom, imagination, and enchantment— an escape from a constraining, mundane reality, and the predominance of regimes of rational meaning and instrumentality—also resounds through Atwood's *Blind Assassin*. In that novel's outer frame, Iris promises to disclose untold stories and attempts to explain her sister Laura's suicide. But these are far from the only functions of storytelling modeled within the novel. In the scenes of the male lover spinning his fantasy tale and the woman's rapt attention to it, Atwood closely links the popular genre material of these sections to erotic pleasure, immersion in a fictional world, and time experienced in suspension from the oppressive conditions of daily life. The fantastic story set on the planet Zycron that the leftist tells his lover is not without its own palpable, allegorical meaning: the blind assassin—enslaved as a child, sightless from "incessant close labour" weaving lavish carpets for aristocrats (22), and forced into prostitution, before escaping and helping liberate a mute, sacrificial virgin—figures class exploitation, and the subordination of women like Iris, who is sold to Richard, but then weaves the narrative that will assassinate his character, and seeks to liberate the story of her silenced, sacrificed sister, Laura. But the novella's unnamed heroine, who lays abed listening to her lover's tale, does not appreciate how it figures her situation, trapped in an unhappy marriage and seeking refuge in trysts. For her, the Zycron tale, linked to the "thick plots" of her lover's pulp magazines (119), is a source of pleasure in the act of listening, not a refiguring of her situation but an escape from it.

Throughout, Atwood has the leftist deride his work for the pulps as mercenary, repetitive, schlock. His flirtatious banter likens the job to sex work. "As a rule I do this for money" (119). Later, when we see him at his typewriter rather than telling a tale orally, Atwood presents his writing as catering to a market that craves a predictable buffet of reheated, salacious fare. "He needs to write something that will sell. It's back to the never-fail dead women, slavering for blood.... The best thing is to picture the cover illustration the boys will likely come up with, and then go on from there" (250). Basing content on the lurid cover art he anticipates, the paperback writer finds his labor tedious and venal, in a way that he again likens to sex work: "He's tired of... the heroes... their ray guns, their metallic skin-tight clothing. Ten cents a thrill. Still, it's a living, if he can keep up the speed, and beggars can hardly be choosers" (250). Necessity urges him on, and Atwood seems to portray genre fiction as relentless commodity production that caters to the lowest common denominator. Later, he wonders:

> Why does he crank out this junk? Because he needs to. . . . He had bigger ambitions once, more serious ones. To write a man's life the way it really is. . . . To expose the workings of the system, the machinery . . . how it uses you up, turns you into a cog or a souse, crushes your face into the muck one way or another. (280)

He had aspired to fuse his revolutionary activities with his writing, produce work of social realism, but concludes that the tastes of the masses are more predisposed toward "junk":

> The average working man wouldn't read that kind of thing, though—the working man the comrades think is so inherently noble. What those guys want is his stuff. Cheap to buy, value for a dime, fast-paced action, with lots of tits and ass. (280)

If this writer is revolutionary in his view of the exploitative capitalist system, he's modernist and elitist in his estimation of what ordinary readers are willing to pay for.

Atwood's depiction of the effects of the pulp writer's narratives on his lover, however, and of the necessity of escape, strains against his self-deprecating lament. Iris recounts that in her and Laura's youth, their housekeeper Reenie frequently brought them "cheap magazines, the pulpy, trashy kind you could buy in drugstores" (152). This is one of many moments in Atwood's fiction that oscillates between the unflattering terms by which popular fiction is often known and an appreciation of its powerful effect on readers, particularly its ability to offer them a temporary journey to other worlds. "Some of" the magazines "were about romance," but Iris preferred "those with stories about other lands or even other planets" (152). Atwood, as she often does—recall her infamous comments about "talking squids from outer space"—gently mocks genre fiction clichés and the objectifying images of women that appear in the pulps: "lithe girls with topaz eyes and opaline skin, dressed in cheesecloth trousers and little metal brassieres like two funnels joined by a chain" (153). But she also, in Iris's love for imaginative transport, pays homage to the deep and abiding allure of putatively "trashy" fare. Again, that fare is not without transmittable meaning. In "the detective magazines, with their pistol-strewn, blood-drenched covers," Iris and Laura find warnings about dangers to girls like them:

> [T]he wide-eyed heiresses to great fortunes were always being conked out with ether and tied up with clothesline . . . and locked into yacht cabins or abandoned church crypts. . . . Laura and I believed in the existence of such men, but we weren't too afraid of them, because we knew what to expect . . . and we would be able to spot them immediately and run away. (153)

Laura and Iris are wrong, however, about the didactic function of such stories. This glimpse of pulp clichés anticipates Laura's fate, as Richard seduces her in the cabin of his yacht (500). Reading about "such men" fails spectacularly in helping Iris and Laura "spot them" and evade their advances. The pulps don't deliver useful information but grant temporary escape. Reenie dismisses them, in familiar fashion, as cheap entertainment and fantasy, but Iris pays tribute to the door they open into other times and places: "*Silly*, Reenie called these. *Like nothing on earth*. But that's what I liked about them" (153).

Atwood intimates the universality of this desire for escape—that even a utopian paradise would produce it, and that narratives derive their energy from this desire. In the chapter "The Peach Women of Aa'a," which Atwood originally published as a stand-alone short story, its title promising the very sound of satisfaction, the pulp writer tries to tell his lover a happy story for once. But he ends up spinning a tale of the relentlessness of human dissatisfaction and desire, and, like the opening of *Anna Karenina*, the stasis of happy stories, the way narrative movement needs conflict. The leftist tells of a pair of intergalactic fighter pilots, who crash-land on a planet where the buxom women of the story's title literally grow on trees and live to satisfy the astronauts' every whim. Atwood seems to render a hyperbolic, objectifying male fantasy. "After some time," however, "this existence, wonderful though it was," for the men anyway, "began to pall" (354). The curse of this seeming utopia is its inescapability. "It's Paradise, but we can't get out of it. And anything you can't get out of is Hell" (355). Later, Atwood has Iris return to this idea, observing in her memoir that in "Paradise there are no stories, because there are no journeys. It's loss and regret and misery and yearning that drive the story forward, along its twisted road" (518). Atwood thus poses the journey, motivated by desire and dissatisfaction, in ideas that hearken to Brooks and Vladimir Propp, as the motor of narrative. At the same time, she points to the desire for escape as that which motivates readers to take refuge in immersive reading. As all three of the plots of *The Blind Assassin* feature characters who try and fail to escape oppressive conditions, the novel shows such escapes as non-instrumental, not a matter of fomenting revolution, but all the more necessary for the brief respites they afford. "Anything you can't get out of is hell."

This recognition of the allure of journeys into fictional worlds that have traditionally been emphasized in genre fiction fields recurs throughout work by genre-bending writers. In Atwood's short story "Alphinland," the aging fantasy writer Constance Starr laments that her avant-garde poet friends "didn't understand" why she takes the genre so seriously. But Atwood's free indirect discourse emphasizes that the world Starr creates is her safe haven. "Alphinland was hers alone. It was her refuge . . . her stronghold; it was where she could go when things with Gavin weren't working out."[66] In Lethem's *Motherless Brooklyn*, the Tourettic orphan Lionel "live[s] . . . in the library" of St. Vincent's Home for Boys, trying to lose himself in its books—until the petty mobster Minna escorts him into the world of gangster movies, which provide a final "escape from [his] doldrums."[67] Anthony Doerr's Pulitzer-winning *All the Light We Cannot See* (2014) is on the surface a work of historical fiction, but it is also constructed as a thriller, with a villainous, syphilitic Nazi in hot pursuit of an accursed, priceless diamond and the blind orphan who guards it. Doerr's novel offers a paean to the power of radio technology to bridge space and time, and of narratives like Jules Verne's *Twenty-Thousand Leagues Under the Sea* (1870), to disclose a world of adventure and the near-infinitude of nonhuman species to the young, sightless Maire-Laure. When she flees Paris to stay with her uncle Etienne in Saint Malo, he "doesn't have any Jules Verne, but he does have Darwin," and he "reads to her from *The Voyage of the 'Beagle'*." These travel tales temporarily lift Marie-Laure out of a world torn to shreds by the Second World War: "it is splendid . . . to feel the sentences hoist her up and carry her somewhere else."[68]

Much of Richard Powers's *Playground* (2024) reads like a modernized Verne adventure, astounding readers with extraordinary visions of undersea voyages. The novel most obviously traffics in journeys to other worlds in depicting the research of one of its multiple protagonists, Evelyn Beaulieu, who is based on the pioneering deep ocean explorer Sylvia Earle. But, as its title indicates, *Playground* is interested in many forms of play, the magic circle of games, and the near infinite possibilities of chess, Go, language, and software. In the novel's sections focalized through Rafi Young, a genius African American child from Chicago's South Side, Powers explores how Rafi's father teaches him to escape via books. In reading, Rafi steps "through the wardrobe, stumbling into the brute particulars of another, more forgiving and beautiful world," one that "was endless, open, and free."[69] Comparing Rafi's transport into the world of books to that of C. S. Lewis's Pevensie children escaping the Blitz into Narnia, Powers emphasizes the necessary reprieve reading can provide, but also how it discloses visions of freedom that propel Rafi into new possibilities: a creative writing degree, graduate work, and becoming an educator.

Telegraph Avenue, Chabon's return to realism, nonetheless traffics in transportation to other worlds through the character of Jules Jaffe, whose name marks his connection with Verne's journeys. Enrolled "in a flame-work class," Jules fashions for his mother's best friend Gwen "a small glass planet, a teardrop of blue alien seas and green continents and polar ice caps tinted ice blue."[70] Gwen reflects that "for as long as" she "had known him, Julie had been a mapper of worlds, on newsprint and graph paper and in the phosphor of a computer screen" (62). Anticipating Powers's depiction of software coding as world-building in *Playground* and Jennifer Egan's fascination with Dungeons & Dragons in *The Candy House* that I discuss in the Coda, Chabon reminds us that novels are but one vehicle to facilitate immersion in fictional worlds. When asked "where he found the inspiration for the tiny glass world," Jules replies "*By living there*" (62). Like the ostracized Oscar Wao, whose "outsized love of genre," in Junot Díaz's novel, "helped him get through the rough days of his youth,"[71] fictional worlds provide Jules a refuge from the cruelty the quotidian world visits upon a queer teen.

Such worlds become available through games, films, fiction, and his first romantic relationship with the aptly named Titus Joyner. After Jules finds himself "literally joining himself by the hand to Titus's shoulder," their bond transforms West Oakland into a "wildly ramifying multiverse of their mutual imagination" (89). When Jules and Titus first meet, at a screening of *Lady Snowblood* (1973) that is part of an evening course on "Source and Allusion in [Quentin Tarantino's] *Kill Bill*" (93), Chabon has a jargony academic lecture give way to a scene of wonder as the lights go down and "Julie dreamed for two hours with his eyes open" (98). Slow to shake off the film's waking-dream, the two boys remain enchanted, extending the make-believe space into the bland hallways of a community center. While the "biomass designated as Julie Jaffee stood up, and its autonomic systems took over and propelled it toward a beige corridor, along beige linoleum tiles, through a beige world," his mind has been catapulted far away, into "another universe," where "his traveler soul honed its katana and ate rice with chopsticks by a fire and tied a thick topknot in its wild black mane" (99). Titus, "whirling an imaginary blade over his head" (99), attacks Julie, and both, in their play-fighting, are "engulfed" in a "strange fizz of wonder" (100). Chabon poses such genre-bending moments of play that mix SF with samurais, as a rest from self-consciousness: "Lost so deep in the dream, they didn't have the sense to be embarrassed" (385). Though these moments exist within the magic circle of the game of make-believe, Chabon intimates that departures into play may transfigure reality, as they initiate the boys' friendship. Titus makes imaginary adventures "happen, driving them, taking them seriously long enough and intensely enough—and in public—to make them somehow *be*" (100). While the arena of play offers its own reward, exercising the imagination can convert mental activity into material results. Play may yield unpredictable benefits, as it creates for Jules a refuge from an inhospitable social world and generates companionship and experience where there was nothing.

As I discuss in the previous chapter, Egan's *The Keep* poses creative writing and literary reading as practice spaces for restoring human connection and the transformative power of the imagination. Like Chabon, Egan links these literary activities to other forms of play and rest. *The Keep* poses children's games as the archetype for transportation in fictional worlds and recalls Marie-Laure Ryan's "frozen metaphor" of immersion by imagining a hotel swimming pool as a place of composure and mental regeneration. In a flashback to a time before Egan's hipster protagonist becomes addicted to what the novel portrays as the spurious forms of human connection offered by mobile communication technology, we glimpse Danny playing a childhood game that his cousin Howie invented called "Terminal Zeus." The game is composed of conventional elements: "there was a hero (Zeus), and there were monsters and missions and runways and airlifts and bad guys and fireballs and high-speed chases" (7). But Egan stresses that the game relies on imagination and communication. "Howie thought most of it up. He'd shut his eyes like he was watching a movie on the backs of his eyelids that he wanted Danny to see" (7). At other times, "he made Danny do the talking—Okay, you tell it: what does the underwater torture dungeon look like?—and Danny would start making stuff up" (7). The boys' creations develop from mental images to oral narrative to a world to be immersed in—one that makes the self and real world temporarily disappear. Danny would get "so deep inside the game he forgot who he was," and when his parents would tell him it was time to go home, he would beg for "another half hour ... *pleasepleaseplease?* Frantic not to be ripped away from the world he and Howie had made" (7–8). Egan contrasts Danny's feeling of "dissolving into that game" (13), with the relentless self-consciousness and self-image maintenance of his adult life.

While for the seven-year-old Danny the imaginary world is so enchanting that he doesn't want to leave, the game provides for Howie a resource to help survive "a *traumatic incident*" (8). When Howie, Danny, and their cousin Rafe explore a cave, Danny tries to impress Rafe by pushing Howie into a subterranean pool and ditching him in the cave. It will be three days before Howie is found. Decades later, when the cousins confront the incident, Howie maintains that his imagination enabled him to survive the hours alone in the cave and the traumatized adolescence that ensued. "I escaped with my mind. I got out of there because I wasn't going to make it otherwise. . . . I left, I went into a game" (217). "*Imagination!* It saved my life. I was a fat kid, adopted, I didn't have many friends. But I made things up. I had a life in my head that had nothing to do with my life" (48). Egan thus poses immersion in imaginary worlds as play with value in its own right that might also furnish resources for a lifesaving escape from traumatic circumstances.

Conclusion: The Permutations of Pleasure and the Pleasures of Permutation

This chapter has shown that writers of literary fiction around the turn of the millennium have sought to extol and provide the pleasures of immersion in fictional worlds, voicing their appreciation of this aspect of the writing of their peers and dramatizing them in self-reflexive moments in their fictions. But I am by no means claiming that the provision of such pleasures is the singular aim of such writers. As previous chapters have shown, genre benders have gravitated to immersive pleasure, while deploying popular genres as frameworks for a wide variety of aesthetic and political projects. Neither is this chapter claiming that immersion is the *only* pleasure such writers want to grant their readers. There are many kinds of pleasure to be had from reading, and pleasures specific to different genres. But the pleasure of immersion cuts across various genres and has historically been emphasized in the fields of genre fiction and relatively deprioritized in the literary field. Rather than advancing an exclusive conception of literary value, these writers' attunement to the delight of getting lost in a book, to being transported via fiction to other worlds, emerges alongside a growing recognition of what Black calls the "multiplicity of the possibilities of reading."

As I discuss in the Introduction, Chabon's "Trickster" essay extends a "new definition of entertainment," which will "encompass everything pleasurable that arises from the encounter of an attentive mind with a page of literature."[72] The encounters Chabon delineates range widely and, as I've noted, attempt to reconcile modernist and popular notions of literary value by converting elements of formal recalcitrance, like "a thousand-word-long sentence" in Proust and the opacities of Foucauldian prose, which might be conceived of as sources of intellectual work, into vehicles for pleasure. One might object to the way Chabon drops all literary "encounters" into an ever-widening basket of entertainment and neglects other goals writers might have: disturbing or upsetting readers, increasing their understanding, critiquing social conditions and calling them to arms on behalf of a cause, seeking to transfigure extant forms of narrative, imagining alternative realities, and many other possibilities.[73] But while he neglects writerly agendas and readerly experiences that are not primarily oriented toward pleasure, there's surely merit to Chabon's insistence that many kinds of reading may yield it and that there are various, polymorphous pleasures of the text.

We might conclude that reading experiences are as varied as texts or readers' routes through those texts and that there are infinite permutations to be had in reading: different combinations of pleasure and exertion, reason and rest, gems of useful knowledge and endless useless arcana about fictional universes, spurs to action in the real world and escapist flights of fancy from living under and even just thinking about such oppressive conditions, the satisfactions of a suspenseful journey to a logical ending, wondrous surprises in narrative innovation, and the delights of aimless wandering. Genre-bending writers have demonstrated their attunement to these permutations of reading experience and to the pleasure of permutation itself, the endless possibilities of varying a given structure—which is to say they have gravitated to the dialectical nature of genre itself. In the culminating instance of self-reflexive moments in Byatt's *Possession*, her narrator reflects that writers may "remake ... for a reader, the primary pleasures of eating, or drinking, or looking on, or sex." But they "do not habitually elaborate on the equally intense pleasure of reading," due to

> the regressive nature of the pleasure ... where words draw attention to the power and delight of words, and so *ad infinitum*, thus making the imagination experience something papery and dry ... without the immediacy of sexual moisture or the scented garnet glow of good burgundy. (510–511)

Byatt points to the way reminders that we're reading a text, like the surfeit of self-reflexivity in postmodernist novels, impede the reader's experience of immersion in a sensuous fictional world. But she violates the principle here.

As we have seen, genre-bending literary writers often *do* self-reflexively ponder the pleasures of reading—suggesting that while they extol immersion, their reflection on the nature of immersive literary experience may obstruct their ability to deliver it. The pursuit of these conflicting agendas is a risk that accompanies a more expansive view of heterodox literary pleasures and affordances. Though Byatt here couches "the pleasure of reading" as singular, she promptly reflects on the multiplicity of ways of reading even the same text and the many pleasures to be found there:

> There are readings—of the same text—that are dutiful, readings that map and dissect, readings that hear a rustling of unheard sounds, that count grey little pronouns for pleasure or instruction.... There are personal readings, which snatch for personal meanings, I am full of love, or disgust, or fear, I scan for love, or disgust, or fear. There are—believe it—impersonal readings—where the mind's eye sees the lines move onwards and the mind's ear hears them sing and sing.
>
> Now and then there are readings that make the hairs on the neck... stand on end ... readings when the knowledge that we *shall know* the writing differently or better or satisfactorily, runs ahead of any capacity to say what we know or how. (511–512)

There is much to unpack in this passage, including Byatt's uncanny anticipation of methods of quantitative literary study often caricatured as counting pronouns.[74] *Possession* pivots on a quest for knowledge, but at the novel's end, it stresses the experiential and sensory aspects of reading, the music of "unheard sounds," the upsurge of gooseflesh, alongside its ability to yield a meaning the reader can extract or articulate.

In addition to reflecting on many modes of reading and the varied pleasures to be derived from them, *Possession* shows a heightened attunement to the possibilities of combination and permutation: to the way genre frameworks enable the remixing of familiar elements and a narrative structure to be repeated with manifold variations. Here we might think of other recent experiments of narrative permutation *within* the same novel, such as Kate Atkinson's *Life After Life* (2013) and Jenny Erpenbeck's *The End of Days* (trans. 2016).[75] In addition to reflecting on tales that cross the threshold between worlds, *Possession*'s Brittany section lingers on the tales told by Christabel's cousin Raoul, a folklorist who delights in retelling the story of Merlin and Vivien. While the constitutive elements of the narrative remain constant ("the end is always the same. So is the essence of the tale"), Sabine declares that her father, "within this framework, has many stories" (383). Christabel similarly observes that "all old stories ... will bear telling and telling again in different ways. What is required is to keep alive, to polish, the simple clean forms of the tale which *must* be there.... And yet to add something of yours, of the writer, which makes all of these things seem new and first seen" (379). Here, Byatt's characters discuss the perpetual malleability of longstanding oral narrative traditions, like the medieval Matter of Britain, Arthurian tales, and *chansons de geste*. But her reflections speak eloquently to genre, as well. For what is a genre but "many stories" built on an extant "framework"—a set of "simple clean forms" to which one may continually "add something" of one's own?

The Blind Assassin even more explicitly reflects on the way working with genre entails adopting a framework that sets certain limits but paradoxically allows a near-infinite set of permutations within them. In Laura's novella, the unnamed pulp writer begins the seduction of his lover by asking her, like a waiter, to choose the kind of story she'd like from a menu of genres. "What will it be, then? ... Dinner jackets and romance, or shipwrecks on a barren coast? You can have your pick: jungles, tropical islands, mountains. Or another dimension of space—that's what I'm best at" (9). Though Atwood gently pokes fun at popular genre conventions, she expounds on how choosing a genre opens certain narrative avenues while foreclosing others. In another tribute to the potentiality of fictional worlds, the leftist insists that "another dimension of space" is an especially "useful address" because "anything you like can happen there" (9). But the woman asks for a desert setting. "Not much scope with deserts. Not many features." But this limitation can be creatively overcome by digging into ostensibly barren narrative ground and stirring in other genres—gothic, SF, and soft pornographic tropes: ". . . unless you add some tombs. Then you could have a pack of nude women who've been dead for three thousand years, with lithe, curvaceous figures, ruby-red lips, azure hair in a foam of tumbled curls, and eyes like snake-filled pits" (9). Despite the man's self-deprecating offer of "lurid" embellishments, tropes designed "for the huddled masses," the woman is delighted and requests helpings of each. She'll have "another dimension of space, and also the tombs and the dead women" (9), please. Though the pulp writer calls this "a tall order," he offers to "throw in some sacrificial virgins" and "a pack of ravening wolves" (9), at no extra charge—all of which turn up in the Zycron narrative that he unfolds during their assignations.

In this witty scene, Atwood again nods at the commercial history of popular genres. The woman selects her order from a menu, and the writer aims to please. At the same time, Atwood propounds a miniature theory of how the apparent limits of generic frameworks may be overcome by the dexterous world-builder, who engineers new combinations and permutations in even the most desolate narrative terrain. The genre-bending writers of the past several decades have exhibited just such dexterity, reforming and deforming extant genres to offer new permutations and narrative wrinkles and provide varied reading pleasures—prominent among them the pleasure of immersion in fictional worlds.

# The Novel of the Global Generic

> It didn't feel like I was in China. It didn't feel like I was anywhere.[1]
> LING MA, *Severance* (2018)

IN LING MA'S *SEVERANCE*, protagonist Candace Chen works for Spectra, a logistics company that helps U.S. publishers subcontract with printers in China. Though the novel unfolds into a postapocalyptic scenario, in which most of the planet's population is wiped out by a pandemic—*à la* Margaret Atwood's *MaddAddam* trilogy and Emily St. John Mandel's *Station Eleven*, and uncannily anticipating COVID-19—it flashes back throughout to realist depictions of Candace's workplace and life in New York City before the Shen Fever strikes. More than a send-up of the mind-numbing routines of white-collar labor that we see in workplace satires like Mike Judge's *Office Space* (1999), Joshua Ferris's *Then We Came to the End* (2006), and the (unrelated) Apple TV sci-fi drama *Severance* (2022), Ma's novel broadens its scope to examine Candace's complicity with exploitative global labor practices. Spectra has "huge collective buying power," which allows it to "drive foreign labor costs down even further" (12).

Candace coordinates the printing of Bibles, which more than "any book," Ma cannily observes, "embodies the purest form of product packaging, the same content repackaged a million times over, in new combinations ad infinitum" (23). Candace oversees the production of a "Gemstone Bible," which is "marketed toward preteen girls" and comes "with a keepsake semiprecious gemstone on a sterling alloy chain," and discovers it has been causing "various forms of lung diseases" in the Chinese laborers who grind and polish the stones, working as they do "in rooms without ventilation systems" (23–24). Here, the Bible resembles the most formulaic of genre fiction—"the same content repackaged a million times over in new combinations"—and anxiety about repetitive literary production fuses with the knowledge that books are like any other commodities, produced and circulated according to the profit imperatives and exploitative manufacturing regimes of global capitalism.[2]

Candace recognizes her complicity in perpetuating this oppressive system, admitting "I was a part of this," while at the same time resorting, not once but three times, to a hollow justification that resounds with echoes of Nazi Germany and the Vietnam War: "I was just doing my job" (85, 151, 235). Ma shows us Candace's unsuccessful repression of the psychic toll of working for companies that accept the poisoning of Chinese workers as the cost of doing business and her failed efforts to self-medicate with artistic pursuits and the consumption of luxury goods. "Me, nothing really weighed on me, nothing unique," she offers—the double caveats signaling that her job does indeed take a toll, along with her sense that she's hardly special in her guilt (11). Ma points to a second-order problem for people like Candace—most of us, that is—whose paycheck is tied up in a violently exploitative and unequal system: she feels late capitalist guilt, but knows that her guilt is commonplace, generic even. Her attempted remedies are shadowed by the awareness that they are not unique either. She "fiddles around with some photography when the moon hit the Gowanus right . . . *the usual ways* of justifying your life, of passing time. With the money I made, I bought Shiseido facial exfoliants, Blue Bottle coffee, Uniqlo cashmere" (11, emphasis added). This is not just the knowing irony of postmodern hipsters recognizing their own triteness and the relative pettiness of their first-world problems. For Ma, like many genre-bending contemporary writers, the problem with global capitalist postmodernity is the problem of the generic: the reproduction and standardization of products, people, places, and reprehensible business practices. And the second-order problem is the realization that literature, though it might critique such practices, is also "a part of this." Here, as we saw in Chapter 3, one thing that makes genre-bending literary fiction *literary* is its self-conscious meditation on that category and on art more broadly, and whether and how they might escape repetitive regimes of popular and consumer culture.

Just as Ma stresses how Candace's complicity and its unsatisfying compensations are unoriginal, *Severance* rehearses familiar anxieties about globalization's tendency to erase local particularity with Westernized sameness. When Candace takes a business trip, she stays at a palatial hotel that bears no signs "that it is located anywhere remotely in Shenzhen, let alone in China" (78). On the hotel grounds, she experiences the strangeness of their detachment from sense of place, thinking, it "didn't feel like I was anywhere" (80). This feeling of dislocation combines with Candace's recognition of her indistinguishability from other business travelers: "they too were all here on manufacturing-related business. . . . They were doing what we were doing" (82). This sense of sameness pervades *Severance*. Though Candace's photoblog *NY Ghost* offers refuge from her job and the devastating pandemic, she views her own artistic practice as derivative,

> clichéd and trope-y . . . basically, variation of the same preexisting New York iconography that permeates calendars, rom-coms, souvenirs, stock art. They could have been hung in any business hotel room. Even the better, more artfully composed images were just Eggleston knockoffs, Stephen Shore derivatives. (14)

Just as the Bibles Candace produces are the same book superficially repackaged, Candace's photography is imitative, revealing anxieties that strike at the heart of literary fiction: What if its products are also knockoffs? What's more, they're produced and circulated by unscrupulous multinationals, part of the same exploitative global system. Ironically, Ma's depiction of the ubiquity of stock NYC images from kitsch and "rom-coms" repeats motifs and concerns from Whitehead's *Zone One*: both novels feature a devastating plague that kills most but leaves others trapped in the mindless routines of their prior lives. *Severance* thus foregrounds a cluster of concerns about neoliberal postmodernity and literature's role within it: global cultural homogenization and the erasure of local particularity; the reduction of places to hackneyed consumable images; the lack of escape for individuals, whose predicaments of guilty complicity or opposition are themselves clichéd; and that art and literature might also be derivative and fatally compromised, mere commodities produced through exploitative global labor.

The notion that literary fiction is just another commodity, a genre that is in essence a market category designed to appeal to an educated, up-market audience, has emerged as a prominent argument in recent literary scholarship.[3] This book has contended that while contemporary literary fiction certainly is a marketable good, it simultaneously insists on its distinction from other repetitively produced commodities, from popular genre fiction, and that it remains recognizably distinct in its institutional location, non-market values, and formal tendencies. As I argue in Chapters 2 and 3, significant markers of literary fiction's effort to differentiate itself lie in its commitment to stylistic and formal innovation and its self-reflexivity about literariness and literary values, which seek to mark it off from repetitive commodity production. I show that writers like Whitehead have expressed a perennial fear about popular culture—that its assembly-line production methods might create mindless consumerist zombies—even as they adopt the genres that have flourished in popular culture.

This chapter argues that in addition to articulating literary values, a significant if less-obvious driver of genre-bending literary fiction has been, as in *Severance*, literary writers' attempt to register contemporary anxieties about global capitalism's production of *genericness*, particularly places and products that become repetitive and standardized, as well as whether literature might escape this production of sameness if not its commodity character. This book has argued that multiple, seemingly contradictory impulses motivate genre-bending literary fiction, such as the desire to provide the pleasures of genre fiction while maintaining literary fiction's distinct values and their formal correlates. These writers take pains to differentiate their literary and innovative uses of genre from what they portray as the repetitive incarnations that dominate genre fiction fields. This chapter argues that genre benders also offer an internally conflicted account of globalization's production of genericness. Even within the same novel, we see writers critique the way late capitalism has rendered people, places, and media generic—erasing their particularity and inundating them in a global media surround made of popular genre franchises—at the same time as they recognize the ways their own deployments of popular genres enable their global circulation and salability. These writers acknowledge this predicament of complicit critique; they acknowledge they are "a part of this," their books produced and circulated by multinational corporations and bound up in capitalism's exploitation and inequality.[4] At the same time, they aim to conserve values—like innovative, meaningful art and uniqueness of place—that they portray as being trampled in that marketplace.

After recounting how fears about standardization of place and culture, including the production and circulation of genre fiction, film, and games, have long accompanied neoliberal globalization, I pose David Mitchell's *Number9Dream* (2001) and Haruki Murakami's *1Q84* (trans. 2011) as paradigmatic examples of the global genre-bending novel. These examples demonstrate the way some of the most prominent and far-reaching contemporary novelists engage the problem of *the global generic*—while also availing themselves of genre's portability, adaptability, and thus marketability. I term these "global genre-bending novels" because they focus attention on generic sites in globalized metropolises, and their works are published by multinationals, translated, and circulated in many nations; the term denotes their global settings as well as the modes of production, circulation, and reception they both depict and participate in. Further, Mitchell and Murakami situate their characters in places that have become recognizable types and in storylines that are overtly and self-consciously rooted in popular genres.

While cities across the world undoubtedly retain distinguishing characteristics and vary in the extent of their late capitalist development, these novels eschew the representation of locational particularity.[5] Instead, *Number 9Dream* and *1Q84*, both of which are set primarily in Tokyo, a location they depict as a consummate site of globalization, represent sites that are increasingly delocalized, similar to sites in postindustrial cities around the world, and saturated with and structured by a global media surround. Mitchell and Murakami take pains to depict the unmooring of subjective experience, the interlayering of reality with fiction, of sense perception with the mediation of prior representations, representing a Tokyo that is image-laden and suggesting the irrevocability of an "actual" Tokyo from its many representations.

Number9Dream and *1Q84* reinforce their depiction of characters' experience of generic spaces by utilizing forms that are shaped by the spread of global media: the genre frameworks of SF, fantasy, and hard-boiled detective novels, and of mafia, disaster, and spy films. Mitchell and Murakami self-consciously deploy popular genres—forms that are recognizable and portable, able to be overlaid onto many settings—though, like all genre benders, they endeavor to transform these genres, blend them in unpredictable configurations, and apply them to fresh concerns. And Mitchell and Murakami cite an extensive range of mostly Western cultural references. These novels thus position themselves for circulation in a global flow of cultural goods. Murakami and Mitchell do not think they might escape this flow—if anything they seem to revel in it—but this playfulness, combined with their anxiety about the homogenizing of space, culture, and persons, shows how global genre-bending literary fiction maintains a deeply ambivalent, even contradictory, position toward the global processes than enable their marketplace success.

Globalization and the Generic

Though the last several decades have seen many and varied accounts of globalization, along with critiques of the concept and its ongoing relevance, including the rise of the "glocal" and renewed anti-globalism and ethnonationalism, anxiety about cultural homogenization has featured centrally in many accounts of its processes and consequences.[6] These have often stressed the intertwining of the expansion of U.S. economic interests with cultural imperialism in the form of American popular culture. Fredric Jameson argues that in accounting for globalization, "ambiguities" surrounding the subject require "talking as much about fantasies and anxieties as about the thing itself."[7] Prominent among these is the fear that U.S. economic and cultural expansion might result in a homogenized global culture:

> The standardization of world culture, with local popular or traditional forms driven out or dumbed down to make way for American television, American music, food, clothes and films, has been seen by many as the very heart of globalization. And this fear that US models are replacing everything else now spills over from the sphere of culture into . . . [economic and social] categories: for this process is clearly, at one level, the result of economic domination—of local cultural industries closed down by American rivals. At a deeper level, the anxiety becomes a social one, of which the cultural is merely a symptom: the fear, in other words, that specifically ethno-national ways of life will themselves be destroyed.[8]

From the outset of debates about globalization, critics have warned that these fears might be overblown, that they neglect the persistence of local heterogeneity, and advocated for rival concepts like "glocalization" and "hybridity." But anxieties about standardization have continued to be registered in cultural criticism and literature alike.[9] Critics have often pointed to the way artistic and media trends reflect a globalizing of markets that threatens to obscure local particularity. For example, in Miwon Kwon's critical genealogy of site-specific art movements, she links the progressive disconnection of site-specific art from physical location as "symptomatic of the dynamics of deterritorialization" and the "spatial undifferentiation and departicularization" characteristic of globalization.[10]

Commentators have recognized the prominent role genre plays in such standardization and the threat of U.S. cultural imperialism. The export of Hollywood franchises has meant that superhero and spy films, crime fictions and westerns, are globally recognizable forms. Genres as a result can appear as both hegemonic—the imposition of U.S. cultural products and their conventions onto disparate locales—and as an opportunity for critical renovation by local producers, who might graft parochial concerns and formal innovations onto globally circulated frameworks and upend audience expectations. To take a prominent recent example, scholars have noted how Bong Joon-ho's films "resituate familiar Hollywood genre staples into specifically Korean settings" to demonstrate the effect of the global propagation of genre tropes "on smaller nations, which grapple with the possibility of development and the desire to hold onto their identities."[11] The movies that result are "a peculiar hybrid" that avail themselves of the recognizability and commercial potential of popular genres, while critiquing "Hollywood's global dominance."[12] In literary production, Sheri-Marie Harrison has argued that "the reach for speculative forms in the present uproots and combines" practices that were once "historically- and geopolitically-situated," in a new "manner that reflects the global circulation of texts and people."[13] Genre's combination of familiarity and flexibility enables forms to travel as producers adapt them to new and particular cultural contexts.

The multinational media conglomerates who control much of the publishing industry today share a great deal with Hollywood in terms of global reach and reliance on genre to make books accessible to far-flung audiences. Rebecca Walkowitz has shown how works of contemporary literature bear the marks of their production for a global marketplace—the fact that they have been designed to circulate in countries and languages outside those from which they originated. "Translation is not secondary or incidental to these works. It is a condition of their production."[14] These novels possess formal characteristics that anticipate their distribution across global literary markets. Not surprisingly, such fictions frequently draw on genre tropes that are recognizable across contexts, due to the global circulation of U.S. popular culture, and often reflect on the conditions of their own production and circulation. Walkowitz shows that "translation" can be extended from a literal, linguistic process to a way of understanding Murakami's "liberal use of generic devices, historical references, and even words culled from Anglophone popular culture," to produce a corpus that "reflects on the translated sources of contemporary Japan and generates works that can appeal to multiple audiences, who recognize both theme and terminology."[15] Global fictions, that is, often use popular genre conventions to appeal across local and national boundaries and also to reflect on the hybrid, transnational character of contemporary culture. Below, I show how *Number9Dream* and *1Q84* depict sites in Tokyo that are saturated with global media—as characters continually encounter large-scale advertisements, images on screens, music piped into buildings—and a thoroughly de-realized urban space that is self-consciously a fictional site: a creation of prior texts in the collective imagination. As real places like Tokyo become overlaid with histories of globally circulated representations and filled with a global-media soundtrack, Mitchell and Murakami envision the way spaces increasingly lose particularity and become generic types.

While this chapter focuses on these two exemplary cases, the threat of standardization of place and the global circulation of genre tropes preoccupies other, seemingly disparate, genre-bending contemporary fictions as well. In Chabon's *Telegraph Avenue*, the novel's two main plots follow Nat Jaffe and Archy Stallings, whose used vinyl store, Brokeland Records, is threatened by the construction of a music and movie megastore, and their wives Gwen Shanks and Aviva Roth-Jaffe, whose small midwifery business runs afoul of a healthcare management conglomerate. In both plots, Chabon's characters are old-school holdouts, desperately seeking "to defend their polder against the capitalist flood tides of consumerist uniformity.[16] Throughout, the novel's metaphors align the onslaught of global market logic with one of the more destructive effects of its extractive practices: sea-level rise due to climate change. Nat and Archy cling to their store as if it were "the last palm tree on the last little atoll in the path of the great wave of late-modern capitalism" (108). The heroes of *Telegraph Avenue* are guardians of non-market values—the record store as cultural institution and meeting place, and midwifery's ethic of care—while the neoliberal profit motive and global cultural homogeneity are its villains.

In a moment that is more noticeable for teasing the reader with the novel's central conceit of magical doors that ferry people across the globe, Mohsin Hamid's *Exit West* (2017) transports readers to "the Tokyo district of Shinjuku."[17] There we encounter a shady character, who seems intent on harming the young women who have just arrived through the mysterious portal—suggesting a human trafficker. Hamid obliquely suggests the man's tastes and nefarious career were inspired by his consumption of Western media. "His whiskey came from Ireland, a place he had never been to but evinced a mild fondness for . . . perhaps because of an Irish gangster film he had gone to see repeatedly in his still-impressionable youth" (29). Just as the magical doors in Hamid's novel are an obvious figure for the migration of people across borders, the novel is also concerned with how goods, images, and genre clichés travel via media and trade.

As I show in Chapter 3, Whitehead's *Zone One* is consumed with worry that popular culture might turn us into imitative, zombified consumers. Throughout, Whitehead's diction emphasizes the category, the type, the generic nature of the retail and living spaces of late capitalism and the consumer and cultural products people devour: "the local megamall's discount appliance emporium"; "the 24-7 gas-and-cigarette vendor"; "that juggernaut clothing empire"; "the desolate consumer-electronics showroom"; and, most ubiquitous, "[t]he coffee company" that started "with a single café . . . and metastasized into an international franchise entity."[18] The novel never specifies proper names of these cancer-like franchises because we know the ones Whitehead means—"*that* juggernaut clothing empire"—but also because there is no longer a difference between the type and the particular. As we have seen, the bland protagonist of his *Apex Hides the Hurt* relishes the sameness of the coffee chain that you can find "no matter what time zone you happened to be in," and Whitehead repeatedly points to the genericness of contemporary retail shops.[19] That novel's nameless hero discovers everywhere "representatives of that contemporary brand of establishment, the kind that dressed itself in rustic sincerity but adhered to the rapacious philosophy of the multinational. They were easily spotted despite their camouflage" (39). Chain stores that hide behind a "homey" veneer are themselves a genre in Whitehead's handling (39), a "kind," a "contemporary brand of establishment," that hides corporate rapaciousness beneath hackneyed, shallow performances of spurious folk authenticity. These novels point to the way far-flung locales are dominated by the global circulation of popular genre fare and global retailers' increasingly generic storefronts.

Literary history is filled of course with the opposite movement, with efforts to render the particularity of the local. Nirvana Tanoukhi eloquently defines the ongoing process of "innovative specification," arguing that "literary history . . . is the story of how places are specified, how depictions of particular places are made." But she also emphasizes how those depictions, once widely circulated, can threaten to harden "into commonplaces." Writers' efforts to specify the particularity of a place can become so prominent that the specific is understood as widely representative, and thus becomes a stereotype.[20] Tanoukhi warns that the threat that representations of the particular will ossify into the generalized type is particularly acute for the "peripheral writer," whose representations, especially when widely imitated, become understood as "the authentic" rendering of a group of people or a place.[21]

While many writers from "peripheral" locations of the global south and elsewhere remain dedicated to specifying places in granular detail, the novels of Mitchell and Murakami that I take up here focus their attention on sites that are already recognizable as types. These writers arrange layers of intertextual references to show how the Tokyo they depict has been produced by the hardening of highly visible, reiterated representations—just as Ma's and Whitehead's New York has become indistinguishable from "iconography that permeates calendars, rom-coms, souvenirs, [and] stock art." Complicating matters further, their novels depict sites that "really" are generic: the experience of sites like megamalls, apartment buildings, and gleaming office towers that have been rendered into cookie-cutter shapes by the economic forces of neoliberal capitalism. The referential and non-referential aspects of these novels converge, as Mitchell and Murakami depict the homogenization of sites into globally recognizable types, and the way subjects' experience of space is thoroughly mediated by the circulation of prior images, within a fictional world that is highly de-realized—self-consciously the stuff of genre fiction and film.

In the remainder of this chapter, I turn to Mitchell's *Number9Dream* and Murakami's *1Q84* to demonstrate how these writers, consummate examples of contemporary novelists who produce for the global literary marketplace, register the "spatial undifferentiation and departicularization" characteristic of globalization, by constructing narratives situated in sites that could be found in almost any postindustrial urban space. Mitchell and Murakami show how nominally Japanese spaces are saturated by globalized media—music, advertisements, video—and homogenizing commercial interests. What's more, the media that suffuses the air their characters breathe bleed into the form of each novel, as each self-consciously adopts forms of genre fiction and lets loose a torrent of popular and high cultural allusions. The sites of these novels are cites, and "generic" names both the homogenized sites of globalization and the literary forms that can be overlaid onto any setting and circulate freely in a global literary market.

In their range of intertextual allusions, and in their overt appropriation of genre fiction tropes, both novels produce elaborate, multi-genre plots that take place less in Tokyo than in the textual space of prior fictions. By depicting a Tokyo that is patently fictional and flooded with media, Murakami and Mitchell specify Tokyo as a mobile site that has been produced intertextually. Murakami has long been criticized by Japanese readers for producing representations of a stylized, cosmopolitan Japan that seems decidedly un-Japanese, for the consumption of Western audiences.[22] And it is easy to see how Mitchell could be accused, in a similar manner, of inauthentically representing a country that is not his own (though he lived in Hiroshima for eight years).

But questions of authenticity are largely beside the point, as both novels self-consciously produce a fantastic Tokyo that is grounded, not in reality, but in prior representations. As Baryon Tensor Posadas writes, *Number9Dream* "is less about any actual Japan and more a self-referential narrative . . . about the impossibility of an authentic and original experience of 'Japan' outside of its global traffic as an image-commodity."[23] Similarly, *1Q84* takes place in a patently fictional Tokyo, in which "the boundary between the real world and the imaginary one has grown obscure. There are two moons in the sky now. These, too, were brought over from the world of fiction."[24] In producing a Tokyo that has been invaded by a fantasy novel, indeed that has become the world of that novel, Murakami points to the way our fictions bleed into and shape our understandings of "reality." I conclude by showing how Murakami and Mitchell figure their enviable position in the global marketplace, as immensely popular and highly regarded writers. Both novelists, that is, gesture toward their ability to combine the formal experiment, stylistic brio, and weighty thematics of literary fiction with the compulsive, immersive, transporting and translatable pleasures of genre fiction. The critical and popular success of Mitchell and Murakami demonstrates how their novelistic specifications of global sites as simultaneously homogenized and mobile are thoroughly embedded in the same global flow of media and circulation of cultural goods they depict.[25]

Generic Sites, Ambient Media, and Popular Genres

"The taxi's radio was tuned to a classical FM broadcast. Janáček's *Sinfonietta*—probably not the ideal music to hear in a taxi caught in traffic" (3). So begins *1Q84*. The reader soon learns that Aomame, one of the novel's co-protagonists, sits "in a hushed Toyota Crown Royal Saloon on the gridlocked elevated Metropolitan Expressway in Tokyo" (6). Though Murakami, for the moment, locates the novel firmly in a realistic Tokyo and at times references particulars of its urban geography, this opening scans like a citation to his own work—exceedingly similar to the first scene of his *The Wind-Up Bird Chronicle* (trans. 1997), which begins with Toru Okada boiling spaghetti and listening to the overture to Rossini's *The Thieving Magpie* on FM radio—and much of what follows takes place in settings that are common in any late-capitalist city.[26] Huge stretches of *1Q84* are set in generic apartments, hotel and hospital rooms, a seat atop a slide on a neighborhood playground. The opening is set in a Crown, a line Toyota only sells in Japan, so this detail particularizes, but Murakami constructs the episode around the generic site of "taxi caught in highway gridlock," which bears conspicuous marks of globalized space.

Aomame escapes the mundane burden of traffic by taking the driver's advice, exiting the taxi to descend a mysterious emergency staircase that leads her to a subway station so she can arrive on time for her urgent appointment. Above the staircase looms "a big billboard advertising Esso gasoline with a smiling tiger holding a gas hose" (11). As Aomame exits the car, she grabs her Ray-Bans. Walking along the highway, her "Charles Jourdan heels clicked against the road's surface" (12). When she climbs over the guardrail, from the window of a Toyota Celica, "Michael Jackson's high-pitched voice provided her with background music. 'Billie Jean' was playing" (14). Czech symphonies; American oil companies, sunglasses, and popular music; French shoes; Japanese cars. *1Q84* opens with a Western soundtrack and the marks of global capitalism dot the landscape. The novel goes on, in typical Murakami fashion, to allude to a host of other musical and literary sources, from Vivaldi, the Rolling Stones, Louis Armstrong, Jeff Beck, and Grand Funk Railroad, to Chekhov, Tolstoy, Kafka, Proust, *The Great Gatsby*, *Out of Africa*, and *Macbeth*. These latter references emerge as one prominent feature of *1Q84*'s literariness. The setting of the novel becomes further layered when we notice that the opening scene seems a more-than-faint echo of the scene in Fellini's *8½* in which Guido climbs out of his car in a traffic jam and flies away over awestruck drivers, especially when Aomame descends the stairs into a world with two moons, a world that has been invaded by the fantastic. *1Q84* assimilates and transforms both particular works and popular genres and increasingly becomes a self-reflexive piece of meta-genre fiction, in which Aomame and co-protagonist Tengo become aware that their world has taken on the characteristics of the fantasy novel he has co-authored.

At one level, then, *1Q84* takes place in Tokyo, a Tokyo in which the phenomenological experience of place is dominated by audiovisual marks of the globalized flow of cultural products and consumer goods. At another level, the ground of the novel is textual and intertextual. This sprawling, intricate book resists efficient summary as it interweaves a host of plots and genres, often self-consciously. Aomame exits the everyday world of traffic, and first enters not fantasy but thriller, as we discover that she has an appointment to assassinate an Armani suit–wearing, Jaguar-driving oil company executive, who beats his wife with a golf club. In addition to using a feminist vigilante frame, like *The Girl with the Dragon Tattoo* (2005), *1Q84* blends existential detective fiction with star-crossed metaphysical romance, chase thriller, in which the pursuing villains are the henchmen of a child-raping cult (which seems to echo a similar one in Mitchell's *A Thousand Autumns of Jacob de Zoet* [2010]), and a tale of literary publishing intrigue with a self-reflexive magical-realist fantasy.

On many occasions the novel nods at its own use of genre tropes. When Tengo's editor Komatsu tells him he has been abducted by cult members, he says: "That's right. A real kidnapping. Like in that old movie, *The Collector*" (651). The "real" world and events in *1Q84* are the stuff of genre and increasingly its characters come to realize that their world has become infiltrated and determined by fiction. Though the cab driver warns Aomame, "There's always only one reality," repeating himself with a heavy metafictional hand, "as if underlining an important passage in a book" (11), she comes to realize this is not exactly true. Literalizing the processes of immersion in a fictional world that I examined in the previous chapter, "Tengo's storytelling ability" has "transported" Aomame "into this other world of 1Q84" (585), a parallel track to the year 1984 that contains two moons and fantastic Little People, who weave strange chrysalises out of air. "To sane people," she thinks "these things would seem like nothing more than the kinds of fabrications that appear in fiction, no more real than the Queen of Hearts or the white rabbit with the watch in *Alice in Wonderland*" (681).

Aomame enters this "other world" of fictional artifice via the rabbit hole of the expressway staircase, and Tengo arrives there through a combination of artistic collaboration and magical sexual intercourse with Eriko Fukada, with whom he has co-authored the fantasy novel *Air Chrysalis*. Tengo comes to discover that "every detail he had put into writing had now become a reality" (734) and eventually finds that "he could no longer distinguish the real world from the fictional" (776). A fiction, in which "real" events are the stuff of Steve McQueen films, and in which Tengo's novel shapes the "real world," *1Q84* literalizes Jean Baudrillard's "precession of simulacra," as the fictional precedes and dictates the shape of the real.[27] The layered sites of *1Q84* are thus at the same time generic spaces in a globalized Tokyo, other fictional texts, and the novel's fiction-within-the-fiction. But the novel's play with its own fictionality and its characters' ontological uncertainty signify more than the winking self-reflexivity of a ludic postmodernism; they convey the way our texts produce our sense of reality, the experience of subjects awash in a global flow of media and unmoored from a stable sense of place.[28]

Mitchell's *Number9Dream*, set several decades later, brims even fuller with a surfeit of surrounding media, and its sites are even more radically homogenized. If the world in which the novel's characters move is ultimately more realistic than that of *1Q84*, the form of *Number9Dream* even more glaringly places its characters in a succession of plots that—as with Mitchell's oeuvre more generally—borrow liberally from literary and popular genres. Mitchell keeps readers guessing repeatedly as to whether disaster sequences and surreal vignettes are "actually" happening in the novel or are irruptions of its narrator protagonist's media-saturated imagination. *Number9Dream* begins as a bildungsroman, updating the genre for a globalized world. Mitchell's protagonist

Eiji Miyake leaves his tiny village for Tokyo, on a quest to find his father, and finds a metropolis that is huge but not entirely disorienting. Steeped in film, pop music, and video games, Miyake arrives already armed with a knowing, cynical wit. The novel's opening scene begins in two generic places characteristic of the globalized city, as Miyake sits in the Jupiter Café outside the PanOpticon, an ominously named "zirconium gothic skyscraper."[29]

Gazing out the windows of the café, Miyake observes this postmodern architectural mash-up and the fluid motion of Tokyo, which blurs the boundaries of humans, nature, and digital information: "City office drones, lip-pierced hairdressers, midday drunks. Nobody is standing still. Rivers, snowstorms, traffic, bytes, generations, a thousand faces per minute. Back on Yakushima you might get a thousand minutes per face" (4). The café's soundtrack is a "Muzak version of 'Imagine'," and Miyake drolly comments: "John Lennon wakes up in his tomb, appalled" (6).

It's not a coincidence that Mitchell's novel is named after a Lennon song and that Murakami is famous for a novel called *Norwegian Wood* (1987); the Beatles serve both authors as emblems of the global spread of Anglo-American media. Though John and Yoko are Miyake's favorites, Mitchell immerses him in stream of popular and high cultural references. Miyake's sister loved *The Wizard of Oz* (388). His girlfriend Ai is a pianist who adores Debussy, Scarlatti, and Bach. Miyake lives above a video store, and throughout *Number9Dream*, TV screens stream in the background *Die Hard* (71), *Titanic* (77), and *Blade Runner* (276). Miyake reads too: "detective stories by Kogoro Akechi," a "novel by Philip K. Dick" (221), and a "Haruki Murakami novel" about "a man stuck down a dry well with no rope" (186). Mitchell positions Murakami's *Wind-Up Bird Chronicle* alongside these other prominent cultural goods and thus anticipates his own novels' circulation in the global flow of media.

Such pre-texts structure Miyake's perception of the world. He describes his friend Suga's "[l]ong dangly E.T. arms" (58). The moonlight looks "bright as a UFO abduction" (60), and a "dying, SF-movie sun sits on a WARNER CINEMA multiplex" (144). After a typhoon, Miyake thinks: "The peaceful Japanese garden I remember is now a demonic-possession movie" (388). Even when a space begins as recognizably Japanese in *Number9Dream*, it is quickly overlaid with the stuff of popular media. This genre-structured worldview is not particular to Miyake; when he tells Ai of his hitchhiking misadventures, she quips: "Sounds like you're stuck in a Nikkatsu trucker film" (365). Mitchell links the blurring of reality and genre fiction/film with a surfeit of media, and with the de-realized life of the contemporary globalized metropolis. In a video arcade, Miyake thinks of "people like my mother paying counselors and clinics to reattach them to reality" while "all of us people here paying Sony and Sega to reattach us to unreality" (101). Postmodernity offers escape into generic fictional worlds as a potentially de-realizing remedy for the disorientation of urban life. When Miyake visits his mother in a psychiatric facility, her doctor opines: "In the cities we Japanese force ourselves to live in, the question should not be 'Why do so many of us suffer from mental illness?' but 'Why do any of us not suffer from mental illness?'" (377–378).

Mitchell also correlates Miyake's apperception of reality through prior mediation with the precarious labor conditions of neoliberalism, as his protagonist joins the ranks of "probationary stop gap employees recruited in the middle of the year" (153). *Number9Dream* also uses filmic metaphor to suggest that the media-saturated "reality" of Tokyo offers a performance of normalcy that conceals its shadowy workings of power: "You straight citizens of Japan are living in a movie set, Miyake. You are unpaid extras. The politicos are the actors. But the true directors, the [Yakuza bosses] Nagasakis and Tsurus—you never see" (160). Though Miyake seems sane enough, at times his cinematic imaginings overwhelm the fiction, and the reader cannot immediately differentiate fantasy or mafia noir from (the fiction's) reality.

Miyake plays amateur sleuth in ways that overtly point to his, and the novel's, imitation of prior genre tropes. A few pages into the novel, he poses as an exotic fish specialist to enter the PanOpticon and obtain information about his estranged father from the latter's lawyer, a Ms. Kato. Miyake confronts her with a canned speech out of an action movie: "We are both busy people, so why not cut the small talk?" Kato responds by asking Miyake if he's sure he isn't Luke Skywalker and if he stole the foregoing lines from a movie. Kato continues to suggest that Miyake must think he's in a film, intoning in movie-preview voice: "One island boy embarks on a perilous mission to discover the father he has never met" (11). Only after Miyake blasts Kato with a tranquilizer, finds out she is a "bioborg" replicant, knocks her unconscious, and escapes the PanOpticon before a fiery explosion, do we realize that Miyake has been absorbed in a cinematic daydream, while sitting in the Jupiter Café the whole time.

Such flights of genre-laden fancy recur throughout the novel. The first few provoke the reader's ontological uncertainty, and they continue to prompt temporary wonderings of what is "actually" happening, as: a flood drowns Tokyo and Miyake wrestles a crocodile to the tune of "Lucy in the Sky with Diamonds" (21); Miyake follows Kato down "an alley that could be from a gangster movie" (27), into the Ganymede Cinema, which is screening a surrealist film called *PanOpticon*, about a Hannibal Lecter–like mental patient who thinks he is god; Miyake, armed with a plasma bazooka, chases mobsters who have kidnapped his father in a futuristic helicopter. Miyake's kaleidoscope dreams are not the hallucinatory effects of LSD. Rather, Mitchell depicts the fantastic imaginings of a media-saturated brain.

Mitchell plays the Dorothy trick throughout, as we realize what we've been reading was just Miyake's daydream, but, in a wrinkle that can only be called Mitchellesque, *Number9Dream* takes the genre fare of these imaginings and injects it into the "actual" plot of the novel, the improbable series of events, in which Miyake gets embroiled. The "reality" of the novel morphs from bildungsroman into mafia caper, as an evening playing video games devolves into a bender with a rich kid whose father has mob ties. Miyake wakes up in a love hotel, finding "the characters ONLY A VIDEO GAME" scrawled on the mirror. "This isn't happening," Miyake thinks. "I try to wake up. I fail. This is definitely happening" (119). Having prepared readers to discount sequences of the novel as Miyake's film- and game-inspired imaginings, Mitchell makes the outrageous series of events that ensue as "real" as anything else in *Number9Dream*. Mitchell has his protagonist self-consciously recognize that his predicament has become the stuff of genre fiction and film but is actually happening. "In movies," Miyake thinks, "people escape along rooftops. . . . What else do people do in movies? 'Out the back way,' they hiss. Where is this 'back way'?" (119).

In a chapter titled "Reclaimed Land," Miyake signs a blood pact with a Yakuza boss and witnesses a series of gruesome mob killings at a giant shopping mall and entertainment complex sited on freshly built terra firma. The height of the novel's deployment of genre fiction tropes coincides with its depiction of the most generic global site: a shiny new consumer wasteland of postmodern pastiche:

> Xanadu, way out beyond Tokyo Bay, is having its grand opening today ... a giant BRIDGESTONE airship floats above the enormous dome.... Valhalla opens in the new year, and Nirvana and its new airport monorail terminus are still under construction.... Flags of the world hang limp. An enormous banner reads "Xanadu Open Today! Family Paradise Here on Earth! Nine-Screen Multiplex! Olympic Pool! Krypton Dance Emporium! Karaoke Beehive! Cuisine Cosmos! California Lido! Neptune Sea Park! Pluto Pachinko! Parking space for 10,000, yes, 10,000!—automobiles." (156)

The mall complex, with once proud symbols of nationalism drooping impotently, is only the most hyperbolic example of globally homogenized space in the novel, promising paradise, international and interplanetary flavor, and delivering instead gridlock and a generic super mall. Though it might not be pure hyperbole. Mitchell's depiction of Xanadu anticipates with eerie precision an account from David Harvey's *Brief History of Neoliberalism* (2005), which describes "Dongguan, just north of Hong Kong," which

> has exploded from a mere town to a city of 7 million inhabitants in a little over twenty years.... It is also the site of construction for what is slated to be the largest shopping mall in the world (built by a Chinese billionaire, it has seven zones modeled on Amsterdam, Paris, Rome, Venice, Egypt, the Caribbean, and California, each constructed with such close attention to detail as to be indistinguishable, we are told, from the real thing).[30]

Mitchell cannily perceives the way global economic developments pastiche world cities and promise paradise but deliver cookie-cutter mega malls that replace the real with simulacra.

Signs of global commerce's replacement of local particularity with generic outposts pop up throughout *Number9Dream*. When Miyake leaves Tokyo for a week, he returns to find "the old shoe repair next to FUJIFILM has been turned into a Kentucky Fried Chicken outlet" (263), and late in the novel Miyake takes a job at Nero's, a sweltering pizza place that features genre-freighted pies like "Chicago Gunfight" and "Hawaii Honeymoon" (313). In all these sites, Mitchell teases readers with the possibility that Miyake is just imagining events. The adjectives he uses to describe Valhalla, an "enormous leisure hotel," suggest Miyake might still be stirring his cup in the Jupiter Café: "Sugar chandeliers, milky carpets, cream walls, silver fittings" (161). Before a mob shootout that ends in a detonation of plastic explosives that Miyake barely survives, he thinks: "Not for the first time today, I feel I have strayed into an action movie" (190). But it turns out that the violence is too real: "This movie is brutal and cheap and fake. If people who dream up violent scripts ever came into contact with real violence, they would be too sickened to write such scenes" (341). While all the metafictional rib-jabbing feels heavy-handed in Mitchell's second novel, his overt acknowledgments that its "realities" are the stuff of genre fiction function as an integral part of his project to depict the citational sites, the departicularized, de-realized, media-saturated spaces of late capitalism, which shape the form of his novel, as well as the experiences of his characters.

Conclusion: Institutional Sites and Hybrid Forms

In the fifth chapter of *Number9Dream*, "Study of Tales," Miyake hides out in a writer's idyllic home and reads her brainstorming warm-up exercises, a ludic, surreal, and metafictional narrative that we read along with him. The barely sensical farce centers on a John Barthian character called Goatwriter, a caprine scribbler, who journeys in search of his stolen writing brush and a manuscript containing "invaluable fragments of a truly untold tale" (198). While this section may strike readers as silly and precious in its allusiveness (Goatwriter drinks from a babbling brook: "'A stream of consciousness!' he reJoyced" [240]), it offers a compelling instance of self-reflexivity about the global literary marketplace that reflects Mitchell's bid to occupy an enviable middle ground in the global literary field, a position that can garner both literary prestige, through genre-bending formal experiment and hybridity, and a worldwide audience by providing the portable, familiar forms and pleasures of genre fiction. Goatwriter is a satirical representation of the authentic, romantic artist engaged in a quest for his voice, brush, and a "truly untold tale." He plumbs his "arborescent soul, far and deep" (236), and searches in "sealed caves, in lost books of learning" (241). His quest culminates in a "sacred pool" in which he "slough[s] off his body" and "[p]eace rain[s]" (249), as pure mind is reunited with brush and he can confront the blank page without the pesky trappings of his goatish body.

Mitchell poses a digitized "two-dimensional" video image called Queen Shrouds as the brush thief and antagonist to this romantic writer, an antagonist who emerges as a portrait of the media-savvy contemporary literary agent, a figure whose power, as Laura McGrath has detailed, has grown exponentially in the contemporary literary marketplace and whose role is to tailor literary fiction for more commercially inclined publishers.[31] Having Queen Shrouds steal Goatwriter's brush, Mitchell references the fear that writers will cede their autonomy to agents, who sacrifice literary and artistic agendas to their concern for marketability. The evil agent queen lives in the crater of a radio telescope, revels in the death of print, and ridicules Goatwriter's literary idealism: "'Fulfillment'? Writing is not about 'fulfillment.' Writing is about adoration! Glamour! Awards!" Queen Shrouds rejects the conventional "language of writers," which brought her only "overdrafts and obscurity" (230) and aims to upload Goatwriter's imagination. "And then his soul . . . and book deals in ninety-nine languages will be mine! Mine!" (231). Couched in more genre parody, Mitchell's muddled allegory "Study of Tales" distances his own work from both the cackling, villainous agents who embrace the digital and ruthlessly strive for fame and fortune, and from those romantic old goats who disinterestedly chase sacred, immaterial values.

1Q84 even more directly comments on its position in the literary marketplace by foregrounding a plot of publishing intrigue, in which Tengo's editor Komatsu asks him to rewrite the raw manuscript of Eriko Fukada (Fuka-Eri), a seventeen-year-old girl, whose *Air Chrysalis* is both a hauntingly compelling fantasy narrative and an extremely shoddy piece of writing. Komatsu describes it as a story with "real power: it draws you in. The overall plot is a fantasy but the descriptive detail is incredibly real . . . it leaves a real impression—it *gets* to you in some strange, inexplicable way" (20). Again, Murakami blurs reality and fiction, as Komatsu mentions three times how "real" this fantastic tale feels.

At the same time, Fuka-Eri's "writing is incredibly bad. . . . She should go back to school and learn how to write a decent sentence before she starts writing fiction" (21). Enter Tengo, who Komatsu hires to rewrite the novel. Tengo reshapes this rough raw material into a crossover work that achieves both critical acclaim and popular appeal, a literary bestseller that garners the Akutagawa Prize. "The Akutagawa prize! Every writer's dream! Huge headlines in the paper! TV news!" (29). It might be tempting to read Tengo's ghostwriting of Fuka-Eri's novel as allegorizing the collaboration of Murakami with his translators, but as Tengo brings not just the techne of "a skilled carpenter" but "style" (84, 85), it is more accurate to understand the collaboration as a figure for the fusion of form (Tengo) and content (Fuka-Eri), of literary language and compellingly immersive "real" feeling, fictional world.

Tengo reflects that Fuka-Eri had no

> intention of leaving behind a work of literature. All she had done was record a story.... She might just as well have used something other than words, but she had not come across a more appropriate medium.... She had never had any literary ambition, no thought of making the finished piece into a commodity, and so she felt no need to pay attention to the details of style. (85)

Tengo and his editor acknowledge literary novels as both the product of an ineffable "literary ambition" and as products, commodities that will be profitable insofar as they are marked by a stylistic signature. Komatsu pragmatically views hiring Tengo to rewrite the book and the resultant "[d]ivision of labor" as a necessity:

> "Mass production would be impossible any other way. In the self-conscious world of literary fiction, of course, such methods are not openly sanctioned. ... If the finished work is good and brings pleasure to a lot of readers, then no harm done, don't you agree?" (32)

Here, in the story of the genesis of the prize-winning novel *Air Chrysalis*, Murakami figures the production and circulation of his own work. Taking up the at times shoddily written but immersive feeling, propulsive storytelling, and global recognizability of popular genre fiction, and rewriting it with style, panache, and literary self-consciousness becomes a perfect recipe for producing a wildly acclaimed work of literary fiction. Murakami admits that literary fiction appears is one segment of "mass production," one that has genteel rules against ghostwriters and an otherwise ordinary capitalistic motive of satisfying consumers. At the same time, he depicts "literary ambition" as undergirded by belief that books may transcend mere commodity status and occasionally become truly original art.

While Komatsu at first appears to be cynically driven by profit and the desire to make *Air Chrysalis* into a bestseller, Tengo comes to believe that his editor "is obsessed with literature. People like him are looking for just one thing, and that is to find, if only once in their lifetimes, a work that is unmistakably the *real thing*" (149). While Tengo's words point again to *1Q84*'s gambit of containing a fantastic novel that turns out to be real, he also suggests that Komatsu truly cares about helping to usher uniquely powerful works of literature into the world. *Air Chrysalis* becomes a number one bestseller, stacks of it are "displayed in the front of all the bookstores" (351), and the "critical reception is wonderful, too. This is no lightweight drama . . ." (352). Exemplary as both a commodity and piece of serious literature, *Air Chrysalis* condenses the site in the literary market of *1Q84* and Murakami's work more broadly. At the same time, Murakami suggests that even critically acclaimed literary bestsellers have the short shelf life of any commodity in a global economy geared toward the incessant production of novelty. After several months have passed,

> *Air Chrysalis* had long since disappeared from the bestseller lists. Number one on the list now was a diet book entitled *Eat as Much as You Want of the Food You Love and Still Lose Weight*. What a great title. The whole book could be blank inside and it would still sell. (776)

While Murakami and Mitchell depict the alienating and dizzying experience of postmodern consumerism, the departicularization of places in globalized, postindustrial cities, and the inundation of subjects and sites in media, their novels balance the literary and generic, the serious and the pleasurable in a manner that makes them eminent commodities, ripe for circulation in an increasingly global, corporate-publishing-dominated literary market, the sites of which are both everywhere and nowhere. At the same time, and as I have argued in Chapters 2 and 3, Mitchell, Murakami, and the broader field of genre-bending writers of literary fiction are "obsessed with literature," evince a belief that their works might be different from ordinary commodities and that they might achieve the standing of great literature, become "unmistakenly the *real thing*." Thus, what looks like contradiction or complicity—genre benders critique globalization while adopting popular forms that enable their global circulation—gets reconciled by the belief that genre benders don't simply reproduce the generic forms that resemble the homogenized spaces of late capitalism but transform and deploy them in novel ways.

In other words, in these novels, globalization poses a threat of homogenization that is also somewhat of a straw man. They worry over the possibility of a flavorless, generic culture that their own innovative deployments and combinations of genre show to be unwarranted. This is why Whitehead's *Zone One* can be both a novel in which imitative consumerism is the zombifying disease and one that thinks all "Last Night Stories" are only superficially the same, that they can be modified to produce "nonetheless heartfelt" narratives that memorialize their creators, escape sameness, and become "the sacred in its current guise" (139). Genre benders express faith in the creative potential of innovating and hybridizing extant forms, as with the colored blocks in *Apex Hides the Hurt*, which can be stacked in near-infinite "permutations" and configurations, giving "the overall impression . . . that there was no end to what you could make" (118).

Similarly, Hamid's *Exit West* guards an optimism that—despite global upheaval caused by war, migration, and climate disaster—novelists will continue to imagine possible futures and generate forms that expand our sense of what art can be. Hamid repeats the familiar formulation that "depression is a failure to imagine a plausible desirable future for oneself," and *Exit West* refuses that condition. Instead, it envisions that in

> places both near and far, the apocalypse appeared to have arrived and yet it was not apocalyptic, which is to say that while the changes were jarring they were not the end, and life went on . . . and plausible desirable futures began to emerge, unimaginable previously, but not unimaginable now. (217)

For Hamid, imagining "desirable futures" is the job of speculative fictions like his, and their desirability is determined at least in part by the cultural production that such futures enable. In *Exit West*, mass migrations help shape a combinatory, genre-bending aesthetic that turns the globalized world into a realm of generative possibility, rather than deadening homogenization. Existing structures, popular genres transformed, offer models for and media through which to imagine futures that are varied and unpredictable:

> Indeed there was a great creative flowering in the region, especially in music. Some were calling this a new jazz age, and one could walk around Marin and see all kinds of ensembles, humans with humans, humans with electronics, dark skin with light skin with gleaming metal with matte plastic . . . (218)

These combinations of human and nonhuman players superficially resemble Miyake's stream of office drones, bytes, and generations, but the result here is not disorientation but the growth of new communities from the germ of new art forms: "Different types of music gathered different tribes of people, tribes that had never existed before, as is always the case" (218). *Exit West*'s co-protagonist Nadia forms a relationship with a cook who "introduces [her] to all sorts of old cuisines, and to new cuisines that were being born, for many of the world's foods were coming together and being reformed in Marin, and the place was a taster's paradise." (218).

While genre-bending writers acknowledge their participation in the global marketplace of late capitalism and freely draw on the recipes of popular genres, they don't view this participation or reliance on well-worn forms as cause for depression, as foreclosing desirable futures or transformative artistic production. Instead, they envision that new tribes and innovative new forms may be born out of old ones, hybrids emerging in "a great creative flowering." This is not to say that such writers are blind to cataclysmic futures, especially those shaped by climate catastrophe. It is to the reckoning with those futures that the next chapter turns.

 # Scalar Modulation and Formal Variation in Literary Climate Fiction

> The animals on the other hand were in the middle of dying, not only one at a time but in sweeps and categories. This he found increasingly distressing. . . . Each time one of the animals disappeared—they went by species or sometimes by organizations of species, interconnected—it was as though all mountains were gone, or all lakes. A certain form of the world. But in the gray that metastasized over continents and hemispheres few appeared to be deterred by this extinguishing or even to speak of it, no one outside fringe elements and elite groups, professors and hippies, small populations of little general importance. The quiet mass disappearance, the inversion of the Ark, was passing unnoticed.[1]
> LYDIA MILLET, *How the Dead Dream* (2008)

LYDIA MILLET'S DARKLY COMIC *How the Dead Dream* centers on T., a real estate developer in Southern California and devout capitalist. Money is his first love and greatest comfort. Millet's protagonist functions both mimetically, as a realistic, if satirically hyperbolic imaginary businessperson, and allegorically, as an archetypal subject of neoliberalism, for whom the pursuit of wealth and self-realization is one and the same. From childhood, T.'s sense of personhood is pegged to the dollar—literally. In "moments of anxiety," Andrew "Jackson's grave and finely etched countenance," on the twenty, "came to him . . . and calmed his heart" (1). Building on his early thrall to currency, T. launches a career in speculative investment, until Millet, braiding character tightly with plot, interrupts his otherwise unbroken pursuit of mammon. One night, while driving to Las Vegas (where else?), T.'s luxury sedan strikes a coyote. As he carries the dying animal off the freeway, he finds himself in an unexpected embrace. A feeling of "fullness," of "terrible sympathy" washes over him, which lingers in the days and weeks ahead as sorrow and memory of communion (37).

The experience hardly prompts a full-scale conversion. T. does not become a model climate citizen or forsake capitalism; he upgrades his Mercedes. But he does experience a modest awakening: a growing attunement to the lives of animals and the huge scale of their dying, due to the growth of human civilization that is the mission of developers like himself. On the framework of this narrative of the flickering into consciousness of one individual, Millet builds a devastating critique of neoliberal capitalism, a call to arms to mitigate the mass extinction event underway and the disruption of climate systems, which threatens the poorest human populations and, increasingly, the built environment and complacency of the wealthiest.

It would be foolish, however, to read *How the Dead Dream* and conclude that Millet believes that hitting a coyote with a car, or another dramatic encounter with an animal, *is required* to jolt one into consciousness of nonhuman life and the destruction human growth is wreaking on the biosphere. This fictional event is a representation, a rendering of a plausible event meant to be *representative*: emblematic of a type of occurrence that might trip the unpredictable wires of epiphany and short-circuit habit.[2] Many kinds of encounter could provoke such awareness. There's more than one way to skin a cat—a proverb Millet's novel makes us see we ought to retire. All roads lead to Rome, let's say, or many might. We can't always predict the method that will yield the best results. That's true of the kind of event that might inspire an individual like T. to question his faith in U.S. capitalism, of what technologies and social systems might yield true progress, and of the kind of stories about climate change and the Anthropocene that might resonate deeply with readers and affect how they view humankind's relationship with the nonhuman world.

The central concern of Millet's novel is the planetary scale of environmental catastrophe—the disappearance of entire "organizations of species" that is "passing unnoticed" on "this hot globe"—but it does not express that concern via a science fictional epic of global scale or vision of a dystopian future. *How the Dead Dream* is acutely focused on ecosystem disruption and nonhuman species, but it relies on a satirical, realist novelistic scaffolding: it depicts the halting journey of a single human protagonist and deftly recounts his deficiencies in free indirect discourse that credits T.'s growing awareness of the mass extinction event underway, encouraging a similar one on its readers, while ironically undercutting the belatedness and inadequacy of T.'s epiphany.

There's more than one way to narrate the Anthropocene. And yet a narrowly prescriptive orthodoxy has emerged in much criticism on literary responses to the climate crisis that contends that certain literary genres are inadequate to the task, while other techniques, forms, or even the dissolution of form are demanded by this ongoing global calamity. Pieter Vermeulen notes the critical "commonplace that climate change constitutes a formal challenge to the customary rhythms, patterns, and scales of the novel."[3] A host of literary and cultural scholars have drawn on influential work by Timothy Clark, Amitav Ghosh, Timothy Morton, and Rob Nixon and concluded that since the causes and effects of climate change and the Anthropocene are vast and widely distributed over time and space, and since they render extraordinary disaster quotidian, they either necessitate particular forms of representation, demand new forms of representation, or "eschew representation" entirely and can only be "intimated" in the "breakdown of literary form."[4] The European realist novel tradition—sometimes *the* novel, sometimes the *literary* novel, sometimes "*serious* fiction"—are the genres most often said to be stymied by climate catastrophe.[5] Novels—so this account goes—are small and quotidian, scaled to individuals and the probable happenings of middle-class and mostly Western experience. (This account might be more accurate for a subset of bourgeois, domestic, realist novels.) Whereas anthropogenic change to planetary systems is big and wild, happening everywhere over a long duration, and scrambling our sense of what is ordinary or incredible. Such assertions reflect tendencies to hypostatize and anthropomorphize genres, attributing to them certain abilities or deficiencies, neatly cleaving them into better- or worse-suited to the exigencies of a given moment, and by turns championing or critiquing genres that are alleged to possess an innate political freight or to perform particular tasks well or ill.

But none of the many challenges posed by climate change and the Anthropocene are challenges to literary form or to a particular genre, since, as this book has maintained, literary form is not rigid or static but plastic and subject to change. If writers of literary fiction have been, like the societies that produce them, torturously slow in their recognition of climate catastrophe and woefully inadequate in their response, if their focus has largely been on the well-being of Western nations instead of those in the global south who bear the brunt of climate change's disastrous consequences, despite having contributed least to its genesis, these failures are not due to the limitations of their forms. Genres are malleable frameworks, adaptable to disparate uses. And only a poor craftsperson blames their tools.

The title of Mahlu Mertens's and Stef Craps's "Contemporary Fiction vs. the Challenge of Imagining the Timescale of Climate Change" summarizes succinctly the critical consensus that the distributed temporality and geographic spread of climate change present an obstacle for fictional narrative; the remainder of the piece lays out a series of interlocking claims that reveals the underlying political and literary formal logic of this position:

> Despite the growing scientific knowledge about the anthropogenic causes and the consequences of climate change—the most salient manifestation of the Anthropocene—little effective action is taken, either by governments or individuals. Cultural responses to the problem might help make people care about and relate to it. Writing about climate change and the Anthropocene, however, confronts writers with formal challenges.[6]

Mertens and Craps suggest that what is perhaps the most salient political impasse in human history—the failure of governments to intervene on a scale that might mitigate the worst effects of planetary climate crisis—might be ameliorated with the aid of "cultural responses" like novels. But the "formal challenges" climate change and the Anthropocene pose to literary representation make it hard for culture to jumpstart us out of our political torpor. According to this logic, the political problem and its solution can be laid at the doorstep of literary form: if writers could only find a form to adequately represent the Anthropocene, Western societies might finally take significant action to combat climate crisis.

A similar logic appears in Ghosh's *The Great Derangement,* which has often been critiqued but has also helped spur the current critical consensus and is representative of a tendency to conflate literary convention with formal constraint. Ghosh laments literary fiction's failures to engage with climate, worrying that "certain literary forms" may be "unable to negotiate these torrents" due to "the peculiar forms of resistance that climate change presents to what is now regarded as serious fiction."[7] Ghosh speculates that the failure of such fictions "will have to be counted as an aspect of the broader imaginative and cultural failure that lies at the heart of the climate crisis."[8] Here we see an immediate confusion of formal and institutional explanations. Is it that "certain literary forms" are "unable" to address the climate crisis? Or does the problem lie with what audiences or tastemakers conventionally "regard as serious fiction"? And is the failure to mount a more strenuous political response largely due to failures of imagination? Despite the fact that Ghosh elsewhere emphasizes material factors—the way the political economy of colonialism generated powerful extractive regimes that have fueled climate change—here he stresses that "the heart" of the climate crisis is "imaginative and cultural failure."[9]

In a similar vein, Ursula Heise draws on the historian Dipesh Chakrabarty to argue that "the Anthropocene *requires*" us "to reimagine what humans are."[10] These accounts foreground a politics of culture and the imagination—what we need now is new art to spur new thinking—while ignoring the many ways non-art disciplines (geological sciences, nonfiction writing and journalism, documentary filmmaking, political economy) have no problems imagining the Anthropocene and its threats and failing to specify the links between imaginative transformation and political reform. While no one would question the idea that art and narrative are important to how we understand ourselves, how we communicate the threats of climate change, and how we might envision both catastrophic and more salutary futures, such emphases fail to delineate how we might translate revised narratives and scaled-up imaginations into large-scale political action, how the political work done by culture might overcome the entrenched interests and government enablers that support the carbon economy.[11]

While here I am pointing to the way such accounts fail to articulate how cultural forms, which fire the imagination, might generate a political praxis that could dislodge such powerful interests, the remainder of this chapter questions their claims about the adequacy of literary forms to the task of confronting climate change and the Anthropocene. At times, commentators have asserted that it is only conventionality or propriety that keeps climate change out of elite literary circles—rather than the recalcitrance of certain forms. Ghosh contends that

> fiction that deals with climate change is almost by definition not of the kind that is taken seriously by serious literary journals: the mere mention of the subject is often enough to relegate a novel or a short story to the genre of science fiction.[12]

Here we find a sociocultural explanation: editors of "serious literary" fiction fail to take environmental subject matter seriously and refuse to publish works that treat it. The novelist Ruth Ozeki offers a similar account, arguing that today's boom in literary fiction concerned with climate marks a shift from an earlier moment, in which literary fiction was expected to be above politics, toward a literary field that values fiction that engages pressing issues of social justice.[13] But Ghosh hypostatizes a literary establishment that always proscribes climate. Since climate change introduces improbable "happenings into a novel," writers who address the subject

> court eviction from the mansion in which serious fiction has long been in residence . . . [and] risk banishment to the humbler dwellings that surround the manor house—those generic outhouses that were once known by names such as "the Gothic," "the romance," or "the melodrama," and have now come to be called "fantasy," "horror," and "science fiction."[14]

Ghosh extends the metaphor congealed in "gatekeeper," arguing that tastemakers exile improbable fiction to the "outhouses" of genre fiction—a play on Henry James's "house of fiction," and perhaps a nod to Kurt Vonnegut's quip that "critics regularly mistake" science fiction "for a urinal."[15] This is a questionable account of how fiction gets published in genre fields: first it's rejected from literary presses. But here the reason climate disturbances don't appear in literary fiction is not so much the resistance of certain forms but "banishment" by those who hold the keys to prestigious literary institutions.

Mark McGurl helps connect the dots between such claims about institutional recognition and how formal regularity is generated within the field of literary fiction. Literary institutions encourage "creativity and originality" but also foster "the humble practice of repetition and reiteration."[16] Meanwhile, *genre fiction* delineates a field that accepts "literary forms willing to risk artistic ludicrousness *in their representation of* the inhumanly large and long."[17] In addition to recalling the absurdism of the highly literary ludic postmodernists, we might note that McGurl's prime example of genre fiction willing to risk ludicrousness in representing inhuman scale is the work of H. P. Lovecraft, which does not actually *represent* deep time in its narrative temporality but *refers* repeatedly in its discourse to the small scale of the human and our inability to correlate that smallness with the vastness of geologic time and the universe, as in the oft-quoted opening of "The Call of Cthulhu": "The most merciful thing in the world is the inability of the human mind to correlate all its contents. We live on a placid island in the midst of black seas of infinity, and it was not meant that we should voyage far."[18]

I will return to the many ways a literary text might convey the vast scales of climate change and of the Anthropocene, or the smallness of humanity relative to the nonhuman universe, without endeavoring *to represent* them. For now, I want to emphasize that the claims Ghosh and McGurl make about the resistance of elite literary institutions to the improbable or to deep time can easily accommodate the belated arrival of many writers of literary fiction to the subject of climate change and the Anthropocene: the literati finally woke up to the threat and now take such fiction seriously. But such institutional diagnoses have repeatedly morphed into claims about the resistance of form, about the inability of certain forms to treat certain subjects, and hence the necessity of new forms.

As Ghosh's *Great Derangement* progresses, he argues that it is not just that novels don't conventionally include long timescales because they want gatekeepers to admit them to the "mansion" of literary distinction, but now a small scale becomes a condition of novelistic narration as such: "it is precisely by excluding those inconceivably large forces, and by telescoping the changes into the duration of a limited time horizon, that the novel becomes narratable."[19] It's not clear why excluding large-scale forces is a condition for narratability in a novel, since a declarative sentence or two would seem capable of registering the potency of such forces and rendering them into narrative. (Here's an amateur effort: The parched river wasn't alone. Due to human carbon emissions, largely from the West, rivers were drying up everywhere.) One wonders if there is a conflation of novels' capacity to *represent the totality* of the climate crisis with the form's ability to apprehend planetary scale. Of course, fiction often functions synecdochally, with the situation of a single character, family, or river standing for a broader class that shares its plight—undercutting the critical commonplace that the realist novel is primarily concerned with isolated individuals.

But claims about the resistance of form are not limited to Ghosh; they become an explicit problem of genre in the work of Heise, who contends that "new forms of art and literature are no doubt called for to" account for "the temporal scales that the Anthropocene challenges us to imagine." Though she also argues "that some of the narrative resources for addressing long time intervals actually lie in narrative forms that preceded the rise of the novel and have accompanied it throughout its history."[20] "Scaling up our imagination of the human, as Chakrabarty challenges us to do, similarly requires different architectures of narrative."[21] Heise singles out science fiction as the genre that has evolved alongside the realist novel and that can address what it allegedly cannot, since SF "has often featured nonhuman agents" and

> has routinely focused on extraordinary events such as the discovery of new planets, encounters with aliens, and revolutionary technological change. Neither is scale . . . a problem for a genre whose settings include entire planets, solar systems, and galaxies.[22]

Although Heise delineates how Richard McGuire's inventive graphic novel *Here* (2014) represents a single place across deep time and acknowledges that "climate change doesn't stymie the narrative imagination," she echoes McGurl's contention that science fiction, since it is "exempt from the constraints Ghosh discusses, would be in a privileged position to tell stories about climate change and the Anthropocene."[23] Scale is a problem for the realist novel and literary fiction, these critics argue, due to their formal "constraints." But, as this book has argued throughout, conventions are not constraints, and form is continually subject to deformation.

This chapter agrees that, undoubtedly, one significant explanation for why so many writers of literary fiction have gravitated to the genres of genre fiction in recent decades—science fiction, particularly of a dystopian bent, but also postapocalyptic, horror, and zombie novels—is their interest in decentering the human, recognizing the agency and huge scales of the nonhuman world, and envisioning futures shaped by climate catastrophe. The felt urgency of literary responses to climate change is a major force behind the accelerated production of genre-bending literary fiction in the early twenty-first century. At the same time, this chapter demonstrates that recent literary writers have also taken creative leaps to bend realism and historical fiction in innovative ways to address climate change and the Anthropocene, and it shows that imagining these subjects does not require particular fictional genres or narrative forms.[24] For that matter, these topics don't require fiction; documentary filmmakers, contributors to scientific journals, nonfiction writers, visual artists, and poets would be surprised to learn that fictional narrative would be required in any way.[25]

While SF has long been concerned with futurity, planetary conflict, utopia, dystopia, and nonhuman actors—and thus offers writers genre frameworks with conventions they can draw on to imagine futures shaped by climate catastrophe and decenter the human—the forms of genres are not fixed and do not resist certain subject matter; they are plastic and can be bent toward new projects and motivated against their conventional, historical tendencies. Recent literary writers have shown that there are many ways to address climate change and the Anthropocene. After considering questions of form and scale, this chapter shows how today's literary writers have bent genres—from the SF epic and postapocalyptic to the realist novella and historical epic—to address climate change and the Anthropocene. If the realist novel has often focused on human problems and scale, been anthropocentric in its emphasis, the writers I treat in this chapter have shown that it doesn't have to be, that its purview can be expanded to networks of human and nonhuman environments, that it can situate individuals within a variety of scales that make visible their smallness, as well as how systemic processes of human extraction, consumption, colonization, and waste—spurred not by *all* humans but a relatively small number in the West—have combined to disrupt planetary ecologic and geologic systems.

Throughout the texts I treat in this chapter, writers, regardless of genre, not only explore scales smaller or larger than those pitched to a single human life but *correlate* scales. If, as I argue in Chapter 2, character and interiority remain enduring concerns in literary writers' deployments of popular genres, these persist in literary climate fiction, but in ways that highlight the entanglement of individuals with objects or organisms that are generally too small or silent to notice, and with far vaster social contexts; biological, geologic, and planetary systems; and durations. In other words, these texts show that writers of literary fiction have not been forced to choose either anthropocentric stories of humans or non- or posthuman narratives of the Anthropocene, but have discovered ingenious methods for dramatizing human lives as they come into contact with vast systems and an incalculably diverse nonhuman world.[26] If ecological awareness is at its core about the interconnection of living things with one another and with inorganic systems, these writers perform ecological thinking at the level of fictional form by showing that the concerns of individual humans cannot be considered in isolation.

Though the conventions of SF, dystopian, and postapocalyptic genres afford the ability to speculate far into the future and warn of terrifying social transformations and cataclysmic events, the novels I analyze in this chapter often deploy literary forms that are not bound to any genre in order to modulate between small and large scales, including radically compressed narration, nested and parallel narratives, metaphor, allegorical characters, and the sometimes-preachy but usefully to-the-point resource of direct discourse. If the writers of literary fiction I consider here have not radically overhauled the novel form to dispense with narrative coherence or wholly displaced human subjects, they have transformed and repurposed existing genres to imbue human narratives with concern for the broader nonhuman world. Demonstrating how genres are not static or discrete but can be perpetually altered and blended with others, today's literary writers have transfigured realism and historical fiction to offer stories of human characters, while lambasting the foolishness of thinking such stories are the whole story, foregrounding how such characters are caught up in networks of nonhuman agents, extractive capitalism, colonialism, and the huge timescales of historic, evolutionary, geologic, and astrophysical change.

But Will It Scale?

The question that typifies tech entrepreneurship is ironically also the one literary and cultural scholars have been asking of literary form. Efforts to marshal literature in the service of environmental movements have unquestionably provoked in writers of literary fiction an interest in scalar modulation—in thinking that can correlate the human with the very large and long (planetary, geologic, and atmospheric systems; mass migrations and extinctions; interplanetary travel; deep time) and the very small (microorganisms, parts per million of chemicals in air, water, soil, and bodies). At question here is not the desirability of scaling up or down the literary imagination, but the approach of various critics who maintain that doing so demands a particular literary form, because novels tend to be scaled to the duration of a human life and rely on dramatic incidents rather than slow accretion.[27] Take Mertens's and Craps's claim that the Anthropocene "confronts writers with formal literary problems" because "*we have to* imagine a future from which organized social memory will have disappeared," because the Anthropocene "will only be detectable as a geological stratum after humans have ceased to exist."[28] Imagining the Anthropocene *requires* a posthuman geologist's perspective. This assertion of necessity comes from Richard Klein, whom they quote: "*we still need to* imagine such a future historian in order to speak in the present about a catastrophic destruction of organized life about which it will not have been possible to speak historically."[29]

We should note several things about this claim regarding what it takes to imagine and speak in the present about the Anthropocene. First, while humans are not done leaving their record in Earth's geologic strata, the Anthropocene has emerged as an urgent if contested concept precisely because the effects of human growth on planetary systems and climate, especially since the Great Acceleration, already "have been measured directly with great accuracy and [have] shown an unmistakable human imprint."[30] Perhaps to perceive *the totality* of the effects of the Anthropocene, we might need to imagine an alien geologist eons hence. But we don't need to witness their totality to understand the massive anthropogenic effects on planetary systems, or to know that what has been done so far is only a fraction of what is likely to occur.

The second feature of Klein's claim cited by Mertens and Craps is its ironic prescriptiveness: "*we still need to* imagine such a future historian . . ." We see this kind of claim made repeatedly in writing about literary engagements with climate and the Anthropocene: the claim that a particular form of representation *is necessary*. But just as scientists already have recorded evidence of human impact on atmospheric carbon, tropical and temperate forests, nitrogen in soil, ocean acidification, and extinction of species—and speak about this impact without any recourse to literary narrative—so I am writing about these anthropogenic changes to planetary systems without reliance on some totalizing future imaginary. Indeed, it's ironic how often literary scholars have argued that "new forms of art and literature are . . . called for" without recognizing their reliance on the rather pedestrian genres of literary and cultural criticism, conference papers, and classroom lectures, with which they have been speaking in the present about the Anthropocene with great frequency, if not efficacy.[31] Indeed, part of the problem here seems to be the determination that a failure of efficacy must mean an inadequate form of address. But the reason a piece of cultural criticism or a lecture to undergraduates about climate change has not succeeded in mitigating the climate crisis is not due to the limitations of literary criticism or the lecture as genres, but rather the indirect and mediated relationship between their audience and the political and economic systems whose transformations are required to begin to ameliorate that crisis.

Further, as in McGurl's reading of Lovecraftian ludicrousness, critics often assume that narratives must *represent* events that span deep time, are dispersed globally, or involve interplanetary travel to convey vast scales of time and space. This is why Heise invokes Gérard Genette's concept of "anisochrony": "the difference between the duration of the narrated events and the duration of the narration itself."[32] For Heise, science fiction is uniquely equipped to cram the "geological or evolutionary time spans to be narrated" into "a few hundred or at most a couple of thousand pages."[33] The assumptions that go unquestioned here are the idea that "narrated events" must transpire over deep time in order to register that temporal scale, that radical compression of narration—like relating the events of millions of years in a paragraph—is not an effective way to convey scale, and that comprehension of deep time is necessary to address the Anthropocene. But in some of Heise's examples, such as H. G. Wells's *The Time Machine*, the narrative does not relate a succession of events over the course of 800,000 years, but is punctuated, only dramatizing events at each of the time traveler's stops; it does not depict the many millennia spanned by each leap. The time machine functions as both a diegetic device or novum that allows the character to move across time in the story world and a narrative device that allows the novel's discourse to dramatically overleap temporal settings. SF texts have often crafted ingenious devices to reference long spans of time and space without having to represent the expanse in between. In *Rocannon's World* (1966), Ursula K. Le Guin's first novel, the prologue alludes to Shakespeare's *The Winter's Tale*, noting that "Unreason darkens that gap of time bridged by our lightspeed ships." The novel envisions an "instantaneous transmitter, the ansible," which allows the Starlord to communicate across millions of light-years, and unmanned drone bombers "that could go from one star to another in no time at all."[34] But the novel does not dramatize events that range across these distances and keeps its action to a single planet.

Radically compressed narrative is another way to comprehend scale. Lovecraft evokes an immense universe indifferent to the puniness of human life not by constructing narratives that transpire over eons, but with adjectives that describe that universe. In "Cthulhu," the narrator recounts what characters in the narrative present have speculated about deep time. Castro, "an immensely aged mestizo," tells of the "Great Old Ones," who came "from the stars," ruled Earth, died "vast epochs of time before men came," and "lay in wait for a glorious resurrection . . . whilst uncounted millions of years rolled by."[35] Lovecraft does not represent these epochs; he has a character mention them in a single sentence. With similar anisochrony but in a far different genre, the prologue to Elizabeth Kolbert's powerful nonfiction book *The Sixth Extinction* (2014) compresses an account of the period from the emergence of homo sapiens approximately 200,000 years ago to the present, when "people come to realize they are causing" the sixth great extinction in the Earth's 4-billion-year history, in just under two pages.[36]

Millet's account of mass extinctions in the epigraph to this chapter neither aims at representing deep time, nor dramatizes the scale of despeciation. But in a few sentences, Millet conveys the magnitude of the extinction event: the "extinguishing" of countless species (140). Such compression gains in efficiency what it might lose in vividness, asking readers to contemplate one of the Anthropocene's most significant ongoing manifestations and critiquing the human social facts that allow such extinctions to occur in relative obscurity. From "where T. stood," such animals "had always been invisible anyway" (140). Millet's telescopic account of animals dying "in sweeps and categories," such that "a third of all species would soon be gone," conveys a terrifying scale of loss, while correlating that scale with an indictment of human obliviousness: a "quiet mass disappearance . . . passing unnoticed" (139). Millet does not represent these extinctions; the fact that they are hidden from view is precisely her point.

We also find deep time and planetary calamity reckoned with in a slim novella like Jenny Offill's *Weather* (2020)—it may be one of the books Joyce Carol Oates had in mind when she complained of the boom in "wan little husks of 'auto fiction' with space between paragraphs to make the book seem longer"— that takes as its ostensible subject the daily trials and musings of a university librarian in New York City.[37] But Offill embeds an ingenious conceit of having her protagonist Lizzie take a second job answering letters for her former dissertation advisor Sylvia, a cultural critic who hosts a climate change podcast *Hell and High Water*. Listeners write in to ask where "will be the safest place" to ride out climate catastrophe, and Lizzie similarly finds herself becoming a "doomer," who googles survival skills for the coming chaos and, like the superrich, wonders where to build her "doomstead."[38]

Via Sylvia's podcast and Lizzie's mounting dread, *Weather* finds inventive ways to embed discussions of deep time, ecology, anthropocentrism, nonhuman agency, and human failures to act in the face of climate disasters in a first-person narrative focused on one woman's guilt at the paltriness of her own concerns. Lizzie listens to an episode of Sylvia's show "about Deep Time," in which "the geologist being interviewed" is a master of compression; he "speaks quickly, sweeping through millions of years in a moment" (30). Another episode features an ecologist, who illustrates interconnection vividly via example "*a species of moth in Madagascar that drinks the tears of sleeping birds*" (67). At a conference, Sylvia skewers the notion that "humans are the height of evolution" (46). Throughout, *Weather* compares the West's inaction on behalf of other species and in the face of climate catastrophe with the bystander silence and slow, incremental rise of terror that characterized the Holocaust. In an extended satire of Lizzie's privilege, Offill has her repeatedly call a livery service rather than take the bus home from work. Asked by her driver what the "the takeaway message" of Sylvia's program is, Lizzie riffs on Martin Niemöller's famous poem: "First, they came for the coral, but I did not say anything because I was not a coral . . ." (41). To an anxious letter writer, Lizzie recalls the Jews who "saw walls being built around the ghetto and thought they still had time," before advising: "Don't be fooled by everyone else's calm" (88). Though it is composed of bite-sized, darkly humorous vignettes about an individual protagonist, is riddled with epigrammatic quips, and takes place over a series of months, *Weather* revolves around the experience of living with foreboding knowledge of the Anthropocene and the torpor of individuals who feel powerless to intervene in problems of tremendous magnitude.

Even in a monumental SF tome like Kim Stanley Robinson's *The Ministry for the Future* (2020), which imagines future climate catastrophe and social breakdown, as well as the international cooperation it might take to adapt to such crises, experiments with nonhuman perspectives and very small scales in chapters narrated by, for example, a neutrino, radical compression and direct discourse help convey the scale of mass extinction and the evolutionary span it might take for a comparable biodiversity to reconstitute itself:[39]

> The current rate of extinctions compared to the geological norm is now several thousandfold faster, making this the sixth great mass extinction event in Earth's history, and thus the start of the Anthropocene in its clearest demarcation, which is to say, we are in a biosphere catastrophe that will be obvious in the fossil record for as long as the earth lasts. . . . Evolution itself will of course eventually refill all these emptied ecological niches with new species. The pre-existing plenitude of speciation will be restored in less than twenty million years.[40]

That expository narration like this embeds the language of popular science writing in a novel suggests an unspoken preference for "showing" over "telling" in recent prescriptive criticism about literary form and the Anthropocene.[41] Huge scales may be conveyed by compressed "telling," and this passage from *Ministry* illustrates the generic hybridity of much climate fiction, the way, as Bakhtin insisted long ago, novels are distinguished by their capacity to ventriloquize and embed other discursive genres. While the bulk of the novel speculates about climate future and envisions possible, even utopian, mitigation and adaptation efforts, taken on its own this passage is neither science fiction nor fiction. Recent climate fictions frequently play with the increasingly blurry line between our current catastrophic reality and likely but as-yet speculative visions of the near future.

Literary Dystopia and Apocalypse

Though we have already seen that SF genres are by no means required for addressing climate change or imagining the Anthropocene, their storehouse of conventions—speculative visions of utopian, dystopian, or apocalyptic futures; extinguished planets; interstellar travel and colonization; nonhuman consciousness—has afforded writers of genre-bending climate fiction a set of resources to borrow from and adapt. As I have stressed, what makes these fictions *literary* and sets them apart from urgent and innovative treatments of climate change in genre fiction fields is no bright dividing line, but rather their often shifting and contested position in the literary field, combined with a tendency to utilize formal features that are prized in that field. By no means does this chapter mean to privilege or suggest that Millet's *How the Dead Dream* or Offill's *Weather* are categorically better, more effective, or higher quality engagements with climate catastrophe than, say, Octavia Butler's *Parable* novels, N. K. Jemisin's Broken Earth trilogy, or Robinson's Science in the Capital trilogy. To say they are works of *literary cli-fi*, is less a claim that they are of superior quality than a claim that they circulate in the field of literary fiction and possess the qualities valued therein, including formal experiment and generic indeterminacy, attention to prose style, interiority, allusiveness, and a self-reflexive consideration of the status and value of the literary—even in blasted future landscapes. Moreover, many of the texts I consider in this chapter seek to overcome any binary that views SF as geared to large-scale social ideas and decentering the human and often-realistic literary fiction that tends to privilege character, interiority, and private experience, allegedly at the expense of broader social, structural, and nonhuman concerns. In other words, these texts shuttle between and correlate scales by extending literary fiction's traditional preoccupation with character and interiority, while showing how individuals respond to, affect, and are entangled in global systems and networks of human and nonhuman agents.

It would be difficult to overstate the number of dystopian and postapocalyptic climate fictions that have proliferated in recent years. Matthew Schneider-Mayerson refers to these as *"cautionary fables of the Anthropocene that offer a blunt critique of fossil-fueled neoliberal capitalism and political passivity"* and asserts that they have not been able muster more than a terrifying vision of the future and a vague "injunction to *do something*."[42] But this range of works cannot be so tidily summarized. Lidia Yuknavitch's *The Book of Joan* does provide a cautionary fable in its vision of a blasted, uninhabitable Earth, but it also takes aim at the intertwining of capitalist resource extraction with reproductive control of women's bodies. Further, the novel's fantastic elements, surrounding the supernatural powers of its title heroine, and its explicit interest in textuality—envisioning stories that literally get under one's skin—ask how narrative might cause changes in readers' bodies, inspire them to revolutionary action, and help prepare the ground for the Earth's slow rebirth. Throughout, Yuknavitch makes explicit her ambition to situate the predicament of the human individual in planetary time and the enormity of the nonhuman universe. *The Book of Joan*'s nested structure, in which its narrator Christine relates both her own experience and the epic battles of Joan, enacts at the level of form this scalar modulation and correlates the large-scale war for the future of the planet with the actions of a seemingly helpless individual.

The Book of Joan begins with a radically compressed prologue that glances back some 66 million years to the volcanic eruptions of the Deccan Traps that blocked out the sun and had "dinosaurs and most manner of living things . . . already at death's door by the time the [Chicxulub] asteroid hit."[43] This opening vignette introduces the idea of life's potential for cataclysm and regeneration across deep time that will be central to the novel, before giving way to its main narrative set in 2049, in the aftermath of ecological cataclysm and world war. Immediately, the novel's setting is decidedly smaller, even claustrophobic. Earth has become a wasteland, and several thousand survivors from the ruling classes orbit the planet in a crudely improvised agglomeration of space junk called CIEL. Its occupants have devolved into pale, hairless, sexless beings—scarier versions of Wells's Eloi, set on the starships of *WALL-E* (2008). A Trumpian TV-celebrity-turned-fascist-dictator, Jean de Men, rules what's left of humanity.

So far this may sound like conventional postapocalyptic fare, but chief among *The Book of Joan*'s highly literary and textual preoccupations is the process of "scarification." CIEL's inhabitants perpetuate the narrative drive by grafting stories onto their skin with electrosurgical pens.[44] Yuknavitch's narrator protagonist Christine Pizan—her allusive name marking her as a reincarnation of the French Renaissance proto-feminist writer—is a body artist and activist intellectual who lives in even greater confinement: imprisoned in a tiny cell in CIEL's Panopticon for critiquing the space station's canon. She "questioned the literary merit" of the work of the dictator de Men, who has written "the most famous CIEL narrative graft . . . hailed, by consensus, as the greatest text of all time" (12). In the restricted terrain of the space station, attacking the way de Men's hegemonic texts perpetuate domination was the "only war [Christine] could wage" (21). She deems his writing "utter pig shit," because "all the women in" it "demanded to be raped . . . served but one purpose in the plot . . . to allow their hole to be plumbed. He took this broken romance trope and elevated it . . . and thus, it permeated consciousness" (20–21). Intriguingly, Yuknavitch poses de Men as a literary genre bender, who has "elevated" a "broken romance trope"—though he perpetuates its ideology. In response, Christine launches a queer "literary resistance movement," whose paltry scale is magnified by its unique form. "What gave my little literary challenge epic impact? . . . skin. The medium itself" (22). Imprisoned for literary resistance and occasionally visited by her clownish friend, the aptly named Trinculo, Christine spends her imprisonment singeing the legend of martyr Joan of Dirt into her skin.

Already we find many of the preoccupations of literary fiction packed into this post-cataclysmic space station. The novel critiques tired "romance tropes" and their ideological valence. It is full of allusions to critical theory and the canon and preoccupied with the continued relevance of the literary. In their final duel, Joan tells the philistine de Men he "should have spent [his] final hours studying literature, history, philosophy" and laments that in the novel's end times, people have forgotten the words: "*Paper. Writing. Books. Libraries*" (161). Though reading has atrophied along with the human body aboard CIEL, Yuknavitch extols the power of stories to build worlds and transform the vast interior scale of consciousness. As Christine burns Joan's epic into her skin, it engraves itself in her mind:

> When you shut your eyes, the universe is internal. I can feel her story . . . rising from my flesh. . . . I can enter a world not limited by any cell, for the mind, the body, even the eye, is a microcosm of the cosmos. (50)

While *The Book of Joan* thus follows a lineage of literary fiction dedicated to journeying deep within the human mind, which roams free even in captivity, the novel foregrounds the relays between story, the human psyche, global catastrophe, and the nonhuman matter of the external world, as Joan's rebellion inspires Christine's, and CIEL's microcosmic dystopia opens onto a grand stage. In what may be a first in the long history of the frame tale, we read the story of Joan as Christine inscribes it onto her body. In Joan's story, the stakes are far greater than a "little literary challenge" to the canon, as she functions as Christ-figure and reborn Joan of Arc, an "epic" or even biblical heroine, who leads an ecofeminist revolution on a planetary scale.

In the legend Christine grafts onto her skin, Yuknavitch embeds the myth of Joan's childhood on Earth and heroism in wars over the fate of the planet. Joan's deep connection with the nonhuman morphs into a supernatural ability to harness the elements. As a child, she has an epiphany as she hears "a song that came in epic waves, about the story of a girl saving the world" (59), a "forest song" that murmurs "The earth . . . she's alive" (69). Yuknavitch weaves the motif of this song throughout, a contemporary physics-inflected music of the spheres, to convey Joan's attunement to the vibrancy of matter and her emergence as the heroine of an epic chanson for the dying biosphere.[45] In school, Joan discovers string theory, "cosmic harmonies—born of the strings" (54). This cosmic lyre plays a song that is increasingly self-reflexive: the epic in which Joan finds herself. As "[t]he verses unraveled and sang, the more her body felt like the source of some larger-than-life vibration. . . . [They] tenored on with grand scale and detail until the ballad was entirely epic, and her place within it" (53). These lines suggest Yuknavitch's effort to reduce the human to one form of vibrating matter, even as Joan gains an outsized significance as the heroine of an "epic battle story she was living one stanza at a time" (77), which will be "a song of the earth's death and resurrection" (137).

From Joan's early animism, she develops a fascination with disparate scales, studying "microbes and quantum physics" in school, the "small and the large inextricably wedded for eons" (71–72). She feels "more kindred with" animals "than with people," but "the world was her deepest intimate. Trees and rocks and rain and ocean and river water compelled her almost completely" (72). Such kinship needn't be science fictional, and Yuknavitch's similes, rather than SF tropes, prompt awareness of nonhuman agency by likening human social organization to the chemical, biologic, and geologic. During the war, alliances "formed or deformed quickly, as in chemistry experiments . . . small powers joined in collectives, like bees in hives. . . . Leaders rose and fell faster than seasons" (74). Christine decries humans' "tsunami-like thirst for never-ending consumption at the price of the planet" (108). Before the war even begins, Joan's song and these metaphors bind her life to quantum and cosmic scales and to the agency of the nonhuman world.

When the battle for Earth arrives, Joan joins the growing ranks of child soldiers but stands out for her miraculous ability to harness the planet's wrath. "When she reached out to touch trees or water or dirt . . . the earth opened up and literally swallowed the tanks and Humvees" (77). Joan's prowess and reputation multiply as she becomes an "Eco-terrorist" in the eyes of the enemy (23), a revolutionary heroine to her partisans; her "first action" is to detonate "thousands of improvised explosive devices covering the Tar Sands in Alberta like malignant cancer cells invading a body" (37). Again, Yuknavitch's similes link disparate scales. Joan fights her final "epic face-off with Jean de Men," sparking an accelerated "[g]eocatastrophy," in which "ice caps speed-melted. The waters rose. Not gradually . . . but in a matter of weeks" (37–38). Here the fantastic acceleration of climate catastrophe—all of which is told, not shown—does not obscure the longer durations with which *The Book of Joan* is concerned. In the "aftermath," "new continents might eventually form" (110). Though the cataclysm is total, in the long view, it is merely a blip. Joan realizes the world will have to be destroyed to be reborn, and her eyes tear up "for a few seconds. About the time humanity has lived on earth compared to the cosmos" (111). Yuknavitch's heroine attempts to capture the paradoxes of the scalar relations of the Anthropocene. The stakes of human action—both ecocide and resistance—are no less than a battle for the future of all life currently on the planet. At the same time, the novel reminds us that human history is a blink relative to the span of the universe.

While the novel centers on two human characters, a form that might be thought anthropocentric, its discourse rejects anthropocentrism throughout. Yuknavitch makes clear her ambition for Joan to function as a new kind of "hero," freed from "a story that is not only man-made but man-centered" (99). Rather than "mythologize" a single human and the species, Joan's epic aims at no "higher truth other than we are matter . . . an energy amid all other energy and matter that emerges, lives, dies, and then changes form" (100–101). Instead of telling a story "to feel better about ourselves" (101), Joan's seeks to decenter the human, insisting "We are not above the organic life we destroyed. We are of it" (225). While the form of the novel centers human characters, its discourse continually rejects the primacy of human life and the scale of the individual, posing a quandary for critics who demand a novelistic form that decenters the human. Further, Yuknavitch emphasizes connection. Instead of a "self-centered species" that intends "to discover, to conquer," Joan pleads for us to "rejoin everything we are made from" (227). It could be argued that these lines are didactic, less artful for their explicitness than a novel that dramatizes humanity's interconnection with all other matter. But it's clear such ideas can be conveyed in direct discourse; even in a novel using an SF framework, their expression is not yoked to a particular genre.

What I've detailed here only scratches the surface of this intricate novel, but what must be stressed is the way Yuknavitch, if often didactically, not only foregrounds the agency of the nonhuman world, critiques a history of anthropocentrism that underwrites "the drive to conquer, colonize, deplete" (106), and shuttles between quantum and cosmic scales. *The Book of Joan* also correlates scales, underscoring the interdependence of the human and nonhuman world and imagining how private acts of reading might spur collective action. One morning Christine nods off while reading her graftstory, a once-familiar action that now feels "nostalgically human and earthbound" (81). She dreams of grafting events "directly onto" her body as they happen, "as if I am history writing itself" (81). This dream reminds her of an unnamed film she saw in childhood, which sounds a lot like David Lean's 1965 *Doctor Zhivago*. In Christine's account of the film and her dream of history's unmediated transcription, we encounter Yuknavitch's ambition for a narrative that would embed the individual human life in history and the flow of deep time—and transmit these into the body of the reader:

> The epic, romantic story, and even its form, got inside me. The micro element of the personal and the macro sweep of the historical seemed to be composed in the film in a way I'd never imagined.... To be human, the film suggested, was to... admit that history was not something in the past but something you might consciously step into.... It was the first time I felt a sense of messianic time, of life that was not limited to the story of a lone human being detached from the cosmos.
>
> When I came out of the theater, I said to my mother, "It's like we're stars in space. It's like space is the theater and we are the bits of stardust and everything everywhere is the story." (82)

The historical epic here, in language reminiscent of Georg Lukács and Fredric Jameson, offers a form that can situate the micro scale of the human within the macro scale of the historic and the cosmic—the human a mote of dust in an infinite totality.[46] Further, Yuknavitch envisions that such a narrative might "get inside," the viewer, transforming her perception of self and history in the process. While *The Book of Joan* seeks to enact this kind of embedding and correlating of scales in its SF and frame narrative, the novel points to an "epic, romantic" film's ability to do the same—and it makes its ambition explicit in an embedded excursus on a classic film, not through its SF elements. Again, relating the individual to the grand sweep of history and deep time is not bound to a particular narrative form.

Christine's account of *Zhivago* further clarifies Yuknavitch's conceit of stories grafted onto the skin as expressing an ideal for the radical political efficacy of narrative, in which the story literally "gets inside" the reader and prompts revolutionary action. Christine declares that Joan's "voice is in my body" (112), but she aims to "collect, fragment, and displace lines from [her] epic body poem onto the bodies of others until we become . . . a resistance movement of flesh" that will launch "plural acts of physical violence" (91). Here, literalizing the way reading might leave its mark, spurring consciousness and action, we see yet another correlation of scales: from the grand scope of epic narrative to the body of the reader, to the revolutionary movement she is inspired to initiate.

In other recent literary dystopias, we find further variation of technique and genre deployed to correlate scales. Published the same year as *The Book of Joan*, Louise Erdrich's *Future Home of the Living God* (2017) shares with it many qualities: it is a feminist dystopia set in the near future, in which humanity has begun a process of devolution—a clear rebuke to narratives of human progress. The cause of this process remains mysterious, but Erdrich suggests it is tied to environmental toxins. Reminiscent of Margaret Atwood's *The Handmaid's Tale*, *Future Home* imagines ecological disruption that threatens human embryonic development and provokes social unrest, resulting in a takeover of the U.S. government by the fundamentalist "Church of the New Constitution," which imprisons pregnant women so it can study genetic alterations in the few surviving infants.[47] This reproductive control is implemented putatively for women's "own safety," though Erdrich quips, with Orwellian irony, that they "are required to go voluntarily" to government hospitals to give birth, and "round[ed] up" if they don't (113). The novel draws from the thriller as well, depicting the efforts of its pregnant protagonist Cedar to flee government forces and citizens who would turn her in. Reproductive control is at stake in both novels, but while Yuknavitch's principal characters are of European descent, Erdrich's novel concerns itself with the historical apocalypse of Indigenous populations and with their efforts at survival and adaptation in the future. Cedar is Ojibwe, but adopted by white Minnesotans, "market-based society suspicious trust-fund liberals" (88). Erdrich emphasizes the varied responses of white settler and Indigenous communities as Cedar's parents worry what devolution will do to culture: "there goes poetry, there goes literary fiction, there goes science, there goes art" (86), while the novel's Native characters "have been adapting" to apocalypse "since before 1492" (43).

Throughout, Erdrich implies that the Earth is taking revenge on humanity and delineates the smallness of humankind in relation to evolutionary and geologic time. Cedar's adoptive father Glen pithily suggests that "Mother Earth has a clear sense of justice. You fuck me up, I fuck you up" (83). As in Offill's podcasts, Erdrich has Cedar and her family watch a paleontologist, author of a book called *Deep Time*, spin devolution theories on television (84). Cedar repeatedly contemplates the impossibility of comprehending vast timescales:

> [W]e do not understand how much time has passed on this planet and we have no concept of our limited place in the enormousness of that time. . . . I can't imagine 4.4 million years . . . the amount of time we've been roughed out as proto-human . . . positively can't go to billions—the 4.6 that is our planet's age. (89)

Such ruminations situate the current crisis in deep time, without representing it, as the novel limits itself to the scale of Cedar's travails and musings, as she is often confined or hiding in small spaces. At the same time, it's clear that Erdrich's focus on this individual pregnant woman is meant to conjure the broader and steadily unfolding specter of reproductive oppression and threats to human flourishing, while maintaining a view of the smallness of human lifespans.

Millet's *A Children's Bible* (2021), a National Book Award Finalist, also projects a near-future dystopia, which centers on a small band of adolescents who take over the affairs of their incompetent parents after a superstorm initiates a comprehensive breakdown of the social fabric. Here, scalar movement is a function of the duality of literary character. Millet uses characters as both mimetic, fleshed-out individuals and allegorical figures who represent a larger social class and phenomenon. Her gaggle of comically inebriated, inept, and mentally ill parents clearly stands for a boomer generation of Western bourgeoisie, whose pursuit of wealth and comfort have wrecked the planet and who are clueless about how to initiate any kind of remedy, and her troupe of resourceful children for the cohort who will inherit the Earth and must adapt to survive. "We knew who was responsible of course," thinks Evie, the novel's narrator protagonist, "it had been a done deal before we were born."[48]

While the novel rebukes the parents for their trivial bourgeois concerns, contrasted with the social chaos initiated by climate catastrophe, Evie offers some measured sympathy for the parents—here likened to a maladapted species—who are victims of their provincial upbringing:

> Specifically adapted to life in their own small niches. . . . My father's habitat had been the art economy. . . . My mother's . . . the university, her articles full of long words and the names of other scholars. Articles five people read. When their habitats collapsed they had no familiar terrain. No map. No equipment. No tools. (206)

Millet skewers scholarly irrelevance and suggests the parents' inability to adapt will soon make them extinct. By contrast, the children homeschool each other on "the story of the planet," presenting a timeline of evolution and "a graph of extinction events" over billions of years (136–137). Again, we see a novel position its human narrative against the scale of deep time. While *A Children's Bible* reduces generations and the breakdown of the "sociocultural order" to a microcosm (213), its project is plainly to critique a self-involved, naïve generation that persisted in its narrow vision, falsely "secure in the knowledge that an orderly future stretched ahead of them" (136).

A dystopian vision of near-future climate catastrophe, Claire Vaye Watkins's *Gold Fame Citrus* foregrounds a solipsistic protagonist, forced to come to grips with the fact "there's a whole great goddamn world out there that has nothing to do with" her.[49] But Watkins embeds Luz Dunn's story in the history of the American West, in particular its spectacular failures of watershed management, which along with global warming have fueled cataclysmic fires and desertification. In a rather different way, Watkins takes up the symbolic function of characters, as Luz has been adopted from birth as the poster child of conservationists, "goddesshead of a land whose rape was in full swing before she was even born" (12). Watkins critiques the way politicians exploit images of children as performative care for future generations—"think of the children!"—as they fail to take meaningful action on their behalf. Watkins's protagonist stands for the generations that will be bequeathed a fiery, waterless West. Luz's partner Ray, a veteran traumatized by the "forever war" (6), represents those asked to serve a nation that fails to protect its homeland or the planet from the ravages of climate change. Watkins positions Ray's willful pursuit of oblivion against a catalogue of the calamities he is seeking to escape:

> He had a mind to surf through all the crises and shortages and conflicts past and present.... He was surfing the day they pronounced the Colorado dead, and he was surfing the day it was dammed, a hundred years before.... He surfed as [L.A.]'s aqueducts went dry. He surfed as she built new aqueducts, wider aqueducts, deeper aqueducts, stretching to the watersheds of Idaho, Washington, Montana, aqueducts veining the West, half a million miles of palatial half-pipe left of the hundredth meridian.... Ray surfed as a concrete waterway crept up to Alaska, surfed as the Mojave and the Sonoran licked the bases of glaciers. He was surfing each time terrorists or visionaries bombed the massive unfilled aqueduct canals at Bend and Boise and Bolder and Eugene. He surfed as states sued states ... as the Central Valley, America's fertile crescent, went salt flat ... as all of the Southwest went moonscape with sinkage, as the winds came and as Phoenix burned and as a white-hot superdune entombed Las Vegas. (20–21)

Putatively about Ray's desire to escape his trauma by surfing, this passage offers a lyrical info-dump that condenses the history of Watkins's speculative near future, its repetitive syntax and sibilant alliteration mimicking the foolish consistency of bureaucrats who persist in applying the same unworkable "fix" again and again. I quote the passage at length to demonstrate both the way narratives may radically compress events that transpire over years and how novelists like Watkins position individual responses—here the escapism of the traumatized veteran—within the macro scale of climate crisis.

As I discuss in Chapter 2, in numerous literary climate fictions that deploy dystopian or postapocalyptic genres, disasters are not played for dramatic effect—often they are not dramatized at all—and long timescales are traversed with a variety of devices. In the Sonmi section of *Cloud Atlas*, we meet a fabricant who has been genetically engineered to work in "deadlands," where extreme heat or radiation would kill an unmodified human. In Chang-rae Lee's *On Such a Full Sea*, the disasters that lead to the dissolution of the United

States, and their settlement by Chinese climate refugees, are passed over in an opening paragraph. But that novel is dedicated to modulating between the individual scale of Fan's story, that of the fish-farming collective of B-Mor, who have invested her with their fears and wishes, and the larger scale of the rigidly stratified dystopia Lee imagines. Michel Faber's *Book of Strange New Things* uses the venerable epistolary form, interspersing the narrative of Peter's missionary work on the planet Oasis with interplanetary email transmissions from his wife Bea, who informs him of an Earth increasingly descending into climate crisis and anarchic unrest.

A similar oscillating structure appears in Richard Powers's *Bewilderment* (2021). Short-listed for the Booker, the novel demonstrates the hybrid blurring of genre categories. Laden with elements of nature writing that exalt the beauty of the forests, streams, and fauna of the Great Smoky Mountains, the novel is largely a realist narrative of Theo Byrne's struggles, after his wife's death, to care for his neuroatypical son Robin. But just as Faber uses Bea's letters to offer a running inventory of earthly tragedies while the main narrative takes place on the planet Oasis, so Powers improvises a number of speculative but increasingly plausible climate and associated social disasters over the bassline of the father-son story. Returning from a camping trip that is aimed to calm Robin's emotional lability, Theo tunes into the news and learns that ecoterrorists have blown up a cruise ship in the Caribbean, right-wing militias attacked a BIPOC organization's peaceful demonstration, and a massive hurricane has "returned a good stretch of the South Fork of Long Island to the sea" while "U.S. and Chinese fleets were playing nuclear cat and mouse off Hainan Island."[50] Though many events catalogued in *Bewilderment* are as yet speculative—Gulf Coast flooding contaminates "the drinking water of thirty million people" and wheat crops fail throughout China (153)—others, like orders to shelter inside from California wildfire smoke, are the stuff of today's current events. Meanwhile the increasingly authoritarian edicts of an unnamed, blustery, white nationalist president seem intentionally designed to blur the boundaries of realism and speculation. The point of such blurring is not hard to discern. Powers intimates that the speculative disasters that haven't happened yet loom so near that it's difficult to disentangle current disaster from future, SF from reality. Put another way, the future of climate catastrophe is now.

In a further blending of genres, *Bewilderment* ingeniously intersperses SF vignettes into its mostly realist frame. Theo is an astrobiologist who uses sophisticated radio telescopes, on the verge of being axed by a neoliberal U.S. Congress that sees little value in pure research, to search for signs of life in distant galaxies. Theo creates simulations of planets that might be hospitable to life. Thus, Powers gives his protagonist a career that is part computational modeler, part author of speculative fictions. "I made worlds by the thousands. I simulated their surfaces and cores and living atmospheres" (64). Powers renders Theo's world-building in embedded science fictions that we read in the nightly bedtime stories he tells Robin, brief tales of imaginary planets, such as the watery Pelagos, with "[d]ozens of dispersed intelligent species" that "spoke millions of languages" (61), or Germinus, where life "split into two kingdoms, one of ice, one of fire, each adapting to half of the bipolar planet" (84). Embedded as they are within the novel's realist frame *as* bedtime stories, these tales are marked as mere speculations. Theo's fictional planets are meant less to convey actual worlds than the infinite possibilities in a mind-blowingly vast universe, within a broader narrative frame that claims plausibility. *Bewilderment* thus intermingles realism with SF, but its interest in other worlds ultimately serves to stress their remoteness and the uniqueness of life on our own planet, and thus the danger of believing there might be a Planet B.

Transformations of Realist and Historical Climate Fiction

While literary scholars have taken notice of realist forays into climate fiction like Barbara Kingsolver's *Flight Behavior* (2012), such novels have proliferated in recent years.[51] It seems almost as if writers of literary fiction in this period have been purposely answering the call issued by Clark, Ghosh, Morton, Nixon, and others to test the capacity of realism to address the varied scales of climate change: from deep time; to climate injustice situated in histories of capitalist and colonialist exploitation; to the lived experience of individuals and communities confronting mounting disasters and who are increasingly conscious of the enormity of what humans, primarily in the West, have done to the planet, and doing what they can to mitigate and adapt to crisis. Many of these novels thus offer a reflexive, self-critical realism that stresses interconnection rather than atomized individuals, that decenters and critiques rather than exalts the human, and that ponders and demonstrates the capacity of realist forms to embed critiques of the ideological commitments of earlier eras of realism.

Bewilderment emphasizes the agency of the "wild" nonhuman world, conveys human smallness in time and space, and critiques private and political inaction in the face of climate catastrophe—and does all of these in its realist sections. Its homonymic title points to Theo's confusion and the rejuvenating potential of wilderness, but it might also suggest a wilding of the supposedly quotidian, individualist form of the realist novel. *Bewilderment*'s critique of anthropocentrism and attunement to the vastness of the nonhuman world emerges through Theo's search for extraterrestrial life, his memory of his deceased wife Alyssa, an environmental lobbyist, and in Robin's love for plants and animals and simmering rage at what humans have done to them. As in Powers's *Playground* and Pulitzer-winning *The Overstory*, *Bewilderment* expresses wonder at the life-forms of *this* planet, often marveling that its biodiversity surpasses the imagination of science fiction. To fulfill a general education requirement in college, Theo takes a biology class, in which his professor shows 500 undergraduates "that none of us had a clue what life can do" (46). "*Astounding Stories* had nothing on Dr. McMillian" (46). Theo becomes her summer research assistant, studying extremophiles, "alien life-forms in a sinkhole under Lake Huron," that "were among the bizarrely creative creatures on this planet—switching like Jekyll and Hyde from anoxic to oxygenic photosynthesis" (46). The references to "aliens" beneath the Great Lakes, pulp magazines, and Stevenson's shilling shocker underscore Powers's project in *The Overstory*, *Bewilderment*, and *Playground*: to show that the Earth's biodiversity, revealed through scientific discovery, is stranger than fiction. In these novels, the task of realism is to restore wonder to the nonhuman real.

Extending the trope of reality one-upping SF to human technology, the grieving Theo scours the web for videos of Alyssa testifying at the Wisconsin state capitol in an effort to outlaw abusive forms of animal husbandry. Theo marvels at the ease with which he can conjure images of his dead wife. "Not even the craziest SF story from my youth predicted it. Imagine a planet where the past never went away but kept happening again and again, forever" (54). Here the speculative planet is our own, and the "crazy" novum is the way we can reanimate our loved ones, after a fashion, via Internet archives. In the videos, Alyssa critiques the instrumentalizing of animals and refers to knowledge that Indigenous Americans have long guarded: "The creatures of this state do not belong to us. We hold them in our trust. The first people who lived here knew: all animals are our relatives" (56). In a series of flashbacks that use the low-tech medium of Theo's narration of his memories, we see Alyssa when alive, plagued by night terrors that rage at human cruelty and inaction. "Why is it so hard for people to see what's happening?" (131). In her dreams, "other kinds of life could talk. . . . And they told her what was really happening on this planet, the systems of invisible suffering on unimaginable scales. Human appetite's final solution" (131). In language reminiscent of other novels that evoke the quotidian genocides and torture chambers that are the meat and animal testing industries, such as Ruth Ozeki's *My Year of Meats* (1998), J. M. Coetzee's *Elizabeth Costello* (2003), and Karen Joy Fowler's *We Are All Completely Beside Ourselves* (2013), Powers has Alyssa evoke the incomprehensible scale of animal suffering that humans hide in slaughterhouses and labs.

Robin is his mother's son in his compassion for all living things and sensitivity to nonhuman agency. Theo too, is nothing if not aware of the scale of the universe and the fact that humans are far from the only life in it. "It takes ninety-three billion years to cross from one end of space to the other. . . . The universe is a living thing" (278). But Robin's neurodivergence hinders his ability to regulate his emotional responses, and Theo refuses to medicate his son—though for a time experimental neural feedback therapy helps. Much of *Bewilderment* is devoted to Robin exploding into violent rages at humanity's destruction of the nonhuman world and inaction in the face of mass extinction and destruction of the planet, followed by prolonged spells of depression. But what is mental health in the face of climate crisis, the novel asks. "Is it the ability to function productively in hard conditions? Or is it more a matter of appropriate response? Constant cheerful optimism might not be the healthiest reaction to" planetary disaster (138).

Powers's novel explores parenting a neurodivergent child in its own right, but also to query the notion of normalcy. Is Robin's rage divergent, or is the calmness of the vast majority the aberration? "The question wasn't why Robin was sliding down again. The question was why the rest of us were staying so insanely sanguine" (138). Evoking the activism of Greta Thunberg, the novel contrasts Robin's energetic political crusading with widespread apathy. Theo takes Robin to the statehouse, then the U.S. Capitol, to protest. Down in the "trenches of Earthly politics," Robin becomes dispirited at how alone he is: "Nobody else is protesting anything? Everyone in the state is perfectly happy with everything just the way it is?" (128). When he and Theo discover how difficult it is to get a permit despite constitutional rights to assemble, Powers expresses cynicism about the potential of such protests: "a civics lesson to show why legal public demonstration was never going to threaten the status quo" (126). The scalar issue Powers confronts here is not the smallness of humanity in comparison with geologic time, but the political question of what dissenting individuals can do in the face of widespread passivity and entrenched interests that throw up legal roadblocks to preserve the status quo.

In keeping with the works of literary SF I've considered in this chapter, *Bewilderment* preserves a concern with the traditional terrain of the realist novel, the human psyche, in exploring Robin's neuroatypicality, neural feedback therapy, Theo's grief over the loss of his wife and his single-parenting challenges, and the eternal mystery that is the human subject. When Robin asks his dad, "Which do you think is bigger? Outer space . . . Or inner," Theo recalls words "from [Olaf] Stapledon's *Star Maker* [1937], the bible of" his youth: "The whole cosmos was infinitely less than the whole of being . . ." "Inner," Theo replies, "Definitely inner" (268). As in *The Book of Joan*, Powers extends the humanistic notion that the mind might be more expansive than the cosmos. And as with his reference to extremophiles that are real "aliens" on our own planet, psychological realism here claims broader reach than intergalactic science fiction. The novel equivocates, however, about the significance of this idea.

Bewilderment knows that exalting the self is a romantic literary practice that is closely aligned with a liberalism that centered individuals in the West, and denied personhood to non-Western peoples, animals, and the natural world in order to instrumentalize them. But as in *Galatea 2.2*, Powers subtly undermines and renders unreliable his narrator protagonist. Theo is hyperconscious of climate calamity but susceptible to self-interest, which he naturalizes as biologically hardwired: the "trap evolution shaped for us: the entire species might have been on the line, and I'd still worry first about my son" (236). Though Theo attributes this flaw to natural selection, and so essentializes it as something inescapably human, he also recognizes prioritizing one's own over the good of the species as a "trap." Individualism, Powers insists, must give way to interconnection: "if some small but critical mass of people recovered a sense of kinship, economics would become ecology" (177). The novel then, especially through Robin's moral vision, critiques the economic logics of self-interest and resource exploitation: "We took over everything!" (36). Reckoning with the fact that "[h]alf the world's species were dying" (156), Robin's verdict is: "We deserve to be alone" (36). And later: "There's something wrong with us, Dad" (119). While Theo at times exalts the human psyche, Robin critiques the violence of anthropocentrism.

Bewilderment thus rejects a binary thinking that views realist novels as small and anthropocentric and SF as capable of dealing with the planetary, cosmic, and nonhuman. Further, it contests that the notion that novels that focus on humans need be in the business of exalting the human. The tensions that emerge in *Bewilderment*'s final passages are less contradictions than espousals of the view that human beings are endlessly complex life-forms and life on Earth precious, even if we are not unique in the cosmos: "[i]n a universe ninety-three billion light-years across, Rare Earths sprang up like weeds" (113). At the same time, humans are life-forms that have adopted instrumental ideologies and exploitative systems that threaten the survival of our own species and much nonhuman life. As the novel ends, Theo composes a requiem: "This endless gift of place is going away" (203). Its final bars sound a proleptic elegy for both the Earth and humanity:

> Oh, this planet was a good one. And we, too, were good, as good as the burn of the sun and the rain's sting and the smell of living soil, the all-over song of endless solutions singing the air of a changing world that by every calculation ought never to have been. (278)

Looking forward to human extinction and that of life on the planet, this ending affirms their goodness. But it does so while acknowledging that we will have destroyed ourselves and the planet's ecological systems. If the novel pays tribute to "goodness," it is one that is fatally undermined by the fact that we "took over everything" and have destroyed "this endless gift of a place." *Bewilderment*'s heartbreaking denouement, Theo's ultimate failure as a parent, ought to be read as an allegorical conclusion about the species: the highly intelligent, supposedly rational scientist can manipulate sophisticated technology, but cannot find a way to avert the most profound catastrophe.

Bewilderment is palpably Powers's effort to scale down *The Overstory*, while nesting the story of Theo and Robin inside broader contexts of mass extinction, the politics of climate inaction, and the vastness of the universe. But *The Overstory* is undoubtedly one of the most ambitious recent efforts to situate human characters in the scales of the nonhuman world and to critique how exclusive attention to human life has led us to the brink of planetary ecosystem collapse. As it intertwines the stories of nine protagonists with excurses on the immense and varied ecosystems of trees, *The Overstory* uses a number of techniques to generate, in the words of Rachel Adams, "an epic that moves from individual stories that are the typical subject of literary realism to a grand vision of the webbed planetary systems—the environment, the internet, the global economy—in which they are enmeshed."[52] Adams stresses the novel's attention to the disruption of "webs of interdependency that have put the world in grave danger and that gesture to an uncertain future," and shows how it "represents varied scales of interdependency at the level of form."[53] In addition to the resourceful methods *The Overstory* uses to intertwine its human stories with planetary systems and the nonhuman world, it internalizes critiques of the realist novel's ability to reckon with the timescales of the Anthropocene—critiques that it seems designed to refute.

The Overstory's Neelay Mehta engineers a gaming platform that bequeaths its players a limitless virtual world—a storyline Powers reprises in *Playground*'s depiction of gamified social media and AI developer Todd Keane. Neelay's game, as its title "Mastery" indicates, reproduces humans' worst tendencies to dominance and accumulation. Prior to a fall from a tree that leaves Neelay partially paralyzed, Powers delineates his love for science fiction—suggesting an origin for his virtual world-building game. "At night he pores over mind-bending epics that reveal the true scandals of time and matter. Sweeping tales of generational spaceship arks . . . that split and bifurcate into countless parallel quantum worlds."[54] Here Powers acknowledges SF's comfort with huge scales and multiple worlds. Further, he embeds a tale that points to ways humans fail to notice action that occurs on timescales that are slower and longer than the individual human life. In one of Neelay's favorite stories, tiny aliens arrive, moving "so fast that Earth seconds seem to them like years" (97). Humans are static "sculptures of immobile meat," by comparison, easy targets for the aliens to capture and cure, "like so much jerky, for the long ride home" (97). Powers inserts this humorous SF vignette as a mini fable of scale that parallels his main narrative; as the aliens mistake slow-moving humans for dumb creatures fit to be jerky, so humans mistake slow-growing trees for simple life-forms suited only to our use. But as in *Bewilderment*, the tale is an embedded fiction, read by a realistic character. Thus, Powers flexes the capacity of realism to embed SF's speculation and interplanetary scales.

While it acknowledges and embeds SF's historic preoccupation with epic scale, *The Overstory* also interpolates a critique of the realist novel's preoccupation with character and human drama, echoing the work of Clark, Ghosh, and others. As Dorothy Cazaly cares for her husband after a massive stroke, she reads to him aloud from the *"Hundred Greatest Novels of All Time"* (382). The books are all Ray has, and he "hangs on the most ridiculous plot crumb, as if the future of humanity hinges on it" (382). The "as if" offers a crucial rebuttal to the premise, and as Powers describes the novels, he suggests their rather narrower significance:

> The books diverge and radiate, as fluid as finches on isolated islands. But they share a core so obvious it passes for given. Every one imagines that fear and anger, violence and desire, rage laced with the surprise capacity to forgive—character—is all that matters in the end. It's a child's creed, of course, just one small step up from the belief that the Creator of the Universe would care to dole out sentences like a judge in federal court. To be human is to confuse a satisfying story with a meaningful one, and to mistake life for something huge with two legs. No: life is mobilized on a vastly larger scale, and the world is failing precisely because no novel can make the contest for the *world* seem as compelling as the struggles between a few lost people. (382–383)[55]

Such moments contend that a preoccupation with human drama has neglected nonhuman life and helped fuel its demise.

But *The Overstory*'s version of this critique forces an insight about novel form that is reminiscent of Bakhtin's theory of the novel, showing how its polyvocality may counterweight its focus on individual characters; by embedding many discourses, novels can critique the limitations of novelistic conventions.[56] What can't fit in a novel, if it can make room for such critiques, Powers seems to ask? *The Overstory* echoes accounts of the novel's anthropocentrism—going so far as to suggest that the "world is failing precisely because" of the failure of novels to confront a grander scale of life. At the same time, Powers's finch simile, likening the novel's forking paths to evolution, suggests its adaptability and variation despite its conventional emphasis on character. It's difficult to read this passage as anything but a self-reflexive account of the challenge Powers has set himself: to see if the novel is flexible enough to decenter humanity, transmit wonder at nonhuman life, and make urgent ongoing drama that holds the fate of the planet's ecosystems in the balance. And the passage suggests that Powers's persistence in depicting domestic dramas of care, like those of Dorothy and Ray, Theo and Robin, are conscious efforts to set the interpersonal novelistic fare that conventionally compels our interest within a larger narrative that makes clear their importance to the individuals involved but their relative insignificance. Further then, Powers's recent novels seem designed to reject binary thinking, to maintain that we can be concerned with the problems that affect individuals, collectives, and vaster scales and systems of human and nonhuman life, at the same time.

The Overstory's interwoven human narratives aim to show the interconnection of living things and inorganic systems. The critique of realist novels' limited purview emerges as part of its broader effort to call attention to human failures to perceive nonhuman life and ecological systems—with trees as the central example. The novel asserts throughout that people are "[p]lant-blind," possessed of a self-centered vision that makes us "only see things that look like us" (114). Much of the novel revolves around the efforts of Patricia Westerford, based on forest ecologist Suzanne Simard and her research into the ways trees communicate, to use her writing to make us see trees as "intricate, reciprocal nations of tied together life" (282). Patricia discovers that writing about such ecosystems presents narrative problems, as there are "no individuals in a forest, no separable events" (218) and often no "drama, no development, no colliding hopes and fears"—only a set of "[b]ranching, tangled, messy plots" (419). Despite these challenges, she figures the novel's efforts to make trees visible to its readers; she relies on personification, penning "biographies of her favorite characters: loner trees, cunning trees, sages and solid citizens," even if, with a debt to Ralph Ellison, "they speak on frequencies too low for people to hear" (432). Throughout, the novel dramatizes its ambitions to estrange readers from our limited field of vision, to dramatize nonhuman life through Patricia's writing, and to depict the transformation of characters who are oblivious to trees but become "primed to see" (165).

Patricia's narratives work to make readers see the long duration of tree life and ecosystem evolution, compared to human spans. We learn of Old Tjikko, a Norway spruce whose roots are 9,000 years old and whose paradoxical "use is to show that the world is not made for our utility" (222). This paradox might also be applied to the novel as a whole: a novel about human characters designed to show us that humans are far from the whole story. At the Pando aspen clone in central Utah, Patricia marvels that underground, "the eighty-year-old trunks are a hundred thousand, if they're a day," and Powers, with a nod to *King Lear*, quips that "trees like to toy with human thought like boys toy with beetles" (131). *The Overstory* devises a range of ingenious methods to make visible disjunctions between human and nonhuman timescales, as characters become aware of human smallness.

Powers opens the novel with the story of the photography project begun by Nicholas Hoel's grandfather: a thousand images of the family chestnut, taken over the course of a century. A flip through the photos becomes an accelerated film of the giant tree, "growing at the speed of wood," while "everything a human being might call the *story*"—the lives of people—"happens outside his photos' frame" (16). The novel's invention and ekphrasis of this idiosyncratic, multigenerational photography project encapsulates its desire to displace the human story from its center, as well as to dramatize the power of works of art to defamiliarize perception. Nicholas's grandfather can't "explain to him the point of the thick flip-book," but concedes in his folksy manner: "Makes you think different about things, don't it?" (19). Similarly, the priceless scroll Mimi Ma inherits from her grandfather depicts "Arhats. Adepts who have passed through the four stages of Enlightenment and now live in pure, knowing joy" (27). When asked to sum up their enlightenment, Mimi's father Winston explains pithily that they see "The True Thing," that "human beings" are "so small" and "life" is "so very big" (30). The novel does not merely juxtapose the fleeting human life with the long lives of trees, but also with the "few hundred million years of evolution" that have led to the biodiversity of the present, and the life that will go on after humans are extinct (224). One character thinks: "Humankind is deeply ill. The species won't last long. It was an aberrant experiment" (56), while another speculates that the "Jungle will get Bangkok, before too long. L.A., one day" (79). Thus the novel continually situates its human stories in contexts that dwarf them.

Though *The Overstory* does not represent planetary disaster as do so many dystopian and postapocalyptic novels, it nonetheless confronts the frightening potential disruptions of the Anthropocene. Further, its interest in correlating timescales leads it to stress that it is precisely the incredible speed with which human activity is upsetting ecosystems that have evolved over millions of years that makes the Anthropocene demand immediate and coordinated response. With heavy irony, Powers depicts logging technology, "human ingenuity at its best," allowing timber companies to raze "in a day what a team of human cutters would need a week to get through" (243). These ruthlessly efficient companies take down "eight-hundred-year-old trees" and are speeding up, "cutting at four times the industry rate," to preempt conservationists and "before legislation can catch up with them" (214). Again, Powers sets this accelerated extraction within a larger frame of ecosystem collapse, stressing that "[d]eforestation" is "a bigger changer of climate than all of transportation put together" and that there is "[t]wice as much carbon in the falling forests than in all the atmosphere" (281). A mere "twenty years" will be "time enough to kill whole ecosystems" (281).

The problem of humans' plant-blindness is thus set within accelerating systems of human growth and resource exploitation. "How is extraction ever going to stop?" Patricia asks her partner:

> The only thing we know how to do is grow. . . . Growth, all the way up to the cliff and over . . . the towering, teetering pyramid of large living things is toppling down already, in slow motion, under the huge swift kick that has dislodged the planetary system. (304)

Despite the challenges *The Overstory* acknowledges are posed by novels' conventional focus on human characters, and the seeming lack of drama of the complex, interconnected lives of trees, Powers has created a novel that emphasizes how we have failed to see them, treated them as raw material for our own use, and how quickly such exploitation will overturn millions of years of evolution, at incalculable cost to us and them.

Millet's *How the Dead Dream* also makes explicit endeavors to position its protagonist against a vast nonhuman world. Millet's free indirect discourse registers both T.'s pride in the housing development he is building and a critique of the extractive practices and infrastructure on which it relies:

It was a modest piece in a patchwork, stitched into the vast fabric by roads and cables and aqueducts, by cheap gasoline and abundant rubber and lumber from the northwest . . . the willingness to drain lakes and damn rivers, the invention of Freon and computers and urea formaldehyde. (86)

Here Millet links T.'s small development to the larger network of extractive industries, policies, and technologies on which it depends. As in *The Overstory*, Millet points to real estate investors' focus on short-term profit and willful blindness to the accelerating environmental threats to their construction projects: "speculators tended to ignore the foreshortened future of the hills, their promise of imminent collapse by mudslide, quake or fire" (28).

T. initially believes "in the wisdom of men" and the thought that "man advanced" (117). But this faith in the progress narrative is shaken as he learns how such "advancement" affects nonhuman life, such as the kangaroo rats, really a species of mouse, who are "displaced by the paving for his subdivision" and are "the last of their kind, on the brink of disappearing" (123). T. begins to confront the enormous scale of the nonhuman world, through its small, non-charismatic species: "The weight of ants, a biologist told him, was equal to fifteen percent of the weight of all land animals; ants roiled beneath the surface in untold billions" (123–124).[57] When T. learns of the rats' imminent extinction, he begins to suspect that "under the foundations" of the cities being "built up into the sky, battlements of convenience and utopias of consumption," the "earth seemed to be shifting and loosening" (125). Just as Powers conjures a "towering, teetering pyramid," Millet has T. recognize the destabilizing of human society and the planet's ecology—in metaphor, without recourse to apocalyptic drama. T.'s dawning awareness prompts a dream, a symbolic device that has always been available to writers of realist novels, in which Millet envisions biosphere upheaval and planetary collapse. The nightmare envisions "the ants abandoning ship" by the billions, "and as they went away holes opened up in the earth, yawning sinkholes into which oceans and mountains poured" (125). Like Powers's "pyramid," but focused on even smaller living things, Millet crafts an image of how human construction of "battlements of convenience" destabilizes their own foundation by upsetting the delicate balance of planetary systems. And Millet reveals the capacity of the realist novel to embed visions of Anthropocene ecological collapse within its character-centric structure.

While a single resonant image may be used to convey despeciation and disruption of planetary systems, Annie Proulx's *Barkskins* (2016), a novel that has been overshadowed to a regrettable degree by *The Overstory*, takes on a far more expansive ambit. *Barkskins* is a 700-page historical epic that examines the vast destruction wrought by timber industries, as well as the intertwining of resource extraction with colonization and genocide of Indigenous peoples. Proulx's novel resists summary, as it lacks any protagonist and instead traces the branching course of two family trees across many generations. It begins with Charles Duquet and René Sel, French indentured servants who arrive in Canada in 1693, and follows their many descendants over more than three centuries. The narrative bifurcates, depicting Duquet's founding of a multigenerational timber dynasty, and Sel's marriage to a Mi'kmaq woman and the struggles of their métis offspring in a North America that annihilates Indigenous peoples and cultures and forces the survivors into brutal labor for subsistence wages. *Barkskins* tracks deforestation from Quebec and Maine, westward to Michigan and California, and on to New Zealand and Brazil.

Alongside the novel's ambitious scope in chronology, setting, and characters, Proulx makes a shrewd intervention into questions of scale and the supposed progress achieved by Western societies, in her depiction of ambitious colonizers and captains of industry. Throughout the novel, these characters marvel at sprawling expanses of forest to be turned to ship masts, railroad ties, and dwellings. Each time, they believe, with poignant dramatic irony, such woodlands to be inexhaustible, "enormous and limitless."[58] Early in the novel, Duquet nearly has an epiphany, observing that the "landscape had been corrupted." "For a moment he was frightened; if miles of forest could be removed so quickly by a few men with axes, was the forest then as vulnerable as beaver?" (118). But this fleeting realization dissolves like smoke from burning slash, as he concludes: "No, the forest returned with vigor, resprouted.... These forests could not disappear. In New France they were vast and eternal" (118). This folly resounds through the novel. Duquet's great-grandson thanks God for the "glorious treasure" that is the forests of Michigan and exclaims that a "thousand men could not cut all this in a thousand years" (466). Another character doesn't worry if cities like Chicago "burned down every two or three years," since "there were more trees in the woods—endless trees" (539). When Duquet's great-great-great-grandson Charlie makes the "same complacent remarks" about Brazil's rainforest, thinking ranchers cannot "harm that massive heart of the world" (646), his father rebukes him: "There is no such thing as a being too large to fall. They all go down when men come" (467). Though Proulx has been criticized for "hammering" home her message, the repetition stresses the vastness of the forests that have been decimated and the irrational hubris of supposedly rational Western businessmen, who repeat the same error rather than learn.[59] Moreover, the mistake is a failure of scalar thinking; the timber barons believe their logging cannot impact the vastness of the Earth's forests.

By interweaving the story of the Duke dynasty with the Mi'kmaq Sels, Proulx contrasts the European Christian belief in a biblical injunction to "replenish the earth, and subdue it, and have dominion over the fish of the sea and every living thing that moveth, and every green tree and herb" (212), with those of Indigenous Americans, who treat the forest as a "living entity" that "one lived with . . . in harmony and gratitude" (51). The Christians ignore the "replenish" part, as under the ax, any sense of ecological interconnection dies: the "wildness of the world receded" and with it "the vast invisible web of filaments that connected human life to animals, trees to flesh and bones to grass shivered as each tree fell and one by one the web strands snapped" (12). Proulx covers this ground carefully, noting white settlers' recourse to an ideology that land was "useless . . . until cleared and planted" (59) and "belongs to the Man who improves it as scriptures show" (179), to justify their violent seizure of territory. And she avoids succumbing to a "myth of pristine primeval forest before the whiteman came" (706).

Proulx depicts some benevolent white settlers like Forgeron, who "deplored wholesale cutting," helping her critique the logging companies' "irresistible urge to take it all, then smash and destroy what they cannot use" (211). In their "insane wastage . . . the destruction of the soil, the gullying and erosion, the ruin of the forest world with no thought for the future," the German Breitsprecher sees simply "[r]apine" (466). But Proulx underscores the majority of the settlers' inability to see human and nonhuman interdependence or plan: "they cannot believe soil has anything to do with forests," ignore erosion, and when they "choke in the fumes of the city they do not make a connection with the purer air in the forest" (480). *Barkskins* repeatedly points to the timber barons' failure to see connections in their rapacious resource exploitation. In New Zealand, the "newcomers did not care to understand the strange new country beyond taking whatever turned a profit. They knew only what they knew. The forest was there for them" (437). At the same time, Proulx counters this instrumentalism with a vision of the forest's interdependence and independent existence, "a kind of grand wild orchestra ... living for itself rather than the benefit of humankind" (643).

As it dramatizes the destruction wrought by settler colonial extraction on both forest ecosystems and native populations, Proulx's novel manifests in striking fashion the overlap and blurriness of generic categories, since *Barkskins* relies on an unquestionably realist historical ontology that is nonetheless apocalyptic. In a chapter entitled "stupendous conflagration," homesteaders clear land with fire, despite drought conditions (381). The resultant wildfire is a "holocaust" accompanied by "hurricane wind" that chases Jinot Sel like "a ravening, demonic beast" (386). Later, logging equipment becomes the diabolical within the actual, as "technology shaped crazy daydreams into real hissing screaming machines that leveled the last of the ancient forests on the continent" (614). As with the similes of Yuknavitch and Powers, Proulx's figurative language establishes the horror that subsists within the real—one doesn't need a gothic framework. Later, when the "noble kauri" forests of New Zealand have been cleared and burned, Proulx shows us "acres of devastation," now indistinguishable from the wastelands of the gum fields, which "were the most desolate landscapes, churned mud where nothing grew, great holes gauged in the wet earth" (645). These realistic visions of the devastating toll of extraction comprise some of *Barkskins* most visceral scenes.

As the deforestation expands globally, so does the novel's apocalyptic rhetoric. The Amazon's "incomprehensible richness ... aloof from its destiny of improving men's lives" is an affront to the American timber barons that makes them "clutch and rend in maenadic frenzies of destruction" (653). The feverish annihilation continues in the novel's depiction of the genocide of Indigenous peoples and cultures. When Jinot Sel's son Aaron returns to his family village outside Halifax, he finds "no dogs, no people," just a solitary soul "dying of violent spasms of coughing" (595). Disease has decimated the population, leaving only bundles of rags covering "emaciated skeletal arms," dead infants, a comatose man. The lone couple able to talk tells him simply: "They die. Everybody sick, no food, die, die, die. Children all die. Mi'kmaw people now walk around, look for food, eat dirt. . . . Now lie down and die" (596). As Aaron looks to buy food to help these starving people, he comes across a pastor who believes "Charity does but delay the inevitable," when "the Red Man passes from the scene" (597). The efforts of European settlers to "civilize" serve as epistemic violence to complement guns, germs, and child torture. Proulx shows us a "residential school where Mi'kmaw children, their culture and language suffered a forty-year implosion as deadly as any munitions ship" (620), and where few "parents knew of the atrocities practiced on their boys and girls by genocidal nuns and priests" (623). The upshot of this litany of terrors in *Barkskins* is clear: for Indigenous Americans and the planet, apocalypse is a matter of history, not the stuff of speculation.[60]

Despite these horrifying visions of genocide and deforestation, Proulx is attuned to what Rebecca Evans calls "the need to narrate a *permeable* apocalypse, an *open* apocalypse" that remains "iterative and incomplete," to address environmental crisis without "craft[ing] an inexorable vision of history in which the end is predestined," and which may "threaten to enervate political will."[61] Or as Robin puts it in *Bewilderment*: "You can't depress people though. That just scares them. You gotta show them the good life" (212). Proulx's *Barkskins* concludes, bringing its historical sweep to the present day, with several chapters that focus on Sapatisia Sel, ecological activist, researcher, and descendent of René Sel, who connects settler colonialism and ecocide:

> Since the conquest the air has been filled with pesticides and chemical fertilizers, with exhaust particles and smoke. We have acid rain. The deep forests are gone and now the climate shifts. The old medicine plants grew in a different world. (696)

But the new world is not without hope, as Sapatisia's grandchildren join her and dozens of conservation groups for a reforestation project in Nova Scotia. Proulx situates their efforts in the broader movement of Indigenous people in "Brazil, Peru, Columbia, Cambodia, Sumatra, Vietnam" and the western United States "to replant forests and resurrect damaged rivers" (706). "Dispossessed people who lived in forests for millennia" are the vanguard who "step forward to do the repair work," despite threats and murders, the ones who "understand how to heal the forest" (706). Even if they will not see the fruits of their labor, as it "will take thousands of years for the great forests to return,"

Sapatisia stresses how "terribly important to all us humans" are the efforts of activists, "even if it is only one or two people" (706).

Proulx thus insists on the consequence of individuals' actions to worldwide environmental movements, even if the forests' recovery will take millennia. And this work in turn inspires and fulfills the individual, as Sapatisia's granddaughter Jeanne discovers not "just a job but a cause, a lifework," that fills her with "joy like a narrow sun ray breaking through heavy overcast" and a sense of "leafy meaning" (709). Thus, *Barkskins* conveys the vast scale of destruction wrought by extraction and colonization, but also how individuals might unite to build worldwide movements to mitigate and adapt to climate disaster, regenerate forests, and secure a future for dispossessed people and the nonhuman world.

Conclusion: Ozeki's Reflexive Magical Realism

Barkskins offers a particularly vivid demonstration of this chapter's central arguments: that speculative genres are not required for writing about climate change and the Anthropocene; that genres—here the novel, the realist novel, and the historical novel—don't have fixed forms or an inherent political freight and don't need to be narrowly focused on individuals, limited in scale, or anthropocentric. Writers of recent literary climate fiction have not abandoned concern with the traditional province of literary novels—human characters with rich inner lives—but they have found innovative ways to adapt realist genres in order to critique the notion that human experience ought to be our only concern, to explore the disastrous consequences of anthropocentric exploitation of the nonhuman world, and to investigate the significance of individual action when it is situated within systems of capitalist extraction and colonialism, and geologic, planetary, and cosmic scales. Further, these writers demonstrate the instability of generic categories, the way claims about the affordances or relative advantages of a given genre rely on a hypostatization that neglects the capacity of writers to modify and deploy genres in novel ways, in the pursuit of varied aims. These writers show that literary form is not restrictive but subject to continual renovation.

Ozeki's *The Book of Form and Emptiness* (2021) stands as a prodigious recent exercise in a reflexive, somewhat magical realism that demonstrates the capacity of novels to move beyond anthropocentrism, combining an interest in human individuals with attention to the vibrant matter of the nonhuman world, colossal scales of time and space, and to the question that has occupied this chapter and book: the question of the plasticity of literary form. Unlike works of postmodernist metafiction, the novel does not foreground its own fictionality or explicitly address its own constructedness or that of all narratives.[62] But the predicament and dialogues of its central characters and its unique formal devices provoke questions about the nature of reality. This is especially true of its most glaring conceit: the fact that alternating chapters of the novel are narrated by a talking book, an object that is both fanciful and real enough. What better example of an agential object than a bundle of wood pulp and ink that communicates and brings to life fictional entities? And Ozeki uses ingenious techniques to contemplate the scale of climate disaster, in a novel that might look to be narrowly focused on the travails of an adolescent boy and his mother, who have recently lost their father and husband.

Benny, the child protagonist of *The Book of Form and Emptiness*, hears voices; the objects of the world talk to him. These voices cause significant distress, as no one else hears them, and at times they ask him to commit disturbing acts. A pair of scissors urges him to stab his teacher, even though Benny really likes her, when she gives a lesson on climate change. The scissors taunt Benny that the informational display he is assigned to construct

> was useless, that it wasn't going to stop climate change, nothing was . . . they were all fucked, this teacher was stupid, she was his enemy and the reason everyone thought he was crazy, which was why it was necessary for him to stab her in the neck. *Now!* [63]

Ozeki thus links Benny's hearing of voices to grief over his father's death, proleptic climate grief, and the sense of his own powerlessness.

One way of viewing the voices, a way he is susceptible to and terrified of, is that he is "crazy." But the ingenious twist of Ozeki's novel is that while Benny's voices might seem a symptom of his mental health struggles, the novel leaves no doubt that the voices *are really there*, as its chapters oscillate between Benny's narration and that of the talking book. In the novel's prologue, an author figure tells the reader the talking book, "it's talking to you," and maintains that "[t]hings speak all the time, but if your ears aren't attuned, you have to learn to listen" (3). One might easily read the novel as a work of magical realism, in which objects possess a marvelous capacity to speak. But Ozeki's work ought to be understood as making a different kind of contention: our "normal" conception of reality, in which we imagine humans to have a unique capacity for agency and speech, fails to see the lives of the things around us; a more "attuned" realism will recognize their agency as a vital part of the real. In other words, to assert that *The Book of Form and Emptiness* is not a realist novel is to align oneself with a rational, purportedly objective epistemology that denies agency to nonhuman objects. Rather than viewing the novel as a venture into magical realism, the fantastic, or the marvelous, Ozeki asks us to reconsider our sense of the real and consider her book part of a more capacious realist project. The talking book enacts this revised realism at the level of narration, while Benny develops a friendship with eccentric artists and poets in the public library, who help him "contemplate [the] nature of reality" (230) and explore "his philosophical question," which is also that of the novel: "*What is real?*" (340). The novel's reflexive realism does not take the answer for granted, and it blends more traditional realism with a kind of it-narrative or novel of circulation to explore ideas central to object-oriented ontology and actor-network theory, as well as Zen ideas about the interconnectedness of being.[64]

Like many novels I've discussed in this chapter, *The Book of Form and Emptiness* seems designed to answer critics who have called for fiction to decenter the human and tackle the confounding scalar oscillations of the Anthropocene. Benny's friend and love interest is a heroin-addicted teenage experimental artist named the Aleph, one of the novel's many Borges references, who produces intricate snow globes containing "miniaturized global catastrophes, frozen in time," that represent "disaster capitalism"; the Aleph considers titling the series "Global Warming," "Desert of the Real," or "State of Emergency" (249–251). The narrating book muses about what gives these microcosmic worlds "the power to enchant," recalling the famous *Blue Marble* photograph shot by Apollo 17 in 1972, an image that "became a symbol of the environmental movement and caused a profound shift in the way people conceived of the planet, shrinking from something incomprehensibly awesome into a fragile, lonely orb that you could ... crush beneath a careless heel" (252–253). At the same time as the photograph shrunk Earth, it "was inflating your sense of importance in relation to it ... The image caused, in other words, a derangement of scale, from which you people still suffer" (253). Ozeki's reference to Clark and the ekphrasis of the Aleph's snow globes embed in the novel an examination of the deformations of scalar perception demanded by life in the Anthropocene. Similarly, in the novel's depiction of the hoarding of Benny's mother Annabelle, who collects news archives for her job at a media-monitoring agency and cannot bear to throw anything away, Ozeki considers the way awareness of the manifold disasters that surround us manifests as an overwhelming volume of information that threatens to engulf our lives.[65]

Annabelle's collection of news media is one instance of the novel's preoccupation with archives and libraries as repositories of great volumes of information and paradigms of the unpredictable agency of things: you never know what might pop up in them. Each of the novel's sections begin with epigraphs from Walter Benjamin, the namesake of Ozeki's protagonist. Benny spends most of his time in the public library, where he discovers slips of paper that the Aleph has left in varied books, as part of her "unauthorized site-specific installation ... consisting of labyrinthine trails that led through the Library's collections" that she calls "Forking Paths" (489). The novel's references to Borges and Benjamin, along with its setting in a library and talking book, make it a bibliophilic piece of literary fiction that poses books as exemplary agential objects. "The Book" admits "writers are necessary," but insists "agency is a matter of perspective"; a writer may be seen as the co-author of books, aided by all those she has read, which have been secretly "colonizing her neural networks" (481).

More pointedly, Ozeki has the narrating book critique instrumental reason, recounting how humans divide the world into "the Made and the Unmade," relegating the latter into a "mere resource, a lowly serf class" of objects "to be colonized, exploited, and fashioned into something *else*" (70–71). In the resulting "hierarchy of matter," books for a time occupied the pinnacle, "were the ecclesiastical caste," "sacred" objects, for whom humans built the "hallowed halls" of libraries (71). But as "new-fangled device[s]" come along, the Book recognizes the "folly" of the belief that "we were so special" (71). Books in turn lose faith in their human creators, as they watch us "mine, instrumentalize and lay waste to our home, this Earth, this sacred planet," and use books as "unwitting tools, forging the destruction of the planet" (72). But in "the end days of the Anthropocene (*your* word, *your* hubris, not ours), Matter is making a comeback. . . . In a neo-materialist world, *Every Thing Matters*" (72). When the Book apologizes for its "rant," Ozeki seems to acknowledge the didacticism of this passage, but the Book offers a potent critique of how instrumentalizing matter, ignoring its vitality, and belief in human mastery have led to planetary crisis (72). As the Book reflects on the declining status of the literary, so it entreats us to recognize the fallacy of our anthropocentrism—the notion that mankind alone has shaped the planet's systems embedded in the word "Anthropocene."

Ozeki's novel asserts that collections of matter like libraries and archives display a complicated agency of their own, persisting as indeterminate assemblages that despite their orderly arrangement are subject to chance encounters and have unpredictable effects on those who wander within them. The Aleph's "strange scraps and leavings" are "like clues in a treasure hunt" that "at first glance seemed random and accidental, and yet you could sense a subtle, underlying pattern, too, a sense of purpose that was controlling the choice of this book over that one" (489). Though the Aleph has arranged the clues according to her purposes, the artist cannot control the encounters that result. Benny only finds his first slip of paper and clue by happening to pick up *Grimm's Fairy Tales* off another library patron's desk. Thus, Ozeki explores the complicated networks of human and nonhuman agency that are co-constituted by writers, the books they read and help produce, libraries, and the forking paths of readers who wander within them.

What kind of book can conjure such networks, foreground nonhuman agents, and reckon with the enormous hyperobjects and scalar derangements generated by climate change and the Anthropocene? "Any kind of book," seems to be Ozeki's answer. In addition to its conceit of the talking book, *The Book of Form and Emptiness* embeds sections from a Marie Kondo–like self-help manual called *Tidy Magic: The Radical Zen Art of Clearing Your Clutter and Revolutionizing Your Life*, written by a Zen monk named Aikon, that jumps into Annabelle's shopping cart (Ozeki herself is a Zen monk). Ever self-aware, Ozeki recognizes the ostensible incongruity of self-help with literary fiction and nods to genre hierarchies by having the talking book observe that "scholarly tomes disparage the more commercial books"; "[l]iterary novels look down on romance and pulp fiction, and there's an almost universal disregard for certain genres like self-help" (94). Thus "the idea of including chapters of a self-help book within these pages caused" the snobby narrating book "some alarm" (94). But Benny insists that *Tidy Magic* is "essential to his mother's story" (95). Annabelle is intrigued by the possibility that it might help her declutter her home, and Ozeki's librarian character Cory, though initially disdainful of self-help, believing "all books are not created equal" (489), decides "this one seemed different"—an outlier that attests to the heterogeneity and pliability of all genres (490). Cory finds that *Tidy Magic* is

> woke to the fucked-upedness of carbon-based consumer capitalism that was wrecking the planet. The problem was systemic. . . . A person's clutter wasn't the result of laziness, procrastination, psychological disorders, or character flaws. It was a socioeconomic and even philosophical problem, one of Marxian alienation and commodity fetishism. (490)

In Ozeki's hands, even self-help need not be individualist, but can be "woke" to the structural problems produced by late-stage, carbon capitalism.

While writers can modify even a genre-like self-help to make it tackle systemic problems, Ozeki's novel, with characteristic humor and brilliance, further reflects on the question of form itself, as its title indicates with reference to the famous verse from the Heart Sutra: "form is emptiness, emptiness is form."[66] It is impossible to concisely render the meaning of this chiastic paradox, the source of voluminous commentary, but the Venerable Zasep Tulku Rinpoche offers a brief and accessible gloss:

> Emptiness is the fact that all things are conditioned to change moment by moment. Each phenomenon has no particular inherent nature of its own, therefore everything is emptiness, yet, at each moment, all phenomena are just as they are. . . . Form is Emptiness and Emptiness is also form because Emptiness is the cause of form and the various aspects of form arise from it. Without Emptiness there would be no form. In this way, the Emptiness of form is essentially not distinct from form. And form also is not essentially distinct from Emptiness. Everything arises from Emptiness, and everything dissolves back into it.[67]

The central Zen notion of "dependent co-arising," of the interdependence and flux of all things, which have no fixed or independent essence, chimes with ecological thought and can of course be applied to literary form as to all phenomena.[68] Literary forms have no fixed essence, coming into being only to be dissolved again and arise again in a different guise. *The Book of Form and Emptiness* explores the arising of form out of emptiness in its imagining of a mystical "Bindery" in the bowels of the public library. There, Benny is surrounded by book covers and blank pages, "like ghosts, waiting for words to be impressed upon . . . their blankness, their emptiness" (288). "Words would animate" these pages "and transform them into semi-living things, but for the time being, they were menacing in their muteness, their meaning not fixed" (288). Though Benny finds the blank pages "menacing" in the creepy basement, for Ozeki, the Bindery's emptiness offers a vision of pure potential: "*The Bindery contains everything. . . . Anything is possible. . . .* The Bindery was primordial, a place of vast boundless silence that contained all sound, and emptiness that contained all form" (289).

The sense that blank pages and unbound books are spaces of endless possibility, emptiness containing and awaiting form, intertwines with Ozeki's aim to contain within her novel the hyperobjects of climate change and the Anthropocene, and even the boundlessness of the universe. With reference to the central ideas of Borges's "El Aleph" and Jane Bennet's *Vibrant Matter*, the talking book calls the Bindery "the point in space that contains all other points," and Benny, within it, is "a boy unbound, a tiny astronaut taking [his] first leap into an infinite and unknowable universe," who can now "see the voices of the things [he'd] been hearing for so long, all that clamorous matter vying for [his] attention" (453). Immediately after these lines, Ozeki connects Benny's vision of the infinite with images of capitalist infrastructure and environmental catastrophe:

> Container ships glittering on a moonlit night off the coast of Alaska . . . Fires rage as the redwoods burn; and in the deep ocean a pilot whale carries her dead baby on her nose, while sea turtles weep briny tears into nets of plastic. . . . How impossible it is to put into words this infinitude of the Unbound! In a single instant, we witnessed constellations on the brink of constellating, assemblages in flux. We perceived the dynamic flow of vibrant matter. (453)

Even as it laments the impossibility of putting infinity into language, the problem of representing scale par excellence, the Book paradoxically manages to convey a sense of the infinite "Unbound" in and through a series of black marks on a white page. Benny accesses the infinite, the dynamic flux of emptiness, "in the Bindery, where phenomena are still Unbound," and stories have not yet learned to behave in a linear fashion, and all the myriad things of the world are simultaneously emergent, occurring in the same present moment, coterminous with you ... the universe becoming ... all that was and ever could be: form and emptiness, and the absence of form and emptiness. (454)

While Benny experiences "what it was to open completely, to merge with matter and let everything in" (454), Ozeki's novel approximates this sensation through its own flow of words, through its upwelling of literary form out of emptiness. The vast scales of climate change and the Anthropocene, the lives of things, the far reaches of the human mind, the infinitude of the universe: all of these might be discovered in a library. Ozeki's book seems to ask: what can't a literary novel find a form for? *Anything is possible.*

Coda
Literary Romance and Social Media Speculation

> Only Gregory Bouton's machine—*this one, fiction*—lets us roam with absolute freedom through the human collective.[1]
> JENNIFER EGAN, *The Candy House* (2022)

IF GENRE BENDING HAS ONLY glancingly touched on literary writers' endeavors to adopt and transform what continues to be the most commercially successful and prolific popular genre, one may not have to look too far for explanations. The romance genre has of course been devalued historically in literary circles, due to both a sexist dismissiveness toward its largely female readership and the relative rigidity of its conventions. Excellent recent scholarship has shown that despite the genre's seeming reliance on a repetitive conventional form and subject matter—to the point where certain players in the field like Harlequin contractually require conventional formal features like the happily-ever-after ending[2]—the romance field is huge and internally varied. Romance is often blended with other genres like fantasy—yielding the "romantasy" sensations of Sarah J. Maas and Rebecca Yarros—or historical period dramas, and writers have folded into their books a near-infinite number of permutations of possible partners, genders, sexual inclinations, rivals intervening, and forms of union—all beneath what might appear from a distance to be the single abiding thematic concern of romantic love.[3] If romance as a genre seems rigid, this is due to practices within its enormous field: publishers demand writers adopt a particular structure, readers want to see their expectations met, and they often are extremely devoted fans of a single genre or subgenre. But the inflexibility or adherence to formula in parts of the romance *field* should not be confused with the rigidity of the romance as a *genre*, which, as this book has argued throughout, is as infinitely plastic and adaptable as any other.

If literary writers have largely hesitated to build their fictions on the romance genre, this is likely due to their efforts to avoid a stigmatized sector of culture, and thus to bend the genre or blend it with others to the point where their books are barely recognizable *as romance*. Byatt's *Possession: A Romance* may remain the novel of high literary ambition that most overtly embraces the designation. But, as I discuss in Chapter 4, even Byatt shows ambivalence toward what the novel calls "vulgar romance" and aligns her book with a "high" romance tradition of quests and fusion of realistic and mythic elements. And, of course, even her "vulgar" romance plot is highly bookish and brainy: the burgeoning relationship of two scholars of Victorian poetry.

This reluctance to embrace the genre does not mean that genre-bending literary writers have avoided consideration of romantic love, sex, and relationships—far from it—but that when they have introduced romance into their fictions, they have frequently blended it with other genres—as in *Possession*, Chabon's *Yiddish Policemen's Union*, Hamid's *Exit West*, Mitchell's *A Thousand Autumns of Jacob de Zoet*, or McCarthy's *All the Pretty Horses*. Like other writers of contemporary literary fiction, genre benders typically refuse the satisfying closure of happy endings and produce frustrated or unsuccessful romances.[4] And they typically subordinate the principal question of romance novels—will they get together?—to other thematic concerns. A novel like Hanya Yanagihara's *A Little Life* (2015) exemplifies these tendencies: its romantic subplot is intertwined with queer melodrama and naturalism; the relationship between Jude and Willem ends tragically; and its concerns with love and romance take a back seat to an excruciating exploration of trauma and self-harm. Or take Elif Batuman's acclaimed *The Idiot* (2017), which is a witty, bibliophilic bildungsroman interested in language and centered on protagonist Selin's confused attraction for Ivan, which is never consummated. And then there is the question of the blurry borders of fields. While works of high literary ambition have tended to blend romance with other genres, bend its conventional plot arc, and foreground other issues at the expense of an exclusive focus on courtship, in the literary/commercial field of general fiction, romance is omnipresent in works from Helen Fielding's *Bridget Jones's Diary* (1996) to Bonnie Garmus's *Lessons in Chemistry* (2022). But if there is one writer in the field of ambitious, critically acclaimed literary fiction who has dedicated her career to bending the romance genre, that writer is undoubtedly Sally Rooney.

Rooney's Literary Romance

What makes Rooney's romances literary? Published in the UK by renowned Faber—whose list boasts thirteen Nobel laureates and six Booker Prize winners—and in the United States by Farrar, Straus and Giroux and the venerable Hogarth—launched by Virginia and Leonard Woolf in 1917 and revived by Penguin Random House in 2011—Rooney's work circulates in the literary subfield—though these publishers have marketed her books aggressively, yielding impressive sales.[5] But their form and what transpires inside them are unmistakably literary, if also unambiguously romance. Rooney's novels revolve around relationships and are chock-full of dialogue and highly bingeable. At the same time, they explore "serious" issues around class, gender, education, religion, and labor. And her characters, their conversations, and milieu are relentlessly bookish: they are writers or editors at literary magazines, English majors who read George Eliot, James Baldwin, and Chris Kraus and name-drop Baudrillard, Spivak, and Zizek.

Rooney's first two novels—spoilers ahead!—are also failed romances, refusing the genre's conventional happy ending. *Conversations with Friends* (2017) ends uncertainly, with the suggestion that Frances and Nick will rekindle their affair, along with the potentially disastrous consequences that will portend for Frances's relationship with Bobbi and Nick's marriage to Melissa. The denouement of *Normal People* (2018) could hardly be more literary in its refusal of tidy closure and subject matter, as Connell and Marianne have reunited and live together in Dublin, but Connell is accepted to pursue an MFA in creative writing at NYU. The novel ends with Marianne encouraging him to go, promising she will "always be here."[6] But we will never know if he does, if doing so spells the end of their romance, or if they will reunite once again. At the end of *Intermezzo* (2024), Ivan and Margaret remain together, and Peter, Sylvia, and Naomi settle into a "throuple" of sorts, an

> experiment bound almost certainly for one kind of failure or another, and yet attaining for these few hours and days to a miraculous success, a perfection of beauty, inexchangeable, meant not to be interpreted, meant only to be lived and nothing more.[7]

Posing this arrangement as "almost certainly" doomed "and yet" a "miraculous success" for the moment, Rooney here seems to reject the very idea of a narrative that presumes to tell how a relationship turns out, "interpret" it as happy, ill-fated, or otherwise—uncertainty and flux being the nature of things. Rooney's *Beautiful World, Where Are You?* (2021) is the outlier here, with its dual romances both ending happily. But that novel, even more than the other three, offers a self-reflexive questioning of the premises of the romance genre and novel reading as such: Just how significant is the happiness of a couple? And how much difference might another novel make in the world?

In other words, the literariness of Rooney's novels arises not only in their adherence to values that predominate in the literary field: a willingness to refuse the romance's conventional ending, an emphasis on character depth and prose style, a bookish milieu, the varied social and political concerns they explore beyond relationships. Her fiction also offers a self-conscious interrogation into these values and the meaning and significance of romantic love and literary production. *Conversations with Friends* is about adultery, but also Frances's battle with endometriosis, against a medical establishment that ignores female pain, and her skepticism toward a literary faith in psychological depth and individuality. When she first meets Nick, he flirts that he is "drawn to the poetic types," and she replies ironically: "Oh, well. I have a rich inner life, believe me."[8] Much later, when Frances begins to cut herself and feel her body to be "completely disposable, like a placeholder for something more valuable," she thinks of "all the things [she] had never told Nick about [her]self," a consoling thought "as if [her] privacy extended all around [her] like a barrier protecting" her body and reassuring her that she is "a very autonomous and independent person with an inner life that nobody else had ever perceived."[9] Here the belief in her unreachable private self serves as a psychic barricade against Frances's suspicion that her body and life are actually "disposable."

Rooney's novels aren't only full of rich inner lives, but they submit that literary value to questioning: Does it really matter if we have unique psyches, if we are treated as disposable by larger social forces and other individuals? Interiority and also style. Even though Rooney's writing prior to *Intermezzo* was largely spare and unadorned, *Normal People* binds Connell's developing aesthetic sense and growth as a writer to its own self-conscious use of poetic language. At Marianne's summer home outside Trieste, "[c]herries hang on the dark-green trees like earrings," and Connell "thinks about this phrase once or twice" (170). Rooney ironizes her own style by pointing to Connell's self-approval at his phrasing and suggests that his literary dreams are motivated by a desire to win "the approval of" other students at Trinity College, "to be a person of status" (219).

This self-reflexive questioning of literary values and the value of the literary persists through Rooney's oeuvre and evinces her avowed Marxist commitments. Connell's literary ambition is evidenced by his application to a creative writing program. But *Normal People*, which foregrounds the tension caused by the opposed class backgrounds of its central couple—Connell's mother cleans the house of Marianne's family—suggests his literary ambition may conceal a working-class boy's efforts to access the intellectual world of elites, and it is skeptical about the difference literature makes in the world. When Connell goes to the reading of a visiting writer, Rooney renders through his perspective a Bourdieusian critique of literature's function as cultural capital. "He knows that a lot of the literary people in college see books primarily as a way of appearing cultured. When someone mentioned the austerity protests that night," his editor Sadie, "threw her hands up and said: Not politics, please!" (228). The succession of Connell's thoughts followed by Sadie's protest against protest make clear Rooney's point that literature serves to legitimate class hierarchy and avoids political commitment that would upend this hierarchy.

Not only elite college students but writers are implicated here:

> All books were ultimately marketed as status symbols, and all writers participated to some degree in this marketing. Presumably this was how literature made money. Literature, in the way it appeared at these public readings, had no potential as a form of resistance to anything. (228)

When Rooney then depicts Connell's work on a story stirring in him the "old beat of pleasure inside his body . . . like the rustling movement of light through leaves, a phrase of music from the window of a passing car," a few consoling "moments of joy despite everything" (228), she poses literary pleasures like her own lyrical similes as fleeting compensations for literature's inability to mount meaningful political resistance. At the same time, her caveat, "in the way it appeared at these public readings," offers some hope it might. When Marianne and Connell go "to a protest against the war in Gaza," she mourns the loss of a time "when she had felt so intelligent and young and powerful that she almost could" believe that she could "stop all violence committed by the strong against the weak" (234). Her loss of confidence in this possibility leaves, however, a more modest hope. Though she finds it "much harder to reconcile herself to the idea of helping a few, like she would rather help no one than do something so small and feeble," she realizes helping no one "wasn't it either" (234). *Normal People* thus suggests more limited goals "of helping a few" people for ambitious young people and novels alike.

But Rooney's most searching interrogation of literature's social function thus far arrives in *Beautiful World, Where Are You?*, in which her co-protagonists, the novelist Alice and her best friend Eileen, correspond via long intellectual emails. (Here literary romance fuses with the epistolary genre.) Alice complains that she can't read contemporary novels anymore, because their fêted authors have become detached from the "ordinary life" they claim to write about, and spend their time "sitting with white linen tablecloths laid out in front of them and complaining about bad reviews."[10] In a novel by a young Irish writer who has shot to fame and written a novel called *Normal People*, it's hard not to read Rooney as indicting herself here. *Beautiful World*'s class critique of literature contrasts these pampered authors with Alice's uneducated love interest Felix, who works in an Amazon warehouse, breaking his body by lugging around commodities like the books she writes for a substantial income.

Beautiful World's blunt challenge to literature is to ask if it can do anything to combat this inequality, or if it merely advances and legitimates it. Alice asserts flatly that the "problem with the contemporary Euro-American novel is that it relies for its structural integrity on suppressing the lived realities of most human beings on earth" (103). "Who can care" what happens in a novel "when it's happening in the context of the increasingly fast, increasingly brutal exploitation of the majority of the human species? Do the protagonists break up or stay together? In this world, what does it matter?" (103). For Alice the utter irrelevance of romance novels relative to the suffering in the world is the problem of romantic entanglements as such: "we can care once again, as we do in real life, whether people break up or stay together—if, and only if, we have successfully forgotten about all the things more important than that, i.e. everything" (103). Alice finds her own work "morally and politically worthless" (244), but she doesn't have the last word on the subject. Eileen responds that Alice's quarrel with the novel is "simply the problem of contemporary life," as we "invest energy in the trivialities of sex and friendship when human civilization is facing collapse" (118). And Eileen muses that civilizations inevitably rise and fall, while to individuals "the meaning of life remains the same—always just to live and be with other people" (169).

For some critics, Rooney thus retreats from the critique she levels at the contemporary novel, failing to envision a world with alternatives to such "trivialities," such as revolutionary struggle against the oppressive regimes she identifies.[11] If this is your hope, that her novels will do more than point out the contradictions of living under late capitalism and function as an instrument in its demise, you will be disappointed. But Rooney's books show that there's no limit to what can be done with the romance genre. It can be used to critique novel reading or our obsession with romantic love—why not start a revolution too? For some the answer here will be that conglomerate publishing suppresses such radicalism. But it's not due to any limitation of the romance genre or novel form.

Egan's Social Media Speculation

Jennifer Egan's *The Candy House*, an expansion of the world of her Pulitzer-winning *A Visit from the Goon Squad*, offers a far more affirmative view of how novels function in the world, illuminating divergent self-reflexive attitudes toward literature within the field of literary fiction. *The Candy House* crystallizes so many of the concerns of *Genre Bending* that it seems almost designed for this book's conclusion. Though its publisher Scribner subtitles it "A Novel," *The Candy House* could be considered a collection of stories as, like its predecessor, it is a set of loosely connected tales in which characters who appear fleetingly in one become the protagonists of the next. These stories take place in different periods and deploy varied genres, but they share and extend concerns from their predecessor: with technology, especially social media, memory, and the difference between authentic art and experience and commodified facsimiles of both.

While the vignettes of *Goon Squad* revolve around record company executive Bennie Salazar and his punk bandmates from his youth, *The Candy House* moves slightly further afield to consider what digital technology has done—not only to the music industry but to contemporary life writ large. The latter volume takes its title from a scene involving Salazar's mentor, record producer Lou Kline, who, upon discovering the invention of the music "sharing" program Napster, has a premonition of "a tidal wave" that portends the "complete annihilation of [his] business" (124). His daughters Lana and Melora encourage him to consider ways to stave off the "sharing" of music, envisioning a media

> campaign to remind people of that eternal law, *Nothing is free!* Only children expect otherwise. . . . *Never trust a candy house!* It was only a matter of time before someone made them pay for what they thought they were getting for free. (125)

Egan's novel thus confronts, and extends into a speculative near future, the pyrrhic victory of contemporary information technology: we think we use social media for "free," when the hidden cost is our privacy, as monopolistic corporations harvest and sell our data, while sowing extremism and division.

Lana and Melora anticipate the central science fiction conceit, or novum, of *The Candy House*—although, as its stories are told nonsequentially, they do so after readers learn about this new technological innovation.[12] They describe music sharing as people "letting the Internet go inside their computers," and the idea makes them "squeamish; it was like letting a stranger rummage through your house—or your brain!" (124). Egan's novel envisions a future that extrapolates the "sharing" of personal data on social media platforms. Mandala, the brainchild of a Zuckerberg-like tycoon Bix Bouton, who makes a brief appearance in *Goon Squad*, has invented a technology called Own Your Unconscious, which literalizes the fears of Lana and Melora, allowing users to "share" the content of their minds to the "Collective Consciousness," where they—but also every other Mandala user—can peruse their every memory and perceive every thought they've ever had.

Adam's dream, in Ian McEwan's *Machines Like Me*, of a cloud-shared collective consciousness that spells "the end of mental privacy," comes true in Egan's *Candy House*. In creating his social media empire, Bix has drawn on the anthropology of Miranda Kline (Lou's ex-wife), particularly her book *Patterns of Affinity*, which contains "algorithms that explain trust and influence among members of a Brazilian tribe" (9). Miranda's work has been "co-opted by social media companies" (9) like Bix's to "quantify human" behavior, to "profit from their actions"—a practice a critical character calls "dehumanizing" (15). Egan's novel critiques the way social media companies profit on harvesting users' private experience, and, echoing McEwan, the notion that the mysteries of human behavior can be quantified and rendered algorithmically.

In a chapter narrated by Lincoln, who readers will remember as the collector of "Great Rock and Roll Pauses" in the PowerPoint section of *Goon Squad*, we learn that a resistance movement of "eluders" has emerged, consisting of old-fashioned types who refuse to upload their consciousness to Mandala's cloud. A non-profit called Mondrian helps the eluders create "proxies: vacant online identities maintained by a third party in order to conceal the fact that their human occupants have eluded" (79). The "most sophisticated proxies are live professionals—usually fiction writers" (79). Egan's future updates her prophetic vision in *Look at Me* (2001): writers have gone from letting readers into the minds of fictional characters to creating fake online identities, so real people can keep their minds to themselves. This satire of the tech world pits quantification-obsessed "empiricists" like Lincoln—who is on the autism spectrum and works for the aptly named "Harvest," which tries to spot eluders and draw them into the Collective—against "impressionists," who "tend toward the romantic" and seek to live outside the quantifying data-collecting regime of technology companies (78). Egan's novel thus offers an updated version of the genre-bending literary novels this book has considered, in which the antagonist of the literary has often been the realm of formulaic and commodified popular culture. In *The Candy House*, the enemies of the literary are the algorithm and surveillance capitalism.[13]

Through a subplot involving Lou Kline's drug-addicted daughter Roxy, who plays Dungeons & Dragons in rehab near the end of her life, the novel links its critique of the notion that human behavior is quantifiable and of the corporations who would mine and sell that data with its celebration of the pleasure of immersion in fictional worlds. The "counters" like Lincoln, "the corporations who buy their numbers," and the "people who measure their own value in clicks and views" quantify and "score real people" the way D&D players roll "dice to assign values to traits" and "acquired skills" (143) in their game play. While scoring real people represents a form of value capture that threatens to standardize and commodify nuanced human traits and values,[14] role playing represents for Egan, as in *The Keep*, an example of the magic of games and fictions that build entire worlds out of the humble ingredients of paper and the imagination. "Roxy marvels at the deep absorption of the players," peering at "hand-drawn" sketches on graph paper, that "represent dungeons, taverns, towns, catacombs, and even outer space: a vast web of interconnected worlds that can be stored, between games, inside a manila envelope" (147).

The Candy House pays tribute to the pleasure of entering such worlds and attempts to offer it, most glaringly in the character of Lulu (another figure brought back from *Goon Squad*). As a kid, Lulu plays D&D and enjoys "going inside a different World and her character Gwenisphere is a Spy who can blend into any Situation and find out people's Secrets" (191). Egan's clever wrinkle is to make Lulu, as an adult, actually enter "the fantastical world where childhood stories are set" (213). She adopts her childhood role, becoming a spy, in the novel's most formally adventurous chapter, "Lulu the Spy, 2032," which Egan first published as "Black Box," in a chain of tweets on the *New Yorker*'s Twitter feed in 2012. This narrative offers the pleasures of a gripping espionage thriller, with conventional elements—a nighttime speedboat ride to a villain's lair, perched high on the cliffs; a helicopter escape—fused with science fictional gadgetry. Lulu has a variety of posthuman cyborg implants. Rather than a tiny camera hidden in a lapel pin, hers is embedded in one eye. Offering the pleasure of immersion, the genre play of this chapter also turns dark in ways that bolster the thematics of the rest of the novel, as Lulu, a "Citizen Agent," sacrifices her individuality to the collective.

Told in the second person, the story takes the form of Lulu's instructions to herself, many of which are repetitions of the lessons of her training, like, "In the new heroism, the goal is to merge with something larger than yourself," and "The power of individual magnetism is nothing against the power of combined selfless effort" (210). These uplifting mantras might sound noble, subordinating oneself to a greater cause, but Lulu's life is endangered by the U.S. security apparatus that employs her, she is forced into sex acts with the targets of her espionage and seriously wounded, and her mental health deteriorates after her traumatic service. Just as the users of Mandala's Own Your Unconscious gain "access to the Collective Consciousness for the small price of making [their] own anonymously" searchable, "never fully reckoning" what they have "surrendered ... to the Internet—and thereby to counters" (86), the companies who harvest their data, Lulu sacrifices her body and mind to the collective at great cost.

Perhaps predictably, *The Candy House*'s preoccupation with the notion that everything can be quantified and submitted to an algorithm drifts from human behavior to narrative genre. A section preciously titled "*i*, the Protagonist," focuses on Chris Salazar, Benny's son, who gets an English degree from Stanford and ditches an editing job to work at the entertainment startup SweetSpot Networks. It's unclear what SweetSpot does exactly. "What was the idea? To make art—or make a *way* to make art—but as far as Chris knew, no product was in sight" (174). His boss Aaron gives Chris a cryptic one-word answer when asked where the work was leading: "DNA" (174). This answer suggests a code for the building blocks of story, perhaps for artificial intelligence to generate narratives and replace human writers—but Egan leaves things murky. What we do know is that Chris's job is to produce algorithms for familiar narrative elements, "algebraizations" of tropes, "scouring movies and TV shows for every possible stock element ('stockblocks'), and then cataloging them and converting them into one algebraic system" (160).

Chris initially thinks the task "impossible," but discovers "that representing stock narratives algebraically was easier than he'd expected" (160); to his chagrin, he finds "much of his life could be described in formulaic clichés" (162). The equations are strange—"*'How Dare You?' (Whispering)* [3Aviiiz]" and "*'Protagonist Hits Bottom Alone, at Night, on City Streets (with Soulful Music)'* [3Aixb]" (160). But Egan's purpose is clear: to envision that genre conventions and clichéd tropes suit perfectly the urge to schematize cultural production and allow tech companies a way to produce AI-generated narratives for film, TV, and literature. Egan makes explicit that SweetSpot's ambition is "to do for entertainment what" Miranda's Kline's "algorithms for predicting human behavior" did to give "social media companies the means to monetize their business" (161). Egan self-reflexively details how Chris's own "caper fails to find a comic resolution" before a "genre switch," in which his "madcap adventure turns serious" (177). As he watches the doors of his startup "disgorge another employee roughly interchangeable with himself" (177), Chris resolves to not be a carbon-copied tech drone or produce more cookie-cutter clichés for the entertainment industry. In a subsequent chapter, we learn that he becomes the "enigmatic" leader of Mondrian's resistance to consciousness sharing, helping "people elude their online identities" (308). Egan thus intertwines the resistance to tech corporations' quantifying and monetizing human behavior and elimination of privacy with the effort to elude formulaic, mechanized cultural production.

The Candy House, then, retains an eminently humanistic and traditional literary belief in the idea that the human mind and artistic practice are unquantifiable, irreducible to algorithms or formulae. Even the "counter" Lincoln offers "testament to the infinitude of an individual consciousness" (86), and Lulu affirms that "Human beings are unknowable; hence the Faustian allure of consciousness sharing" (221). This novel's faith in the novel as such comes to the fore most explicitly in its penultimate chapter, focalized through Gregory Bouton, the son of Bix the tech magnate, who has sunk into a deep depression after his father's death. Gregory grieves not because he and Bix were close but because they never saw eye to eye. Gregory cared nothing for "Technology, wealth, and fame," the values of Bix's world—one in which "the things that mattered to" Gregory, "namely books and writing, counted for nothing" (313).

After getting an MFA at NYU—perhaps the classmate of Rooney's Connell in some imaginary cohort—the morose Gregory has abandoned his novel in progress and sells "vintage" marijuana, "the weed equivalent of vinyl" (305). (Even with drugs, Egan pits romantics against high tech business.) But Gregory is roused out of his torpor when he is called to deliver an order to his onetime professor Athena. In workshop, Athena taught Gregory to abhor trite and worn-out expression, proclaiming her profound aversion to

> word-casings and phrase-casings: gutted language she likened to proxies. "Find the eluder.... I want words that are still alive.... Give me the bullet, not the casing—fire it right in my chest. I'll gladly die for some fresh language." (306)

Egan reprises her concern with the hollowing out of language; "word-casings" are "words that had been shucked of their meanings and reduced to husks," in *Goon Squad*.[15] The earlier novel clearly links this linguistic problem to neoliberal market dynamics, in which all values are subsumed by market value. Words like "identity" are "drained of life by their Web usage," and "democracy" comes "to be used in an arch mocking way."[16] And young people learn in marketing class to dismiss people who do things for reasons other than money as dedicated to "atavistic purism."[17] Near the end of *Candy House*, Egan repeats her Orwell-like insistence that to retain values in a world shorn of them requires the use of language that retains vividness and meaning. Athena's plea for language that "eludes" the hollowing out of meaning explicitly ties hackneyed diction to the surveillance regimes of *Candy House*'s social media corporations. Just as eluders seek to avoid data collection, so powerful writing gives cliché the slip. Here again, we see how the literary field's valuing of innovative prose style and individual consciousness is bound to a critique of powerful market actors that erase both in their singular pursuit of profit.

Gregory smokes with Athena, an old-school literary joint "cloned from an actual crop grown by Beats in California in the 1960s," in a redwood forest that "burned up in the early '20s," an experience Egan poses as another form of imaginative transport: "Space travel: We're going to a real place that doesn't exist" (319). Nostalgia for the Beat Generation here fuses with proleptic visions of climate disaster and immersive imaginative experience. After Athena tells Gregory to "finish [his] fucking book" (321), he wanders into a snowy Central Park that has been filled with a "lavender lunar radiance" and transformed into a magical "world from childhood: castles and forests and magic lamps and princes scaling walls of brambles" (322). Looking up into the snow in a scene reminiscent of the ending of James Joyce's "The Dead," Gregory has an epiphany, a vision of "human lives past and present . . . a galaxy of human lives hurtling toward his curiosity. From a distance they faded into uniformity, but they were moving, each propelled by a singular force." Gregory realizes that he is "feeling the collective without any machinery at all" and that "its stories, infinite and particular, would be his to tell" (323). Egan affirms, in the lines that I take as the epigraph to this Coda, that "[o]nly Gregory Bouton's machine—this one, fiction—lets us roam with absolute freedom through the human collective" (333). Egan's unabashedly sentimental scene poses the literary imagination as superior to any digital technology, a superiority that inheres in its freedom to roam and dedication to the snowflake-like "singular" and "particular" human story, over the reductive "uniformity" of formulae and algorithms.

"From a distance . . . uniformity." Singularity up close. This is a pretty neat encapsulation of this book's conception of genre and of the efflorescence of genre-bending literary fiction that is its subject. *The Candy House* gives the idea that genres are constituted by a plastic framework that is modified with each instantiation a final turn of the screw in its last chapter, "Middle Son (Area of Detail)," which takes the risk of staging an utterly trite scenario: scrawny Little Leaguer Ames Hollander hasn't hit a home run all season and steps up to the plate in the bottom of the ninth inning with the bases loaded. But Egan self-reflexively and paradoxically embraces the scene's conventionality to argue for its uniqueness: with Ames's mother watching, "her emotions cliché to anyone who's read a book or seen a movie about children playing sports and how their mothers feel, and yet—how is this possible?—fiercely specific" (325). "There are so many boys in the world. From a distance they look alike even to her, especially in uniform" (326). Introducing but rejecting the brilliant pun on his attire, Egan has the mother wish that her son's "uniqueness, so manifest to her lovestruck eyes, be revealed to all: a singularity" (325). But this picture "turns generic the instant you cease to have a stake in it" (326). Here, Egan poses a challenge to jaded critiques of liberal individualism. Do you feel like your kid is "generic," socially determined by their category, exactly the same as any other of their race, gender, class, and geographical origin? Egan rejects categorical thinking. From a distance they may all look alike. When you look closely, when you "have a stake in it," the category doesn't do them justice.

Conclusion: Generic Singularity

The same is true of the genres literary writers like Egan have gravitated to in recent decades. From a distance, all detective fictions, all science fiction and fantasy, all romance, spy novels, westerns, and zombie novels may look alike. "From a distance . . . uniformity." Singularity up close. The same is true of genre-bending literary fiction. At a glance, it might be easy to see uniform motives for the literary writers who have adopted popular genres in recent decades. They're trying to sell more books. But they also want to gain literary prestige. They're attracted to immersive pleasure and world-building. They have abandoned any snobby disdain toward popular genres. But *Genre Bending* has argued that none of these generalizing claims tell the full story of contemporary literary fiction in its particularity. These writers have disparate, even contradictory motives for their genre play. What unites them is no particular agenda, save their commitment to singularity, their recognition that all genres, even the ones that have been seemingly done to death in popular fiction, can be used to produce something new and unique. Genres are useful frameworks—but not for doing just one thing. They are useful because they are plastic, infinitely adaptable. No genre is better than any other; it all depends on what you do with it. And what genre-bending writers have done is wildly varied. *Anything is possible.* But only by looking closely can we see the singularity.

Notes

Preface

1. See Andrew Hoberek, "Cormac McCarthy and the Aesthetics of Exhaustion," *American Literary History* 23, no. 3 (Fall 2011): 483–499.

2. "Spaghettii," featuring Linda Martell and Shaboozey, track 12 on Beyoncé's *Cowboy Carter*, Parkwood, 2024. Elizabeth Leach first pointed out the relevance of the album to this book.

3. See Ben Beaumont-Thomas, "Beyoncé: Texas Hold 'Em and 16 Carriages Review—Country Gets Brilliantly Beyoncéfied," *Guardian*, February 12, 2024, https://www.theguardian.com/music/2024/feb/12/beyonce-texas-hold-em-and-16-carriages-review-country-gets-brilliantly-beyoncefied

4. Tanner Davenport, "I Saw Beyoncé Get Booed at the CMAs. I've Been Waiting for 'Cowboy Carter,'" *MSNBC*, March 29, 2024, https://www.msnbc.com/opinion/msnbc-opinion/saw-beyonce-get-booed-cmas-ve-waiting-cowboy-carter-rcna144981

5. For a discussion of Jemisin's fiction and "Puppygate," see Jenny Bonnevier and Mark Soderstrom, "On N. K. Jemisin and Speculative Fiction as a Liberatory Space," *Socialism and Democracy* 36, no. 3 (2022): 135–149.

6. Melinda Newman, "Did Beyoncé Need to Submit 'Cowboy Carter' and 'Texas Hold 'Em' to Be Eligible for a CMA Award Nomination?" *Billboard*, September 10, 2024, https://www.billboard.com/music/awards/beyonce-cma-awards-submitted-cowboy-carter-texas-hold-em-1235771470/

7. Davenport, "I Saw Beyoncé."

8. David Duff, "Introduction," in *Modern Genre Theory*, ed. David Duff (Routledge, 2014), 1.

9. Ibid., 7.

10. Tressie McMillan Cottom, "Beyoncé Asks, and Answers, a Crucial Question in

Her Latest Album," *New York Times*, April 4, 2024, https://www.nytimes.com/2024/04/04/opinion/beyonce-cowboy-carter-country.html

11. See, for example, Avishay Artsy, "Beyoncé's Country Roots: A Century of History of Black Country Music, Explained by Alice Randall," *Vox*, March 26, 2024, https://www.vox.com/2024/3/26/24111978/beyonce-album-cowboy-carter-black-country-history

12. See Linda Hutcheon, *A Theory of Adaptation* (Routledge, 2006).

13. Glen Duncan, *The Last Werewolf* (Vintage, 2012), 81, 82. All further references cited parenthetically.

Introduction

1. Chris Tennant, "Interview with Marlon James," *Man of the World*, no. 14, https://tennant.nyc/marlon-james-man-of-the-world-no-14-christopher-tennant/

2. Lila Shapiro, "A Conversation with Marlon James and Victor LaValle," *Vulture*, February 5, 2019, https://www.vulture.com/2019/02/marlon-james-and-victor-lavalle-have-a-conversation.html

3. For James's move into fantasy as "surprise" and "departure," see: Jeff VanderMeer, "Marlon James' 'Black Leopard, Red Wolf' Unleashes an Immersive African Myth-Inspired Fantasy World," *Los Angeles Times*, January 30, 2019, https://www.latimes.com/books/la-ca-jc-black-leopard-red-wolf-marlon-james-review-20190103-story.html; and Kevin Nguyen, "African *Game of Thrones*? Marlon James Is on It," *GQ*, January 11, 2017, https://www.gq.com/story/marlon-james-african-game-of-thrones

4. Kaiama L. Glover, "Womanchild in the Oppressive Land," *New York Times*, February 26, 2009, https://www.nytimes.com/2009/03/01/books/review/Glover-t.html

5. Michiko Kakutani, "Jamaica Via a Sea of Voices," *New York Times*, September 21, 2014, https://www.nytimes.com/2014/09/22/books/marlon-jamess-a-brief-history-of-seven-killings.html; see also Sheri-Marie Harrison, "Excess in *A Brief History of Seven Killings*," *Post45*, October 24, 2015, https://post45.org/2015/10/excess-in-a-brief-history-of-seven-killings/

6. Jia Tolentino, "Why Marlon James Decided to Write an African 'Game of Thrones,'" *New Yorker*, January 21, 2019, https://www.newyorker.com/magazine/2019/01/28/why-marlon-james-decided-to-write-an-african-game-of-thrones

7. For the Booker's prestige, see Heloise Wood, "Booker Remains World's Most Visible Literary Prize, Research Shows," *Bookseller*, December 22, 2021, https://www.thebookseller.com/news/booker-remains-most-visible-literary-prize-research-shows-1296568

8. China Miéville, "The Future of the Novel," *Guardian*, August 21, 2012, https://www.theguardian.com/books/2012/aug/21/china-mieville-the-future-of-the-novel

9. See: Tim Lanzendörfer, "Introduction: The Generic Turn? Toward a Poetics of Genre in the Contemporary Novel," in *The Poetics of Genre in the Contemporary Novel*, ed. Tim Lanzendörfer (Lexington, 2016), 3.

10. For the contention that literary writers adopt a "grit aesthetic," see Günter Ley-

poldt, "Social Dimensions of the Turn to Genre: Junot Díaz's *Oscar Wao* and Kazuo Ishiguro's *The Buried Giant*," *Post45*, March 31, 2018, https://post45.org/2018/03/social-dimensions-of-the-turn-to-genre-junot-diazs-oscar-wao-and-kazuo-ishiguros-the-buried-giant/

11. For the circulation of literary culture online, see Jessica Pressman, *Bookishness: Loving Books in a Digital Age* (Columbia University Press, 2020).

12. See: Arthur Krystal, "Easy Writers," *New Yorker*, May 28, 2012, https://www.newyorker.com/magazine/2012/05/28/easy-writers; Laura Miller, "National Book Awards: Genre Fiction Dissed Again," *Salon*, October 11, 2012, https://www.salon.com/2012/10/11/national_book_awards_genre_fiction_dissed_again/; Arthur Krystal, "It's Genre. Not That There's Anything Wrong with it!" *New Yorker*, October 24, 2012, https://www.newyorker.com/books/page-turner/its-genre-not-that-theres-anything-wrong-with-it#:~:text=Hybridization%20has%20been%20around%20since,their%20ability%20to%20modulate%20them.; Elizabeth Edmondson, "The Genre Debate: 'Literary Fiction' Is Just Clever Marketing," *Guardian*, April 21, 2014, https://www.theguardian.com/books/booksblog/2014/apr/21/literary-fiction-clever-marketing-genre-debate; Joshua Rothman, "A Better Way to Think About the Genre Debate," *New Yorker*, November 6, 2014, https://www.newyorker.com/books/joshua-rothman/better-way-think-genre-debate; Stephen Marche, "How Genre Fiction Became More Important Than Literary Fiction," *Esquire*, March 11, 2015, https://www.esquire.com/entertainment/books/a33599/genre-fiction-vs-literary-fiction/; Damien Walter, "Literature vs Genre Is a Battle Where Both Sides Lose," *Guardian*, November 20, 2015, https://www.theguardian.com/books/booksblog/2015/nov/20/literature-vs-genre-is-a-battle-where-both-sides-lose; Lincoln Michel, "When Popular Fiction Isn't Popular: Genre, Literary, and the Myths of Popularity," *Electric Literature*, April 2, 2016, https://electricliterature.com/when-popular-fiction-isnt-popular-genre-literary-and-the-myths-of-popularity/#.nlwz48dth

13. Lev Grossman, "Literary Revolution in the Supermarket Aisle: Genre Fiction Is Disruptive Technology," *Time*, May 23, 2012, https://entertainment.time.com/2012/05/23/genre-fiction-is-disruptive-technology/

14. Laura Miller, "Dark Futures: What Happens When Literary Novelists Experiment with Science Fiction," *Slate*, May 25, 2017, https://slate.com/culture/2017/05/literary-fiction-is-borrowing-the-tools-of-the-science-fiction-genre.html

15. See Andrew Hoberek, "Cormac McCarthy and the Aesthetics of Exhaustion," *American Literary History* 23, no. 3 (Fall 2011): 483–499.

16. The classic account of modernism's "anxiety of contamination by its other" is Andreas Huyssen, *After the Great Divide: Modernism, Mass Culture, Postmodernism* (Indiana University Press, 1986), vii. Huyssen later clarified that the divide was "a powerful imaginary insisting on the divide while time and again violating that categorical separation in practice." Quoted in Robert Scholes, "Exploring the Great Divide: High and Low, Left and Right," *Narrative* 11, no. 3 (October 2003): 245. For modernist attempts to "reinvent [the novel] as fine art," from "within the institutions of an ex-

panding mass market," see Mark McGurl, *The Novel Art: Elevations of American Fiction After Henry James* (Princeton University Press, 2001), 6. Fredric Jameson argues that the "fundamental feature shared by all the modernisms is . . . their hostility to the market itself." Jameson, *Postmodernism, or, the Cultural Logic of Late Capitalism* (Duke University Press, 1991), 305.

17. For the mass culture debate, see John Storey, *Cultural Theory and Popular Culture: An Introduction*, 5th ed. (Pearson, 2009). For canonical critiques of mass culture, see: Clement Greenberg, "Avant-Garde and Kitsch," in *Art and Culture: Critical Essays* (Beacon, 1989), 3–21; Max Horkheimer and Theodor Adorno, "The Culture Industry: Enlightenment as Mass Deception," in *The Dialectic of Enlightenment: Philosophical Fragments*, ed. Gunzelin Schmid Noerr and trans. Edmund Jephcott (Stanford University Press, 2000): 94–136; and Dwight Macdonald, "Masscult and Midcult," in *Masscult and Midcult: Essays Against the American Grain*, ed. John Summers (New York Review Books, 2011), 3–71.

18. Tony Bennett argues that "popular culture is . . . an area of negotiation between" an "imposed mass culture that is coincident with dominant ideology" and "spontaneously oppositional cultures." Quoted in Storey, *Cultural Theory*, 10.

19. Quoted in Charles Nicol, "Nabokov and Science Fiction: 'Lance,'" *Science Fiction Studies* 14, no. 1 (March 1987): 9. William Faulkner provides another classic example of a writer whose career was "[s]plit . . . between high modernist achievement and popular magazine deadlines, between formal experimentalism and generic sensationalism . . . autonomous creation and commodity circulation." See Devan Bailey, "Allegory, Culture Industry, and William Faulkner's *Sanctuary*," *Studies in American Fiction* 47, no. 1 (2020): 73–74.

20. Duncan White, *Nabokov and His Books: Between Late Modernism and the Literary Marketplace* (Oxford University Press, 2017), 3.

21. See Marianne DeKoven's discussion of "postmodern egalitarian . . . pastiche: the open-ended, free mixing of previously distinct modes of cultural practice and form." DeKoven, *Utopia Limited: The Sixties and the Emergence of the Postmodern* (Duke University Press, 2004), 17.

22. John Barth, "The Literature of Replenishment," in *The Friday Book: Essays and Other Nonfiction* (Putnam, 1984), 203.

23. Ibid.

24. Hoberek notes that rather than ironize popular genres, contemporary literary writers offer "at least a version of" their conventional pleasures. Andrew Hoberek, "Literary Genre Fiction," in *American Literature in Transition, 2000–2010*, ed. Rachel Greenwald Smith (Cambridge University Press, 2018), 65. Dan Sinykin contrasts the "ironic, heady" parody of detective tropes in Pynchon's *Crying of Lot 49* (1966) with *Inherent Vice* (2009), which "plays hard-boiled noir . . . a lot closer to straight." Sinykin, "The Conglomerate Era: Publishing, Authorship, and Literary Form, 1965–2007," *Contemporary Literature* 58, no. 4 (Winter 2017): 478–479.

25. Hoberek, "Literary Genre Fiction," 62–65. As I elaborate below, I prefer the term

"genre-bending literary fiction" to signal the way this body of fiction by and large seeks to differentiate itself from genre fiction and values transformation of its adopted genres.

26. For Lee's genre switching, see Min Hyoung Song, "Between Genres: On Chang-rae Lee's Realism," *Los Angeles Review of Books,* January 10, 2014, https://www.lareviewofbooks.org/article/chang-rae-lees-realism

27. For claims that the genre turn marks genre fiction's elevated status or a breakdown in barriers between literary and popular fiction, see: Grossman, "Literary Revolution"; Hoberek, "Cormac McCarthy," 486; Andrew Hoberek, "Introduction: After Postmodernism," *Twentieth-Century Literature* 53, no. 3 (Fall 2007): 240; Hoberek, "Literary Genre Fiction," 66; Theodore Martin, *Contemporary Drift: Genre, Historicism, and the Problem of the Present* (Columbia University Press, 2017); Matthew Eatough, "'Are They Going to Say This Is Fantasy?': Kazuo Ishiguro, Untimely Genres, and the Making of Literary Prestige," *Modern Fiction Studies* 67, no. 1 (2021): 40–66; James Dorson, "Cormac McCarthy and the Genre Turn in Contemporary Literary Fiction," *European Journal of American Studies*, December 3, 2017, https://doi.org/10.4000/ejas.12291

28. Andrew Goldstone, "Origins of the US Genre-Fiction System, 1890–1956," *Book History* 26, no. 1 (2023): 203–233, quote at 205.

29. See most famously Janice Radway, *Reading the Romance: Women, Patriarchy, and Popular Literature* (University of North Carolina Press, 1984). For debates over popular culture's aesthetic and political merits, see: Storey, *Cultural Theory*; John Fiske, *Understanding Popular Culture* (Unwin Hyman, 1989); and Evan Brier, *A Novel Marketplace: Mass Culture, the Book Trade, and Postwar American Fiction* (University of Pennsylvania Press, 2012), 5–6.

30. For one marker of scholarly recognition of SF's potential, see the *PMLA* special topic "Science Fiction and Literary Studies: The Next Millennium," *PMLA* 119, no. 3 (May 2004). For science fiction's registering of the need for utopian imagining, even as it fails to conceive of utopia, see Fredric Jameson, *Archaeologies of the Future: The Desire Called Utopia and Other Science Fictions* (Verso, 2005).

31. For the view that most genre fiction is deservedly viewed as ephemeral, even within science fiction studies, see Gerry Canavan and Benjamin Robertson, "Guilty Pleasures: Late Capitalism and Mere Genre," *Extrapolation* 58, nos. 2–3 (2017): 123–128.

32. John Rieder writes that it is "not any coincidence that the paradigm shift in genre theory . . . corresponds closely in time with such calls to end the othering of mass culture," but that "the hierarchical divide between the traditional and the mass cultural genres still has considerable force." Rieder, *Science Fiction and the Mass Cultural Genre System* (Wesleyan University Press, 2017), 43, 44.

33. Jeffrey J. Williams, "Generation Jones and Contemporary US Fiction," *American Literary History* 28, no. 1 (Spring 2016): 94–122.

34. "Interview: Kazuo Ishiguro," *Lightspeed Magazine* 63 (August 2015), https://www.lightspeedmagazine.com/nonfiction/interview-kazuo-ishiguro/. Bradley's novel

is the book most frequently shelved under "Arthurian" on Goodreads.com: https://www.goodreads.com/shelf/show/arthurian. See also McEwan's discussion of science fiction below.

35. Ramón Saldívar, "Historical Fantasy, Speculative Realism, and Postrace Aesthetics in Contemporary American Fiction," *American Literary History* 23, no. 3 (Fall 2011): 575.

36. Dan Sinykin, *Big Fiction: How Conglomeration Changed the Publishing Industry and American Literature* (Columbia University Press, 2023), 10, 14, 121. See also Paul Crosthwaite, *The Market Logics of Contemporary Fiction* (Cambridge University Press, 2019).

37. For genre as strategy for conglomerate publishers to target preexisting audiences and minimize risk, see Jeremy Rosen, *Minor Characters Have Their Day: Genre in the Contemporary Literary Marketplace* (Columbia University Press, 2016).

38. Michael Chabon, "The Editor's Notebook: A Confidential Chat with the Editor," in *McSweeney's Mammoth Treasury of Thrilling Tales*, ed. Michael Chabon (Vintage, 2003), 5–8, quote at 6.

39. For the centrality of world-building to popular culture, see Marta Boni, ed., *World Building: Transmedia, Fans, Industries* (Amsterdam University Press, 2017).

40. For plot as the primary allure of popular genres, see: Grossman, "Literary Revolution"; Hoberek, "Literary Genre Fiction"; Krystal, "Easy Writers."

41. Genre-bending literary fiction might seem an example of what Rachel Greenwald Smith describes as "compromise aesthetics." But this book argues that genre benders don't view as a binary choice either pursuing formal innovation and political intervention or providing pleasurable, marketable books. They reject the equation of formal recalcitrance with political radicalism, the notion that accessibility fatally compromises political critique. Rachel Greenwald Smith, *On Compromise: Art, Politics, and the Fate of an American Ideal* (Graywolf, 2021).

42. For the argument that race and genre operate together to generate understandings of the world, see Mark C. Jerng, *Racial Worldmaking: The Power of Popular Fiction* (Fordham University Press, 2017).

43. Tzvetan Todorov summarizes the persistent opposition that the literary is transformative and popular fiction repetitive: "we grant a text the right to figure in the history of literature . . . insofar as it produces a change in our previous notion of the . . . activity. . . . Texts that do not fulfill this condition automatically pass into another category: that of the so-called 'popular' or 'mass' literature." Todorov, *The Fantastic: A Structural Approach to a Literary Genre* (Cornell University Press, 1975), 6. See also Frank Kermode, who writes that "it is the popular story that sticks most closely to established conventions; novels the clerisy calls 'major' tend to vary them, and to vary them more and more as time goes by." Kermode, *The Sense of an Ending: Studies in the Theory of Fiction with a New Epilogue* (Oxford University Press, 2000), 17. John Rieder notes that "in modern Western artistic practices more prestige accrues to violating [genre] boundaries than to conforming to them. . . . The peculiar sense of 'literature'

as the category whose members defy categorization is an integral part of the history of the sense of 'genre' that is one of SF's conditions of existence." Rieder, *Science Fiction*, 24.

44. An *Esquire* interview with David Mitchell refers to his "seminal genre-bender, *The Bone Clocks*." Jill Krasny, "Talking to David Mitchell About Twitter, Ghosts, and His New Novel *Slade House*," *Esquire*, October 23, 2015, https://www.esquire.com/entertainment/books/q-and-a/a38690/david-mitchell-on-his-new-novel/. See also Susann Cokal's "Jews with Swords," *New York Times*, October 28, 2007, https://www.nytimes.com/2007/10/28/books/review/Cokal-t.html, which notes that Chabon "delights in reinventing genres."

45. Amy Hungerford's work is emblematic of institutional studies of contemporary literature in examining how "workers who are largely invisible to the public . . . collaborate . . . to create literary worlds." Hungerford, *Making Literature Now* (Stanford University Press, 2016). 3. For the unstudied literary agent as "the central figure in the literary field," see Laura McGrath, "Literary Agency," *American Literary History* 33, no. 2 (2021): 350. See also Jeremy Rosen, "The Institutional Turn," *Oxford Research Encyclopedia of Literature*, June 25, 2019, https://doi.org/10.1093/acrefore/9780190201098.013.1028. For studies of popular genres, see: Eva Illouz, *Hard-Core Romance*: Fifty Shades of Grey, *Best-Sellers, and Society* (University of Chicago Press, 2014); Kinohi Nishikawa, *Street Players: Black Pulp Fiction and the Making of a Literary Underground* (University of Chicago Press, 2018); and Brooks Hefner, *Black Pulp: Genre Fiction in the Shadow of Jim Crow* (University of Minnesota Press, 2021).

46. Mark McGurl, *Everything and Less: Fiction in the Age of Amazon* (Verso, 2021), 166, xxvii, 14–15, xviii.

47. McGurl's explicit aim is to consider contemporary literature from Amazon's perspective. McGurl, *Everything*, 22.

48. For genres as "recipes," see Thomas Pavel, "Literary Genres as Norms and Good Habits," *New Literary History* 34, no. 2 (Spring 2003): 210. For definitions of "genre fiction," see: David Duff, "Key Concepts," in *Modern Genre Theory*, ed. David Duff (Routledge, 2014), xiii; and Chris Baldick, "Genre Fiction," *The Oxford Dictionary of Literary Terms*, 4th ed. (Oxford University Press, 2015), 150.

49. John Frow, *Genre* (Routledge, 2005), 22.

50. John Rieder, "On Defining SF, or Not: Genre Theory, SF, and History," *Science Fiction Studies* 37, no. 2 (July 2010): 193.

51. Paul Kincaid, "On the Origins of Genre," *Extrapolation* 44, no. 3 (2003): 413.

52. Fowler recalls that Ruskin put Dickens "out of the pale of great authors," but several decades later Henry James could "aver that 'the novel remains . . . under the right persuasion, the most independent, most elastic, most prodigious of literary forms.'" Alastair Fowler, *Kinds of Literature: An Introduction to the Theory of Genres and Modes* (Oxford, 1982), 226.

53. For the relation between the evolving formal features of a literary genre and its institutional market context, see: Rosen, *Minor Characters*; and Kim Wilkins, Beth

Driscoll, and Lisa Fletcher, *Genre Worlds: Popular Fiction and Twenty-First Century Book Culture* (University of Massachusetts Press, 2022).

54. "[T]he fundamental stake in literary struggles is the monopoly of literary legitimacy... the power to consecrate producers or products." Pierre Bourdieu, "The Field of Cultural Production," in *The Field of Cultural Production*, ed. and trans. Randal Johnson (Columbia University Press, 1993), 42.

55. Ken Gelder taxonomizes the opposing values of literary fiction (complexity, life, cerebral pleasure, restraint, seriousness, "formal artistry," and ambivalence toward the marketplace) and genre fiction (simplicity, fantasy, sensuous pleasure, excessiveness, excitement, and the desire to please large audiences). Gelder, *Popular Fiction: The Logics and Practices of a Literary Field* (Routledge, 2004), 19–28.

56. Radway, *Reading the Romance*, 26.

57. Ibid.

58. See Duff for "the modern period" as "characterized by... aesthetic programmes which" advocated the "dissolution of genres," "an apparently liberating ambition that links the otherwise radically opposed poetics of Romanticism and Modernism." Duff, "Introduction," 1.

59. Michael Levenson, "Introduction," in *The Cambridge Companion to Modernism*, ed. Michael Levenson (Cambridge University Press, 1999), 3.

60. Claire Squires, *Marketing Literature: The Making of Contemporary Writing in Britain* (Palgrave, 2007), 5.

61. Ibid., 6, 4, 4.

62. Ibid., 4.

63. Squires, *Marketing*, 72–73; Perry Anderson, "From Progress to Catastrophe," *London Review of Books*, July 28, 2011, https://www.lrb.co.uk/the-paper/v33/n15/perry-anderson/from-progress-to-catastrophe; James F. English, "Now, Not Now: Counting Time in Contemporary Fiction Studies," *Modern Language Quarterly* 77, no. 3 (September 2016): 395–418; and Alexander Manshel, "The Rise of the Recent Historical Novel," *Post45*, September 29, 2017, https://post45.org/2017/09/the-rise-of-the-recent-historical-novel/. For the prominence of autofiction see Sinykin, "The Conglomerate Era"; and McGurl, *Everything*.

64. McGurl taxonomizes postwar literary fiction into "technomodernism," "high cultural pluralism," and "lower-middle-class modernism." McGurl, *The Program Era: Postwar Fiction and the Rise of Creative Writing* (Harvard University Press, 2009), 42, 32.

65. For Grove's history, see Loren Glass, *Counterculture Colophon: Grove Press, the Evergreen Review, and the Incorporation of the Avant-Garde* (Stanford University Press, 2013).

66. Michael Chabon, *The Amazing Adventures of Kavalier & Clay* (Random House, 2000), 363. All further references cited parenthetically. For the declaration that "all literary genres are created equal," see Marleen S. Barr, "Introduction: Textism: An Emancipation Proclamation," *PMLA* 119, no. 3 (May 2004) 429–441, quote at 436.

67. Here I refer to an "aesthetic form" in the loose sense of "kind"—not to a text's

structural composition. "Form" is "often used synonymously with *genre* to mean simply a type or category of literary work." Duff, "Key Concepts," xiii. The relation between genre and form (in the sense of "structure") is a complicated topic, but most complex literary genres combine formal and thematic attributes. For comics as a medium, see Scott McCloud, *Understanding Comics (The Invisible Art)* (Harper, 1994).

68. Colson Whitehead, "What to Write Next," *New York Times,* October 29, 2009, https://www.nytimes.com/2009/11/01/books/review/Whitehead-t.html

69. Glen Duncan, "A Plague of Urban Undead in Lower Manhattan," *New York Times,* October 28, 2011, https://www.nytimes.com/2011/10/30/books/review/zone-one-by-colson-whitehead-book-review.html

70. For the umbrage of horror partisans, see Paul Constant, "NYT on Colson Whitehead Writing Zombies," *The Stranger,* November 1, 2011, https://www.thestranger.com/books/2011/11/01/10559768/nyt-on-colson-whitehead-writing-zombies-like-an-intellectual-dating-a-porn-star

71. Ron Charles, "'Zone One,' by Colson Whitehead: Zombies Abound," *Washington Post,* October 19, 2011, https://www.washingtonpost.com/entertainment/books/zone-one-by-colson-whitehead-zombies-abound/2011/10/09/gIQAGrMMvL_story.html; Andrew Hoberek, "Living with PASD," *Contemporary Literature* 53, no. 2 (Summer 2012): 406–413.

72. Search for "Zone One," and "Whitehead" at Zombies Defined, http://www.zombiesdefined.com; Zombiepedia fan wiki, https://zombie.fandom.com; and Zombie Research Society, https://zombieresearchsociety.com

73. For the debate between Atwood and Le Guin, see Gerry Canavan and Patricia Wald, "Preface," *American Literature* 83, no. 2 (June 2011): 237–249.

74. Doubtless, the market segmentation of bookselling into genres can limit readers' exploration. But the prevalent metaphor of genre "ghettos" misrepresents the relation between literary and genre fiction. The impoverishment of SF relative to "literary" fiction is a deficiency in symbolic capital, while economically SF is quite lucrative. Urban ghettos have material, not just symbolic, deficiencies. See also Rieder, *Science Fiction*, 58–59.

75. Alexandra Alter, "For Kazuo Ishiguro, 'The Buried Giant' Is a Departure," *New York Times,* February 10, 2015, https://www.nytimes.com/2015/02/20/books/for-kazuo-ishiguro-the-buried-giant-is-a-departure.html

76. Ursula K. Le Guin, "Are They Going to Say This Is Fantasy?" *Ursula K. Le Guin Blog,* March 2, 2015, https://www.ursulakleguin.com/blog/95-are-they-going-to-say-this-is-fantasy

77. Ibid.

78. Ibid.

79. Ibid.

80. Sarah Ditum, "'It Drives Writers Mad': Why Are Authors Still Sniffy About Sci-Fi?" *Guardian,* April 18, 2019, https://www.theguardian.com/books/2019/apr/18/it-drives-writers-mad-why-are-authors-still-sniffy-about-sci-fi

81. Kurt Vonnegut, "Science Fiction," in *Wampeters, Foma & Granfaloons (Opinions)* (Dial, 2006), 1.

82. Quoted in Tina Jordan, "'Call Me a Science Fiction Writer, I'll Come to Your House and Nail Your Pet's Head to a Coffee Table,'" *New York Times*, May 2, 2019, https://www.nytimes.com/2019/05/02/books/review/ian-mcewan-machines-like-me-john-sandford-rules-of-prey-best-seller.html

83. Pierre Bourdieu argues "the fields of cultural production" are "universes of belief," which rely on "denial of the ordinary practices of 'the economy'" and "[t]he opposition between the 'commercial' and the 'non-commercial.'" Bourdieu, "The Production of Belief: Contribution to an Economy of Symbolic Goods," in *The Field of Cultural Production*, 82.

84. For conglomerate "imprints and divisions" "explicitly" dedicated to literary rather than commercial publishing, see John B. Thompson, *Merchants of Culture: The Publishing Business in the Twenty-First Century* (Polity, 2012), 139.

85. Tolentino, "Why Marlon James."

86. Ibid.

87. When *Black Leopard*'s antihero Tracker addresses the Inquisitor to whom his tale is narrated, James poses storytelling as a value in its own right, not determined by the truth it purports to contain. "What you wanted was testimony, but what you really wanted was story, is it not true? Now you sound like men I have heard of, men coming from the West for they heard of slave flesh, men who ask, Is this true? When we find this, shall we seek no more? Is it truth as you call it, truth in entire? . . . Truth is just another story." Likening the pursuit of truth to the slave trade, James poses a non-instrumental proliferation of stories as opposed to a Western emphasis on objectivity and usable knowledge. Hence the novel's refrain "The child is dead. There is nothing else to know." Marlon James, *Black Leopard, Red Wolf* (Riverhead, 2019), 523. For the novel's diasporic queer sensibility, see Amber Jamilla Musser, "Queer Talk: *Black Leopard Red Wolf* and the Black Diaspora," *ASAP/Journal* 6, no. 2 (2021): 290–294. For its emphasis on story over knowable reality, see Benjamin J. Robertson, "But That Is Not the Story: On Marlon James's 'Black Leopard, Red Wolf,'" *Los Angeles Review of Books*, April 20, 2019, https://lareviewofbooks.org/article/but-that-is-not-the-story-on-marlon-jamess-black-leopard-red-wolf/

88. See, for example, Larry McCaffery, ed., *Avant-Pop: Fiction for a Daydream Nation* (Fiction Collective Two, 1993).

89. Tolentino, "Why Marlon James."

90. For fanfiction as "playing in someone else's sandbox," see Anne Jamison, *Fic: Why Fanfiction Is Taking over the World* (BenBella, 2013), 17.

91. James, *Black Leopard*, 389.

92. Ibid.

93. Tolentino, "Why Marlon James."

94. Ibid.

95. Kasey Moore, "'A Brief History of Seven Killings' TV Adaptation Eying Move

to Netflix," *What's on Netflix*, March 22, 2022, https://www.whats-on-netflix.com/news/a-brief-history-of-seven-killings-adaptation-moving-to-netflix/

96. "Talks at Google: Carmen Maria Machado," https://www.youtube.com/watch?v=d3UMPS3vJzk, 1:04. Like James, Machado is both highly literary and also unafraid to joke about her desire to earn a living from her writing: "If anyone is hiring a fiction writer here at Google, please email me. I like your kitchens." 0:20–0:34.

97. Ibid., 1:42.

98. Lara Jones, "Radioactive: Interview with Carmen Maria Machado," *KRCL Radio*, October 4, 2023, https://krcl.org/blog/radioactive-100423/ 29:40–30:46.

99. Fredric Jameson famously argues that "[g]enres are essentially literary institutions, or social contracts between a writer and a specific public, whose function is to specify the proper use of a particular cultural artifact." Jameson, *The Political Unconscious: Narrative as a Socially Symbolic Act* (Cornell University Press, 1981), 106.

100. David Mitchell, *Utopia Avenue: A Novel* (Random House, 2020), 291. All further references cited parenthetically.

101. For *Telegraph Avenue* as Chabon's return to realism, see Hoberek, "Literary Genre Fiction," 62.

102. Michael Chabon, *Telegraph Avenue: A Novel* (Harper, 2012), 373. All further references cited parenthetically.

103. For the hybrid aesthetic in contemporary fiction, see Kate Marshall, "New Wave Fabulism and Hybrid Science Fictions," in *American Literature in Transition, 2000–2010*, 76–87.

104. For a contemporaneous publication of writers that trouble the border between literary and genre fields, see Peter Straub, ed., *Conjunctions 39: The New Wave Fabulists* (Bard College, 2002).

105. Michael Chabon, ed., *McSweeney's Mammoth Treasury of Thrilling Tales* (Vintage, 2002). The "more" included stories by Neil Gaiman, Sherman Alexie, Karen Joy Fowler, Rick Moody, and Chabon.

106. Michael Chabon, "Introduction," in *McSweeney's Enchanting Chamber of Astonishing Stories*, ed. Michael Chabon (Vintage, 2004), ix–xv. Chabon, "Introduction," in *The Best American Short Stories 2005*, ed. Michael Chabon (Houghton Mifflin, 2005), xiii–xvii. Chabon, "The Pleasure Principle," *Los Angeles Times*, April 27, 2008, https://www.latimes.com/archives/la-xpm-2008-apr-27-bk-chabon27-story.html; Chabon, "Trickster in a Suit of Lights: Thoughts on the Modern Short Story," in *Maps and Legends: Reading and Writing Along the Borderlands* (McSweeney's, 2008), 13–26.

107. Hungerford, *Making Literature Now*, 8.

108. https://www.mcsweeneys.net/articles/issue-no-10-your-questions-are-answered

109. Ibid.

110. Ibid.

111. Chabon, "Trickster," 18.

112. See, for example, John Plotz, "The Realism of Our Times: Kim Stanley Robin-

son on How Science Fiction Works," *Public Books*, September 23, 2020, https://www.publicbooks.org/the-realism-of-our-times-kim-stanley-robinson-on-how-science-fiction-works/

113. Sheri-Marie Harrison, "New Black Gothic," *Los Angeles Review of Books*, June 23, 2018, https://lareviewofbooks.org/article/new-black-gothic/

114. Chabon, "Trickster," 14.

115. Ibid., 16.

116. Ibid., 14.

117. Ibid., 14–15.

118. Ibid., 15.

119. Ibid., 17.

120. Ibid., 24.

121. Jane Tompkins, "Introduction," in *West of Everything: The Inner Life of Westerns* (Oxford University Press, 1992), 6.

122. Percival Everett, *God's Country* (Beacon, 1994).

123. For the argument that the conglomeration of publishing encouraged literary writers to adopt the forms of popular genres in order to write "more crowd-pleasing" books, see Sinykin, *Big Fiction*, 10.

Chapter 1

1. Nikesh Shukla, "Colson Whitehead: Each Book an Antidote," *Guernica*, April 24, 2013, https://www.guernicamag.com/colson-whitehead-each-book-an-antidote/

2. Michael Chabon, *The Amazing Adventures of Kavalier & Clay* (Random House, 2000), 360. All further references cited parenthetically.

3. For an anthropomorphizing, evolutionary account of genres, see Franco Moretti's argument that a literary form's "journey 'down the inevitable road from birth to death' can . . . be explained by focusing . . . on the relationship between . . . the form and its historical context: a genre exhausts its potentialities—and the time comes to give a competitor a chance—when its inner form is no longer capable of representing the most significant aspects of contemporary reality." Moretti, *Graphs, Maps, Trees: Abstract Models for a Literary History* (Verso, 2005), 17n7.

4. Jeremy Keehn, "*Zone One*: Six Questions for Colson Whitehead," *Harper's Magazine*, October 17, 2011, https://harpers.org/2011/10/six-questions-for-colson-whitehead/

5. John Rieder, *Science Fiction and the Mass Cultural Genre System* (Wesleyan University Press, 2017), 19.

6. *Merriam-Webster Dictionary*, s.v. "plastic," accessed February 3, 2025, https://www.merriam-webster.com/dictionary/plastic

7. In referring throughout this book to the "plasticity of form" and to "flexible" and "malleable" "frameworks," I am using physical, material *metaphors* for genre. To use or work with extant literary genres is more literally to perform a set of practices, to write in ways that both imitate and diverge from a constellation of formal, thematic, and what Thomas Pavel calls "extratextual properties." Pavel writes that

The vocabulary of literary genres ... includes "content" terms that are shared with our moral and existential vocabulary ("tragedy," "comedy"), terms of art that have a simple formal definition (for example, "sonnet"), and terms of art that refer to what I called "extratextual properties" and therefore require from their users a certain level of hermeneutic dexterity ("fiction," and, ... "novel").

Pavel, "Literary Genres as Norms and Good Habits," *New Literary History* 34, no. 2 (Spring 2003): 205. See also David Fishelov, *Metaphors of Genre: The Role of Analogies in Genre Theory* (Pennsylvania State University Press, 1993).

8. Colson Whitehead, *Apex Hides the Hurt* (Anchor, 2006), 118. All further references cited parenthetically.

9. For the paradigm shift in genre theory, see: John Frow, *Genre* (Routledge, 2005); Rieder, *Science Fiction*. Some resistance to categorization persists; see Alex Clark, "The Big Idea: Should We Abolish Literary Genres," *Guardian*, November 27, 2023, https://www.theguardian.com/books/2023/nov/27/the-big-idea-should-we-abolish-literary-genres

10. Alexander Manshel, "Colson Whitehead's History of the United States," *MELUS* (Winter 2020): 1.

11. Shukla, "Colson Whitehead."

12. Ibid.

13. Colson Whitehead, *John Henry Days* (Anchor, 2001), 29, 29, 59. All further references cited parenthetically. Ironically deflating John Henry's mythic battle with a steam drill, Whitehead's protagonist J. Sutter's contest is for the most consecutive days a freelancer has collected free food, drink, or swag at a press junket.

14. *Cleveland Plain Dealer* blurb on cover of Whitehead's *John Henry Days*.

15. John Updike, "Tote That Ephemera: An Ambitious New Novel from a Gifted Writer," *New Yorker*, April 30, 2001, https://www.newyorker.com/magazine/2001/05/07/tote-that-ephemera

16. Jonathan Franzen, "Freeloading Man: Review of Colson Whitehead, *John Henry Days*," *New York Times*, May 13, 2001, https://archive.nytimes.com/www.nytimes.com/books/01/05/13/reviews/010513.13franzt.html

17. M. M. Bakhtin, "Epic and Novel," in *The Dialogic Imagination: Four Essays*, ed. Michael Holquist, trans. Caryl Emerson and Michael Holquist (University of Texas Press, 2004), 5.

18. Ramón Saldívar asserts that *John Henry Days* takes part in the aesthetic formation he calls "speculative realism." "The Second Elevation of the Novel: Race, Form, and the Postrace Aesthetic in Contemporary Narrative," *Narrative* 21, no. 1 (January 2013): 13. But despite deploying many genres, *John Henry Days* does not utilize the speculative forms of fantasy, science fiction, or magical realism.

19. For zombie-like forms, see Fredric Jameson: "The older generic categories ... persist in the half-life of the subliterary genres of mass culture." Jameson, *The Political Unconscious: Narrative as a Socially Symbolic Act* (Cornell University Press, 1981), 93.

20. For the growing consensus, see David Duff, "Introduction," in *Modern Genre Theory*, ed. David Duff (Routledge, 2014), 15.

21. Franco Moretti, "The Soul and the Harpy: Reflections on the Aims and Methods of Literary Historiography," in *Signs Taken for Wonders: On the Sociology of Literary Forms* (Verso, 1983), 12.

22. Caroline Levine, *Forms: Whole, Rhythm, Hierarchy, Network* (Princeton University Press, 2015), 7, emphasis added.

23. Ibid., 22. Langdon Hammer notes the agency of forms in Levine's account in "Fantastic Forms," *PMLA* 132, no. 5 (October 2017): 1200–1205. For a constructivist account of form facilitating new possibilities, see Anna Kornbluh, *The Order of Forms: Realism, Formalism, and Social Space* (University of Chicago Press, 2019).

24. Nicholas Brown, *Autonomy: The Social Ontology of Art Under Capitalism* (Duke University Press, 2019), 25–26.

25. What are the *requirements* of SF or even a detective novel? Complex genres like SF, or the police procedural or rock 'n' roll (the latter two are Brown's examples), do not have a *single* formal problem. Further, one wonders: Who decides whether an existing "requirement" is varied enough to count as an autonomous artistic gesture, versus the degree of variation that occurs even within frequently formulaic popular genres?

26. Mark McGurl, *Everything and Less: Fiction in the Age of Amazon* (Verso, 2021), xvii.

27. Jameson uses the notion of contract but later articulates a "dialectical" "structural model" he calls the *"combinatoire,"* in which "the deviation of the individual text from some deeper narrative structure directs our attention to those determinate changes in the historical situation which block a full manifestation of the structure on the discursive level." Jameson, *Political Unconscious*, 146.

28. For the neoclassical tragedy as an unusual example of rigidly codified generic norms, see Pavel, "Literary Genres," 210. For Harlequin's publishing practice see Kim Wilkins, Beth Driscoll, and Lisa Fletcher, *Genre Worlds: Popular Fiction and Twenty-First Century Book Culture* (University of Massachusetts Press, 2022), 40.

29. Rieder, *Science Fiction*.

30. Michael McKeon, *The Origins of the English Novel 1600–1740* (Johns Hopkins University Press, 2002), 20.

31. Ibid., 8.

32. Ibid., 12–13. See also Ralph Cohen, "Introduction," *New Literary History* 34, no. 2 (Spring 2003): v.

33. See also Yury Tynyanov: "a static definition of genre, one which would cover all its manifestations, is impossible: the genre dislocates itself; we see before us the broken line, not a straight line, of its evolution. "The Literary Fact," trans. Ann Shukman, in *Modern Genre Theory*, 32.

34. Wai Chee Dimock, "Introduction: Genres as Fields of Knowledge," *PMLA* 122, no. 5, "Special Topic: Remapping Genre" (October 2007): 1378.

35. David Duff argues that "genres confer *expressive* power, serving the needs of

writers." Duff, *Romanticism and the Uses of Genre* (Oxford University Press, 2009), 7.

36. Pavel, "Literary Genres," 210.

37. Ursula K. Le Guin, "Science Fiction and Mrs. Brown," in *The Language of the Night Essays on Fantasy and Science Fiction* (Perigee, 1979), 119, 119, 115.

38. Inge Birgitte Siegumfeldt, "Paul Auster: I Don't Even Know if *The New York Trilogy* Is Very Good: An Author Looks Back at His Most Well-Known Book," *LitHub*, October 2, 2017, https://lithub.com/paul-auster-i-dont-even-know-if-the-new-york-trilogy-is-very-good/

39. Ibid.

40. Colson Whitehead, "I Have Been on a Fried Chicken Journey: The 2019 AWP Annual Conference & Bookfair Keynote Address," *The Writer's Chronicle* 52, no. 2 (November 2019): 19. All further references cited parenthetically.

41. See Lauren Berlant, "Genre Flailing," *Capacious* 1, no. 2 (2018): 156–162.

42. Adam Kelly argues that "the enthusiastic adoption by celebrated authors of standard genre forms" is an "aesthetic manifestation" of a widespread "praise . . . of convention" in contemporary fiction. "Formally Conventional Fiction," in *American Literature in Transition, 2000–2010*, ed. Rachel Greenwald Smith (Cambridge University Press, 2018), 47. Rather than adhering to convention, genre benders argue that conventions can be used in ways that enable freedom from them.

43. "2.1: Fiction as Streaming, Genre as Portal: Jennifer Egan and Ivan Kreilkamp," *Novel Dialogue Podcast*, September 16, 2021, https://noveldialogue.org/2021/09/16/2-1-fiction-as-streaming-genre-as-portal-jennifer-egan-and-ivan-kreilkamp-jp/

44. Ibid.

45. Ibid.

46. Ibid.

47. Michael Chabon, "Trickster in a Suit of Lights: Thoughts on the Modern Short Story," in *Maps and Legends: Reading and Writing Along the Borderlands* (McSweeney's, 2008), 22.

48. Neil Gaiman and Kazuo Ishiguro, "'Let's Talk About Genre': Neil Gaiman and Kazuo Ishiguro in Conversation," *New Statesman*, June 4, 2015, https://www.newstatesman.com/2015/05/neil-gaiman-kazuo-ishiguro-interview-literature-genre-machines-can-toil-they-can-t-imagine. Gaiman argues that genre grants creators the "advantage" of having "something to play to and to play against." Gaiman, "The Pornography of Genre, or the Genre of Pornography," in *The View from the Cheap Seats: Selected Nonfiction* (New York: HarperCollins, 2016), 45.

49. See Merja Makinen, who argues against the "received assumption" that popular genres are "inherently conservative formats." Instead, she discovers "subversive and challenging" texts and the "gargantuan mutability" of popular genres. Makinen, *Feminist Popular Fiction* (Palgrave, 2001), 1.

50. Ramón Saldívar, "Historical Fantasy, Speculative Realism, and Postrace Aesthetics in Contemporary American Fiction," *American Literary History* 23, no. 3 (Fall 2011): 585.

51. Richard Crownshaw adapts Saldívar's "speculative realism" and Kate Marshall's "speculative memory" to argue that speculative fictions attempt to "recalibrate" memory "to the scales of the Anthropocene." Crownshaw, "Speculative Memory, the Planetary and Genre Fiction," *Textual Practice* 31, no. 5 (2017): 892. See also Kate Marshall, "What Are the Novels of the Anthropocene? American Fiction in Geological Time," *American Literary History* 27, no. 3 (Fall 2015): 523–538.

52. See Laura Savu Walker, "'A Balance of Power': The Covert Authorship of Ian McEwan's Double Agents in *Sweet Tooth*," *Modern Fiction Studies* 61, no. 3 (Fall 2015): 493–514.

53. For "metageneric," see Duff, *Romanticism*, 18.

54. Madhu Dubey, *Signs and Cities: Black Literary Postmodernism* (University of Chicago Press, 2007), 2.

55. Jeffrey Allen Tucker, "'Verticality Is Such a Risky Enterprise': The Literary and Paraliterary Antecedents of Colson Whitehead's *The Intuitionist*," *NOVEL: A Forum on Fiction* 43, no. 1 (Spring 2010): 154.

56. Sean Grattan, "I Think We're Alone Now: Solitude and the Utopian Subject in Colson Whitehead's *The Intuitionist*," *Cultural Critique* 96 (Spring 2017): 146.

57. Colson Whitehead, *The Intuitionist* (Anchor, 1999), 61. All further references cited parenthetically.

58. For a classic exploration of the novelist's representation of torture, see J. M. Coetzee, "Into the Dark Chamber: The Novelist and South Africa," *New York Times*, January 12, 1986, https://www.nytimes.com/1986/01/12/books/into-the-dark-chamber-the-ovelist-and-south-africa.html

59. Mark McGurl, *The Program Era: Postwar Fiction and the Rise of Creative Writing* (Harvard University Press, 2009), 42.

60. Colson Whitehead, *Zone One: A Novel* (Anchor, 2012), 240. All further references cited parenthetically.

61. For the posthuman as blurring "bodily existence and computer simulation," see N. Katherine Hayles, *How We Became Posthuman: Virtual Bodies in Cybernetics, Literature, and Informatics* (University of Chicago Press, 1999), 3. Leif Sorensen reads the humans in *Zone One* as "forced" into "adaptation." But Whitehead's humans are zombie-like before the plague. Sorensen, "Against the Post-Apocalyptic: Narrative Closure in Colson Whitehead's *Zone One*," *Contemporary Literature* 55, no. 3 (Fall 2014): 568.

62. Leo Tolstoy, *Anna Karenina*, trans. Richard Pevear and Larissa Volokhonsky (Penguin, 2000), 1.

63. Andrew Hoberek notes this tension, arguing *Zone One* echoes Eliot's aestheticism, making style "the preserve of the individualism lacking in the world." While Hoberek views this as a "fantastic" resolution, I contend it is pragmatic: insofar as writers make tangible objects, their production is not an imaginary solution to deindividuation, but a material addition of novelty in a world of homogenizing forces. Hoberek, "Living with PASD," *Contemporary Literature* 53, no. 2 (Summer 2012): 409, 410.

64. "The job of the detective is to restore the state of grace in which the aesthetic

and the ethical are as one." W. H. Auden, "The Guilty Vicarage: Notes on the Detective Story, by an Addict," *Harper's Magazine*, May 1948, https://harpers.org/archive/1948/05/the-guilty-vicarage/. For Sherlock Holmes consolidating "values associated with the integrity of 'Englishness,'" see Derek Longhurst, "Sherlock Holmes: Adventures of an English Gentleman 1887–1894," in *Gender, Genre and Narrative Pleasure*, ed. Derek Longhurst (Unwin Hyman, 1989), 60.

65. Andrew Pepper, "Black Crime Fiction," in *The Cambridge Companion to Crime Fiction*, ed. Martin Priestman (Cambridge University Press, 2000), 210.

66. Susan Elizabeth Sweeney, "Unusual Suspects: American Crimes, Metaphysical Detectives, Postmodernist Genres," in *A History of American Crime Fiction*, ed. Chris Raczkowski, (Cambridge University Press, 2017), 221. See also William W. Stowe, "Critical Investigations: Convention and Ideology in Detective Fiction," *Texas Studies in Literature and Language* 31, no. 4 (Winter 1989): 570–591.

67. Jim Collins, "Review of: *The Pursuit of Crime: Art and Ideology in Detective Fiction* by Dennis Porter," *SubStance* 13, no. 1 (January 1984): 105.

68. Ibid., 105. For the hard-boiled tradition, see Lee Horsely, *The Noir Thriller* (Palgrave, 2009).

69. Jim Collins, *Uncommon Cultures: Popular Culture and Post-Modernism* (Routledge, 1989), 32, 34.

70. Ibid., 45.

71. Andrew Pepper, *The Contemporary American Crime Novel: Race, Ethnicity, Gender, Class* (Edinburgh University Press, 2000), 54.

72. Pepper, "Black Crime Fiction," 212.

73. Collins, *Uncommon Cultures*, 30.

74. Laura Marcus, "Detection and Literary Fiction," in *The Cambridge Companion to Crime Fiction*, ed. Martin Priestman (Cambridge University Press, 2000), 246.

75. Patricia Merivale and Susan Elizabeth Sweeney, "The Game's Afoot: On the Trail of the Metaphysical Detective Story," in *Detecting Texts: The Metaphysical Detective Story from Poe to Postmodernism*, eds. Patricia Merivale and Susan Elizabeth Sweeney (University of Pennsylvania Press, 1999), 3.

76. Marcus, "Detection," 261.

77. See Albert Mobilio, "What Makes Him Tic," *New York Times*, October 17, 1999, https://archive.nytimes.com/www.nytimes.com/books/99/10/17/reviews/991017.17mobilot.html?em_pos=large&emc=edit_bk_20161014&nl=bookreview

78. Jonathan Lethem, *Motherless Brooklyn* (Vintage, 2000), 233. All further references cited parenthetically.

79. James Peacock, "'We Learned to Tell Our Story Walking': Tourette's and Urban Space in Jonathan Lethem's *Motherless Brooklyn*," in *Diseases and Disorders in Contemporary Fiction: The Syndrome Syndrome*, eds. James Peacock and Tim Lustig (Routledge, 2013), 71, 81.

80. Jennifer Fleissner, "Symptomatology and the Novel," *NOVEL: A Forum on Fiction* 42, no. 3 (Fall 2009): 391.

81. Ibid., 391.

82. Ibid., 390.

83. For the novel's dramatization of language's poetic function, see Ronald Schleifer, "The Poetics of Tourette Syndrome: Language, Neurobiology, and Poetry," *New Literary History* 32, no. 3 (Summer 2001): 563–584.

84. Hélène Machinal, "*When We Were Orphans*: Narration and Detection in the Case of Christopher Banks," in *Kazuo Ishiguro: Contemporary Critical Perspectives*, eds. Sean Matthews and Sebastian Groes (Continuum, 2009), 89, 90. For Banks's unreliability, see also Bert Olivier, "Literature After Ranciére: Ishiguro's *When We Were Orphans* and Gibson's *Neuromancer*," *Journal of Literary Studies* 29, no. 3 (September 2013): 23–45.

85. Matthew Hart, *Extraterritorial: A Political Geography of Contemporary Fiction* (Columbia University Press, 2020), 209.

86. Kazuo Ishiguro, *When We Were Orphans* (Knopf, 2000), 116. All further references cited parenthetically.

87. For Banks's culpability, see Brian Finney, "Figuring the Real: Ishiguro's *When We Were Orphans*," *Jouvert: A Journal of Postcolonial Studies* 7, no. 1 (Autumn 2002), https://legacy.chass.ncsu.edu/jouvert/v7is1/ishigu.htm

88. Michael Chabon, *The Yiddish Policemen's Union* (Harper Perennial, 2008). See also Daniel Anderson, "Planet of the Jews: Eruvim, Geography, and Jewish Identity in Michael Chabon's *The Yiddish Policemen's Union*," *Shofar* 33, no. 3 (2015): 86–109; and Adam Rovner, "Alternate History: The Case of Nava Semel's *IsraIsland* and Michael Chabon's *The Yiddish Policemen's Union*," *Partial Answers: Journal of Literature and the History of Ideas* 9, no. 1 (2011): 131–152.

89. Louise Erdrich, *The Round House* (Harper Perennial, 2012).

90. Jessica Hurley and Dan Sinykin, "Apocalypse: Introduction," *ASAP/Journal* 3, no. 3 (September 2018): 451.

91. Ibid.

92. Heather Hicks, *The Post-Apocalyptic Novel in the Twenty-First Century: Modernity Beyond Salvage* (Palgrave Macmillan, 2016), 21.

93. Jeanette Winterson, *The Stone Gods* (Mariner, 2007), 7.

94. Sequoia Nagamatsu interweaves ecocatastrophe and contagion, as melting permafrost unleashes a dormant virus. Nagamatsu, *How High We Go in the Dark* (William Morrow, 2022).

95. Mark McGurl, "The Zombie Renaissance," *n+1*, no. 9 (Spring 2010), https://www.nplusonemag.com/issue-9/reviews/the-zombie-renaissance/

96. Emily St. John Mandel, *Station Eleven* (Vintage, 2014), 119. All further references cited parenthetically.

97. See: Diana Adesola Mafe, "Ghostly Girls in the 'Eerie Bush': Helen Oyeyemi's *The Icarus Girl* as Postcolonial Female Gothic Fiction," *Research in African Literatures* 43, no. 3 (Fall 2012): 21–35; Sheri-Marie Harrison, "Marlon James and the Metafiction of the New Black Gothic," *Journal of West Indian Literature* 26, no. 2 (November 2018):

1–17; and Lily G. N. Mabur, "Breaking Gods: An African Postcolonial Gothic Reading of Chimamanda Ngozi Adichie's *Purple Hibiscus* and *Half of a Yellow Sun*," *Research in African Literatures* 39, no. 1 (Winter 2008): 203–222.

98. See Emily Johansen, "The Neoliberal Gothic: *Gone Girl*, *Broken Harbor*, and the Terror of Everyday Life," *Contemporary Literature* 57, no. 1 (Spring 2016): 30–55.

99. Mark B. N. Hansen, "The Digital Topography of Mark Z. Danielewski's *House of Leaves*," *Contemporary Literature* 45, no. 4 (Winter 2004): 597–636.

100. Jason Molesky, "Gothic Toxicity and the Mysteries of Nondisclosure in American Hydrofracking Literature," *MFS Modern Fiction Studies* 66, no. 1 (Spring 2020): 52–77; and Olivia Vázquez-Medina, "Samanta Schweblin's *Fever Dream*: Watery Toxicity, Percolating Disquietude," *Contemporary Literature* 62, no. 1 (2021): 1–34.

101. Manshel, "Colson Whitehead's History," 2.

102. Ibid., 19, 3.

103. Ibid., 3, emphasis added.

104. Madhu Dubey, "Museumizing Slavery: Living History in Colson Whitehead's *The Underground Railroad*," *American Literary History* 32, no. 1 (Spring 2020): 125, 130.

105. Colson Whitehead, *The Underground Railroad* (Anchor, 2016), 70. All further references cited parenthetically.

106. The ambiguity of this ending and the novel's innovative fusion of genres complicate Stephanie Li's contention that *The Underground Railroad* "is inescapably caught in generic and long-standing social discourses," and thus is "the most predictable, and certainly the most generic, of [Whitehead's] six novels and, perhaps for that reason, the most commercially successful." Li, "Genre Trouble and History's Miseries in Colson Whitehead's *The Underground Railroad*," *MELUS* 44, no. 2 (Summer 2019): 4–5.

Chapter 2

1. Viet Than Nguyen, *The Sympathizer* (Grove, 2015), 318. All further references cited parenthetically.

2. Kazuo Ishiguro, *Klara and the Sun* (Vintage, 2021), 207–208. All further references cited parenthetically.

3. For "the production of the value of cultural goods," see Pierre Bourdieu, "The Field of Cultural Production," in *The Field of Cultural Production*, ed. and trans. Randal Johnson (Columbia University Press, 1993), 76.

4. Claire Squires, *Marketing Literature: The Making of Contemporary Writing in Britain* (Palgrave, 2007), 5.

5. Ibid., 4–5.

6. See Cary Wolfe, *What Is Posthumanism?* (University of Minnesota Press, 2009).

7. For "literariness" as "the single most important question" for the Russian formalists, see Victor Erlich, *Russian Formalism: History—Doctrine* (De Gruyter, 2012), 172. Jonathan Culler notes that despite the reign of theory, there has been a dearth of theorizing about what constitutes the literary. Culler, *The Literary in Theory* (Stanford University Press, 2006), 10.

8. Chris Baldick's *Oxford Dictionary of Literary Terms* is representative. Lacking an entry for "literary fiction," it refers, in its definition of "genre fiction," to "its presumed opposite, now increasingly referred to as 'literary fiction,'" which is "expected to go beyond generic boundaries and offer more original imaginative exploration." Baldick, "Genre Fiction," in *The Oxford Dictionary of Literary Terms*, 4th ed. (Oxford University Press, 2015).

9. Richard Todd, *Consuming Fictions: The Booker Prize and Fiction in Britain Today* (Bloomsbury, 1996), 3.

10. Dan Sinykin, *Big Fiction: How Conglomeration Changed the Publishing Industry and American Literature* (Columbia University Press, 2023), 18, 20.

11. Alexander Manshel, *Writing Backwards: Historical Fiction and the Reshaping of the American Canon* (Columbia University Press, 2024).

12. For "vernacular criticism," see Nika Mavrody, Laura B. McGrath, Nichole Nomura, Alexander Sherman, Stanford University Literary Lab, "Voice," *Post45 x Journal of Cultural Analytics*, no. 7, ed. Richard Jean So, April 21, 2021, https://post45.org/2021/04/voice/

13. Joyce Saricks, *The Readers' Advisory Guide to Genre Fiction* (American Library Association, 2009), 165.

14. Ibid., 165–166.

15. Ibid., 166.

16. For the classic application of Wittgenstein's theory, see Alastair Fowler, *Kinds of Literature: An Introduction to the Theory of Genres and Modes* (Oxford, 1982).

17. Günter Leypoldt, "Social Dimensions of the Turn to Genre: Junot Díaz's *Oscar Wao* and Kazuo Ishiguro's *The Buried Giant*," *Post45*, March 31, 2018, https://post45.org/2018/03/social-dimensions-of-the-turn-to-genre-junot-diazs-oscar-wao-and-kazuo-ishiguros-the-buried-giant/. See also Pieter Vermeulen, "The Field of Restricted Emotion: Empathy and Literary Value in Valeria Luiselli's *Lost Children Archive*," *Contemporary Literature* 63, no. 1 (Spring 2022): 79.

18. Leypoldt, "Social Dimensions."

19. Mark McGurl, *Everything and Less: Fiction in the Age of Amazon* (Verso, 2021), 177.

20. See Susan Mandala, *Language in Science Fiction and Fantasy: The Question of Style* (Bloomsbury, 2010).

21. Kurt Vonnegut, *Slaughterhouse-Five* (Dial, 2005), 140.

22. Margaret Atwood, *The Blind Assassin* (Anchor, 2000), 22. All further references cited parenthetically.

23. "You will give distinction to your style if an ingenious combination makes a familiar word new." Horace, "Ars Poetica," in *The Norton Anthology of Theory and Criticism*, 2nd ed., ed. Vincent B. Leitch (Norton, 2010), 123.

24. George Orwell, "Politics and the English Language," in *All Art Is Propaganda: Critical Essays* (Mariner, 2009), 285.

25. David James, *Discrepant Solace: Contemporary Literature and the Work of Consolation* (Oxford University Press, 2019), 6.

26. Michael Dango examines detox, binge, filter, and ghost, as four aesthetic styles for repairing contemporary crises. Dango, *Crisis Style: The Aesthetics of Repair* (Stanford University Press, 2021).

27. Jesmyn Ward, *Sing, Unburied, Sing* (Scribner, 2017), 186. For Ward's use of the road novel to consider constraints on freedom and mobility for African Americans, see Nicole Dib, "Haunted Roadscapes in Jesmyn Ward's *Sing, Unburied, Sing*," *MELUS* 45, no. 2 (Summer 2020): 134–153.

28. Ward, *Sing*, 190.

29. David Mitchell, *The Bone Clocks* (Random House, 2014), 294.

30. See the page-long sentence in David Mitchell, *A Thousand Autumns of Jacob de Zoet* (Random House, 2010), 451–452.

31. James Wood, "Soul Cycle: David Mitchell's 'The Bone Clocks,'" *New Yorker*, September 1, 2014, https://www.newyorker.com/magazine/2014/09/08/soul-cycle

32. Ibid.

33 Colson Whitehead, *Zone One: A Novel* (Anchor, 2012), 83. All further references cited parenthetically.

34. Andrew Hoberek argues that "the turn to genre pushes contemporary fiction" toward "the poetic delight in language" that "has always stood . . . disreputably close to pulp." Hoberek, "Cormac McCarthy and the Aesthetics of Exhaustion," *American Literary History* 23, no. 3 (Fall 2011): 496. But pulp often narrates action with a minimum of ornament. Consider the parallel scene of frozen traffic in Max Brooks's *World War Z*:

> Even before the crisis, the bridge had been a nightmare of traffic jams. Now it was crammed with evacuees. . . . Cars were everywhere, little Lags and old Zhigs, a few Mercedes, and a mammoth GAZ truck sitting right in the middle, just turned over on its side! We tried to move it, get a chain around the axle, and pull it free with one of the tanks. Not a chance.

Brooks, *World War Z: An Oral History of the Zombie War* (Three Rivers, 2006), 117.

35. For modernist aesthetic opposition, see: Andrew Hoberek, "'But—What Can Anyone Do About It?': Modernism, Superheroes, and the Unfinished Business of the Common Good," *Journal of Modern Literature* 39, no. 2 (Winter 2016): 115–125; and Patrick Bixby, "Becoming 'James Overman': Joyce, Nietzsche, and the Uncreated Conscience of the Irish," *Modernism/modernity* 24, no. 1 (January 2017): 45–66.

36. See: James Dorson, "Demystifying the Judge: Law and Mythical Violence in Cormac McCarthy's *Blood Meridian*," *Journal of Modern Literature* 36, no. 2 (Winter 2013): 105–121; and Dana Phillips, "History and the Ugly Facts of Cormac McCarthy's *Blood Meridian*," *American Literature* 68, no. 2 (June 1996): 433–460.

37. Cormac McCarthy, *Blood Meridian, or, The Evening Redness in the West* (Vintage, 1992), 4–5. All further references cited parenthetically.

38. See Dorson, who summarizes the scholarly consensus that novel is a critique of liberal humanism. Dorson, "Demystifying," 107.

39. The novel generally narrates brutality without commentary, allowing the possi-

bility that it naturalizes such violence. But McCarthy's narrator at times offers subtle cues that the reader should resist the Judge's nihilism, referring to him as a "vast abhorrence" (254).

40. For the novel's critique of "commensurability," the amoral neoliberal principle that "everything has its price," see Dorson, "Demystifying," 112.

41. Vladimir Nabokov, *Lolita* (Vintage, 2010), 9.

42. See Philip Caputo, "'The Sympathizer,' by Viet Thanh Nguyen," *New York Times*, April 2, 2015, https://www.nytimes.com/2015/04/05/books/review/the-sympathizer-by-viet-thanh-nguyen.html

43. For Roth's engagement with Ellison, see Timothy L. Parrish, "Ralph Ellison: The Invisible Man in Philip Roth's 'The Human Stain,'" *Contemporary Literature* 45, no. 3 (Autumn 2004): 421–459.

44. Ellison's narrator famously begins: "No, I am not a spook like those who haunted Edgar Allan Poe; nor am I one of your Hollywood-movie ectoplasms." Ralph Ellison, *Invisible Man* (Vintage, 1995), 3.

45. Critics often include Díaz's novel in discussions of the genre turn. But, except for brief appearances of an uncanny mongoose and a man with no face, which might be distressed characters' hallucinations, most of *Oscar Wao* is a historical novel and family saga, that uses SF and comics metaphors for Oscar's ostracism. "You really want to know what being an X-Man feels like? Just be a smart bookish boy of color in a contemporary U.S. ghetto." Junot Díaz, *The Brief Wondrous Life of Oscar Wao* (Riverhead, 2007), 22.

46. Leypoldt, "Social Dimensions." Such deflation argues against McGurl's claim that "writers of high literary ambition have been trying to produce . . . genre effects," scenes that are "the equivalent of special effects in movies." Mark McGurl, "The Novel's Forking Path," *Public Books*, April 1, 2015, https://www.publicbooks.org/the-novels-forking-path/

47. Jeremy Keehn, "*Zone One*: Six Questions for Colson Whitehead," *Harper's Magazine*, October 17, 2011, https://harpers.org/2011/10/six-questions-for-colson-whitehead/

48. Michael Chabon, *Gentlemen of the Road: A Tale of Adventure* (Del Rey, 2007), 3.

49. Chang-Rae Lee, *Native Speaker* (Riverhead, 1995), 147. All further references cited parenthetically.

50. David Mitchell, *Cloud Atlas* (Random House, 2004), 186. All further references cited parenthetically.

51. Michel Faber, *The Book of Strange New Things* (Hogarth, 2014), 272. All further references cited parenthetically.

52. Dorothy J. Hale, *The Novel and the New Ethics* (Stanford University Press, 2020), 27.

53. Ibid., 28, 4.

54. See Dorrit Cohn, *The Distinction of Fiction* (Johns Hopkins University Press, 2000).

55. "2.1: Fiction as Streaming, Genre as Portal: Jennifer Egan and Ivan Kreilkamp," *Novel Dialogue Podcast*, September 16, 2021, https://noveldialogue.org/2021/09/16/2-1-fiction-as-streaming-genre-as-portal-jennifer-egan-and-ivan-kreilkamp-jp/

56. Timothy Aubry, *Reading as Therapy: What Contemporary Fiction Does for Middle-Class Americans* (University of Iowa Press, 2006), 2.

57. See, for example, Fredric Jameson, who opposes the "psychological landscape of the realistic" narrative with the "figural (SF) narrative." Jameson, *Archaeologies of the Future: The Desire Called Utopia and Other Science Fictions* (Verso, 2005), 304. Le Guin asserts "that in fantasy, character is often less important than role (also true of Greek tragedy and much of Shakespeare.)" Ursula K. Le Guin, "Some Assumptions About Fantasy," June 4, 2004, https://www.ursulakleguin.com/some-assumptions-about-fantasy

58. Andrew Hoberek, "Popular Genres and Interiority," *Amerikastudien / American Studies* 64, no. 4 (2019): 568, 570.

59. Ibid., 570.

60. Fredric Jameson, *The Antinomies of Realism* (Verso, 2015), 267.

61. Timothy Aubry, *Reading as Therapy: What Contemporary Fiction Does for Middle-Class Americans* (University of Iowa Press, 2006), 152.

62. Mark McGurl, *The Program Era: Postwar Fiction and the Rise of Creative Writing* (Harvard University Press, 2009), 32. Caren Irr, *Toward the Geopolitical Novel: U.S. Fiction in the Twenty-First Century* (Columbia University Press, 2013).

63. David Mitchell, *Ghostwritten: A Novel* (Vintage, 2001), 153.

64. For Mitchell's effort to achieve global scale by accumulating individuals, see Berthold Schoene, "'Tour Du Monde': David Mitchell's 'Ghostwritten' and the Cosmopolitan Imagination," *College Literature* 37, no. 4 (Fall 2010): 42–60. Mitchell explains that his "über-novel" enables scalar oscillations, "creating a world that is enormous," through "self-contained narratives about milieus with boundaries." Mitch R. Murray, "Thinking Polyphonically: A Conversation with David Mitchell," *Los Angeles Review of Books*, September 11, 2020, https://lareviewofbooks.org/article/thinking-polyphonically-a-conversation-with-david-mitchell/. Murray contends that Mitchell's "work is fundamentally at odds with the enclosure, interiority, and finality typically understood to be characteristic of literary fiction." But his novels demonstrate the compatibility of interiority with large-scale world-building. Mitch R. Murray, "David Mitchell's Storytelling and the Metalife of Utopia," *ASAP/Journal* 5, no. 1 (January 2020): 185.

65. Mitchell, *Ghostwritten*, 154.

66. Mitchell adapted Goose's law from a Japanese proverb, itself adapted from the eight-century Tang dynasty poet Han Yu. See Lisa Wallin, "Weekly Japanese Idiom: 'Jakuniku-kyoushoku'—Survival of the Fittest," *Tokyo Weekender*, February 12, 2021, https://www.tokyoweekender.com/art_and_culture/japanese-culture/weekly-japanese-idiom-jakuniku-kyoushoku-survival-fittest/

67. For *Cloud Atlas* as a novel that does justice to our "historical past" and "our historical futures," see Jameson, *Antinomies*, 312–313.

68. Ander Monson, "Living in Your Head," *New York Times*, September 3, 2010, https://www.nytimes.com/2010/09/05/books/review/Monson-t.html

69. Charles Yu, *How to Live Safely in a Science Fictional Universe* (Vintage, 2010), 164–165. All further references cited parenthetically.

70. See also Frances Tran, "Time Traveling with Care: On Female Coolies and Archival Speculations," *American Quarterly* 70, no. 2 (June 2018): 189–210.

71. Charles Yu, *Interior Chinatown: A Novel* (Vintage, 2020), 176. All further references cited parenthetically.

72. Kazuo Ishiguro, *Never Let Me Go* (Vintage International, 2006), 261. All further references cited parenthetically.

73. For the failure of the students' artworks to ameliorate their condition, see Sarah Brouillette, *Literature and the Creative Economy* (Stanford University Press, 2014), 200–205.

74. Sheryl Vint, "Introduction," in *After the Human: Culture, Theory, and Criticism in the 21st Century* (Cambridge University Press, 2020), 7.

Chapter 3

1. Gary Shteyngart, *Super Sad True Love Story* (Random House, 2010), 52. All further references cited parenthetically.

2. Richard Powers, *Galatea 2.2: A Novel* (Harper Perennial, 1996), 260. All further references cited parenthetically.

3. For metafiction, see Linda Hutcheon, *A Poetics of Postmodernism: History, Theory, Fiction* (New York: Routledge, 1988).

4. See Wendy Brown, *Undoing the Demos: Neoliberalism's Stealth Revolution* (Zone Books, 2015).

5. The reference is to Raymond Williams's schema in "Dominant, Residual, Emergent," in *Marxism and Literature* (Oxford University Press, 1977), 121–127.

6. Andrzej Gąsiorek and David James, "Introduction: Fiction Since 2000: Postmillennial Commitments, *Contemporary Literature* 53, no. 4 (2012): 616.

7. For allegories of contemporary authorship in the era of publishing's conglomeration, see Dan Sinykin, *Big Fiction: How Conglomeration Changed the Publishing Industry and American Literature* (Columbia University Press, 2023).

8. See Biwu Shang, "From Alan Turing to Ian McEwan: Artificial Intelligence, Lies and Ethics in *Machines Like Me*," *Comparative Literature Studies* 57, no. 3 (2020): 443–453.

9. See Pieter Vermeulen for the claim that contemporary literary fictions often proceed by "interrogating the unreflexive empathy they attribute to commercial literature . . . and replacing it with complex, self-reflexive, and even self-sabotaging empathy." Vermeulen, "The Field of Restricted Emotion: Empathy and Literary Value in Valeria Luiselli's *Lost Children Archive*," *Contemporary Literature* 63, no. 1 (Spring 2022): 80.

10. Ian McEwan, *Machines Like Me: And People Like You* (Anchor, 2019), 213. All further references cited parenthetically.

11. Michael Cunningham, *Specimen Days* (Picador, 2006), 239. All further references cited parenthetically.

12. Walt Whitman, "Song of Myself," from *Leaves of Grass* in *Walt Whitman: The Complete Poems*, ed. Francis Murphy (Penguin, 2004), 124.

13. Jessica Pressman, *Bookishness: Loving Books in a Digital Age* (Columbia University Press, 2020), 41.

14. Ibid., 45–46.

15. Sarah Brouillette, *Literature and the Creative Economy* (Stanford University Press, 2014), 207.

16. Jennifer Egan, *The Keep* (Anchor, 2006), 6. All further references cited parenthetically.

17. Michael Chabon, *The Amazing Adventures of Kavalier & Clay* (Random House, 2000), 486. All further references cited parenthetically.

18. Nikesh Shukla, "Colson Whitehead: Each Book an Antidote," *Guernica*, April 24, 2013, https://www.guernicamag.com/colson-whitehead-each-book-an-antidote/

19 Colson Whitehead, *Zone One: A Novel* (Anchor, 2012), 26. All further references cited parenthetically.

20. William Shakespeare, *King Lear*, in *The Riverside Shakespeare*, 2nd ed., eds. G. Blakemore Evans and J. J. M. Tobin (Houghton Mifflin, 1997), 3.4.107–108.

21. Margaret Atwood, *The Blind Assassin* (Anchor, 2000), 154–156.

22. Emily St. John Mandel, *Station Eleven* (Vintage, 2014), 296. All further references cited parenthetically.

23. Charles Yu, *How to Live Safely in a Science Fictional Universe* (Vintage, 2010), 168. All further references cited parenthetically.

24. Ling Ma, *Severance* (Picador, 2018), 199. All further references cited parenthetically.

25. Jonathan Lethem, *The Fortress of Solitude* (Vintage, 2003), 230.

26. Margaret Atwood, *Oryx and Crake* (Anchor, 2004), 40. All further references cited parenthetically.

27. Carmen Maria Machado, "The Resident," in *Her Body and Other Parties* (Harper Perennial, 2018), 172–194.

28. Leo Corry and Renato Giovanolli, "Jorge Borges, Author of *The Name of the Rose*," *Poetics Today* 13, no. 3 (1992): 426. For the novel's semiotic theory, see Christoph Prang, "The Creative Power of Semiotics: Umberto Eco's *The Name of the Rose*," *Comparative Literature* 66, no. 4 (Fall 2014): 420–437.

29. For *Possession* and *The Marriage Plot* as novels that blend realism and metafiction, see: Jane Campbell, *A. S. Byatt and the Heliotropic Imagination* (Wilfrid Laurier University Press, 2004), 111; and Sharon Marcus, "The Euphoria of Influence: Jeffrey Eugenides's 'The Marriage Plot,'" *Public Books*, November 10, 2011, https://www.publicbooks.org/marcus-tribute-2020-the-euphoria-of-influence-jeffrey-eugenidess-the-marriage-plot/

30. Ian McEwan, *Sweet Tooth: A Novel* (Anchor, 2013), 101.

31. Mark McGurl, *The Program Era: Postwar Fiction and the Rise of Creative Writing* (Harvard University Press, 2009).

32. Bennett Sims, *A Questionable Shape* (Two Dollar Radio, 2013), 83. All further references cited parenthetically.

33. For Sims's seeming antipathy for the zombie genre, see Benjamin Rybeck, "Review: *A Questionable Shape*, by Bennett Sims," *Electric Literature*, June 3, 2013, https://electricliterature.com/review-a-questionable-shape-by-bennett-sims/

34. Tobias Carroll, "The Thinking Man's Zombie," *Los Angeles Review of Books*, July 28, 2013, https://lareviewofbooks.org/article/the-thinking-mans-zombie/

35. For *Galatea's* literariness, see Steven Moore, "Soul of a New Machine," *Washington Post*, July 9, 1995, https://www.washingtonpost.com/archive/entertainment/books/1995/07/09/soul-of-a-new-machine/918914e5-7861-484a-8af7-077106a03c1e/. For Powers's "encyclopedic" novels, see Trey Stecker, "Ecologies of Knowledge: The Encyclopedic Narratives of Richard Powers and His Contemporaries," *Review of Contemporary Fiction* (January 1, 1998): 67–72. For Powers's intertextual references and bridging of the "two cultures," see J. D. Thomas, "Science and the Sacred: Intertextuality in Richard Powers's *The Gold Bug Variations*," *Critique: Studies in Contemporary Fiction* 51, no. 1 (2010): 18–31.

36. N. Katherine Hayles, "The Posthuman Body: Inscription and Incorporation in *Galatea 2.2* and *Snow Crash*," *Configurations* 5, no. 2 (Spring 1997): 247.

37. Kathleen Fitzpatrick, "The Exhaustion of Literature: Novels, Computers, and the Threat of Obsolescence," *Contemporary Literature* 43, no. 3 (Autumn 2002): 556.

38. Fitzpatrick, "Exhaustion," 554; for Rick's unreliability, see Hayles, "Posthuman Body," 255–257.

39. See Georg Lukács, *The Theory of the Novel: A Historico-Philosophical Essay on the Forms of Great Epic Literature*, trans. Anna Bostock (MIT Press, 1971), 41.

40. Walter Benjamin, "Theses on the Philosophy of History," in *Illuminations*, ed. Hannah Arendt, trans. Harry Zohn (Schocken, 2007), 253–264.

41. The final turn of *Galatea 2.2*'s screw, in which we discover that Helen was a hoax perpetrated on Rick, reveals that it wasn't a machine making these conclusions about the awfulness of the human world. Still, this only bolsters Powers's critical view of humanity since it adds the computer scientists' jesting at the expense of the naïf humanist to the list of human ills, and it hardly undermines the accuracy of Helen's judgment.

Chapter 4

1. Margaret Atwood, *The Blind Assassin* (Anchor, 2000), 142. All further references cited parenthetically.

2. Jennifer Egan, *The Keep* (Anchor, 2006), 6. All further references cited parenthetically.

3. Michael Chabon, "The Editor's Notebook: A Confidential Chat with the Editor," in *McSweeney's Mammoth Treasury of Thrilling Tales*, ed. Michael Chabon (Vintage, 2003), 6.

4. Michael Chabon, "Trickster in a Suit of Lights: Thoughts on the Modern Short Story," in *Maps and Legends: Reading and Writing Along the Borderlands* (McSweeney's, 2008), 19; Chabon, "Editor's Notebook," 7.

5. Chabon, "Editor's Notebook," 7–8.

6. Arthur Krystal, "Easy Writers," *New Yorker*, May 28, 2012, https://www.newyorker.com/magazine/2012/05/28/easy-writers

7. Lev Grossman, "Literary Revolution in the Supermarket Aisle: Genre Fiction Is Disruptive Technology," *Time*, May 23, 2012, https://entertainment.time.com/2012/05/23/genre-fiction-is-disruptive-technology/

8. Ibid.

9. Ibid.

10. Andrew Hoberek, "Literary Genre Fiction," in *American Literature in Transition, 2000–2010*, ed. Rachel Greenwald Smith (Cambridge University Press, 2018), 61, 62.

11. Andrew Hoberek, "Popular Genres and Interiority," *Amerikastudien / American Studies* 64, no. 4 (2019): 570.

12. Ibid., 568.

13. For the conservatism of crime fiction, see Stephen Knight, *Form and Ideology in Crime Fiction* (Indiana University Press, 1980); and Dennis Porter, *The Pursuit of Crime: Art and Ideology in Detective Fiction* (Yale University Press, 1981). For the western's patriarchal nationalism, see Jane Tompkins, *West of Everything: The Inner Life of Westerns* (Oxford University Press, 1992). Janice Radway's classic account "does not challenge absolutely the notion that mass-produced art forms like the romance are ideologically conservative," but also contends the genre in "contradictory ways . . . protests the weakness of patriarchy and the failure of traditional marriage even as it apparently acts to assert the perfection of each." Radway, *Reading the Romance: Women, Patriarchy, and Popular Literature* (University of North Carolina Press, 1984), 220.

14. Jed Esty notes the legacy of modernism in literary theories in which "the problem of bourgeois subjectivity or psychic depth [was] seen as the baleful provenance of realism as against more direct, plot-driven fiction or experimental, language-driven fiction," but this "pattern of attribution repeats itself across various realism wars to simplify the messy empirical facts of literary history at any given moment." Esty, "Realism Wars," *NOVEL: A Forum on Fiction* 49, no. 2 (August 2016): 321.

15. I'm grateful to Scott Black for this insight.

16. Peter Brooks, *Reading for the Plot: Design and Intention in Narrative* (Harvard University Press, 1992), 5. All further references cited parenthetically.

17. See also Caroline Levine, *The Serious Pleasures of Suspense: Victorian Realism and Narrative Doubt* (University of Virginia Press, 2003), 8: "Narrative fiction emerges, here, as a particularly effective way to introduce readers to the activity of hypothesizing and testing in order to come to knowledge."

18. For the literary field's relative indifference to readers' pleasure and popular fiction's desire to please audiences, see Ken Gelder, *Popular Fiction: The Logics and Practices of a Literary Field* (Routledge, 2004), 13, 24.

19. Wyatt Mason, "David Mitchell, the Experimentalist," *New York Times Magazine*, June 25, 2010, https://www.nytimes.com/2010/06/27/magazine/27mitchell-t.html

20. See, for example: Nicholas Brown, *Autonomy: The Social Ontology of Art Under Capitalism* (Duke University Press, 2019); and Walter Benn Michaels, "Neoliberal Aesthetics: Fried, Rancière and the Form of the Photograph," *nonsite*, no. 1, January 25, 2011, https://nonsite.org/neoliberal-aesthetics-fried-ranciere-and-the-form-of-the-photograph/

21. Ursula K. Le Guin, "*The Bone Clocks* by David Mitchell—Dazzle of Narrative Fireworks," *Guardian*, September 2, 2014, https://www.theguardian.com/books/2014/sep/02/the-bone-clocks-david-mitchell-review-novel

22. Mason, "Mitchell, the Experimentalist," *New York Times Magazine*, June 25, 2010, https://www.nytimes.com/2010/06/27/magazine/27mitchell-t.html

23. See Henry Jenkins, *Convergence Culture: Where Old and New Media Collide* (New York University Press, 2006).

24. Michael Saler, *As If: Modern Enchantment and the Literary Prehistory of Virtual Reality* (Oxford University Press, 2012), 6.

25. Marie-Laure Ryan, *Narrative as Virtual Reality: Immersion and Interactivity in Literature and Electronic Media* (Johns Hopkins University Press, 2003), 94. All further references cited parenthetically.

26. Constance Grady, "*Black Leopard, Red Wolf* Was Sold as an African *Game of Thrones*. It's a Weirder Book Than That," *Vox*, February 6, 2019, https://www.vox.com/culture/2019/2/6/18212431/black-leopard-red-wolf-marlon-james-review. See also Amber Jamilla Musser, "Queer Talk: *Black Leopard Red Wolf* and the Black Diaspora," *ASAP/Journal* 6, no. 2 (2021): 293, for James's "withholding" of readerly pleasures.

27. Min Hyoung Song explains how his "desire for immersion" was disrupted by Chang-rae Lee's use of "language [that] kept calling attention to its obfuscations," in *A Gesture Life* (1999). Min Hyoung Song, "Between Genres: On Chang-rae Lee's Realism," *Los Angeles Review of Books*, January 10, 2014, https://www.lareviewofbooks.org/article/chang-rae-lees-realism

28. David James, *Modernist Futures: Innovation and Inheritance in the Contemporary Novel* (Cambridge University Press, 2012), 18.

29. Ibid., 11.

30. Ibid., 18, emphasis added.

31. Ibid., 25.

32. Michael Chabon, "Fan Fiction: On Sherlock Holmes," in *Maps and Legends*, 44.

33. Margaret Atwood, "Introduction," in *In Other Worlds* (Nan A. Talese/Doubleday, 2011), 8.

34. Margaret Atwood, "Flying Rabbits," in *In Other Worlds*, 23.

35. For readings of the map sequence of *Game of Thrones*, see: Michael Szalay, "HBO's Flexible Gold," *Representations* 126, no. 1 (May 2014): 112–134; and Kate Marshall, "Atlas of a Concave World: *Game of Thrones* and the Historical Novel," *Critical Quarterly* 57, no. 1 (April 2015): 61–70. While these are brilliant readings of the title

sequence, its mapping of Westeros functions at a more basic level to invite the viewer into its imaginative geography.

36. Scott Black, "Reading Adventures," *English Language Notes* 51, no. 2 (Fall/Winter 2013): 36–37. Black quotes Rita Felski, *The Uses of Literature* (Blackwell, 2008), 135.

37. Black, "Reading Adventures," 36.

38. Ibid., 37.

39. Ibid.

40. Barry Weller, "Pleasure and Self-Loss in Reading," *ADE Bulletin* 99 (Fall 1991): 9.

41. Ibid.

42. Michael Chabon, "Afterword," in *Gentlemen of the Road* (Del Rey, 2008), 200.

43. Michael Chabon, *The Amazing Adventures of Kavalier & Clay* (Random House, 2000), 575. All further references cited parenthetically.

44. For Chabon's rejection of "a binary of complicit pleasure or critical action," that the critic ironically reinstates, see Iain Bernhoft, "The Politics of Escapistry: Harry Houdini, Nostalgia, and the Turn from Critique in Michael Chabon's *The Amazing Adventures of Kavalier & Clay*," *Modern Fiction Studies* 64, no. 1 (Spring 2018): 1–26.

45. Ursula K. Le Guin, "Why Americans Are Afraid of Dragons?" in *The Language of the Night: Essays on Fantasy and Science Fiction*, ed. and introduction by Susan Wood (Putnam, 1979), 40.

46. Ibid.

47. Ibid., 41.

48. Ibid.

49. Samuel R. Delany, "The Necessity of Tomorrow," in *Starboard Wine: More Notes on the Language of Science Fiction* (Dragon Press, 1984), 29.

50. Ibid.

51. Ibid. Elsewhere, Delany makes similar claims that SF's central mechanism is to activate the play of difference between the actual and imaginary worlds. Samuel R. Delany, "Science Fiction and 'Literature'—or, The Conscience of the King," in *Starboard Wine*, 120.

52. David Mitchell, *Cloud Atlas* (Random House, 2004), 5. All further references cited parenthetically.

53. In Chapter XX of *Don Quixote*, Sancho binds Rocinante's legs to make Quixote wait through the night before taking on more dangers. "'There's no reason to cry,' responded Sancho, 'I'll entertain your grace, telling you stories until daylight.'" Of course, the comedy here comes from the fact that Sancho aims to put Quixote to sleep with his monotonous tale. Miguel de Cervantes, *Don Quixote*, trans. Edith Grossman (Ecco, 2015), 144.

54. "Yarn," *Online Etymology Dictionary*, https://www.etymonline.com/word/yarn

55. Black, "Reading Adventures," 39.

56. A. S. Byatt, "Choices: The Writing of *Possession*," *The Threepenny Review* 63 (Autumn 1995): 17.

57. Umberto Eco, *The Name of the Rose*, trans. William Weaver (Harvest, 1984), 5. All further references cited parenthetically.

58. A. S. Byatt, *Possession: A Romance* (Vintage, 1990), 460. All further references cited parenthetically.

59. See the famous opening line of Stephen Greenblatt, *Shakespearean Negotiations: The Circulation of Social Energy in Renaissance England* (University of California Press, 1988), 1: "I began with the desire to speak with the dead."

60. For Atwood's depiction of reconstructing history, see Alan Robinson, "'Alias Laura': Representations of the Past in Margaret Atwood's 'The Blind Assassin,'" *Modern Language Review* 101, no. 2 (April 2006): 347–359.

61. For the postscript, see Armelle Parey, "Unsettling Postscripts and Epilogues in A. S. Byatt's *Possession* and Ian McEwan's *Atonement*," *Sillages Critiques* 24 (July 2018), https://journals.openedition.org/sillagescritiques/5751?lang=en

62. Byatt, "Choices," 17, emphasis added.

63. See Dorrit Cohn, *The Distinction of Fiction* (Johns Hopkins University Press, 2000).

64. Nathaniel Hawthorne, "Preface" in *The House of the Seven Gables* (Project Gutenberg, 1993), https://www.gutenberg.org/files/77/77-h/77-h.htm#pref02

65. Chabon, "Trickster," 12–13.

66. Margaret Atwood, "Alphinland," in *Stone Mattress: Nine Tales* (Nan A. Talese, 2014), 22.

67. Jonathan Lethem, *Motherless Brooklyn* (Vintage, 2000), 37–38.

68. Anthony Doerr, *All the Light We Cannot See* (Scribner, 2014), 135.

69. Richard Powers, *Playground: A Novel* (Norton, 2024), 68.

70. Michael Chabon, *Telegraph Avenue: A Novel* (Harper, 2012), 62. All further references cited parenthetically.

71. Junot Díaz, *The Brief Wondrous Life of Oscar Wao* (Riverhead, 2007), 21–22n6.

72. Chabon, "Trickster," 2.

73. For a compendium of things fictions can do, see Joshua Landy, *How to Do Things with Fictions* (Oxford University Press, 2012).

74. See James F. English, "The Resistance to Counting, Recounting," *Representations*, January 13, 2015, http://www.representations.org/reponse-to-ulysses-by-numbers-james-f-english/

75. Kate Atkinson, *Life After Life* (Reagan Arthur, 2013); Jenny Erpenbeck, *The End of Days*, trans. Susan Bernofsky (New Directions, 2016).

Chapter 5

1. Ling Ma, *Severance* (Picador, 2018), 80. All further references cited parenthetically.

2. For contemporary book production, see Matthew Kirschenbaum, "Bibliologistics: The Nature of Books Now, or A Memorable Fancy," *Post45*, April 9, 2020, https://post45.org/2020/04/bibliologistics-the-nature-of-books-now-or-a-memorable-fancy/

3. See: Sarah Brouillette, *Literature and the Creative Economy* (Stanford University Press, 2014); Mark McGurl, *Everything and Less: Fiction in the Age of Amazon* (Verso, 2021); Dan Sinykin, *Big Fiction: How Conglomeration Changed the Publishing Industry and American Literature* (Columbia University Press, 2023).

4. For complicit critique as the predicament of postmodernism, see Linda Hutcheon, *A Poetics of Postmodernism: History Theory Fiction* (New York: Routledge, 1988).

5. For the unevenness of capitalist penetration across global sites, see Warwick Research Collective, *Combined and Uneven Development: Towards a New Theory of World-Literature* (Liverpool University Press, 2015).

6. See, for example: Arjun Appadurai, ed., *Globalization* (Duke University Press, 2001); Joseph Stiglitz, *Globalization and Its Discontents* (Norton, 2003); Victor Roudometof, *Glocalization: A Critical Introduction* (Taylor & Francis, 2016); and Matthew Sparke, "The Crisis of Globalisation," in *The Routledge Handbook of Social Change*, eds. Richard Ballard and Clive Barnett (Routledge, 2023).

7. Fredric Jameson, "Globalization and Political Strategy," *New Left Review* 4 (July-August 2000): 49–68, quote at 49.

8. Ibid., 51.

9. See, for example, Roland Robertson, "Glocalization: Time-Space and Homogeneity-Heterogeneity," and Jan Nederveen Pieterse, "Globalization as Hybridization," in *Global Modernities*, eds. Mike Featherstone, Scott Lash, and Roland Robertson (Sage, 1997), 25–44 and 45–68.

10. Miwon Kwon, *One Place After Another: Site-Specific Art and Locational Identity* (MIT Press, 2002), 157.

11. Joshua Schulze, "The Sacred Engine and the Rice Paddy: Globalization, Genre, and Local Space in the Films of Bong Joon-ho," *Journal of Popular Film and Television* 47, no. 1 (2019): 21–29, quote at 22.

12. Ibid., 22.

13. Sheri-Marie Harrison, "Global Horror: An Introduction," *Post45*, April 4, 2019, https://post45.org/sections/contemporaries-essays/global-horror/

14. Rebecca Walkowitz, *Born Translated: The Contemporary Novel in an Age of World Literature* (Columbia University Press, 2015), 4.

15. Ibid., 15.

16. Michael Chabon, *Telegraph Avenue: A Novel* (Harper, 2012), 401. All further references cited parenthetically.

17. Mohsin Hamid, *Exit West* (Riverhead, 2017), 29. All further references cited parenthetically.

18. Colson Whitehead, *Zone One: A Novel* (Anchor, 2012), 22, 23, 46, 61, 184.

19. Colson Whitehead, *Apex Hides the Hurt* (Anchor, 2006), 38. All further references cited parenthetically.

20. Nirvana Tanoukhi, "The Movement of Specificity," *PMLA* 128, no. 3 (May 2013): 671.

21. Ibid., 678, 680.

22. See Jay Rubin, *Haruki Murakami and the Music of Words* (Harvill, 2002), esp. 6–7; and Sam Anderson, "The Fierce Imagination of Haruki Murakami," *New York Times Magazine*, October 21, 2011, https://www.nytimes.com/2011/10/23/magazine/the-fierce-imagination-of-haruki-murakami.html. For Murakami's use of popular genre, especially noir, see Steffen Hanke, "Postmodernism and Genre Fiction as Deferred Action: Haruki Murakami and the Noir Tradition," *Critique* 49, no. 1 (Fall 2007): 3–23.

23. Baryon Tensor Posadas, "Remediations of 'Japan' in *Number9Dream*," in *David Mitchell: Critical Essays*, ed. Sarah Dillon (Gylphi, 2011), 92.

24. Haruki Murakami, *1Q84*, trans. Jay Rubin and Philip Gabriel (Vintage, 2013), 901. All further references cited parenthetically.

25. Many have recognized Mitchell and Murakami as consummate global novelists. See: Wendy Knepper, "Toward a Theory of Experimental World Epic: David Mitchell's *Cloud Atlas*," *Ariel* 47, no. 1 (2006): 93–126; Aaron Francis Schneeberger, "The Genre Spaces of David Mitchell's *Cloud Atlas*," *College Literature* 46, no. 3 (2019): 543–572; Berthold Schoene, "'Tour Du Monde': David Mitchell's 'Ghostwritten' and the Cosmopolitan Imagination," *College Literature* 37, no. 4 (Fall 2010): 42–60; and Karolina Watroba, "World Literature and Literary Value: Is 'Global' the New 'Lowbrow?'" *Cambridge Journal of Postcolonial Literary Inquiry* 5, no. 1 (2018): 53–68.

26. Haruki Murakami, *The Wind-Up Bird Chronicle*, trans. Jay Rubin (Vintage International, 1998).

27. Jean Baudrillard, *Simulacra and Simulation*, trans. Sheila Faria Glaser (University of Michigan Press, 1994), 2.

28. For the ontological uncertainty of postmodernist fiction, see Brian McHale, *Postmodernist Fiction* (Methuen, 1987). For unmooring from place, see David Harvey, "From Space to Place and Back Again: Reflections on the Condition of Postmodernity," in *Mapping the Futures: Local Cultures, Global Change*, eds. Jon Bird et al. (Routledge, 1993), 2–29.

29. David Mitchell, *Number9Dream* (Random House, 2003), 3. All further references cited parenthetically.

30. David Harvey, *A Brief History of Neoliberalism* (Oxford, 2005), 132.

31. See Laura McGrath, "Literary Agency," *American Literary History* 33, no. 2 (2021): 350–370.

Chapter 6

1. Lydia Millet, *How the Dead Dream* (Mariner, 2009), 139. All further references cited parenthetically.

2. For the contention that post-postmodernist fiction has stopped using representation to critique neoliberalism, see Mitchum Huehls, *After Critique: Twenty-First-Century Fiction in a Neoliberal Age* (Oxford University Press, 2016).

3. Pieter Vermeulen, "Beauty That Must Die: *Station Eleven*, Climate Change Fiction, and the Life of Form," *Studies in the Novel* 50, no. 1 (Spring 2018): 9.

4. Ibid. See also Timothy Clark, *Ecocriticism on the Edge: The Anthropocene as a Threshold Concept* (Bloomsbury, 2015), 181.

5. Amitav Ghosh, *The Great Derangement: Climate Change and the Unthinkable* (University of Chicago Press, 2016), 8; emphases added.

6. Mahlu Mertens and Stef Craps, "Contemporary Fiction vs. the Challenge of Imagining the Timescale of Climate Change," *Studies in the Novel* 50, no. 1 (Spring 2018): 134.

7. Ghosh, *Derangement*, 8.

8. Ibid.

9. For Ghosh's attention to colonial systems, see Amitav Ghosh, *The Nutmeg's Curse: Parables for a Planet in Crisis* (University of Chicago Press, 2021).

10. Ursula Heise, "Science Fiction and the Time Scales of the Anthropocene," *English Literary History* 86, no. 2 (Summer 2019): 278, emphasis added. Clark's work suggests that the Anthropocene might prove resistant to the human mind: "does the Anthropocene form a threshold at which art and literature touch limits to the human psyche and imagination themselves?" Clark, *Ecocriticism*, 175–176.

11. David James writes of the scholarly delusion he calls "the romance of consequentiality": the

> alluring ... collective refusal of the notion that literary critics by and large don't substantively redress the realms of structural inequity, everyday violence, systemic oppression, or ongoing exploitation that they so tenaciously examine through the literature they anatomize and the curriculums they build.

James, "The Romance of Consequentiality," *American Literary History* 34, no. 1 (Spring 2022): 399.

12. Ghosh, *Derangement*, 7.

13. "In the Editing Room with Ruth Ozeki and Rebecca Evans," *Novel Dialogue Podcast*, March 3, 2022, https://noveldialogue.org/2022/03/03/3-3-in-the-editing-room-with-ruth-ozeki-and-rebecca-evans-eh/.

14. Ghosh, *Derangement*, 24.

15. Kurt Vonnegut, "Science Fiction," in *Wampeters, Foma & Granfaloons (Opinions)* (Dial, 2006), 1.

16. Mark McGurl, "The Posthuman Comedy," *Critical Inquiry* 38, no. 3 (Spring 2012): 541.

17. Ibid., 539, emphasis added.

18. H. P. Lovecraft, "The Call of Cthulhu" in *The Complete Fiction of H. P. Lovecraft*, vol. 2 (Chartwells, 2016), 381.

19. Ibid., 61.

20. Heise, "Science Fiction," 279.

21. Ibid., 301.

22. Ibid., 281.

23. Ibid., 300, 282.

24. For less prescriptive accounts that recognize the heterogeneity of climate fiction, see: Matthew Schneider-Mayerson, "Climate Change Fiction," in *American Literature in Transition, 2000–2010*, ed. Rachel Greenwald Smith (Cambridge University

Press, 2018): 309–310; Stef Craps and Richard Crownshaw, "Introduction: The Rising Tide of Climate Change Fiction," *Studies in the Novel* 50, no. 1 (Spring 2018): 1.

25. For postwar lyric poetry's response to ecocatastrophe, see Margaret Ronda, *Remainders: American Poetry at Nature's End* (Stanford University Press, 2018).

26. For Clark and his adherents, novels that rely on the "still-dominant conventions of plotting, characterization and setting . . . [are] pervaded by anthropocentric delusion." Clark, *Ecocriticism*, 164–165. See also Adeline Johns-Putra, "The Rest Is Silence: Postmodern and Postcolonial Possibilities in Climate Change Fiction," *Studies in the Novel* 50, no. 1 (Spring 2018): 26–42. Stephanie LeMenager, by contrast, argues that "cli-fi, like its older sibling sci-fi, indicts the privatization of human experience even as it participates in novelistic modes of action," and that "the novelistic mode of cli-fi is not restricted to any subgenre." LeMenager, "Climate Change and the Struggle for Genre," in *Anthropocene Reading: Literary History in Geologic Times*, eds. Tobias Menely and Jesse Oak Taylor (Pennsylvania State University Press, 2017), 223, 225.

27. For the challenge of dramatizing slow violence, see Rob Nixon, *Slow Violence and the Environmentalism of the Poor* (Harvard University Press, 2011).

28. Mertens and Craps, "Contemporary Fiction," 135, emphasis added.

29. Ibid., 135–136, emphasis added.

30. Will Steffen et al., "The Anthropocene: Conceptual and Historical Perspectives," *Philosophical Transactions of the Royal Society* (2011) 369: 842–867.

31. Heise, "Science Fiction," 279.

32. Ibid., 283–284.

33. Ibid., 284.

34. Ursula K. Le Guin, "Rocannon's World," in *Worlds of Exile and Illusion* (Orb Books, 2016), e-book 24, 67.

35. Lovecraft, "Call of Cthulhu," 394.

36. Elizabeth Kolbert, *The Sixth Extinction: An Unnatural History* (Holt, 2014), 3.

37. See Oates's comment at https://twitter.com/joycecaroloates/status/1371859718650597387?lang=en

38. Jenny Offill, *Weather* (Vintage, 2021), 52–53, 89, 157. All further references cited parenthetically.

39. For biodiversity discourse, see Elizabeth Callaway, *Eden's Endemics: Narratives of Biodiversity on Earth and Beyond* (University of Virginia Press, 2020).

40. Kim Stanley Robinson, *The Ministry for the Future* (Orbit, 2020), 44.

41. For innovative translation of information into artistic forms, see Heather Houser, *Infowhelm: Environmental Art and Literature in an Age of Data* (Columbia University Press, 2020).

42. Schneider-Mayerson, "Climate Change Fiction," 314, 315.

43. Lidia Yuknavitch, *The Book of Joan* (HarperCollins, 2017), 3. All further references cited parenthetically.

44. For the skin grafting, see Anne Jamison, "Retrofuturist Feminism: Lidia Yuknavitch's 'The Book of Joan,'" *Los Angeles Review of Books*, April 18, 2017, https://lareviewofbooks.org/article/retrofuturist-feminism-lidia-yuknavitchs-book-of-joan/

45. See Jane Bennett, *Vibrant Matter: A Political Ecology of Things* (Duke University Press, 2010).

46. For Jameson's *Antinomies of Realism* as an update of Lukács's account of the historical novel, see Ian Duncan, "History and the Novel After Lukács," *Novel: A Forum on Fiction* 50, no. 3 (November 2017): 388–396.

47. Louise Erdrich, *Future Home of the Living God* (HarperLuxe, 2017), 169. All further references cited parenthetically.

48. Lydia Millet, *A Children's Bible* (Norton, 2021), 27. All further references cited parenthetically.

49. Claire Vaye Watkins, *Gold Fame Citrus* (Riverhead, 2015), 213. All further references cited parenthetically.

50. Richard Powers, *Bewilderment* (Norton, 2021), 39. All further references cited parenthetically.

51. See, for example, Schneider-Mayerson, "Climate Change Fiction," 313.

52. Rachel Adams, "An Overstory for Our Time," *American Literature* 92, no. 4 (December 2020): 801. See also Monica Manolescu, "'Arboretum America' in Richard Powers's *The Overstory*," *Polysèmes*, June 30, 2021, https://journals.openedition.org/polysemes/8565

53. Adams, "Overstory," 801.

54. Richard Powers, *The Overstory* (Norton, 2018), 97. All further references cited parenthetically.

55. Walter Benn Michaels suggests of this moment that Powers disdains the "very idea of character." While it's clear that character is not all that matters to Powers, it's difficult to argue that the novel centered on the intersecting lives and experiences of nine human protagonists disdains the very idea. Michaels, "Commentary," *American Literary History* 34, no. 1 (Spring 2022): 420.

56. For the novel as vehicle for rendering the "diversity of social speech types," which he calls "heteroglossia," see M. M. Bakhtin, "Discourse in the Novel," in *The Dialogic Imagination: Four Essays*, ed. Michael Holquist, trans. Caryl Emerson and Michael Holquist (University of Texas Press, 2004), 262, 263.

57. For charismatic endangered species, see Ursula Heise, *Imagining Extinction: The Cultural Meanings of Endangered Species* (University of Chicago Press, 2016).

58. Annie Proulx, *Barkskins* (Scribner, 2016), 51. All further references cited parenthetically.

59. See William T. Vollman, "Review of 'Barkskins,' by Annie Proulx," *New York Times*, June 17, 2016, https://www.nytimes.com/2016/06/19/books/review/barkskins-by-annie-proulx.html

60. See Kyle Powys Whyte, "Indigenous Science (Fiction) for the Anthropocene: Ancestral Dystopias and Fantasies of Climate Change Crises," *Environment and Planning* 1, nos. 1–2 (2018): 224–242; and Gerald Horne, *The Apocalypse of Settler Colonialism: The Roots of Slavery, White Supremacy, and Capitalism in Seventeenth-Century North America and the Caribbean* (Monthly Review Press, 2017). *Barkskins*'s depiction of this apocalypse within a historical novel troubles the idea that "the longue durée of

catastrophe across the hemisphere raises questions that cannot be answered by recourse to European frameworks of knowledge production." Anna Brickhouse, "Elsewhere Catastrophe," *American Literary History*, 34, no. 1 (Spring 2022): 39.

61. Rebecca M. Evans, "The Best of Times, the Worst of Times, the End of Times?: The Uses and Abuses of Environmental Apocalypse," *ASAP/Journal* 3, no. 3 (September 2018): 502–503.

62. For historiographic metafiction, see Linda Hutcheon, *A Poetics of Postmodernism: History, Theory, Fiction* (New York: Routledge, 1988).

63. Ruth Ozeki, *The Book of Form and Emptiness* (Penguin, 2021), 96. All further references cited parenthetically.

64. See Bruno Latour, *Reassembling the Social: An Introduction to Actor-Network-Theory* (Oxford University Press, 2005).

65. For efforts to shape the overwhelming deluge of climate information into legible artistic form, see Houser, *Infowhelm*.

66. Donald S. Lopez calls the line the most famous in Buddhism. Lopez, *Elaborations on Emptiness: Uses of the Heart Sūtra* (Princeton University Press, 2016), 5.

67. Zasep Tulku Rinpoche, "Commentary on The Heart Sutra," https://buddhaweekly.com/commentary-heart-sutra-zasep-tulku-rinpoche-form-emptiness-emptiness-form/

68. For Ozeki's discussion of this concept in relation to her novel, see Nancy Chu, "The Creative Force: In Conversation with Novelist Ruth Ozeki," *Lion's Roar*, September 23, 2021, https://www.lionsroar.com/the-creative-force-in-conversation-with-novelist-ruth-ozeki/

Coda

1. Jennifer Egan, *The Candy House* (Scribner, 2022), 333, emphasis added. All further references cited parenthetically.

2. For rigidity of romance conventions due to publishers' requirements, see Kim Wilkins, Beth Driscoll, and Lisa Fletcher, *Genre Worlds: Popular Fiction and Twenty-First Century Book Culture* (University of Massachusetts Press, 2022), 40.

3. For the permutations and scale of romance, see Mark McGurl, *Everything and Less: Fiction in the Age of Amazon* (Verso, 2021); and J. D. Porter, Angelina Eimannsberger, James English, May Hathaway, and Ashna Yakoob, "Genre Juggernaut: Measuring 'Romance,'" *Public Books*, November 10, 2023, https://www.publicbooks.org/genre-juggernaut-measuring-romance/

4. For literariness as "secured" by "the failure" of "happily ever after," see McGurl, *Everything*, 221.

5. For the marketing of Rooney, see Kate Dwyer, "Beautiful Merch, Where Are You?" *New York Times*, September 2, 2021, https://www.nytimes.com/2021/09/02/style/sally-rooney-book-merch.html

6. Sally Rooney, *Normal People* (Hogarth, 2018), 273. All further references cited parenthetically.

7. Sally Rooney, *Intermezzo: A Novel* (Farrar, Straus and Giroux, 2024), 430, 431.

8. Sally Rooney, *Conversations with Friends* (Hogarth, 2017), 14.

9. Ibid., 275.

10. Sally Rooney, *Beautiful World, Where Are You?* (Picador, 2021), 102. All further references cited parenthetically.

11. See Sarah Brouillette, "Sally Rooney's Couple Form," *Post45*, June 16, 2020, https://post45.org/2020/06/sally-rooneys-couple-form/

12. For the novum, see Darko Suvin, *Metamorphoses of Science Fiction: On the Poetics and History of a Literary Genre*, ed. Gerry Canavan (Peter Lang Verlag, 2016).

13. See Shoshana Zuboff, *The Age of Surveillance Capitalism: The Fight for a Human Future at the New Frontier of Power* (PublicAffairs, 2019).

14. See C. Thi Nguyen, "Value Capture," *Journal of Ethics and Social Philosophy* 27, no. 3 (May 2024): 469–504.

15. Jennifer Egan, *A Visit from the Goon Squad* (Knopf, 2010), 324.

16. Ibid.

17. Ibid., 319.

Index

Absalom, Absalom! (Faulkner), 144
Ace Books, 17
Acker, Kathy, 65
actor-network-theory, 250
Ada, or Ardor (Nabokov), 4
Adams, Rachel, 238
Adventures of Augie March, The (Bellow), 19
Adventures of Huckleberry Finn, The (Twain), 139–40
Agamben, Giorgio, 136–37
airport fiction, 31
Alice in Wonderland (Carroll), 196
All the Light We Cannot See (Doerr), 174–75
All the Pretty Horses (McCarthy), 7, 257
"Alphinland" (Atwood), 174
alterity, 102
Amazing Adventures of Kavalier & Clay, The (Chabon), 6, 20–21, 30, 41–42, 90, 125; comics, 42, 125, 127, 129, 153; comics, as plastic, 20, 21; escapist reading, in defense of, 153; genre-bending ethos, 43; *Golem, The*, 129–30, 134

Amazon, 48–49, 84, 277n47
American Psycho (Ellis), 19
Amis, Martin, xii; *Money,* 19
Aniston, Jennifer, 128
Anna Karenina (Tolstoy), 174
Anthropocene, 39, 208–11, 213–16, 218–21, 226, 241–43, 248, 250–52, 286n51, 303n10; climate fictions, 222; future imaginary, 217; representation, form of, 217; timescales, 238; totality of effects, 217
anthropocentrism, 220, 226–27, 234, 237, 239–40, 248–49, 252, 304n26
anti-globalism, 188
Apex Hides the Hurt (Whitehead), 44–45, 191, 205; marketing, satire of, 59; as metageneric commentary, 56; multinational corporations, critique of, 55–56; protagonist of, 59–60
apocalyptic fiction, 14; as malleable, 73
Ariosto, 170–71
Aristotle, 42–43
Arnold, Matthew, xii
artificial intelligence (AI), 85, 109–113, 116–122, 137–140

309

Asimov, Isaac, 44, 110, 154
Atkinson, Kate: *Life After Life*, 180
Atwood, Margaret, ix, 2–3, 7, 14, 22–24, 30, 44–45, 73, 95–96, 103, 133, 153, 164–65, 172, 182; "Alphinland," 174; *Blind Assassin, The*, 6, 47, 83, 89–90, 107–8, 128, 141, 157, 163–64, 171–74, 181; genre fiction clichés, mocking of, 173; great range of, 163; *Handmaid's Tale, The*, 6, 9–11, 163, 228; *In Other Worlds*, 151; *MaddAddam*, 6, 82–83, 183; *Oryx and Crake*, 73–74, 132, 163; otherness, 151; "Peach Woman of Aa'a, The," 173–74; popular genre conventions, poking fun at, 181
Aubry, Timothy, 103–4
Auden, W. H., 286–87n64; "Guilty Vicarage, The," 65
Auster, Paul, 44; *City of Glass*, 6, 135; *New York Trilogy, The*, 51, 66
authorship: conglomerate, 87; gender, 54–55
autofiction, 219

Bakhtin, Mikhail, 46–47, 50, 221, 239; heteroglossia, 305n56
Baldacci, David, 20
Baldick, Chris: *Oxford Dictionary of Literary Terms, The*, 290n8
"Ballad of John Henry" (song), 58–59
Baldwin, James, 258
Bantam Books, 17
Barkskins (Proulx): apocalyptic rhetoric, 246–47; longue durée of catastrophe, 305–6nn60; Indigenous peoples, colonization and genocide of, 244–45, 247–48
Barrett Browning, Robert, 128
Barth, John, 5
Batuman, Elif: *Idiot, The*, 257
Baudrillard, Jean, 196, 258
Beatles, x, 197

Beautiful World, Where Are You? (Rooney), 259, 261
Beckett, Samuel: *Texts for Nothing*, 5; *Waiting for Godot*, 51
Bellow, Saul, xii; *Adventures of Augie March, The*, 19
Beloved (Morrison), 6, 9–10, 52, 76–77, 87
Bender, Aimee, 30
Benjamin, Walter, 140, 251; "Storyteller, The," 34
Bennett, Jane: *Vibrant Matter*, 254
Bennett, Tony, 274n18
Beowulf, 23
Bewilderment (Powers), 235, 238–39, 247; anthropocentrism, critique of, 234; binary thinking, rejection of, 237, 240; climate catastrophe, 232, 234; denouement of, 237; exalting the self, 236; as hybrid, 232; science fiction elements, 232–34, 236
Beyoncé, viii–x
Bezos, Jeff, 101
Big Sleep, The (Chandler), 67–68
binary thinking, 153–54, 237, 240
"Blackbird" (song), x
Black Leopard, Red Wolf (James), 1, 11, 24–26, 149, 280n87
Black Panther (film), 24
Black, Scott, 153, 157, 297n15; multiplicity of possibilities of reading, 178; reading adventures, 151–52, 167
Blade Runner (film), 197
Blind Assassin, The (Atwood), 6, 47, 83, 89–90, 108, 128, 141, 157, 172–73, 181; nested plots in, 163–64, 174; romance, 171; structure of, as embedding many genres, 107
Blood Meridian, or, The Evening Redness in the West, (McCarthy), 6, 96, 291–2n39; horrific violence, aestheticized language of, 93; pseudo-objectivity of, 108; style of, 93–94

Bone Clocks, The (Mitchell), 91–92; as enjoyable, 147
Book of Form and Emptiness, The (Ozeki), 248–50, 252–55
Book of Joan, The (Yuknavitch), 76, 222, 224, 236; anthropocentrism, rejection of, 226–27; climate catastrophe, 226; *Doctor Zhivago*, reference to, 227–28; eco-terrorism, 225–26; nonhuman agency, 225; scalar modulation, 223; scarification, 223
Book of Night Women, The (James), 1, 26
Book of Strange New Things, The (Faber), 99–102, 119, 127–28, 232
Borges, Jorge Luis, 34, 65, 135, 250, 254; "Pierre Menard, Author of the Quixote," 49
Bourdieu, Pierre, 17, 24, 260, 278n54, 280n83
Boyle, T. C.: *Budding Prospects: A Pastoral*, 19
Bradley, Marion Zimmer: *Mists of Avalon, The*, 9, 275–76n34
Bradshaw, Gillian, 22
Bridget Jones's Diary (Fielding), 257
Brief History of Neoliberalism, A (Harvey), 200
Brief History of Seven Killings, A (James), 1, 26
Brief Wondrous Life of Oscar Wao, The (Díaz), 76–77; genre turn, 292n45; ostracized, 176, 292n45; otherness, 95
Brookner, Anita, 34
Brooks, Max, 22; *World War Z*, 291n34
Brooks, Peter, 148–49, 152, 158, 160–61; plot, as universal, 143–45; *Reading for the Plot: Design and Intention in Narrative*, 143, 145
Brouillette, Sarah, 123
Brown, Nicholas, 48–49, 284n25
Bruckheimer, Jerry, 33
Budding Prospects: A Pastoral (Boyle), 19

Buffy the Vampire Slayer (television series), xii
Butler, Octavia, 10, 44, 101; *Parable*, 222
Byatt, A. S., 34, 44, 171; "Choices," 158, 166; pleasure of reading, as singular, 180; *Possession: A Romance*, 6, 19, 47, 135–36, 157–70, 179–81, 257

"Call of Cthulhu, The" (Lovecraft), 212–13
Calvino, Italo, 34, 155
Candy House, The (Egan), 7, 40, 118, 175–76, 256, 262, 265; climate disaster and immersive experience, fusing with, 268; epiphany in, 268; science fiction conceit of, 263; singularity, 268–69; social media, 263–64, 266–67
Carlyle, Thomas, xii
Carver, Raymond, 19
Cervantes, Miguel de: *Don Quixote*, 16, 51, 135, 299n53
Chabon, Michael, 2, 7, 9, 11–12, 23, 31–35, 45, 53, 95, 141–42, 147, 169, 176–79; *Amazing Adventures of Kavalier & Clay, The*, 6, 20–21, 30, 41–42, 43, 90, 125, 127, 129, 130, 134, 153; "Fan Fiction: On Sherlock Holmes," 151; *Final Solution, The*, 6; *Gentlemen of the Road*, 6, 96, 153; *Maps and Legends: Writing along the Borderlands*, 151; *Mysteries of Pittsburgh, The*, 145; popular genres, adoption of, 96; *Telegraph Avenue*, 28–29, 175, 190; *Yiddish Policemen's Union, The*, 6, 72, 83, 257
Chakrabarty, Dipesh, 211, 214
Chandler, Raymond, 44, 65; *Big Sleep, The*, 67–68; *Raymond Chandler: Stories and Early Novels*, 8
Chang, David, 51–52
Chaplin, Charlie, 68
Chicks, The, ix

Children's Bible, A (Millett), 229; climate catastrophe, 230
"Choices" (Byatt), 158, 166
Christie, Agatha, 65; *Murder of Roger Ackroyd, The*, 49
Citizen Kane (film), 41, 43
City of Glass (Auster), 6, 135
Clancy, Tom, 20
Clark, Timothy, 209, 233, 239, 251, 303n10, 304n26
cliché, xii, 2, 4, 81, 84, 90–91, 94, 115, 173, 191, 266–69
cli-fi, 304n26. *See also* climate fiction
climate catastrophe, 39, 60, 206, 209–10, 214, 215, 220–21, 222, 226, 230, 232, 234, 248, 268
climate change, 39, 54, 60, 73, 208, 210, 213–14, 220–22, 233, 248, 252, 254; literary responses to, 209; science fiction, 211–12
climate fiction, 215, 221–22, 233, 248
clones, 54, 97–98, 108–9, 112, 115, 125, 156, 241
Cloud Atlas (Mitchell), 7, 47, 73, 83, 91, 103–4, 115, 121; linguistic flair, 97; "Orison of Sonmi-451" section, 97–99, 108, 156–57, 231; pleasure of, 155; "Sloosha's Crossin' an' Ev'rythin' After" section, 156; as smorgasbord of thought, 157; storytelling, as tribute to, 156; "yarn," use of, 155–56, 161
Coetzee, J. M.: *Elizabeth Costello*, 235
Cohen, Ralph, 49
Cold War, 7, 54–55
Coleridge, Samuel Taylor, 128
Cole, Teju, 103–4
Collector, The (film), 195
Collins, Jim, 65
Collins, Wilkie, 65
comics, 20–21, 42, 125, 128–30, 153, 292n45
Conan Doyle, Arthur, 6–7, 65, 135; *Study in Scarlet, A*, 49

Conrad, Joseph, 155; *Heart of Darkness*, 127–28, 144
"Contemporary Fiction vs. the Challenge of Imagining the Timescale of Climate Change" (Mertens and Craps), 210
Conversations with Friends (Rooney), 258–59
COVID-19 pandemic, 73
Cowboy Carter (Beyoncé), viii–xi; commercial character, x
Craps, Stef, 210, 216–17
Crichton, Michael, 30
crime fiction, viii, 72, 82–83; as conservative genre, 65; ideological heterogeneity, 65–66
Crook Manifesto (Whitehead), 7, 45
Crownshaw, Richard, 286n51
Crying of Lot 49, The (Pynchon), 274n24
Culler, Jonathan, 289n7
cultural capital, 96, 115, 260
cultural imperialism, 188–89
Cunningham, Michael, 125; *Hours, The*, 120; *Specimen Days*, 120–22
Curious Incident of the Dog in the Night-Time, The (Haddon), 72, 88
Cyrus, Miley, x

"Daddy Lessons" (song), ix
Dango, Michael, 291n26
Danielewski, Mark Z.: *House of Leaves*, 77
Darwin, Charles, 165; *Voyage of the Beagle, The*, 175
"Dead, The" (Joyce), 268
deep time, 214, 219–20, 233
deformation, 16, 32, 50, 68, 78, 214
Delany, Samuel R., 10, 44, 158, 299n51; *Dhalgren*, 17; enchantment and political critique of science fiction, balance between, 154; imaginative transport, pleasure of, 154

DeLillo, Don, 65
detective fiction, 7, 12, 18, 35, 45, 51, 55, 64–67, 70, 76, 83, 135, 158, 195, 269, 284n25; metageneric deployments, 72
Dhalgren (Delany), 17
Díaz, Junot: *Brief Wondrous Life of Oscar Wao, The*, 76–77, 95, 176, 292n45
Dickens, Charles, 128, 277n52
Dick, Philip K., 8, 44, 65, 197; *Do Androids Dream of Electric Sheep?* 110
Die Hard (film), 197
Do Androids Dream of Electric Sheep? (Dick), 110
Doctor Zhivago (film), 227–28
Doerr, Anthony: *All the Light We Cannot See*, 174–75
Don Quixote (Cervantes), 16, 51, 135, 299n53
Dostoevsky, Fyodor, 103–4
Dubey, Madhu, 78
Du Bois, W. E. B., 93; *Souls of Black Folk, The*, 94–95
Duff, David, 278n58, 284–85nn35
Duncan, Glen, 21; *Last Werewolf, The*, xi, xiii–xiv, 5–6; self-consciousness, xii
dystopian fiction, 7, 10, 39, 67, 83, 120, 156, 214, 216, 221–22, 230–31, 241–42

"Eagle, The" (Tennyson), 138
Earle, Sylvia, 175
Eco, Umberto, 44, 159, 167; *Name of the Rose, The*, 6, 9–10, 16, 135, 158
ecocide, 39, 54
ecology, 220
Egan, Jennifer, 2, 9, 45, 55, 102, 122, 125, 141, 178; *Candy House, The*, 7, 40, 118, 175–76, 256, 262–69; genre, as lifeline, 53; *Keep, The*, 7, 77, 122–24, 141, 177, 264; social media, as rival of literary, 40; *Visit from the Goon Squad, A*, 7, 262–65, 267

Eggers, Dave, 30–31
8 1/2 (film), 195
826 Valencia writing school, 31
Eliot, George, 258, 286n63
elitism, 23–24
Elizabeth Costello (Coetzee), 235
Ellis, Brett Easton: *American Psycho*, 19
Ellison, Harlan, 23
Ellison, Ralph, 93, 139–40, 240, 292n44; *Invisible Man*, 94–95
End of Days, The (Erpenbeck), 180
Erdrich, Louise, 2; *Future Home of the Living God*, 7, 228–29; *Round House, The*, 7, 72
Erpenbeck, Jenny: *End of Days, The*, 180
escapism, 153–54, 231
espionage genre, 20
ethnonationalism, 188
Esty, Jed, 297n14
Eugenides, Jeffrey: *Marriage Plot, The*, 19, 136
Evans, Rebecca, 247
Everett, Percival: *God's Country*, 35
Exit West (Hamid), 191, 205–6, 257

Faber, Michael, 103; *Book of Strange New Things, The*, 99–102, 119, 127–28, 232
"Fan Fiction: On Sherlock Holmes" (Chabon), 151
fantasy, 10, 18, 22–23, 25, 35, 82, 103, 256, 269, 293n57
Faulkner, William, 274n19; *Absalom, Absalom!*, 144
Faerie Queene (Spenser), 170–71
Ferris, Joshua: *Then We Came to the End*, 183
Fever Dream (Schweblin), 77
Fielding, Helen: *Bridget Jones's Diary*, 257
Final Solution, The (Chabon), 6
Fitzpatrick, Kathleen, 138, 140
Flaubert, Gustave, 33

Fleissner, Jennifer, 68
Flight Behavior (Kingsolver), 233
Flynn, Gillian: *Gone Girl*, 77
Forster, E. M., 34, 102
Fortress of Solitude, The (Lethem), 131, 133–34
Foucault, Michel, 33, 178
Fowler, Alistair, 16, 277n52
Fowler, Karen Joy: *We Are All Completely Beside Ourselves*, 235
Fowles, John, 34
France, 49
Frankenstein (Shelley), 95
Franzen, Jonathan, 19, 46
Free Life, A (Jin), 88
Friends (television series), 126
Frow, John, 16
Frye, Northrup, 57–58
Fuseli, Henry, xii
Future Home of the Living God (Erdrich), 7; historical apocalypse of Indigenous populations, 228–29

Gaiman, Neil, 54, 285n48
Galatea 2.2 (Powers), 7, 113, 128, 137–39, 236, 296n42; Turing Test, 140
Game of Thrones (television series), 298–99nn35
Garmus, Bonnie: *Lessons in Chemistry*, 257
Gasiorek, Andrzej, 114–15
Gass, William, 17
Gee, Maggie, 150–51
Gelder, Ken, 278n55, 297n18
generic fiction, 8–9, 193; homogenization of spaces, depiction of, 192
genericness, 186, 191
Genette, Gérard: anisochrony, concept of, 218
genre, xii, xiv, 2, 7–9, 11–12, 18, 35, 56, 84, 181–82, 191–92, 215, 282n3, 284n33, 285n42, 285n48; as adaptable, 269; adaptive reuse, 53–54; conventions, 48–49, 53; correlating scales, 215; dialectical approach to, 49–50; expressive power, 284–85nn35; familiarity and flexibility, combination of, 189; as flexible form, 50–51, 54, 70; genre film, 39; genre slumming, 3; ghettos, 279n74; as heterogeneous, 54; historical change, 49; innovation, enabling of, 53, 55; as literary institutions, 281n99; as malleable, 47, 54, 77, 210; material metaphors, 282–83nn7; perfecting set of techniques, 52; plasticity of, viii, x–xi, 14, 16, 20, 37, 42–43, 51, 53, 60, 65–66, 81, 269; popular, as subversive, 285n49; protean, 65; repetitive nature of, 60; reproductive functions of, 47–48; rigidity of, 48; as rule bound, 48–49; self-consciousness, 53; textuality, 16; tropes, 189–90; as useful frameworks, 47; value judgment, 51–52; as variable recipe, 51–53.
genre-bending literary fiction, viii–xi, xiii–xiv, 2, 4–6, 8, 12, 14, 19–20, 26–27, 30, 34, 37, 51, 53–54, 84, 86, 89, 91, 95, 105, 108, 111, 115, 118, 121–22, 129, 146, 157, 174, 182, 223–24, 256–57; allusions, 127; boom in, 11; as compromise aesthetics, 276n41; dialectical nature of genre, 13; genre, difference from, 15–16; global capitalism, anxieties about, 186–88; globalization, critiquing of, 204; heterogeneous of, 102–3, 143; homogenization, 204, 205; as hyperliterary, 128, 135–36, 140; immersion, 102–3, 149, 179, 269; innovative new-forms, faith in, 205–6; interiority, 102, 115; as literary, 112, 184; metageneric moments, 55, 72; as meta-immersive, 146; obsessed with literature, 204; pleasure, 146, 158;

pleasures of reading, 179; plot, 36, 38, 145; serious work and enchantment, balancing of, 155; posthumanism, 132; self-reflexivity, 114; spillovers, 50; style, importance of, 115, 134; as term, 15, 274–75nn25; textual pleasures, 151; world-building, 147, 269

genre fiction, 5, 9, 12–13, 15–16, 18–20, 23, 39, 51, 212; condescension toward, 21–22; gaining respect, 3; literary fiction, distinct from, 81; overt appropriation of, 193; pleasure, 146; plot, pleasures of, 142–43; popular fiction, as synonymous with, 17; as subfield, 24, 86

genre theory, ix, 11, 36, 47; paradigm shift in, 9, 275n32

genre turn, vii, 4, 8–10, 12, 88, 103, 142, 291n34, 292n45

Gentlemen of the Road (Chabon), 6, 96, 153

Ghosh, Amitav, 209, 211–12, 214, 233, 239; *Great Derangement, The*, 210, 213

Ghostwritten (Mitchell), 104

Gibson, William, 65

Giddens, Rhiannon, ix

gig economy, 57

Girl with the Dragon Tattoo, The (Larsson), 195

Girl in Landscape (Lethem), 67

global capitalism, 55, 74, 125; genericness, 186

global generic, 187

globalization, 38, 184, 188–89, 192–93; genericness, 186; neoliberal, 186–87; as threat of homogenization, 204–5

global south, 192, 209–10

glocalization, 188

God's Country (Everett), 35

Goethe, Johann Wolfgang von, 116

Gold Fame Citrus (Watkins), 76, 230

Goldstone, Andrew, 8–9, 17

Gone Girl (Flynn), 77

gothic: resurgence of, 76–77

Gravity's Rainbow (Pynchon), 1

Great Acceleration, 217

Great Derangement, The (Ghosh), 210, 213

Great Divide, 4–5

Greene, Graham, xii–xiii

Grimm's Fairy Tales (Brothers Grimm), 252

Grossman, Lev, 142–43, 145; *Magicians Trilogy, The*, 3

Grove Atlantic, 20

"Guilty Vicarage, The" (Auden), 65

Haddon, Mark: *Curious Incident of the Dog in the Night-Time, The*, 72, 88

Haigh, Jennifer: *Heat and Light*, 77

Hale, Dorothy J., 102

Hamid, Mohsin, 191; *Exit West*, 191, 205–6, 257

Hammer, Langdon, 284n23

Hammett, Dashiell, 8, 44, 65

Handmaid's Tale, The (Atwood), 6, 9–11, 163, 228

Handmaid's Tale, The (television series), 103

Han Yu, 293n66

Hard-Boiled Wonderland and the End of the World (Murakami), 6

Harlequin, 49, 168–69

Harrison, Sheri-Marie, 32, 189

Hart, Matthew, 70

Harvey, David: *Brief History of Neoliberalism, A*, 200

Hawthorne, Nathaniel, 169; *House of the Seven Gables, The*, 168

Hayles, N. Katherine, 138, 140, 286n61

Heart of Darkness (Conrad), 127–28, 144

Heat and Light (Haigh), 77

Heidegger, Martin, 136–37

Heise, Ursula, 211, 213–14, 218

Her Body and Other Parties (Machado), 26–27, 76–77
Here (McGuire), 214
heterogeneity, 11, 17, 34–36, 65, 121, 134, 143, 188, 253; of literary fiction, 54; recognition of, 9
Hicks, Heather, 73
Himes, Chester, 66
Hiroshima (Japan), 193
historical fantasy, 54
historical fiction, 2, 10, 19, 39, 45, 77, 87, 163, 174–75, 214, 216
historical novels, 1, 6, 19, 55, 79, 103, 248, 248, 292n45
Hoberek, Andrew, 6, 103–4, 145, 274n24, 286n63; genre turn, 4, 142, 291n34
Horace, 90
Hornby, Nick, 30
horror, 10, 214
Hours, The (Cunningham), 120
House of Leaves (Danielewski), 77
House of the Seven Gables, The (Hawthorne), 168
How the Dead Dream (Millet), 222, 242; environmental catastrophe, 208; neoliberal capitalism, critique of, 207–8
How to Live Safely in a Science Fictional Universe (Yu), 130; as metasciencefictional novel, 105; science fiction and immigrant novel, fusion of, 106; time travel, 105–6
Human Stain, The (Roth), 94–95
Hungerford, Amy, 30–31, 277n45
Hurley, Jessica, 73
Huyssen, Andreas, 4, 273–74nn16
hybridity, 54, 77, 78, 188, 201, 221
hybridization, 32
hyperliterary fiction, 128, 135–36, 140
Hyde, Lewis: *Trickster Makes This World*, 34

Icarus Girl, The (Oyeyemi), 76–77
Idiot, The (Batuman), 257
"Imagine" (song), 197
immersion, 12, 25–26, 38, 102–3, 147, 151, 167, 177, 196, 268–69, 298n27; accessibility, 149–50; cosplay, 149; devaluing of, 148; escapist pleasure of, 32; fan fiction, 149; in fictional worlds, 86, 146, 149, 175–76; obstacles to, 149–50; pleasure of, 153, 178–79, 182; pleasure of in fictional world, 143, 145; popular genre fiction, conducive to, 150
Infinite Jest (Wallace), 1
Inherent Vice (Pynchon), 274n24
In Other Worlds (Atwood), 151
Interior Chinatown (Yu), 106–7
Intermezzo (Rooney), 258–59
Intuitionist, The (Whitehead), 7, 43; as amalgam of alternate history, noir, and racial allegory, 56; generic hybridity, 77–78; as innovative, 57; screaming as singing, 57
Invisible Man (Ellison), 94–95
Iowa Writers' Workshop, 136
I, Robot (Asimov), 110
Irr, Caren, 104
Ishiguro, Kazuo, ix, 2, 9, 22–24, 45, 54, 72, 120, 137, 146–47, 152–53; conventional detective novel, and British imperial worldview, 70–71; genre, flexibility of, 70; *Klara and the Sun*, 7, 81, 108, 110–11, 113–14, 116, 121; *Never Let Me Go*, 7, 52, 54, 108–9, 111, 115, 121; repetitive generic narratives, power of, 69; rescue narrative, endless variability, 70; *When We Were Orphans*, 7, 69–71

James, David, 90, 114–15, 150–51; romance of consequentiality, 303n11
James, Henry, 102, 143, 212, 277n52
James, Marlon, 2–3, 6, 14, 27, 29, 35; *Black

Leopard, Red Wolf, 1, 11, 24–26, 149, 280n87; *Book of Night Women, The*, 1, 26; *Brief History of Seven Killings, A*, 1, 26; Dark Star trilogy, 13, 24–25; *John Crow's Devil*, 26

Jameson, Fredric, 49, 103, 188, 227, 281n99, 283n19, 293n57; combinatoire, 284n27

James, P. D., 65

Japan, 193–94, 198

Jaws (Benchley), 143–45

Jemisin, N. K., ix, 222

Jin, Ha: *Free Life, A*, 88

John Crow's Devil (James), 26

John Henry Days (Whitehead), 45–47, 64, 77, 283n13; "Bob is hip," utility of, 57–58; "clarity of the trinity," 57–58; gig economy, 57; as miniature theory of genre, 57; mythic figures in, 57; as speculative realism, 283n18

Johnson, Charles, 52

"Jolene" (song), x

Joon-ho, Bong, 15, 189

Joyce, James, 17, 136; "Dead, The," 268; *Ulysses*, 46

Joy Luck Club (Tan), 19

Jubilee (Walker), 19

Judge, Mike, 183

Jung, Carl, 33

Kafka, Franz, 33

Kant, Immanuel, 146

Keaton, Buster, 68

Keats, John, xii

Keep, The (Egan), 7, 77, 122, 141, 177, 264; bookish sensibility, 123; technological capitalism, 123–24

Kelly, Adam, 285n42

Kermode, Frank, 276–77n43

Kill Bill (film), 176

Kincaid, Paul, 16

King Lear (Shakespeare), 127, 241

Kingsolver, Barbara: *Flight Behavior*, 233

King, Stephen, 8, 30, 141–42

Klara and the Sun (Ishiguro), 7, 81, 108, 116, 121; artificial friend (AF), as protagonist, 110–11; interiority, commitment to, 113–14; prose style, originality of, 113–14

Klein, Richard, 217

Kolbert, Elizabeth: *Sixth Extinction, The*, 219

Kondo, Marie, 252–53

Kraus, Chris, 258

Krystal, Arthur, 142

Kubrick, Stanley, 5

Kwon, Miwon, 188–89

Lacan, Jacques, 33, 136

"Lance" (Nabokov), 4

Larkin, Philip, 117

Last Werewolf, The (Duncan), xi, xiii–xiv, 5–6; self-consciousness, xii

late capitalism, 60, 64, 75, 92, 131, 186, 191, 201, 204, 206, 262

Lean, David, 227

Leaves of Grass (Whitman), 120

Lee, Chang-rae, 2–3, 298n27; *Native Speaker*, 6–8, 54, 96–97, 99; *On Such a Full Sea*, 7, 83, 103, 231–32; *Surrendered, The*, 7

Le Guin, Ursula K., 8, 10, 17, 22–23, 44, 147, 171; character, in fantasy, 293n57; free play of mind, extolling of, 153–54; *Rocannon's World*, 218; "Science Fiction and Mrs. Brown," 51; "Why Are Americans Afraid of Dragons?" 153–54; works of fantasy, American dismissal of, 153–54

LeMenager, Stephanie, 304n26

Lennon, John, 197

Leonard, Elmore, 30

Lessons in Chemistry (Garmus), 257

Lethem, Jonathan, 9, 23, 30; *Fortress of Solitude, The*, 131, 133–34; *Girl in Landscape*, 67; *Motherless Brooklyn*, 6, 11, 66–69, 72, 90, 174
Levine, Caroline, 48, 284n23, 297n17
Lewis, C. S., 175
Leypoldt, Günter, 88, 95
Library of America, 17
Life After Life (Atkinson), 180
Lil Nas X, x
Li, Stephanie, 289n106
literary fiction, 1–3, 7, 10, 12–18, 23, 45, 47, 66, 69, 81–82, 95, 99, 104, 150, 152, 193–94, 212, 215, 224, 234, 257, 258, 262, 290n8; artful language, commitment to, 96; avant-garde, difference between, 25; bookish characters, 115; cliché, avoidance of, 90–91; climate change, 209–10, 213; consciousness, as primary site of experience, 85; definition of, 86; genre fiction, embracing of, 5, 83, 142; genre turn, vii; genre frameworks, drawn on, 19; historical fiction in, 87; innovative deployments of familiar genres, 84–85; interiority, emphasis on, 85; intellect genres, 87–88; interiority, 103, 111–12, 222; literary novel of artificial consciousness, 109–10; originality, 90; personal and psychological, 103; plot, allure of, 142, 145; as plotless, 143; popular fiction, distinctions between, 21, 83–84, 86, 102–3, 115, 185–86; prose style, 89–91, 103, 111–12; realism and historical fiction, drawn on, 19; resurgence of, 102; scalar modulation, 216; style, formal experiment and topicality, as central to, 88; as subfield, 84, 86–87, 91, 134; variations, 50; writers of color, historical fiction, 87
literary history, 16, 82; particularity of local, 192

literary genre fiction, 6, 10
literary reading, 83–84, 114–15, 121–22, 133, 139, 177
literary romanticism, x
literary studies, 86
Little Life, A (Yanagihara), 257
Lolita (Nabokov), 4–5, 94, 97, 139
Longfellow, Henry Wadsworth, 128
Look at Me (Egan), 264
Lopez, Donald S., 306n66
Lord of the Rings (Tolkien), 23
Lovecraft, H. P., 8, 218; "Call of Cthulhu, The" 212–13, 219; deep time, 212–13
"Lucy in the Sky with Diamonds" (song), 199
Ludlum, Robert, 20
Lukács, Georg, 103, 140, 227

Maas, Sarah J., 256
Machado, Carmen Maria, 3, 29, 281n96; *Her Body and Other Parties*, 26–27, 76–77
Machinal, Hélène, 70
Machines Like Me (McEwan), 7, 23, 116–18, 263; posthumanist exploration, 120; Turing character, 119–20, 138
MaddAddam (Atwood), 6, 183; as science fiction, 82–83
magical realism, 19, 248–50
Magicians Trilogy, The (Grossman), 3
Makinen, Merja, 285n49
Ma, Ling, 3, 192; *Severance*, 73, 131, 137, 183–86
Mandel, Emily St. John, 3; *Station Eleven*, 11, 73–76, 103, 127–29, 183
Mann, Thomas, 5
Manshel, Alexander, 77, 87
Maps and Legends: Writing along the Borderlands (Chabon), 151
Marcus, Laura, 66
Marley, Bob, 1
Marriage Plot, The (Eugenides), 19, 136

Marshall, Kate: speculative memory, 286n51
Martell, Linda, viii–x
Martin, George R. R., 24
Marx, Karl: simple abstraction, 49
McCarthy, Cormac, 2–3, 33–34; *All the Pretty Horses*, 7, 257; *Blood Meridian*, 6, 93–94, 96, 108, 291–92n39; *No Country for Old Men*, 7, 14; *Road, The*, 7, 52, 73, 88, 103
McEwan, Ian, ix, 2, 24, 137, 140, 264; immersion, 150–51; *Machines Like Me*, 7, 23, 116–20, 138, 263; *Sweet Tooth*, 7, 54–55, 128, 136
McGrath, Laura, 202
McGuire, Richard, 214
McGurl, Mark, 15, 48–49, 58, 74, 89, 104, 212–13, 218, 277n47, 278n64, 292n46
McKeon, Michael, 49
McQueen, Steve, 196
McSweeney's (magazine), 30–31, 34, 141
McSweeney's Mammoth Treasury of Thrilling Tales, 30
Melville, Herman, 33, 56, 155; *Moby Dick*, 46
Mertens, Mahlu, 210, 216–17
metafiction, 114; historiographic, 19; postmodernist, 2, 249
Michaels, Walter Benn, 305n55
Miéville, China, 2, 30
Miller, Laura, 3
Millet, Lydia, 219, 243; *Children's Bible, A*, 229–30; *How the Dead Dream*, 207–8, 222, 242
Milton, John, 135
Ministry for the Future, The (Robinson), 220–21
Mists of Avalon, The (Bradley), 9, 275–76nn34
Mitchell, David, 2–3, 29–30, 35–36, 38–39, 92, 95–96, 120, 146–47, 153, 188, 194–95, 257; *Bone Clocks, The*, 91–92, 147; *Cloud Atlas*, 7, 47, 73, 83, 91, 97–99, 103, 108, 115, 121, 155–57, 161, 231; emblem of Anglo-American media, 197; genre-bending ethos of, 27; genre fiction tropes, overt appropriation of, 193; *Ghostwritten*, 104; Goose's law, 293n66; homogenization of spaces, depiction of, 192; Japanese spaces, as saturated by globalized media, 193; *Number9Dream*, 186–87, 190, 192–93, 196–202, 204; *Thousand Autumns of Jacob de Zoet, The*, 26, 36, 195, 257; *Utopia Avenue*, 27–28; works, as über-novel, 27–28, 104–5, 293n64
Moby Dick (Melville), 46
modernism, x, 32, 144, 146, 150–51, 297n14; form over content, 149; literary, 4
Momofuku, 51
Monaco, Richard, 22
Money (Amis), 19
Monson, Ander, 105
Moretti, Franco, 48, 282n3
Morrison, Toni, 44, 103–4; *Beloved*, 6, 9–10, 52, 76–77, 87
Morton, Timothy, 209, 233
Mosely, Walter, 65
Motherless Brooklyn (Lethem), 6, 11, 72, 174; Tourette syndrome, as metaphor, 66–69, 90; wordplay, 66–68, 90
Murakami, Haruki, 2, 7, 38–39, 188; as emblem of Anglo-American media, 197; genre fiction tropes, overt appropriation of, 193; *Hard-Boiled Wonderland and the End of the World*, 6; homogenization of spaces, depiction of, 192; Japanese spaces, as saturated by globalized media, 193; *Norwegian Wood*, 197; *1Q84*, 186–87, 190, 192–96, 202–3, 204; *Wind-Up Bird Chronicle, The*, 194, 197
Murder of Roger Ackroyd, The (Christie), 49

Murray, Mitch R., 293n64
Mysteries of Pittsburgh, The (Chabon), 145
My Year of Meats (Ozeki), 235

Nabokov, Vladimir, xii, 17, 33, 65, 139; *Ada, or Ardor*, 4; "Lance," 4; *Lolita*, 4–5, 94, 97, 139; *Pale Fire*, 5
Nagamatsu, Sequoia, 288n94
Name of the Rose, The (Eco), 6, 9–10, 16, 135, 158
Native Speaker (Lee), 6–8, 54, 96–97, 99
Nelson, Willie, x
neoliberal capitalism, 207–8, 222; cookie-cutter shapes, 192; as generic, 192
neoliberalism, 118, 123, 130, 132, 154, 207; globalization, 186–87
Never Let Me Go (Ishiguro), 7, 52, 54, 108–9, 111, 115, 121
New Historicism, 161
New York (New York), 192
New Yorker (magazine), 141
New York Trilogy, The (Auster), 51, 66
New Weird, 2
Niemöller, Martin, 220
Nightmare, The (Fuseli), xii
Nguyen, Viet Than, 3; *Sympathizer, The*, 7, 20, 54–55, 81, 87, 94–95, 115
Nixon, Rob, 209, 233
No Country for Old Men (McCarthy), 7, 14
nonhuman agency, 220, 225
Normal People (Rooney), 258–61
Northanger Abbey (Austen), 16
Norwegian Wood (Murakami), 197
Number9Dream (Mitchell), 186, 190, 192, 197–98; Dorothy trick, 199; globally homogenized space, 200; as global genre-bending novel, 187; late capitalism media-saturated spaces, 201; literary and generic, balancing of, 204; literary and popular genres, borrowing from, 196, 199–200; as self-referential narrative, 193, 201–2; "Study of Tales" section, 201–2

Oates, Joyce Carol, 30, 219
Odyssey (Homer), 150
Office Space (film), 183
Offill, Jenny, 229; *Weather*, 219–20, 222
"Old Town Road" (song), x
1Q84 (Murakami), 186, 190, 192, 202–3; fictional Japan, setting of, 193; genre tropes, nod to, 195; as global genre-bending novel, 187; globalized space, 194; immersion, 196; layered sites, 196; literary and generic, balancing of, 204
Ono, Yoko, 197
On Such a Full Sea (Lee), 7, 83, 103, 231–32
Orwell, George, 228, 267; "Politics and the English Language," 90
Oryx and Crake (Atwood), 73–74, 132, 163
otherness, 95, 140, 151
Overstory, The (Powers), 142, 234, 241, 243–44; anthropocentrism of, 239–40; ecosystem collapse, 238, 242; non-human world, 238; science fiction vignettes, 238–39
Oyeyemi, Helen, 3; *Icarus Girl, The*, 76–77
Oxford Dictionary of Literary Terms, The (Baldick), 290n8
Ozeki, Ruth, 212, 251; *Book of Form and Emptiness, The*, 248–50, 252–55; *My Year of Meats*, 235

Pale Fire (Nabokov), 5
Parable novels (Butler), 222
Paretsky, Sara, 65
particularity: peripheral writers, 192; of place, 192; as stereotype, 192

Parton, Dolly, x
Patterson, James, 20
Pavel, Thomas, 50–51, 282–83nn7
"Peach Woman of Aa'a, The" (Atwood), 173–74
Peacock, James, 67
Pepper, Andrew, 65–66
"Pierre Menard, Author of the Quixote," 49
Pilot's Wife, The (Shreve), 104
Playground (Powers), 175–76, 234, 238
plot, 149, 152; desire for meaning, 145; Freudian psychoanalysis, 145; as structuring operation, 144; as universal, 143–45
Plot Against America, The (Roth), 2–3, 52
Poe, Edgar Allan, 292n44; "William Wilson," 135
"Politics and the English Language" (Orwell), 90
popular genre fiction, vii, xiii, 5, 8, 11, 15, 21, 31, 37, 47, 84, 87, 89, 126, 144, 173, 181, 185–86, 191–92; global recognizability of, 203; as immersive experience, 149; immersive pleasure, conducive to, 150, 171; plot, 143–44; transnational character, 190
popular media studies, 147
Posadas, Baryon Tensor, 193
Possession: A Romance (Byatt), 6, 19, 47, 135–36, 157–58, 164–66, 179, 257; Brittany section, 170, 180–81; combination and permutation, possibilities of, 180; dramatic irony, 165; gothic turn, 161–63; high Romance, 160, 167–69; postscript, 166; as satire of 1980s academia, 159; spy novel, dabbling in, 161–62
postapocalyptic fiction, 55, 64, 73–76, 133, 214–16, 231, 241–42
posthumanism, 109, 132, 217, 286n61
postmodernism, 1, 134, 146, 150–51, 184–85, 196, 198; consumerism, 204; irony, 12, 184; ludic, 19; metafiction, 2, 114; pastiche, 199–200; popular genres, deployments of, 10
poststructuralism, 102, 167
Powers, Richard, 2, 233, 246, 296n41; *Bewilderment*, 232–40, 247; character, idea of, 305n55; *Galatea 2.2*, 7, 113, 128, 137–40, 236, 296n42; individualism, and interconnection, 236–37; *Overstory, The*, 142, 234, 238–44; *Playground*, 175–76, 234, 238; Turing Test, 137–38
Pressman, Jessica, 122–23
Prince, 69
Propp, Vladimir, 62
Proulx, Annie: *Barkskins*, 244–48, 305–6n60
Proust, Marcel, 33, 178
publishing industry, 8, 10–11, 15–16, 31; comics, 21; conglomerate, 10, 89, 262; consolidation of, 10; corporate, 84, 204; imprints, 9, 24; multinational, 131; romance, 18–19; segmentation of market, 10. *See also* individual publishers
pulp fiction, 34, 88, 172–73, 181; comics, 125; fiction, 9, 252, 291n23; magazines, 31, 163–64, 171, 234
Pynchon, Thomas, 5, 34, 46, 65; *Gravity's Rainbow*, 1; *Inherent Vice*, 274n24

Questionable Shape, A (Sims), 128, 136–37

Radway, Janice, 17–18, 297n13
Raymond Chandler: Stories and Early Novels (Chandler), 8
Readers' Advisory Guide to Genre Fiction, The (Saricks), vernacular criticism, 87
Reading for the Plot: Design and Intention in Narrative (Brooks), 143, 145

322   Index

realism, 32, 35, 143; interiority, devotion to, 142
realist novels, 74, 102, 134, 143–44, 168, 209, 213–15, 234, 236–37, 240, 243, 248, 250
Reed, Ishmael, 5, 46, 65
Renaissance (Beyoncé), ix
Rieder, John, 49, 275n32, 276–77n43
Road, The (McCarthy), 7, 52, 73, 88, 103
Robbe-Grillet, Alain, 65
Robinson Crusoe (Defoe), 16, 73
Robinson, Kim Stanley, 222; *Ministry for the Future, The*, 220–21
Rocannon's World (Le Guin), 218
romance fiction, 35, 39–40, 82, 168–69, 171, 269; as genre, 256–58
Romero, George, 21
Rooney, Sally, 2, 39–40, 262, 267; *Beautiful World, Where Are You?* 259, 261; *Conversation with Friends*, 258–59, *Intermezzo*, 258–59; Marxist commitments, 260; *Normal People*, 258–61; romance genre, bending of, 257–59
Roth, Philip, 33, 93; *Human Stain, The*, 94–95; *Plot Against America, The*, 2–3, 52
Round House, The (Erdrich), 7; as bildungsroman and crime novel, 72
Rushdie, Salman, 19, 46
Ruskin, John, 277n52
Russell, Karen, 3
Russ, Joanna, 10
Ryan, Marie-Laure, 38, 149–51, 167–68; frozen metaphors, 147, 177; immersive reading, devaluing of, 148; readers' participation in fictional worlds, 147–48

Sad Puppies, ix
Sag Harbor (Whitehead), 45
Saldívar, Ramón, 10, 54; speculative realism, 283n18, 286n51

Saler, Michael, 147, 151, 168
Saricks, Joyce, 88; *Readers' Advisory Guide to Genre Fiction, The*, 87
Sayers, Dorothy, 65
Schiller, Friedrich, 116
Schneider-Mayerson, Matthew, 222
Schweblin, Samantha: *Fever Dream*, 77
science fiction, 4, 10, 16, 18, 26, 35, 49, 82–83, 87–89, 103, 105–7, 110, 121–22, 137, 142, 218, 221–22, 227–28, 232–33, 236, 238–39, 263, 269, 276–77n43, 285n25, 293n57, 299n51, 304n26; climate change, 211–12; dystopian, 214–16; as economically lucrative, 279n74; enchantment and political critique, balance between, 154; pleasure, as vital to, 154–55
"Science Fiction and Mrs. Brown" (Le Guin), 51
Scribner, 262
Severance (Ma), 73, 131, 137, 183, 185–86; globalization, anxieties about, 184
Severance (television series), 183
Shaboozey, ix
Shakespeare, William, 116, 128–29, 293n57; *King Lear*, 127, 241; *Tempest, The*, 117, 140; *Winter's Tale, The*, 218
Shelley, Mary: *Frankenstein* (Shelley), 95
Shreve, Anita: *Pilot's Wife, The*, 104
Shteyngart, Gary, 9, 136; *Super Sad True Love Story*, 113, 133
signification, 148
Sims, Bennett: *Questionable Shape, A*, 128, 136–37
singularity, 268–69
Sing, Unburied, Sing (Ward), 76–77, 90
Sinykin, Dan, 10, 73, 87, 274n24
"16 Carriages" (song), viii–ix
Sixth Extinction, The (Kolbert), 219
Slaughterhouse-Five (Vonnegut), 89
Smith, Rachel Greenwald, 276n41

Smith, Zadie, 46
social media, 7, 40, 238, 262–64, 266–67
Song of Ice and Fire, A (Martin), 24
Song, Min Hyoung, 275n26, 298n27
sonnets, 50
Sontag, Susan, xiii; erotics of art, call for, 144
Sorensen, Leif, 286n61
Souls of Black Folk, The (Du Bois), 94–95
"Spaghettii" (song), viii
Specimen Days (Cunningham): "Children's Crusade," 120; "In the Machine," 120; "Like Beauty," 120–22; structure of, 120
speculative fiction, 20, 205, 232–33
speculative realism, 54
Spivak, Gayatri Chakravorty, 258
spy fiction, 37, 54–55, 94, 161–62, 269
Squires, Claire, 18, 82
Star Trek, 75
Station Eleven (Mandel), 11, 73, 76, 103; as allusive, 127; backward-facing structure, 74; COVID-19, anticipating of, 183; postapocalyptic world, 75; Shakespeare, as focal point, 127–29
Sterne, Laurence, 46
Stevenson, Robert Louis: romance tradition of, 152; *Strange Case of Dr. Jekyll and Mr. Hyde*, 234
Stone Gods, The (Winterson), 73
"Storyteller, The" (Benjamin), 34
Strange Case of Dr. Jekyll and Mr. Hyde (Stevenson), 234
Study in Scarlet, A (Conan Doyle), 49
Super Sad True Love Story (Shteyngart), 113, 133
Surrendered, The (Lee), 7
Sweet Tooth (McEwan), 7, 54–55, 128, 136
Sympathizer, The (Nguyen), 7, 20, 54–55, 81, 87, 115; allusive language of, 94–95; otherness, 95; as spy novel, 94

Tan, Amy: *Joy Luck Club*, 19
Tanoukhi, Nirvana, 192
Tarantino, Quentin, 176
Telegraph Avenue (Chabon), 29, 175, 190; genre-scrambling ethos, 28
Tempest, The (Shakespeare), 117, 140
Temple, Johnny, 26
Tennyson, Alfred Lord: "Eagle, The," 138
"Texas Hold 'Em" (song), ix
textuality, 16, 147–48, 222
Texts for Nothing (Beckett), 5
Then We Came to the End (Ferris), 183
Thousand Autumns of Jacob de Zoet, The (Mitchell), 26, 36, 195, 257
Thunberg, Greta, 235
Time Machine, The (Wells), 218
Titanic (film), 197
Todd, Richard, 86
Todorov, Tzvetan, 276–77n43
Tokyo (Japan), 187, 190–93, 195–98, 200
Tolentino, Jia, 24–26
Tolstoy, Lee, 62; *Anna Karenina*, 174
Tompkins, Jane, 35
Tor, 24
translation, 189–90
Trickster Makes This World (Hyde), 34
Twenty Thousand Leagues under the Sea (Verne), 175
Two Dollar Radio, 136
Tynyanov, Yury, 284n33

Ulysses (Joyce), 46
Underground Railroad, The (Whitehead), 11, 36, 44, 52, 79–80, 87, 90, 289n106; generic hybridity of, 77–78; historical novel and neo-slave narrative, deforming of, 55; as metageneric text, 55
United States, 76; works of fantasy, dismissal of, 153–54
Updike, John, 46

Utopia Avenue (Mitchell), 27; genre-bending style, 28

Vermeulen, Pieter, 209, 294n9
Verne, Jules: *Twenty Thousand Leagues under the Sea*, 175
Vibrant Matter (Bennett), 254
Vintage, 17, 30–31
Visit from the Goon Squad, A (Egan), 7, 262–65, 267
Vonnegut, Kurt, 23, 34, 212; *Slaughterhouse-Five*, 89
Voyage of the Beagle, The (Darwin), 175

Waiting for Godot (Beckett), 51
Walker, Margaret: *Jubilee*, 19
Walkowitz, Rebecca, 189–90
Wallace, David Foster, 5, 136; *Infinite Jest*, 1
WALL-E (film), 223
Ward, Jasmyn, metaphors, 91; *Sing, Unburied, Sing*, 76–77, 90
Watkins, Claire Vaye, 231; *Gold Fame Citrus*, 76, 230
Weather (Offill), 219–20, 222
We Are All Completely Beside Ourselves (Fowler), 235
Weller, Barry, 152
Welles, Orson, 41
Wells, H. G., 223; *Time Machine, The*, 218
westerns, 36, 269; settler colonial heroes, 35
When We Were Orphans (Ishiguro), 7, 71; narrator protagonist of, 69–70
Whitehead, Colson, 2–3, 9, 14, 23, 27, 35, 37, 41, 47, 125, 153, 186, 192; adjectival agility, 92; *Apex Hides the Hurt*, 44–45, 55–56, 59–60, 191, 205; *Crook Manifesto*, 7, 45; "fried chicken journey" metaphor, 51–52; genre switching, 21, 45; historical fiction, as writer of, 77; *Intuitionist, The*, 7, 43, 56–57, 77–78; *John Henry Days*, 45–47, 57–58, 64, 77, 283n13, 283n18; metageneric moments, 55–56, 64; multinational corporations, critique of, 55; mutability, 56; *Sag Harbor*, 45; *Underground Railroad, The*, 11, 36, 44, 52, 55, 77–80, 87, 90, 289n106; use of language, 95; *Zone One*, 11, 21–22, 44, 52, 60–64, 73–76, 92, 95–96, 101, 126–27, 131, 136, 185, 191, 205, 286n61, 286n63
white nationalists, ix, 232; white supremacy, 13–14
Whitman, Walt, 121; *Leaves of Grass*, 120
"Why Are Americans Afraid of Dragons?" (Le Guin), 153–54
Whyte, Jack, 22
Williams, Jeffrey J., 9
"William Wilson" (Poe), 135
Wind-Up Bird Chronicle, The (Murakami), 194, 197
Winterson, Jeanette: *Stone Gods, The*, 73
Winter's Tale, The (Shakespeare), 218
Wittgenstein, Ludwig, 137
Wizard of Oz (film), 197
Wolfe, Tom, 46
Wood, James, 92
Woolf, Leonard, 258
Woolf, Virginia, 33, 102–4, 120, 258
world-building, 13, 26, 95–96, 147, 182, 269
World War Z (Brooks), 291n34
Wright, Richard, 139–40

X-Men, 95

Yanagihara, Hanya: *Little Life, A*, 257
Yarros, Rebecca, 256
Yiddish Policemen's Union, The (Chabon), 6, 257; alternate history and noir, combination of, 72, 83

Yu, Charles: *How to Live Safely in a Science Fictional Universe*, 105–6, 130; *Interior Chinatown*, 106–7

Yuknavitch, Lydia, 246; *Book of Joan, The*, 76, 222–28, 236

Zizek, Slavoj, 258

zombie fiction, 14, 37, 52, 60, 136–37, 214, 269

Zone One (Whitehead), 11, 21–22, 44, 52, 95–96, 131, 136, 185, 191, 286n63; character and genre, links between, 62; disaster elements, 127; *Friends*-like show, aping of, 126; humans, as robotic dummies, 61; individual agency, attacking notion of, 60; Last Night stories, 62–63, 74, 205; late capitalism, 60, 64, 75, 92, 191; as literary fiction, 95; Mark Spitz, as protagonist, 61–64, 74, 92, 127; metageneric moments, 64; metaphor, 92; Obituary, 63–64; repetitive action, focus on, 60–61, 74; thorough, power of, 64; zombies, 60–62, 73–76, 101, 286n61

Sara Kippur, *New York Nouveau: How Postwar French Literature Became American*

Francisco E. Robles, *Coalition Literature: Aesthetics on the Move in Midcentury US Multiethnic Writing*

Myka Tucker-Abramson, *Cartographies of Empire: The Road Novel and American Hegemony*

Michael Shane Boyle, *The Arts of Logistics: Artistic Production in Supply Chain Capitalism*

Adam Kelly, *New Sincerity: American Fiction in the Neoliberal Age*

Adrienne Brown, *The Residential Is Racial: A Perceptual History of Mass Homeownership*

Patrick Whitmarsh, *Writing Our Extinction: Anthropocene Fiction and Vertical Science*

Rebecca B. Clark, *American Graphic: Disgust and Data in Contemporary Literature*

Palmer Rampell, *Genres of Privacy in Postwar America*

Joseph Darda, *The Strange Career of Racial Liberalism*

Jordan S. Carroll, *Reading the Obscene: Transgressive Editors and the Class Politics of US Literature*

Michael Dango, *Crisis Style: The Aesthetics of Repair*

Mary Esteve, *Incremental Realism: Postwar American Fiction, Happiness, and Welfare-State Liberalism*

Dorothy J. Hale, *The Novel and the New Ethics*

Christine Hong, *A Violent Peace: Race, U.S. Militarism, and Cultures of Democratization in Cold War Asia and the Pacific*

Sarah Brouillette, *UNESCO and the Fate of the Literary*

Sophie Seita, *Provisional Avant-Gardes: Little Magazine Communities from Dada to Digital*

Guy Davidson, *Categorically Famous: Literary Celebrity and Sexual Liberation in 1960s America*

Joseph Jonghyun Jeon, *Vicious Circuits: Korea's IMF Cinema and the End of the American Century*

Lytle Shaw, *Narrowcast: Poetry and Audio Research*

Stephen Schryer, *Maximum Feasible Participation: American Literature and the War on Poverty*

Margaret Ronda, *Remainders: American Poetry at Nature's End*

Jasper Bernes, *The Work of Art in the Age of Deindustrialization*

Annie McClanahan, *Dead Pledges: Debt, Crisis, and Twenty-First-Century Culture*

Amy Hungerford, *Making Literature Now*

J. D. Connor, *The Studios After the Studios: Neoclassical Hollywood (1970–2010)*

Michael Trask, *Camp Sites: Sex, Politics, and Academic Style in Postwar America*

Loren Glass, *Counterculture Colophon: Grove Press, the Evergreen Review, and the Incorporation of the Avant-Garde*

Michael Szalay, *Hip Figures: A Literary History of the Democratic Party*

For a complete listing of titles in this series, visit the Stanford University Press website, www.sup.org.

The authorized representative in the EU for product safety and compliance is:
Mare Nostrum Group
B.V Doelen 72
4831 GR Breda
The Netherlands

www.ingramcontent.com/pod-product-compliance
Lightning Source LLC
Chambersburg PA
CBHW030605230426
43661CB00053B/1849